The Limits of Utilitarianism

The Limits of Utilitarianism

Edited by
Harlan B. Miller
and
William H. Williams

University of Minnesota Press, Minneapolis

Copyright © 1982 by the University of Minnesota.
All rights reserved.
Published by the University of Minnesota Press,
2037 University Avenue Southeast,
Minneapolis, Minnesota 55414

Library of Congress Cataloging in Publication Data
Main entry under title:

The Limits of utilitarianism.

   Bibliography: p.
   Includes index.
   1. Utilitarianism. I. Miller, Harlan B.
II. Williams, William H. (William Hatton), 1934-
B843.L55   144'.6   81-14698
ISBN 0-8166-1044-4   AACR2
ISBN 0-8166-1047-9 (pbk.)

The University of Minnesota
is an equal-opportunity educator
and employer.

In Memory of Louis Werner

Contents

Preface and Acknowledgments		ix
Introduction	*William H. Williams*	3

Section I: The Principle of Utility

1	Mill's "Proof" of the Principle of Utility	*Henry R. West*	23
2	Egalitarianism and the General Happiness	*John Marshall*	35
3	Benevolence and Justice in Mill	*David Lyons*	42
4	Inchoately Utilitarian Common Sense: The Bearing of a Thesis of Sidgwick's on Moral Theory	*Allan Gibbard*	71
5	Utilitarianism and Unconscious Utilitarianism	*A. John Simmons*	86

Section II: Utilitarianism and Contractarianism

6	Utilitarianism and Contractarianism	*B. J. Diggs*	101
7	Fairness to "Justice as Fairness"	*Alan E. Fuchs*	115
8	Rawls and Utilitarianism	*Jan Narveson*	128
9	On the Refutation of Utilitarianism	*David Gauthier*	144

Section III: Welfare

10	Two Concepts of Utility	*Richard B. Brandt*	169
11	Self-Interest and Getting What You Want	*Mark Carl Overvold*	186
12	Human Welfare: What It Is Not	*Thomas Schwartz*	195

Section IV: Utilitarianism and the Moral Community

13	Benevolence, Collective Action, and the Provision of Public Goods	*Rolf Sartorius*	209
14	The Free-Rider Problem	*Lawrence C. Becker*	217
15	Utilitarianism and Aiding Others	*Dan W. Brock*	225
16	Utilitarianism and World Poverty	*Thomas L. Carson*	242
Bibliography			255
Index			303

Preface and Acknowledgments

With one exception the essays presented here arose out of papers and comments delivered at our conference, The Moral Foundations of Public Policy: The Limits of Utilitarianism, held on the campus of Virginia Polytechnic Institute and State University, May 18-21, 1978. That conference was made possible by a grant from the Virginia Foundation for the Humanities and Public Policy and matching funds from VPI & SU. We are grateful for their support. We are indebted as well to the participants in that conference, especially the panelists. We thank those panelists whose essays appear here both for their contributions and for their patience during the lengthy period between the conference and the publication of this collection. In addition we wish to express our gratitude to those panelists whose contributions to the conference could not (for various reasons) be represented by essays in this volume: James M. Buchanan, Holly Goldman, Frederic Schick, Jerome Schneewind, T. Nicolaus Tideman, and Gordon Tullock. We also acknowledge with appreciation the assistance of those who served as moderators of sessions of the conference: I. J. Good, Norman Grover, Guy B. Hammond, Dorothy B. James, Frank A. MacDonald, the late Charles L. Stevenson, and Anthony D. Woozley. David Lyons, who was unable to present a paper at the conference, generously provided us with the fruits of a sabbatical year: his essay in this volume.

To our departmental secretaries, Betty Davis and Jeanne Keister, who have no equals, we express our gratitude for their many labors (labors of love) without which neither the conference nor this book would have come about. We also thank Sarah Williams for her help with the bibliography and index. Thanks are due too to the University of Minnesota Press staff and to the referees whose reports, commissioned by the Press, provided us with helpful criticism. Finally, we appreciate the encouragement, cooperation, and patience of our departmental colleagues and others on the faculty and in the administration of VPI

& SU, including Henry Bauer, Dean of the College of Arts and Sciences and Anita Malebranche and Dorothy McCombs of the Carol M. Newman Library for their financial assistance and expert help respectively in the gathering of bibliographical sources. Especially we are indebted to Roger D. Rosenkrantz, our former colleague and department head, who participated in the early planning of the conference. Without his urgings we should never have gotten under way.

The conference was held in memory of our late friend and colleague, Louis Werner. This volume also is dedicated to his memory.

The Limits of Utilitarianism

Introduction

William H. Williams

The traditional questions about utilitarianism are still with us. In the main they comprise the agenda of current debate. Is the final test of conduct the good or evil that results therefrom? If so, how might that be demonstrated, and what is the good by which conduct is to be appraised? Is the good the same as happiness, or the satisfaction of desires, or something else? How might we establish the answer to that question? If goodness is the test of conduct, how does the test apply? What precisely is the bearing of goodness (or of evil) on the morality of the actions that produce it? Should we seek in every instance to perform an act that will produce more good than (or at least as much good as) any available alternative? Or is the relationship of good to right in particular acts less direct? Are there moral obligations that require of us something other than the maximization of the good? Can a theory of right action that makes production of desirable states of affairs the final test allow for such a possibility? Can such a theory accommodate, for example, considerations of rights and of justice, which seem to operate as constraints on what is permitted, even in the bringing about of good? How could a theory that makes the production of desirable states of affairs the test of morality recognize such constraints? Many have held that considerations of rights and justice presuppose notions of a *person* and of a *moral community* not acknowledged in the mere concern for production of the good. Is that true? Or may it not be that the rights and principles of justice constitutive of such an ideal community of persons reflect an ultimate commitment to promote the good conjoined with certain assumptions about the facts of life—in particular, about the ways and means by which the good can be promoted? These familiar issues dominate the present volume. They are reflected in its division into four sections, the first of which is devoted to discussion of some of their classical sources.

I

One of the sources is John Stuart Mill. His is perhaps the most suggestive and perplexing account of utility and of its bearing on morality that we have. When we examine Mill's writings, we find support for different interpretations of his claim that the general happiness is the only thing desirable as an end, that it is the test of human conduct and thus of morality. Because these different interpretations provide markedly different but plausible views about happiness in relation to morality, they are of interest in themselves as theories of the good and the right and not just as interpretations of Mill.

The standard interpretation of Mill's account of the *summum bonum* is that each person's happiness (happiness understood as pleasure or the absence of pain) is a good in itself. The putative evidence for this is that each person desires his own happiness (and that only) as an end. Mill invokes the principle that the sole evidence that anything is desirable (i.e., good) is that it is desired. Now, since according to such evidence each person's happiness is good, Mill concludes that all these happinesses taken together (the general happiness) constitute a good, the greatest good. Many objections have been raised against this proof: objections to Mill's principle of evidence, to his psychological hedonism, and to his inference from the goodness of the happiness of each to the goodness of the happiness of all. For example, it has been urged against Mill's principle of evidence that what is desired is often undesirable; against his psychological hedonism, that we often desire the happiness of others for its own sake; and against his inference, that it does not follow from each person's desiring his own happiness that anyone desires the happiness of all.

In his essay on Mill's "proof," Henry West[1] undertakes to defend something like the standard account of Mill's view against such objections. West endeavors to show that Mill's principle of evidence and his psychological hedonism withstand familiar objections and that they are plausible. In addition, West maintains that on the proper understanding of Mill's conception of the general happiness, the inference from the claim that the happiness of each is a good to the claim that the general happiness is a good commits no fallacy and is supported by Mill's principle of evidence. According to West, the general happiness is shown to be a good inasmuch as it comprises the happy states of the several happy individuals, each of which instances of happiness has been shown to be a good by virtue of its being desired as an end by that individual whose happiness it is. Just as A's desire for his own happiness shows it to be good, and B's desire for his own happiness shows *it* to be good, so these individual desires taken together show that A's happiness and B's happiness, etc., taken together (that is, the general happiness) constitute a good. There is no need that anyone desire the happiness of anyone else, let alone the happiness of everyone, to show that the general happiness is, in an appropriate sense, desired and thus a good. In other words, on Mill's account, A's desire of his own happiness shows it to be *a good for A*, not in the sense merely that it is considered *a good from A's point of view*, but rather in the sense that it is shown to be *a good that has A as its location*. In this way, the sum of the individual happinesses of the aggregate of persons is a good to the aggregate of persons, that is, the aggregate of persons is its location.

In "Egalitarianism and the General Happiness," John Marshall rejects the view that we can sensibly talk of a sum of happiness. If Mill must be understood to treat the good as a sum then, according to Marshall, Mill is mistaken. However, Marshall suggests another way in which to construe Mill's proof. If each person's desire of his own happiness is evidence for everyone that that person's happiness is a good—and Marshall concurs with West that this is what Mill maintains—then we may conclude that each person has a reason to hold that any other person should be happy, and as much reason to hold this as to hold that he himself should be happy. This idea in turn provides the basis for asserting, as Mill does in Chapter V of *Utilitarianism*[2] that every person has an equal claim to happiness. This, according to Marshall, may be seen as the upshot of Mill's proof. We need not understand Mill to be arguing that happiness is a measurable sum whose maximization is the test of conduct, but rather that persons have an equal claim to happiness, which involves "an equal claim to all the means of happiness" and "a *right* to equality of treatment, except when some recognized social expediency requires the reverse."[3] However, Marshall grants that the text yields support for both interpretations.

Traditionally Mill has been read as an act utilitarian, i.e., as one who holds that we ought always act so as to maximize the aggregate happiness. As Marshall sees it, his treatment of Mill's proof of the principle of utility entails a contrary view of Mill's theory of right action. In particular, Marshall holds that on his account, Mill occupies a position akin to that of contractualist thinkers like John Rawls. West's account of Mill's proof, on the other hand, has implications only for a theory of the good. On West's account, Mill can consistently hold virtually any view of right action, including act utilitarianism. In his essay West advances no view about Mill's theory of the right.

Among those who have recently challenged the act-utilitarian reading of Mill, David Lyons is perhaps the most persuasive and illuminating. In his essay, "Mill's Theory of Morality,"[4] Lyons proposes that although Mill makes general happiness or utility the test of conduct, in that actions are ranked and preferred in accordance with their expediency, he is not committed thereby to regarding an act that fails to maximize the aggregate happiness as morally wrong. On Lyons's reading, utility, for Mill, bears on the morality of acts indirectly, by way of rules or obligations whose warrant lies not simply in the utility of acts that accord with them but also in the expediency of sanctions (legal punishment, social disapprobation, and feelings of guilt) against those persons whose conduct violates them. Such conduct alone is morally wrong. Thus, on Lyons's reading, Mill espouses a form of ideal rule utilitarianism—one which, unlike some versions of that theory, takes account not only of the utility to be gained from the wide acceptance of a moral rule but also of the disutility of the sanctions by which compliance with the rule tends to be secured.

In his "Benevolence and Justice in Mill," presented here, Lyons is concerned to show that Mill distinguishes different kinds of obligations. In particular, Lyons wishes to trace or reconstruct a distinction drawn by Mill between obligations of justice (obligations that on Mill's account are correlated with others' rights) and what Lyons terms "non-justice obligations." He wants to show, moreover, that Mill's kind of utilitarianism can accommodate a further distinction between morally required acts and acts of supererogation.

Lyons suggests that in *On Liberty* Mill distinguishes three sorts of moral requirements or obligations and correspondingly three sorts of conduct properly subject to coercive social control. These are the obligations: first, to respect those interests of others that according to law or to tacit understanding ought to be deemed rights; second, to bear one's fair share of the burden of defending society or its members from injury; and third, to refrain from conduct that "may be hurtful to others or wanting in due consideration of their welfare"[5] even if it does not violate their rights. These are the minimal requirements of harm-prevention augmented by considerations of reciprocity. Of these only the first are requirements whose violation would, per se, constitute an infringement of others' rights. They alone on Mill's view would properly be considered obligations of justice. Violations of the remaining requirements, which do not constitute infringements of rights—or do so only by way of the second-order obligation of reciprocity—would constitute nonjustice obligations, for example, the obligation to act as a good samaritan.

In contrast with these varieties of obligated conduct stand acts of sheer beneficence or generosity. These do not constitute harm-prevention, nor do they involve, even indirectly, the rights of others. These acts are desirable by virtue of their utility, and are praiseworthy, but one's failure to perform them on given occasions does not amount to wrongdoing. Their performance (at least those cases in which substantial disutility is incurred or risked by the agent) is supererogatory.

Lyons contends that Mill errs in making correlation with a right a sufficient as well as a necessary condition of an obligation's being one of justice. The obligation to keep a promise, for example, correlates with another's right but does not seem to raise a question of justice. Nevertheless, Mill's form of utilitarianism, Lyons argues, is not deficient by failing in general to recognize moral rights or considerations of justice, or by failing to allow for acts of supererogation. These failings, many allege, mar more typical accounts of right action in which promotion of the good is made the ultimate test of conduct.

From Hume to Sidgwick a line of argument[6] runs to the effect that the utilitarian principle that we ought to promote the general happiness provides the best explanation of the various rules of conduct and obligations recognized by common sense. Inasmuch as the principle is here seen to apply to rules rather than particular acts, this line of argument may appear to support some form of rule utilitarianism. However that may be, it seems to involve one or more of at least three different claims. First is the Humean contention[7] that common-sense morality is a repository of our accumulated wisdom about the effects of different sorts of acts on the general happiness. Second, the view is found in Mill,[8] among others, that the utilitarian principle provides the best ordering and systematization of the rules and obligations acknowledged by common sense. Finally, there is the claim of Sidgwick[9] that as common-sense morality in a society alters over the course of history, it manifests a tendency, however imperfect, in the direction of utilitarianism. It is not always clear precisely how these different assertions are to be understood, how plausible each is, and what bearing each might have on the truth of utilitarianism as a theory about how we ought to act. In their respective essays, Allan Gibbard[10] and John Simmons[11] examine aspects of this approach to the proof of the utilitarian theory of right action.

If common-sense morality has per se some authority, some presumption of truth, then if indeed its requirements could be explained only by the desire of people to promote the general happiness, that would appear to constitute a strong case for the truth of utilitarianism. However, it is doubtful, to say the least, that the wide acceptance of any particular moral rules can be explained by the *conscious* common end of promoting the general happiness. In the first place, there would seem to be no evidence that such a conscious purpose exists among the members of any society. To show on the other hand the existence of an unconscious purpose to promote the general happiness, we would probably have to appeal to the existence of the prevailing rules themselves as evidence of that. But these rules appear to be consistent with contrary principles of right action, so that apart from wide recognition, on reflection, by those who accept the rules that they do so because they view their acceptance as a means to the general happiness, no support would be provided for utilitarianism. It seems unlikely that we could ever elicit such recognition. Additional doubt is shed on the hypothesis that common-sense convictions are explained by an underlying commitment to utilitarianism by the evident fact that many such convictions sanction practices of questionable utility. Finally, even if the moral rules popularly subscribed to were perfect instruments to promote utility, it would no more follow that their subscription was to be explained by a perception, conscious or not, that they in fact subserve utility than it would follow that a common preference for salt is to be explained by an understanding that its consumption promotes health. For even if such a connection were perceived, it would no more follow that the rules were approved because of a commitment to utility than it would follow that salt was preferred because of a commitment to sound dietary principles.[12]

The argument that the utilitarian principle provides the best ordering and systematization of common-sense morality fares differently. It involves no hypothesis of allegiance, conscious or unconscious, to utility, and it accommodates rules that may in particular applications diverge noticeably from the end of utility maximization. It derives its support from common-sense morality (on the presumption that the latter is by-and-large correct) by virtue of the consistency, coherence, and systematic order it introduces. Its support is drawn from what it corrects and perfects, and by virtue of that correction. The principal weakness of this argument is that common-sense morality can be systematized and corrected in a number of seemingly plausible ways. Apart from some further considerations in favor of the principle of utility as against other accounts, its acceptance in virtue of this argument would seem to be largely a matter of adopting a convention, and largely unmotivated. If, on the other hand, a plausible argument somewhat like that suggested by Hume could be developed, it might make good the deficiency of this second approach.

Sidgwick's proposal that, over time, systems of popular morality tend toward utilitarianism recommends itself to our consideration. Although it is not altogether clear what Sidgwick means, he does not appear to propose that alterations of common-sense morality are the result of the conscious commitment of many or most ordinary people to utilitarianism. Nor does he seem to hypothesize an unconscious utilitarianism in the sense discussed above: that people could be brought by some reflection on their convictions to recognize that they had all along been moved by an implicit belief in the utilitarian principle. Rather, it seems more likely that what Sidgwick has in mind is that when adherence to traditional canons of conduct results in substantial disutilities, those canons change: What was condoned comes to be proscribed, what was forbidden to be permitted — that at least is the tendency, though various factors such as cultural lag may impede change in the utilitarian direction. This theory postulates, then, a kind of unconscious utilitarianism, if you like, a tendency whose goal utilitarianism as a first principle makes explicit.

In a searching examination of its implications,[13] Allan Gibbard argues that from the point of view of certain moral epistemologies, and given somewhat plausible auxiliary assumptions, Sidgwick's thesis entails a form of rule utilitarianism: "An act is right if and only if it is permitted by those rules that are most felicitous for the society of its agent."[14] The entailment is shown by way of a kind of reflection by means of which we are led to acknowledge rule utilitarianism if we accept Sidgwick's thesis. Gibbard's suggestion is that our moral judgments may properly be influenced by considerations about the sociopsychological process that shapes moral convictions, because that process has epistemic implications. Suppose, for example, we hold, as Ross does,[15] that some of our moral beliefs are apprehensions. Those that count as apprehensions are presumably the ones that we arrive at under ideal epistemic circumstances — circumstances, for instance, in which belief is free from influences we think would make it unreliable or its truth a matter of coincidence. Is it not at least somewhat plausible to assume that such ideal circumstances include that one judges acts in one's own society and in accordance with a shared morality that is the outcome of a natural sociopsychological process of belief formation, undistorted by influences like cultural lag, that considered judgment would deem to be morally irrelevant?

If that is so, then if Sidgwick's thesis is correct, our judgments in ideal epistemic circumstances will be made in accordance with rule utilitarianism. Parallel considerations can be developed in connection with such quasi-naturalist epistemologies as Brandt's qualified attitude method.[16] The ideal epistemic position here will be determined by those factors that qualify reliable attitudes. Again these would include freedom from distorting influences, which is best guaranteed when one is judging acts in one's own society, where that society is in what Gibbard calls "Sidgwickian equilibrium" (that is, its morality has reached the unique point toward which common-sense moralities by nature tend). Now, suppose we are *not* members of a society in Sidgwickian equilibrium, but we are serious moral persons. We shall want our attitudes to conform with qualified ones. If we accept Sidgwick's thesis and if we know that qualified attitudes are those of persons who are evaluating acts in their societies and who are members of societies in Sidgwickian equilibrium (i.e., societies whose common morality has according to Sidgwick's thesis come naturally to accord with rule utilitarianism for domestic cases), we shall choose to judge in accordance with rule utilitarianism — we will accept rule utilitarianism as true.

But is Sidgwick's thesis true? Granted that there is a rough coincidence between utilitarianism and common sense, it might still seem as reasonable to suppose that the latter is determined by factors other than the avoidance of infelicitous practices as that it is determined by such avoidance alone. As John Simmons argues in his "Utilitarianism and Unconscious Utilitarianism," it is plausible to suppose that utility is *an* end, but not the only end, that shapes common sense. Suppose, as Gibbard speculates,[17] that historically in societies great survival advantage attaches to cooperation and the avoidance of conflict, with the result that moral significance is attributed to whatever common expectations may develop among the members of a society regarding the division of benefits in bargaining situations. Since a great variety of distributive schemes of a nonutilitarian sort may emerge in different circumstances, it may be expected that common-sense morality will commonly deviate from utilitarianism in a systematic way. Sidgwick's thesis, then, will not provide the true account of the sociopsychological generation of moral beliefs. Should we say in that case — appealing to the same sort of reflection that Gibbard suggests — that common sense supports, for example, a conservative sentiment of justice in societies where change is slow enough, a morality that will almost certainly conflict with the rule utilitarian requirement that distributions be felicitous? It might appear indeed that uncertainty over the answer to this question puts in doubt the claim that Sidgwick's thesis supports utilitarianism, even if the thesis is true. For if what is in fact a non-Sidgwickian tendency of change in common-sense moralities results in principles that seem wrong, we shall not regard their being natural outcomes of a universal, sociopsychological process as supporting their validity. Why then should we think that their so being supports utilitarianism if Sidgwick is right? Thus, it appears that Simmons's and Gibbard's essays together show us that the complex line of argument in support of utilitarianism that they examine is doubtful in all of its aspects.

II

The discussion of utilitarianism in recent years has centered on its merits and deficiencies in comparison with those theories of right action that reflect the contractarian tradition in moral philosophy flowing from Rousseau and Kant. The major stimulus for this emphasis is without question the work of John Rawls.[18] Rawls draws together the insights of several traditional approaches to questions of both normative and critical ethics under a concept of morality and, more specifically, of justice, which has as its model a set of conditions called "the original position." In the original position rational choosers would concur (hence the contract) in the selection, *inter alia*, of fundamental principles to regulate the basic institutions within which they will pursue their lives and receive the benefits and burdens of their joint effort. The principles chosen in the original position are thereby justified, according to Rawls, by virtue of the fact that the conditions constituting the original position are conditions of fairness. The principles selected are the outcome of a choice procedure exhibiting the impartial regard for persons with their different interests and prospects that is assumedly essential to a considered notion of morality, one that would be acknowledged on reflection by proponents of rival principles of right action and justice. This reconstruction of the putatively common concept of justice, Rawls calls "justice as fairness."

Justice as fairness yields, Rawls claims, two basic principles. The first of these requires, roughly, that institutions be designed to secure for citizens the greatest possible equal liberty. On what Rawls terms his "special conception," this principle of liberty takes priority over his second principle, "the difference principle." The difference principle mandates an equal distribution of wealth, income, etc. (those means surely necessary to the achievement of one's life goals whatever they may be—Rawls calls these means "primary goods") except where inequalities will result in everyone's, and in particular the least advantaged person's, being better off. Unequal distributions are constrained by equality of opportunity to hold advantaged positions. Rawls considers utilitarianism to be the chief rival of this view of justice.

In "Fairness to 'Justice as Fairness'," the second essay of Section II, Alan Fuchs reminds us that Rawls appeals to what he terms our "considered judgments in reflective equilibrium" to secure additional support for the two principles. Fuchs contends that this move actually compromises Rawls's argument. It both detracts from the force of the derivation from the original position and obscures its significance as what Fuchs maintains is an importantly antirelativistic method of ethics. The damage results, according to Fuchs, from the fact that Rawls alters (or appears to alter) the original position so that its yield will accord with considered judgments about what is just. To the extent that this occurs, the authority of the original position as a model of our common concept of justice is destroyed, together with its relevance to the issue of what is just.

Fuchs undertakes to argue that those elements of the original position included in the description of the choosers—as self-interested but mutually disinterested parties operating behind a "thick" veil of ignorance concerning their identities, tastes, talents, social advantages, and the time and society in which they will live, but possessing a capacity for a sense of justice and a knowledge of the laws of human nature and society—serve adequately to model our concept of morality and of justice. He further maintains that these features entail what Rawls calls the "formal constraints of the concept of right," viz. that principles of right action must be general in form, universal in application, and publicly recognized and must order conflicting claims and provide final decisions. The formal constraints, therefore, are shown to add nothing to justice as fairness as explicated above, and justice as fairness is, thereby, shown to be simpler and more elegant than it might otherwise appear to be. Once we are convinced of the adequacy of justice as fairness as a theoretical construct of morality, it remains only to derive the two principles to demonstrate their validity as an account of what is just. Fuchs does not attempt this final demonstration.

In "Rawls and Utilitarianism," Jan Narveson rejects the assumption that utilitarianism is incompatible with Rawls's two principles. He argues that, indeed, it is possible to derive the two principles from the utilitarian position construed as Rawls construes it and that Rawls's own argument from the original position, if sound, would appear to show that the net utility of a society is maximized by arranging institutions according to Rawls's principles.

The heart of Narveson's argument is that given certain assumptions that Rawls appears to use in his derivation of the two principles from the original position, the principles can be derived as well from the utilitarian mandate to arrange institutions so as to maximize utility. The assumptions in question are that the primary goods are subject to declining marginal utility and that the curve expressing this tendency is the same for all persons. These establish for the utilitarian a benchmark of equality, departures from which need to be justified as bettering the lot of some (the least advantaged in particular) without worsening that of others. Declining marginal utility of primary goods entails that we look to improve the position of the worst off under unequal distribution because doing so will result in the greater gain in utility. To accommodate the priority of liberty on Rawls's special conception of justice we must make an additional assumption about the value of liberty relative to other primary goods at appropriate levels of those goods.

Narveson rejects Rawls's contention that the derivation of the two principles from the utilitarian principle is too indirect and risky, and that it is better to secure our ideal of justice "straightway"[19] by embodying it in basic principles. Narveson argues that Rawl's derivation from the original position of the principles that secure this ideal rests on the same "shaky" assumptions. The crux of the matter, Narveson says, is Rawl's insistence that the choice strategy called for in the original position is the maximin: that of choosing those principles that will guarantee a better worst possible outcome for choosers than any others. Rawl's reasons for adopting the maximin strategy, according to Narveson, are (a) that choosers can't know the probability of their ending up in a given position (they choose under uncertainty rather than risk), (b) persons care relatively little about what they might receive in the way of primary goods above the minimum guaranteed by choice according to the maximin strategy, and (c) alternatives rejected on the maximin strategy have disastrous outcomes. Quite apart from his disagreements with Rawls about (a), Narveson argues that (b) and (c) are grounded on the assumptions already mentioned, which utilitarians can accept and with whose aid they may derive the two principles according to their strategy of maximizing expected utility. Narveson contends that if maximin is invoked, it is properly at the point of deciding the scheme by which primary goods are to be distributed, rather than utility. The choice of maximin at this juncture can be justified, given the assumptions, on utilitarian grounds.

Narveson disclaims any intention to show by his argument that Rawls is a utilitarian or that the two principles cannot be defended from a nonutilitarian perspective, which Rawls might well prefer. Moreover, he does not intend to defend the assumptions of declining marginal utility and the relative utility of liberty appealed to above. These he regards as highly doubtful. His thesis is that the two principles may not constitute an alternative to utilitarianism and that the illusion that they must is fostered by one's failing to bear in mind the distinction between principles regarding utility and principles governing the distribution of primary goods.

But even granted cardinal comparisons of utility, can utilitarianism itself be justified by derivation from something like the original position, as Narveson seems to suggest? One argument to show that average utilitarianism (the injunction that we maximize the average utility) can be so justified is offered by John Harsanyi.[20] Harsanyi holds that moral judgments manifest an impartial concern for the preferences of all parties, which would be guaranteed in decisions affecting other parties if the persons making the judgments (or choices) had to choose among alternatives in disregard or ignorance of what their own resulting social positions would be. A rational individual according to modern decision theory would always choose to maximize his expected utility, which in this condition of ignorance would mean choosing to maximize the average per capita utility.

In his elegant essay "On the Refutation of Utilitarianism," David Gauthier maintains that this argument is not sound. According to Gauthier, a chooser on this model would be concerned not with calculating the utility of a situation for this or that person who would occupy it as the result of a given choice, but the utility of his (the chooser's) *being* this or that person *in* the resulting situation. Unless the utilities were the same, in these two cases his maximizing of expected utility would not amount to choosing the highest level of average utility for the individuals affected. But, Gauthier contends, they need not be the same. Using Mill's famous example of Socrates dissatisfied and the fool satisfied, Gauthier argues that the utility for a given chooser of being Socrates dissatisfied may exceed that of his being the fool satisfied, although the chooser knows that the utility to Socrates of being dissatisfied is less than the utility to the fool of being satisfied. If one objects that the chooser, on this account, knows who he is (although not who he will be), and that impartiality requires that he be ignorant even of who he is, then, Gauthier argues, the chooser logically cannot express any preferences. Although he can calculate the average value of a prospect for those involved in it, "he can not identify this value with *his preference* since he cannot identify himself."[21] Thus the conditions for individual choice cannot be satisfied here. One can function as an arbitrator in these circumstances, determining a fair compromise among individual preferences, but one cannot be a chooser. If this is so, Gauthier contends, then Harsanyi's argument fails. It insures impartiality by sacrificing individuality. "Average utilitarianism is not shown to be a principle to which a person would conform in any circumstances appropriate to individual choice."[22] Put another way, suppose it be allowed that a chooser might choose in ignorance of his identity and would do so in accordance with average utilitarianism. Again the case for utilitarianism fails. Because whereas normally one cannot complain about the unfairness of what results from one's impartial choice, if, as here, impartiality requires that one cannot know his own identity, that does not follow. Such impartial choice would not be regarded as fair by a chooser aware of his own identity. The upshot of this according to Gauthier is that the impartiality appropriate to moral decision is that "of an ideal bargain, in which the outcome reflects equally the partially conflicting preferences of the several bargainers."[23] The correct ethical theory will be, Gauthier concludes, "contractarian rather than utilitarian in its basic structure."[24]

Contractarianism turns on respect for persons, for their rationality and capacity for choice. It views morality as a voluntary mode of social control to which all members of a society can freely subscribe for good and decisive reasons. Section II is introduced by B. J. Diggs's "Utilitarianism and Contractarianism," in which these traditional contractualist themes and their implications for utilitarianism are explored independently of the formalities of decision theoretic treatments of such thinkers as Rawls, Narveson, Harsanyi, and Gauthier.

III

The essays in Section III are devoted to an examination of the nature of utility or welfare, that is, the good, which, according to utilitarian theories, our acts or moral rules and institutions should serve to maximize. As Richard Brandt explains in his "Two Concepts of Utility," different thinkers have opted in the main for one of three major kinds of theories of the good. First are accounts of the good in terms of the satisfaction of desires—either of desires persons actually have or so-called "corrected" desires, those, for example, persons would have were they fully informed about the objects of their desire, vividly aware of those facts about them, and were their desires *not* the results of one or another personal defect or logical abnormality. Other accounts identify the good with happiness rather than with desire-satisfaction, which may or may not be enjoyed. Finally, there is the view advanced by utilitarians like G. E. Moore, according to which goodness is an indefinable quality that many attach to a variety of things such as pleasure, knowledge, friendship, or beauty. Because the last of these has few if any proponents nowadays, Brandt confines his attention to desire and happiness accounts of welfare or utility.

The great problem for a desire-satisfaction account, Brandt holds, is how welfare is to be determined and how a program of welfare maximization is to be conceived for the individual and the community. The biggest obstacle here is that a person's desires change over time. How are we to determine which of his changing desires we should satisfy to maximize his welfare? If an individual's desires were fixed, we could, as Brandt suggests, identify his fixed long-term preferences—his ordering of biographies or world scenarios—and then undertake to move him up as many stages as we can from one indifference curve to another.[25] Alas, they are not fixed, which suggests that no program of welfare maximization that is both intelligible and plausible can be formulated on the desire-satisfaction account of welfare.

On the happiness account, however, the program of welfare maximization seems to be, in principle at least, straightforward. Brandt conceives of happiness in terms of enjoyment as follows: A person enjoys an experience if the experience makes him want to continue or repeat it for itself. (Since enjoyment involves desire, we can distinguish actual and corrected enjoyments.) At any moment a person's experience may include a number of enjoyments of greater or lesser intensity (where intensity is the strength of his desire that that part of his experience continue for its own sake). The level of a person's welfare at a given time is identified on this account, then, with his total happiness level at that time. Now assuming that we know what the consequences of alternative acts will be for an individual—what differences the performance of each will make in his life at each future moment—and assuming further that we can make measurements, we can determine how much happier he will be made by the performance of one of the acts than by the performance of the other. Denoting the acts as A and B, we can graph the times at which he is happier if A is done by plotting those points on a broken curve above the time axis. The distance of a point above the axis represents how much happier he is at that time because of A than he would have been, given B. Similarly, we can represent the times he is happier given B by points at appropriate distances below the axis. To determine whether A or B contributes more to the happiness of the person, we simply measure and compare the areas thus marked out above and below the axis.[26] To determine the relative effects of A and B for the general welfare, we construct curves for the happiness levels of all concerned and sum.

Brandt opts for the happiness theory of welfare principally because it allows for a coherent account of how one should go about promoting or maximizing the well-being of another and the general good. He suggests that it enjoys another telling advantage. When we reflect what it is we desire for those we care for, or for persons generally when we are moved by benevolence, it is surely their happiness, not the satisfaction of their desires. We want the latter, Brandt suggests, only insofar as (and to the extent that) we think that satisfaction will be enjoyed. Finally, the happiness theory of welfare allows us to distinguish between actions that are in one's self-interest and actions that constitute self-sacrifice. It is not easy to accommodate this and related distinctions on a desire-satisfaction account. Indeed, Brandt's preference for happiness over desire-satisfaction as constituting welfare represents a change of view partly induced by Mark Overvold's development of criticisms based on this consideration.[27]

Overvold's objection to Brandt's earlier view (that an agent's welfare is to be understood in terms of that act he would most want to do if he possessed all relevant information regarding the act and his desires and aversions were rational) is that it renders the idea of self-sacrifice incoherent. It is conceptually impossible on this view that one could wittingly, freely, and rationally sacrifice one's own welfare on behalf of another person or a cause. On this view what one wittingly, freely, and rationally does is by definition an act in the enhancement of his welfare. In "Individual Welfare and Getting What You Want," Overvold proposes a desire-satisfaction account of welfare that accommodates a distinction between what one wants and what pertains to one's welfare, as well as a distinction between acts that may (or may not) maximize the agent's welfare and acts that are self-interested or selfish. Finally, Overvold suggests as a virtue of his account that it makes psychological egoism (the thesis that persons are motivated only by a concern to maximize their own welfare) a substantive view, rather than one that follows trivially from the definition of welfare, and that it provides a framework for the evaluation of psychological egoism. It accomplishes these ends by distinguishing between those desires of an agent, and situations desired, that are pertinent to his welfare and those that are not, so that it is conceptually possible for him to seek ends in fact impertinent to his welfare or ends pertinent thereto, but without regard for their pertinence.

Briefly, Overvold proposes that the desires and aversions of an individual relevant to the determination of his welfare are precisely those for those states of affairs in which the agent's existence at given times is a logically necessary condition of those states of affairs' obtaining at those times. Moreover, an act that maximizes an agent's welfare is one that he would most want performed were he fully informed, and were he choosing in the light of his rational desires and aversions for those features and outcomes of the act in which his existence at a time was a logically necessary condition of their obtaining at that time. Overvold adds the qualification that if the fact that the state of affairs' occurring at a time entails the agent's existence at that time plays no role in explaining the agent's desire that it occur, then his desire does not pertain to his welfare.

By way of illustration, consider the example of a father whose daughter is badly in need of medical treatment, as he is himself.[28] Treatment cannot be afforded both. The father chooses that tomorrow he forego treatment so that his daughter can be treated then. *Prima-facie* he does not choose with an eye to his own welfare, but solely out of concern for his daughter's. On Overvold's account, however, *minus the qualification*, it might appear that his desire does count as pertaining to his welfare, because as formulated, the state of affairs that he desires involves his existence—his foregoing treatment at the time in question. Since, however, his desire for the state of affairs is not explained, we suppose, by the fact that it involves him in this way, the qualification excludes it, and his desire, as irrelevant to his welfare.[29]

The final essay of this section is an attack by Thomas Schwartz[30] on all attempts to account for welfare in terms of want satisfaction, happiness, or the like. Schwartz's rejection of "subjectivist" theories (those formulated in terms of person's desires, attitudes, or beliefs) is grounded, first, on the implausibility of treating the satisfaction of actual desires as good for the person satisfied, given the many defects to which desires are subject. (They may be based on misinformation or ignorance, weakness of will, inability to enjoy certain worthwhile things, or untoward conditioning.) Second, Schwartz doubts that an account of welfare can be given in terms of corrected desires that does not in effect incorporate the notion to be explained. Finally, he is convinced that subjectivist accounts entail psychological egoism.

Whatever the force of these criticisms for views like Brandt's or Overvold's, they are presented as a prelude to an account of welfare in terms of essential needs. According to Schwartz, welfare is related to *needs*, not wants, but not to all needs—not to all that would have to be met for one to carry out a particular life plan. Rather, welfare involves just those essential needs the meeting of which is necessary if one is to be able to live any satisfactory sort of life. Thus, what is good for one is understood objectively—not in terms of wants, preferences, or the like. Schwartz recommends his account of welfare as appropriate to a correct view of the ends of public policy as seen from the perspective of distributive justice.

IV

The final section of this volume is devoted to two moral issues affecting consideration of public policy. The first of these is the question of the conditions under which act utilitarianism would require of agents that they cooperate in the provision of public goods and whether those conditions are satisfied with respect to such pressing issues as population control and fuel conservation, in which effective action depends on the efforts of large groups of people. In his contribution to the discussion of this issue,[31] Rolf Sartorius concludes that with respect to many of the issues of greatest public concern, act utilitarianism provides no foundation in moral principle for voluntary cooperation. The reason for this, briefly, is that such cooperation (for example, turning back one's thermostat) will be without effect as regards the existence or nonexistence of a sufficient number of cooperating parties to produce the good in question (conservation). In general, Sartorius argues, one's cooperation will contribute to the general good in such cases only where by example it will serve to produce the necessary number of cooperating parties or where it is highly likely that the number will just fail of sufficiency by reason of one's noncooperation. But one's example is likely to be effective only in small groups. Moreover, it is only where small groups are involved that it is likely that one's cooperation will otherwise constitute the crucial difference.

Lawrence Becker takes issue with Sartorius here.[32] He argues that with regard to issues of public policy (even in the nation-state), we have the opportunity to cultivate in people a set of attitudes (for example, "feelings of solidarity, conviviality, and fraternity") that serve to offset the costs of cooperation. In addition, people can be trained in wide areas of life to dispense with calculation, to act spontaneously (as in loving another person). A rational maximizer of his own utility can understand these possibilities and realize that he stands to gain through the instilling of such attitudes and dispositions in people generally. Thus self-maximizers have reason to undertake to bring that about. But once such a task is undertaken, act-utilitarian considerations may require that agents behave cooperatively by reason of the fact that even self-maximizers are now disposed to cooperate.[33]

The second issue concerns what utilitarianism requires of us with respect to aiding others. It is often alleged that utilitarianism exaggerates our moral duty to meet the needs of others to whom, for example, we owe no special obligation by reason (say) of some significant relationship or whom we are in no wise bound to assist on grounds of distributive justice. It is often argued, moreover, that utilitarianism fails in these matters to reflect a proper respect for the interests of individuals. In his "Utilitarianism and Aiding Others," Dan Brock asks whether "utilitarianism is defective."[34] His answer is, first, that utilitarianism is indeed defective, especially in its failure to respect "the particularity and separateness of individual persons" and to acknowledge limits to the ways in which "we may deliberately use a person to further the ends of others."[35]

In "Utilitarianism and World Poverty," on the other hand, Tom Carson argues that utilitarianism captures, more nearly than many thinkers or the common-sense morality will allow, our very stringent duty to assist those peoples less fortunate than we who live in the industrialized nations of the northern hemisphere. Indeed, he contends that other plausible theories of right action prove on examination to have the same consequence.

Notes

1. "Mill's Proof of the Principle of Utility," Chapter 1 of this volume.
2. J. S. Mill, *Utilitarianism* (New York: Bobbs-Merrill Co., Inc., 1957), pp. 76, 77.
3. *Ibid.*, pp. 77-78.
4. David Lyons, "Mill's Theory of Morality," *Nous* 10 (1976): 101-120.
5. J. S. Mill, *On Liberty* (1859) Chapter IV, Para. 3, as cited in David Lyons, "Benevolence and Justice in Mill," this volume.
6. In the next four paragraphs, I have drawn upon remarks by Jerome Schneewind at Session I of our conference "The Moral Foundations of Public Policy: The Limits of Utilitarianism," May 18, 1978, and upon A. J. Simmons, "Utilitarianism and Unconscious Utilitarianism," this volume.
7. Dave Hume, *A Treatise of Human Nature*, edited by L. A. Selby-Bigge, Second Edition (Oxford University Press, 1978), p. 577. Also, *An Enquiry Concerning the Principles*

of Morals in *Enquiries Concerning Human Understanding and Concerning the Principles of Morals*, edited by L. A. Selby-Bigge, Second Edition (Oxford University Press, 1902), pp. 188, 192-204.

8. E.g., *Utilitarianism*, Chapter V.

9. Henry Sidgwick, *Methods of Ethics*, Seventh Edition (New York: Dover Publications, Inc., 1966), p. 425. See also Allan Gibbard, "Inchoately Utilitarian Common Sense: The Bearing of a Thesis of Sidgwick's on Moral Theory," chapter 4, this volume.

10. Gibbard, "Inchoately Utilitarian Common Sense."

11. Simmons, "Utilitarianism and Unconscious Utilitarianism."

12. Sidgwick, *Method of Ethics*, p. 424, notes that Adam Smith rejects the idea that utility "is either the first or the principal source of our approbation or disapprobation" while admitting "the objective coincidence of Rightness or Approvedness and Utility." My example is taken from Schneewind's remarks.

13. Gibbard, "Inchoately Utilitarian Common Sense."

14. *Ibid*.

15. W. D. Ross, *The Right and the Good* (Oxford: Clarendon Press, 1930), pp. 39-41.

16. Richard Brandt, *Ethical Theory* (Englewood Cliffs, N. J.: Prentice-Hall, Inc., 1959), pp. 244-252 and pp. 264-269.

17. Gibbard, "Inchoately Utilitarian Common Sense."

18. John Rawls, *A Theory of Justice* (Cambridge: Harvard University Press, 1971).

19. *Ibid*., p. 160 (as cited by Narveson).

20. Especially John Harsanyi, "Rule Utilitarianism and Decision Theory," *Erkenntnis* 11 (1977).

21. David Gauthier, "On the Refutation of Utilitarianism," Chapter 9, this volume.

22. *Ibid*.

23. *Ibid*.

24. *Ibid*.

25. Richard Brandt, "Two Concepts of Utility," p. 172.

26. In this case B produces more happiness for P than A would.

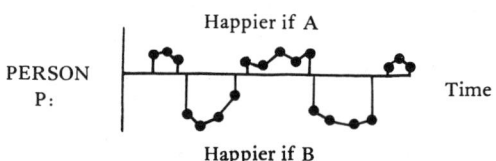

27. Brandt, "Two Concepts."

28. I adapt this example from T. Schwartz, "Human Welfare: What It Is Not," this volume. Schwartz uses it to exemplify his contention that subjectivist theories of welfare, including the desire satisfaction variety, entail psychological hedonism. Overvold's version of such a theory appears not to do so.

29. One may wonder whether Overvold's distinction works for an agent who desires to discharge an obligation he has to someone at the earliest possible time, which is, let us say, tomorrow. Does his desire count on Overvold's definition as one pertinent to his welfare? It seems that it does, but ought not.

30. Thomas Schwartz, "Human Welfare: What It Is Not," Chapter 12, this volume.

31. Rolf Sartorius, "Benevolence, Collective Action, and the Provision of Public Goods," this volume.

32. Lawrence C. Becker, "The Free-Rider Problem," this volume.

33. Those who wonder if the free rider problem will now arise at the second level will want to examine closely Becker's first "Objection" and "Reply," p. 221.

34. Dan Brock, "Utilitarianism and Aiding Others," this volume.

35. *Ibid*.

Section I: The Principle of Utility

The papers in this section are concerned mainly with the meaning, status, and justification of some version or other of the principle of utility. All of them, moreover, address these issues through the examination of classical sources, especially the works of J. S. Mill and Henry Sidgwick.

Although utilitarianism is understood to be a theory chiefly about what makes actions right or wrong, what has been advanced as "the principle of utility" has not always been a principle of right action: one asserting that the rightness of actions is determined by the value of their consequences or by their conformity to rules whose validity rests on the good that results from their general, effective acceptance. Mill, for instance, in *Utilitarianism*, uses the term "principle of utility" to refer to the thesis that the general happiness or utility is the one and only thing desirable as an end. Thus the principle for Mill concerns the good rather than the right. Nevertheless, it is clear that Mill takes the general happiness to be the basis of what he terms "the art of life" and thus of morality, which, on his account, is a division of that art. Moreover, he certainly seems to hold that the proof of his principle of the good establishes, through the connection of will and desire, the correctness of the utilitarian position that morality or right conduct is determined somehow in reference to utility, though leaving open the precise way in which it is so determined.

Two related issues concerning Mill's principle are its meaning and the adequacy of the "proof" he offers of it. Henry West defends Mill's proof of the principle on its traditional interpretation, according to which the general happiness is a sum of individual states of pleasure or contentment. John Marshall rejects Mill's proof of the principle so understood. He proposes an unorthodox reading of the principle as incorporating the ideal of the equal consideration of person's welfare. These readings suggest different accounts of the incidence of the principle on morality. West's points toward some form or other of utilitarianism, while Marshall's, according to which the principle is one of entitlement, indicates a more nearly contractarian theory of right action.

Mill's defense of utilitarianism is not limited to his proof of the principle of utility. At various places in *Utilitarianism* Mill provides further arguments for that account. These, moreover, indicate, in a sketchy way that invites differing interpretations, the bearing of utility on the morality of conduct. David Lyons develops one such interpretation that, he argues, allows Mill to distinguish obligations of justice from other moral obligations, and both of these from beneficence, generosity, or acts of supererogation. Most would regard the recognition of these distinctions by a theory as essential to its validity. Many have charged that utilitarianism fails to accommodate them.

Mill's arguments for utilitarianism appear to include two related sorts, either or both of which can be found in some form in the writings of other classical figures, e.g., Hume and Sidgwick. One is that utilitarianism provides the only plausible systematization of more specific moral principles acknowledged by common sense. Another, which Sidgwick developed at length, is that commonsense morality in any society tends naturally to alter in the direction of that set of rules whose general acceptance in that society will result in the greatest happiness. Alan Gibbard and A. John Simmons examine the force of these arguments, with special attention to the latter.

1 Mill's "Proof" of the Principle of Utility

Henry R. West

Utilitarianism, in every one of its forms or formulations, requires a theory for the evaluation of consequences. Whether the units of behavior being judged are acts, rules, practices, attitudes, or institutions, to judge them by their utility, that is, by their contribution to good or bad ends, requires a theory of what count as good or bad ends. In the philosophies of the classical utilitarians, Jeremy Bentham and John Stuart Mill, some variety of hedonism served this purpose. Mill calls this

> the theory of life on which this theory of morality is grounded — namely that pleasure, and freedom from pain, are the only things desirable as ends; and that all desirable things (which are as numerous in the utilitarian as in any other scheme) are desirable either for the pleasure inherent in themselves, or as means to the promotion of pleasure and the prevention of pain.[1]

In Chapter IV of his essay entitled *Utilitarianism*, Mill addresses himself to the question of what sort of proof this principle is susceptible. The twelve paragraphs of the chapter present an argument which, if successful, is one of the most important arguments in all of moral philosophy, for, although Mill says questions of ultimate ends are not amenable to "direct proof," he believes that considerations may be presented capable of determining the intellect to give its assent to the doctrine.[2]

Unfortunately, few commentators on Mill have had their intellects convinced, and perhaps even fewer have agreed on the correct interpretation of the argument. J. B. Schneewind says of it:

> A greater mare's nest has seldom been constructed. It is now generally agreed that Mill is not, in this chapter, betraying his own belief that proof of a first moral principle is impossible, but there is not a general agreement

as to what he is doing. In the last fifteen years there have been more essays dealing with the topic of "Mill's Proof" than with any other single topic in the history of ethical thought.[3]

Mill does say of the Utilitarian formula of ultimate ends that it is impossible to give a proof in the "ordinary or popular meaning of the term," but he continues,

> We are not, however, to infer that its acceptance or rejection must depend on blind impulse or arbitrary choice. . . . The subject is within the cognizance of the rational faculty, and neither does that faculty deal with it solely in the way of intuition. Considerations may be presented capable of determining the intellect either to give or withhold its assent to the doctrine, and this is the equivalent of proof.[4]

Furthermore, at the end of Chapter IV, he says that if the doctrine he has argued for is true, "the principle of utility *is proved*."[5]

Given the claim, that he has proved his principle or presented something equivalent to proof, I think it is worthwhile to lay out the structure of the argument in deductive form. In that way we can determine the nature of the premises he introduces, locate the gaps that prevent it from being a valid deduction, and see if plausible assumptions can be formulated or interpretations offered that will support the premises and bridge the gaps. I shall present what I believe to be a reasonable interpretation of what Mill had in mind, and I shall claim that the assumptions necessary to make the argument sound are—though controversial—at least plausible.

The conclusion he is seeking is stated in Paragraph 2: "The utilitarian doctrine is that happiness is desirable, and the only thing desirable, as an end, all other things being only desirable as a means to that end." The connection between this idea and morality is mentioned at the end of Paragraph 9, where he says that the promotion of happiness is the test by which to judge all human conduct, "from whence it necessarily follows that it must be the criterion of morality, since a part is included in the whole." Mill has a complex view of the way the ultimate standard of the promotion of happiness is to be applied in morality, and morality is only one of the "three departments" of what he calls the "Art of Life." These general teleological views on testing conduct, and the place of morality within this teleological framework, are found elsewhere in the essay and in the *Logic*.[6] They are not part of this "proof," and I shall not be discussing them in this paper. I shall be examining only how he gets to the conclusion that happiness is desirable and the only thing desirable as an end.

The structure of the argument is very simple. In Paragraph 3 he argues that happiness is desirable. In the remainder of the chapter he argues that happiness is the only thing desirable. The outline of the argument can be given in Mill's own words:

(1) "The sole evidence it is possible to produce that anything is desirable is that people do actually desire it." (Paragraph 3)

(2) "Each person, so far as he believes it to be attainable, desires his own happiness." (Paragraph 3)

(Therefore,)

(3) "Happiness is a good." (Paragraph 3)

He substitutes the expression "is a good" for the expression "is desirable," but I presume that this is only for stylistic reasons. I think he would regard his use of these two as interchangeable in this context.[7]

The argument to show that happiness is the only thing desirable is likewise based on the evidence of actual desire:

(4) "Human nature is so constituted as to desire nothing which is not either a part of happiness or a means of happiness." (Paragraph 9, but argued throughout Paragraphs 5-10)

(Therefore,)

(5) "Nothing is a good to human beings but in so far as it is either pleasurable or a means of attaining pleasure or averting pain." (Paragraph 11)

Here his use of "pleasure" and "pleasurable" instead of "happiness" is merely stylistic. Throughout the essay he says that by happiness he means pleasure and freedom from pain.

This is the simple outline of the argument. It is complicated by the fact that each individual's desire is for *his own* happiness, whereas the utilitarian doctrine that Mill is seeking to establish is that the *general* happiness is the foundation of morality.[8] In Paragraph 3, this distinction is explicit. Having said that each person desires his own happiness, Mill says we have all the proof it is possible to require

> that happiness is a good, that each person's happiness is a good to that person, and the general happiness, therefore, a good to the aggregate of all persons.

These propositions we may state as separate theses:

(3A) "Each person's happiness is a good to that person."

(Therefore,)

(3B) "The general happiness [is] a good to the aggregate of all persons."

The distinction also can be introduced into the second part of the argument. Without doubt the psychological premise (4) means:

(4′) Each person desires nothing which is not either a part of his happiness or a means of his happiness.[9]

And parallel to (3A) and (3B) the distinction between each person and the aggregate of all persons can be introduced. This would give:

(5A) Nothing is a good to each person but insofar as it is either a part of his happiness or a means of his happiness.

(Therefore,)

(5B) Nothing is a good to the aggregate of all persons but insofar as it is either a part of the general happiness or a means of the general happiness.

From (3B) and (5B), we can then deduce an interpretation of the "utilitarian doctrine," as follows:

(6) "[The general] happiness [or a part of the general happiness] is desirable, and the only thing desirable, as an end, all other things being only desirable as means to that end." (Paragraph 2)

Examining the argument, it can be seen that (1) is a methodological premise; (2) and (4) are factual psychological premises; (3) or (3A) and (5) or (5A) are supported by (2) and (4), respectively. (3B) and (5B) putatively follow from (3A) and (5A), respectively. The premise (2) is probably noncontroversial. The controversial premises are (1) and (4), and the controversial steps are from the fact of happiness being desired to its being normatively desirable, and from each person's happiness being desirable to that person to the conclusion that the general happiness is desirable to the aggregate of all people. There seem, then, to be three central issues: (A) Mill's methodology, which is to argue for what is desirable on the evidence of what is in fact desired; (B) his psychological hedonism, that each person desires his own happiness as an end and nothing as an end which is not a part of his happiness; and (C) the argument that if each person's happiness is a good and inclusive of the only good for him, as an end, the general happiness is a good, and encompasses the only good, as an end, to the aggregate of all persons. I shall take these issues up in turn.

A. DESIRE AS EVIDENCE OF DESIRABLE

I think it is hardly necessary to point out that Mill did not say that "desirable" or "the good" *means* "desired," as Moore says he does.[10] He is not committing a naturalistic or definist fallacy.[11] Mill is quite explicit in demarcating factual and normative propositions.[12]

I also think it is not likely he was misled by the similarity of the verbal endings of "visible" and "audible" into thinking that "desirable" means "able to be desired."[13] The significance of the analogy with visible and audible is announced in the first paragraph of the chapter: The first premises of our knowledge do not admit of proof by reasoning, but are subject to a direct appeal to the senses; he suggests that the first premises of conduct are subject to a direct appeal to our desiring faculty. It does not follow that he regards what is desirable as a "permanent possibility of desire." That would be to regard it as a matter of fact. The analogy is that as judgments of existence are based on the evidence of the senses and corrected by further evidence of the senses, so judgments of what is desirable are based on what is desired and corrected by further evidence of what is desired. The only evidence on which a recommendation of an end of conduct can be based is what is found appealing to the desiring faculty.

Mill also supports his appeal to desire by what is a pragmatic argument:

> If the end which the utilitarian doctrine proposes to itself were not, in theory and in practice, acknowledged to be an end, nothing could ever convince any person that it was so.[14]

Nothing about the logic of recommending an end of conduct prevents any end whatsoever from being recommended, but only one based on actual desires will be convincing. This is one respect in which the "proof" is not a proof in the ordinary sense. There is no necessity about accepting desire as the sole evidence for desirability. It is logically possible that ends of conduct that are not in fact desired by recommended without contradiction. The force of the appeal to what is desired is only to convince, not logically to rule out all other possibilities.

The import of premise (1), however, is primarily negative. It denies the existence of an intellectual intuition of the normative ends of conduct. The faculty to which Mill appeals is one that takes "cognizance" of practical ends, but by way of feeling or "sensibility" rather than intellect or moral sense. He is denying that we intuit what is intrinsically a good in some directly cognitive way.

The only way to argue a negative claim such as this conclusively would be to take each putative intuition and examine it critically to try to show that it can be reduced to desire or else to absurdity. I can obviously not do this to defend Mill's proof. I can only state that I find unconvincing all claims to intuit values, independent of desires (or likes and dislikes); so I find his skeptical starting point a plausible one. However, the desires we do have provide practical ends that will be pursued unless frustrated by the pursuit of the ends of other desires. This provides an arena in which practical reason can seek to bring order out of disorder by analyzing desires to determine which, if any, are illusory; which, if any, are fundamental; what, if anything is the common object of them all. It is this last question that Mill's psychological hedonism claims to answer.

B. PSYCHOLOGICAL HEDONISM

Mill's argument for (4) has two parts. One is in Paragraph 11, which classifies as mere habit those ends of conduct that are sought neither as means to happiness nor as a part of happiness. He claims that they have become ends of conduct

> Will is the child of desire, and passes out of the domination of its parent only to come under that of habit. That which is the result of habit affords no presumption of being intrinsically good.[15]

That argument leaves him with everything that affords any presumption of being intrinsically good an object of conscious desire. I think it is unnecessary to accept Mill's Associationist account of all habitual conduct or his account of all nondeliberative nondesiring willed behavior as habit. It is enough if actions that are not the result of deliberation and conscious desire afford no presumption that their ends help to identify for us what is desirable. Evolutionary ethicists, natural law theorists, and many others would perhaps deny this, but I find it a plausible skepticism.

The other part of his argument is to claim that every object of conscious desire is associated with pleasure or the absence of pain, either as a means or an end. Many desires are acquired, such as the desire for virtue or for the possession of money, and have come to be desired through the mechanism of their association with pleasure or the absence of pain. Whether acquired or not, the ultimate ends of the desires can be regarded as experiences or states of affairs with a pleasure component: They are pleasures or "parts of happiness." Although they may fall under various other descriptions, it is the fact that they are ingredients of happiness that provides a common denominator and a unified account of desire.

If Mill is correct that there is a pleasure component to the ultimate end of every desire, and if no other common denominator provides a unified account of desire, then Mill has a persuasive claim that it is the pleasure component (i.e., being part of happiness) that is the element in all objects of desire that makes them desirable as ends, which recommends them to the intellect as the basis for action and which can provide for critical assessment in case of conflict between desires.

It is tempting to read into Mill the claim that it is the agreeable quality of the state of consciousness desired that is the real object of desire. Just as the sense-data theorist claims that one sees only sense data, although it is palpable that he sees things that, in common languages, are decidedly distinguished from sense data (i.e., from whatever common language words are sense data words—"sights," "sounds," "appearances," or whatever), so Mill might be thought to hold that one desires only the pleasure component of desired experiences, although it is palpable that people "do desire things, which, in common language, are decidedly distinguished from happiness."[16] I think this is impossible to reconcile with Mill's talk of the objects of desire as being "music," "health," "virtue," "power," "fame," "possession of money," not just the agreeable feeling attending these. Furthermore, he does not need to make such a strong claim. He only needs to claim that, as a psychological fact, music, health, etc., would not be desired if no pleasure or freedom from pain or past association with these were connected with music, health, etc. Desire is evidence of desirability, but it does not confer desirability. This is obvious in the case of things desired as means. On reflection, it is obvious in the case of things desired as ends. The possession of money is desired by the miser. This desire does not make the possession of money a normative object of action for a reasonable person. The evidence furnished by desire must be analyzed; it is only by analysis of the fact that the miser desires the possession of money as part of his happiness—that he would be made happy by its possession—that the evidence of desire fits into a comprehensive theory. It is this comprehensive theory that identifies the pleasure inherent in desirable things as what makes them desirable. The pleasure inherent in them does not itself have to be discriminated as the *object* of desire.

Some commentators also have thought that Mill reduces the relation between desire and pleasure to a trivial one in the passage where he says that:

> desiring a thing and finding it pleasant, aversion to it and thinking of it as painful, are phenomena entirely inseparable, or rather two parts of the same phenomenon—in strictness of language, two different modes of naming the same psychological fact; that to think of an object as desirable (unless for the sake of its consequences), and to think of it as pleasant, are one and the same thing; and that to desire anything, except in proportion as the idea of it is pleasant, is a physical and metaphysical impossibility.[17]

This statement is certainly puzzling to the twentieth-century reader, but in context Mill is asking the reader to engage in "practiced self-consciousness and self-observation." If the terms were reducible to one another independent of observation, it is hard to see why he would invite one to attempt what appears to be an empirical discovery. A clue to interpretation is that "metaphysical" means approximately "psychological" for him.[18] In his notes on his father's *Analysis of the Phenomena of the Human Mind*, Mill takes issue with his father's statement, "The term 'Idea of a pleasure' expresses precisely the same thing as the term Desire. It does so by the very import of the words."[19] J. S. Mill says that desire:

> is more than the idea of pleasure desired, being, in truth, the initiatory state of Will. In what we call Desire there is, I think, always included a positive stimulation to action.[20]

According to J. S. Mill, then, a distinction is to be made between desiring a thing and thinking of it as pleasant. Desire is psychologically more complex and conceivably could have an object not thought of as pleasurable. It is obvious that it may have a more inclusive object, as is the case in desiring the means to an end when the means are unpleasant. In any case the question is a psychological, not a linguistic one.

Mill's substantive claim is that desire and pleasure (or the avoidance of pain) are psychologically inseparable. If this is true, two things follow: First, (4) is established—each person desires nothing that is not either a part of his happiness or a means of his happiness; second, since attainment of pleasure and avoidance of pain are the common denominators of desire, the evidence of desire supports the theory that it is the pleasure and pain aspects of the objects of desire and aversion that make them desirable and undesirable and that should serve as the criteria of good and bad consequences in a normative theory of conduct.

An adequate defense of Mill's position would require a more thorough analysis of desire and of pleasure and pain, happiness and unhappiness. I believe, however, that the interpretation given above shows that the position does not completely lack plausibility and that it might be supported by such a refined analysis.

C. FROM EACH PERSON'S HAPPINESS TO THE GENERAL HAPPINESS

If the intellect is convinced that the person's happiness is good and the sole good to that person, does it follow that it will be convinced that the general happiness is a good and the sole good to the aggregate of all persons? Mill presumably thinks this is obvious, simply asserting it without argument. He apparently thinks he has practically established (3B) when he has established (3A), and (5B) when he has established (5A). I think Mill has been misinterpreted in this argument because commentators have thought his conclusion to be a much stronger claim than it is. He is making a very weak claim, which is seen when we notice what he means by "the general happiness."

According to Mill "the general happiness" is a mere sum of instances of individual happiness. Just as personal happiness is not a "collective something" but simply a sum of pleasures,[21] so we can take Mill as holding that the general happiness is simply a sum of individual pleasures. There are still two ways of understanding the argument. One is that "to that person" represents the point of view of the agent when he is making prudential decisions; "to the aggregate" represents the point of view of the benevolent man when he is acting morally. Some things can be said in support of this interpretation, but I do not think that it is the correct one. I think rather that he believes that his analysis of desire shows that happiness is the *kind* of thing that constitutes intrinsic welfare, wherever it occurs. All instances of happiness will be parts of the personal welfare of someone, that is, "a good *to someone*," but being instances of happiness, they have a common denominator that makes them the same kind of thing wherever they occur—whether in different experiences of a given individual or in the experiences of different individuals. Moreover, Mill assumes that the value of different instances of happiness can be thought of as summed up to generate a larger good. These assumptions are explicit in a letter Mill wrote regarding the move from (3A) to (3B):

> As to the sentence you quote from my *Utilitarianism*, when I said the general happiness is a good to the aggregate of all persons I did not mean that every human being's happiness is a good to every other human being, though I think in a good state of society and education it would be so. I merely meant in this particular sentence to argue that since A's happiness is a good, B's a good, C's a good, etc., the sum of all these goods must be a good.[22]

His assumptions are even more explicit in a footnote to Chapter V of *Utilitarianism*. There, answering the objection that the principle of utility presupposes the anterior principle that everybody has an equal right to happiness, Mill says:

It may be more correctly described as supposing that equal amounts of happiness are equally desirable, whether felt by the same or by different persons. This, however, is not a presupposition, not a premise needful to support the principle of utility, but the very principle itself; . . . If there is an anterior principle implied, it can be no other than this—that the truths of arithmetic are applicable to the valuation of happiness, as of all other measurable quantities.[23]

It seems clear, then, that the "to each person" in (3A) and (5A) does not represent a "point of view," but simply the location or embodiment of welfare that cannot exist without location or embodiment, and the "to the aggregate of all persons" in (3B) and (5B) refers to the location or embodiment of welfare in a group of individuals, not a point of view. A good to the aggregate of A, B, C, etc., is interpreted by Mill to be a sum of goods to A, plus goods to B, plus goods to C, etc. He assumes both that happiness is arithmetical, capable of being summed up to find a total, "general" happiness, and that goods to different people are arithmetical, capable of being summed up to find a total good "to the aggregate of all persons."

With these assumptions, (3B) does follow from (3A), for to say that the general happiness is a good to the aggregate of all persons is merely to say that A's happiness, plus B's happiness, plus C's happiness, etc., constitutes a good to A, plus a good to B, plus C's happiness, etc. And (5B) follows from (5A). If nothing is a good to each person but in so far as it is a part of his happiness (or a means to it), then nothing will be part of the sum of goods to A, plus goods to B, plus goods to C, etc., but insofar as it is a part of the happiness of A or part of the happiness of B, etc., or a means to these. This interpretation explains why Mill did not bother to state (5A) and (5B) explicitly and why he passed from (3A) to (3B) in one sentence. The evidence of desire shows that happiness is the *kind* of thing desirable as an end. It is not a different kind of thing when it is located in A's experience from what it is when it is located in B's experience. Thus, whether or not any single individual desires the general happiness, if each of its parts is shown to be desirable by the evidence of desire, because of the kind of thing each part is, then the sum of these parts will be desirable because it is simply a summation of instances of the same kind of thing.[24] Given this interpretation the "utilitarian doctrine," represented by (6) is perhaps better stated by making clear that Mill believes happiness, wherever it occurs, is what is desirable as an end. This could be restated with the following reinterpretation:

(6) "Happiness is [the kind of thing which is] desirable, and the only [kind of] thing desirable, as an end, all other things being desirable only as means to that end."

From this, the connection with morality is said to follow:

(7) "The promotion of [happiness] is the test by which to judge of all conduct from whence it necessarily follows that it must be the criterion of morality, since a part is included in the whole."[25]

If my earlier elucidation of Mill's argument for happiness as the kind of thing that makes the objects of desires desirable was convincing, then the argument has some plausibility. Desire does not confer desirability; it is evidence for what kind of thing constitutes welfare. Thus, that one desires only his own happiness does not restrict the desirability of happiness to one's own happiness. If the desirability of happiness *as such* is identified (and not created) by one's own desire for it in one's own experience, its desirability—wherever it is located—can be admitted by the intellect.

That the value of different instances of happiness is arithmetical is certainly controversial, but not, I think, indefensible. Without an operational definition for measurement, it is difficult to know how happy two different individuals are, but it seems plausible that if two people do happen to be equally happy, then twice as much happiness exists. Mill recognizes the difficulty in determining how happy a person is. He thinks Bentham's measure of intensity and duration are inadequate to capture the complex hedonic dimensions of experience, asserting that the only test of the comparative pleasure of two experiences is the unbiased preference of those who have experienced both. This is not a direct measurement of felt experience, since the experiences are seldom if ever simultaneous. It is a judgment based on memory. In making interpersonal comparisons, it is even less reliable, since one can assume only a rough equality of sensibility between persons or make a rough estimate of difference in case evidence based on behavior or physiology shows a basis for difference. Thus summations of instances of happiness will be imprecise, but we do make judgments that one course of action will make oneself or another person more or less happy. These are not meaningless judgments; even if only rough estimates, they assume (and, I think, justifiably) that different instances of happiness are commensurable.

That the general happiness is simply the sum of the happiness of all individuals and that the good to the aggregate of all is simply the sum of the goods to each is, like Mill's methodological principle, primarily negative in its import. He is denying that there is any happiness or any value that cannot be analyzed without remainder as the happiness or the good of some individual or individuals. To prove this would require refutation of every claim to such an irreducible social good. So, again, I simply assert that I find his skepticism plausible.

If Mill's proof is plausible, as I have suggested, it does not follow that anyone will act on it. The intellect may be convinced that it is plausible or even that it is correct, without one thereby being moved to conduct his life in such a way as to maximize his own happiness or thereby being moved to identify the general happiness with his own and become a practicing utilitarian. That, according to Mill, requires a good state of society and education. But convincingly the intellect may be a first step.

Notes

1. John Stuart Mill, *Utilitarianism*, Chapter II, Paragraph 2. *Utilitarianism*, published in 1861, is reprinted in *Collected Works of John Stuart Mill*, Volume X: *Essays on Ethics, Religion and Society*, ed. J. W. Robson (Toronto: University of Toronto Press, 1969), pp. 203-259, and in various other editions. References will be to chapter and paragraph. Unless otherwise noted, references will be to paragraphs of Chapter IV.
2. Chapter I, Paragraph 5.
3. "Introduction" to *Mill's Ethical Writings*, edited with an introduction by J. B. Schneewind (London: Collier-Macmillan Ltd.; New York: Collier Books, 1965), p. 31. In the years following 1965 when Schneewind wrote this, the frequency of essays on the topic even increased.
4. Chapter I, Paragraph 5.
5. Paragraph 11. (Emphasis added.)
6. Book VI, Chapter XII. For an analysis of these complex views, see D. P. Dryer, "Mill's Utilitarianism," in *Collected Works of John Stuart Mill*, Volume X: *Essays on Ethics, Religion and Society*, pp. lxiii-cxiii, especially xcv-cxiii, and David Lyons, "Mill's Theory of Morality," *Nous* 10 (1976): 101-120.
7. In her essay, "Mill's Theory of Value," *Theoria* 36 (1970): 100-115, Dorothy Mitchell makes a distinction between "desirable" and "good" based on an analysis of the use of "desirable" in contexts of ordinary language. I think she is correct that they are not synonyms in English, but I think, nevertheless, that Mill is using them as such in this essay.
8. For a discussion of this point, see H. R. West, 'Reconstructing Mill's "Proof" of the Principle of Utility,' *Mind* 81 (1972): 256-257.
9. This part of Mill's psychological doctrine is stated explicitly in his essay on "Whewell's Moral Philosophy." He quotes Whewell as saying that "we cannot desire anything else unless by identifying it with our happiness." To this Mill says he should have nothing to object, "if by identification was meant that what we desire unselfishly must first, by a mental process, become an actual part of what we seek as our own happiness; that the good of others becomes our pleasure because we have learnt to find pleasure in it; this is, we think, the true philosophical account of the matter." ("Whewell's Moral Philosophy," *Collected Works*, Volume X: *Essays on Ethics, Religion and Society*, p. 184 note; Schnewind, ed., *Mill's Ethical Writings*, p. 192 note.)
10. George Edward Moore, *Principia Ethica* (Cambridge: at the University Press, 1948 [first edition 1903], p. 66.
11. Moore's interpretation of Mill as committing the "naturalistic fallacy" is analyzed and refuted by E. W. Hall in "The 'Proof' of Utility in Bentham and Mill," *Ethics* 61 (1950-51): 66-68. R. F. Atkinson in "J. S. Mill's 'Proof' of the Principle of Utility," *Philosophy* 32 (1957): 158-167, calls attention to the continuing difficulty presented by a footnote in Chapter V where Mill says ". . . for what is the principle of utility, if it be not that 'happiness' and 'desirable' are synonymous terms." This is a puzzling use of "synonymous" but I do not think that it has to be interpreted (absurdly) as claiming that "Happiness is desirdesirable" is a tautology. He may simply mean that the two terms are applicable to the same phenomena, one descriptively, the other normatively.
12. This is found in Book VI, Chapter XII, Section VI of the *Logic* where he says that a first principle of an Art (including the Art of Life, which embodies the first principles of all conduct) enunciates the object aimed at and affirms it to be a desirable object. It does not assert that anything is, but enjoins that something should be. "A proposition of which the predicate is expressed by the words *ought* or *should be*, is generically different from one which is expressed by *is*, or *will be*."
13. Another of Moore's charges, in *Principia*, p. 67.

14. Paragraph 3.

15. Paragraph 11.

16. Paragraph 4. J. S. Mill's father, James Mill, apparently did hold such a view "... we have a desire for water to drink, for fire to warm us, and so on." But, "... it is not the water we desire, but the pleasure of drinking; not the fire we desire, but the pleasure of warmth." (James Mill, *Analysis of the Phenomena of the Human Mind*, 2nd edition, ed. John Stuart Mill, Chapter XIX.)

17. Paragraph 10.

18. For example, he says that "the peculiar character of what we term *moral* feelings is not a question of ethics but of metaphysics." ("Whewell's Moral Philosophy," p. 185.) This interpretation of the term "metaphysical" is argued forcefully in M. Mandelbaum, "On Interpreting Mill's *Utilitarianism*," *Journal of the History of Philosophy* 6 (1968): 39.

19. James Mill, *Analysis of the Phenomena of the Human Mind*, 2nd edition, Chapter XIX. The passage continues: "The idea of a pleasure, is the idea of something good to have. But what is desire, other than the idea of something good to have; good to have, being really nothing but desirable to have? The term, therefore, "idea of pleasure," and "desire," are but two names; the thing named, the state of consciousness, is one and the same."

20. James Mill, *Analysis of the Phenomena of the Human Mind*, 2nd edition, Volume ii, Note 36.

21. Paragraph 5 and Paragraph 6.

22. *The Letters of John Stuart Mill*, 2 volumes, ed. H. S. R. Elliot (London: Longmans, Green, and Co., 1910), Vol. 2, p. 116; *Collected Works of John Stuart Mill*, Vol. XVI: *The Later Letters of John Stuart Mill 1819-1873*, edited by Francis E. Mineka and Dwight N. Lindley (Toronto: University of Toronto Press, 1972), p. 1414. Quoted in Schneewind (ed.), *Mill's Ethical Writings*, p. 339.

23. Chapter V, the second from the last paragraph of the chapter.

24. John Marshall, in "The Proof of Utility and Equity in Mill's Utilitarianism," *Canadian Journal of Philosophy* 3 (1973-74): 13-26, especially p. 16, points out the ambiguity in the question, "What is desirable as an end?" It can be taken to ask "What kind of thing?" or "What specific thing?" He interprets Mill as thinking more in terms of the first question in arguing that each person's happiness is desirable. I am claiming that Mill's proof is concerned only with the first question and believe that Marshall is reading in too much in finding a proof of equity as well. For a further statement of Marshall's position, see "Egalitarianism and the General Happiness" in this volume.

25. Paragraph 9.

2 Egalitarianism and the General Happiness

John Marshall

It is commonly supposed as beyond dispute that utilitarianism is a maximizing theory, that the utility to be promoted, directly by individual actions, indirectly by moral rules, moral virtues, or public institutions, is maximum utility, either maximum utility altogether (on the classical view) or maximum average utility (on most modern views). J. S. Mill's *Utilitarianism* is read, sometimes one way, sometimes the other, but it is almost always read in one way *or* the other. Of course, utilitarianism, in many of its traditional and perhaps in all its modern elaborations is a maximizing theory. And it is anything but forced so to construe Mill's *Utilitarianism;* some passages may be thought next to impossible to explain in any other way. Yet, some others, which at first seem to demand a maximizing account, can, I think with equal ease, be illuminatingly interpreted quite differently. Still others can hardly bear a maximizing construction at all. So any internally consistent reconstruction of Mill's theory, whether maximizing or not, must encounter some hostile text. In this paper, however, although I propose a nonmaximizing alternative to the traditional reading of Mill, I shall provide for this reading only an abbreviated defense, leaving most of the questions it poses unventilated. The *point d'appui* of my proposal is Mill's proof of utility, and my intention is to show that this proof, when consistently worked out, leads not to a maximizing conception of utility, but to one that is in an important sense egalitarian.

I

Mill's proof has three stages. In the first he argues that "Each person desires his own happiness" is intellectually determining evidence for "Each person's happiness is desirable." This is said to follow, in part, from a general principle (which I shall call Mill's principle of evidence) that the only evidence that something is desirable is that it is in fact desired by someone. For the purposes of this paper I shall simply accept this principle; my main aim is to show where it must lead if accepted. In the second stage, Mill argues that the only thing anyone desires as an end is his own happiness; this too I shall accept.[1] In the third stage, combining the conclusions of the first two, Mill argues that the general happiness and it alone is desirable.

On one account—the more or less standard account of this stage—the general happiness is taken to be a sum of individual happinesses.[2] Each individual's happiness, itself measurable and a sum of pleasures, is said to be a part of a still greater sum, the general happiness. Accordingly, that the general happiness is desirable follows directly from the conjunction, "Smith's happiness is desirable," "Jones' happiness is desirable," and "n's happiness is desirable"; the general happiness just is the sum of all the desirable happinesses of each individual.

Although there is much textual support for the standard account as an interpretation of Mill—an explanatory letter Mill wrote in 1868 might be thought to decide the matter[3]—as an argument it will not hold up. In the first place, it is doubtful (and I think false) that happiness is additive in the required way; in any case, that it is certainly does not follow from the fact, if it is a fact, that one person's happiness is commensurable with that of another. My height may be not only commensurable with but exactly the same as that of Smith, but there is not even clear sense, certainly no truth, in saying that in the two of us there is twice as much height as there is in either of us considered alone; there is even less sense in the corresponding claim about happiness. This is not to deny that, if Jones' happiness and Smith's happiness are individually desirable, both Jones and Smith should be made happy; after all, to make only one happy when both might have been could be condemned simply as a failure to promote a possible, intrinsically good state of affairs.

In the second place, and far more important to my argument, the standard account plainly violates Mill's principle of evidence. What that principle requires for the desirability of x is that x be desired by someone. There is no single individual, however, who desires the general happiness (the aggregate of all individuals is not itself an individual); therefore, even if the general happiness were a sum, its desirability could not be licensed by Mill's evidentiary principle. It is of no consequence that each part of this sum is desired by someone or other.

The problem here is not, or not just, that anyone who infers "the whole is desirable" from "Each part of the whole is desirable" must commit the fallacy of composition. This difficulty could be obviated with the help of supplementary premises. But the needed premises would have to contradict either Mill's principle of evidence or his contention that a person desires only his own happiness as an end. These, though not themselves indisputable, are in the present context fixed points.

II

Sidgwick, raising substantially the same objection, concluded that Mill's argument was a failure.[4] And so long as the general happiness is conceived as a sum of individual happinesses, it is a failure. But the general happiness need not be constructed from individual happiness in the standard way. One entirely different conception, which I here propose, is that "Each person's happiness is desirable" is simply equivalent to "The general happiness is desirable"; the change in terminology, though striking the intended note of universal beneficence, does not signal any logical advance.

What Mill's principle of evidence required is that each person's happiness be judged desirable. My desiring my happiness is evidence that it is desirable. The desire is, of course, mine, both as a psychological state and as a motivating reason, but as evidence for the desirability of my happiness it is evidence for everyone. My desiring my own happiness places the cognitive faculty of every other individual under the same rational constraint to acknowledge the desirability of my happiness as it does mine. On Mill's view, a desirability judgment is normative; it is one that does not simply assert that something is the case, but enjoins or recommends that something should be the case.[5] Accordingly, I have as much reason to hold that any other person should be happy as I have for holding that I should be. To say, then, that the general happiness is desirable is to say that it is desirable that each person be happy — as happy as possible. To be sure, that each should be as happy as possible is an ideal of the utilitarian theory of life; it remains to determine what steps should be taken to promote it. But, whatever the means, their end would be, not to maximize some chimerical sum of individual happinesses (or to maximize the average), but to give equal weight to each person's rational claim against all that his happiness be as great as the circumstances and their claims against him allow. (This rational claim, based on Mill's principle of evidence, is not itself a claim of justice — a matter I will explain below.) When Mill, adapting Bentham's phrase, says that each is to count as one and none for more than one, the logic of his argument demands not just the principle that when counting noses, we must count all, and none twice, say, because it is the nose of a prince, but also demands the strong principle that avoidable inequalities are ideal only if they work to the advantage of the less well off. In this sense, Mill's ideal is egalitarian.

To bring this abstract conception of general happiness, in Kant's phrase, closer to intuition, we might think in terms of an ideal equi-benevolent parent, a natural model for Mill's conception. If we suppose, to indulge in the fantasy I have disdained above, that the happiness of one person is not only commensurable with that of another but that both can be added together to make a definite sum, then we may imagine the equi-benevolent parent as having control over the distribution of all the happiness to be visited on his children, a control that also may indirectly determine the amount to be distributed. In the case in which the maximum possible happiness would be exhausted whatever the pattern of distribution, the parent must be seen as dividing all of it equally among all his children. Equi-benevolence precludes making one person happier than another when the inequality is avoidable and the unequal distribution would leave one child less happy than he would be under the equal distribution. On the other hand, if the sum would not be exhausted by maximal equal distribution, then so long as giving more to some than to others would not entail giving less to any than would equal distribution, benevolence demands the unequal distribution. In this case, the alternatives might be as follows: A, B, and C are the possible patterns of distribution, A permitting the largest total, B less than this maximum, and C less still, A distributing happiness unequally and leaving some below some level, x, B distributing happiness unequally and leaving all above some level, x plus n, and C distributing equally at a level between x and x plus n. A simple maximizer would elect A; a simple egalitarian C, but the equi-benevolent parent B.

The ideal equi-benevolent parent is only an imaginative model, in which respect it is like the more familiar impartial, sympathetic spectator; both models express the same substantive egalitarianism. That the impartial but sympathetic spectator is egalitarian has often been denied. John Rawls, for example, supposes that such a spectator would necessarily favor acts or policies that maximized happiness, equalizing distributive shares only when compatible with the maximum. Rawls' supposition is mistaken. A sympathetic person takes an interest in the happiness of each person, individually; nothing in his sympathy can explain an interest in the maximum amount of happiness altogether. Nor is any such explanation to be found in his impartiality. A simple maximizer would be indifferent, not sympathetic to the interests of individuals.

It has been said also that utilitarianism ignores the difference among persons, taking impersonality for impartiality. This is no doubt an apt criticism of some forms of the theory, but not of that which issues from Mill's proof. This form is egalitarian in a strong sense. Moreover, even if happiness were additive, the conception of general happiness implied by this proof would still not be maximizing.

III

The proposed conception of the general happiness bears a close resemblance to Rawl's general conception of justice as fairness:

> All social values—liberty and opportunity, income and wealth, and the bases of self-respect—are to be distributed equally unless an unequal distribution of any, or all, of these values is to everyone's advantage.[6]

This similarity calls for comment. To begin with a minor point of difference, Rawl's conception incorporates a theory of social primary goods (liberty, opportunity, etc.); these are, on the one hand, goods that it is rational to want more of rather than less, whatever one's particular view of the good life may be, and, on the other, goods whose distribution is largely governed by the basic institutions of society. Generally speaking, the more of such goods one has the happier one is likely to be. There is reason to question this theory of primary goods, but if it were true, it would in any case be neutral between contractarian and utilitarian theories and accordingly could be conjoined with the egalitarian conception of the general happiness, to yield something very like Rawls's general principle of justice. It is a requirement of justice, according to Rawls, that the means to happiness, that is, the primary goods, be distributed equally unless an unequal distribution leads to everyone's advantage. Similarly, on the assumption that one's supply of these means is directly proportional to one's degree of happiness, to promote the general happiness also would be to seek this same distribution of the means.

Here, however, the similarity ends. Rawls's conception is one of social justice; it expresses a basic moral constraint—a constraint of right—on the design of basic social institutions. The requirement laid on the design of public institutions directly by utility, however, is not a moral one, not a constraint of right. On Mill's view, a constraint of right is subordinate to utility. In this sense, his theory is teleological. But this utility—the general happiness—incorporates as part of its analysis the same distributive ideal as we find in Rawls; only in Mill's case, the egalitarian constraints on distribution are in the first instance constraints of reason, not of morality or justice; they issue directly from the proof of utility and are logically prior to the (Millian) concept of right (which is not introduced until chapter five of *Utilitarianism*).

The general happiness is, for Mill, the goal of what he calls a theory of life. It is, so far as the proof is probative, a rationally well-founded goal. But it is not thought to place us directly under any moral constraint always to seek it. Effective rules of morality are vital to the general happiness, but they do not regulate all of our practical decisions, not even all of those that might affect the general happiness. Moral right and wrong, as these are analyzed in Chapter V, have to do only with types of action that are peculiarly vital to the general happiness. One salient condition of the general happiness, for example, is the security of each individual, of which Mill writes.

> The moral rules which forbid mankind to hurt one another (in which we must never forget to include wrongful interference with each other's freedom) are more vital to human well-being than any maxims, however important, which only point out the best mode of managing some department of human affairs.[7]

This is not the place to work out the details, according to Mill, of the connection of morality and justice, or of these to expedience, but the main lines of the account are clear.[8] Justice is a part of morality. An unjust act is not only morally wrong—of a type that ought to be discouraged by the force of conscience if not by the threat of public opprobrium as well—it violates a right, something that ought to be protected not only by conscience, public opinion and public censure but, in the case of basic liberties, by law. The "ought," here, is *not* the moral "ought," but the "ought" of expedience utility.

Among the precepts of justice that can be derived from utility, Mill cites "that first of judicial virtues, impartiality."[9] This, he says, is justified, in part "as being a necessary condition of the fulfillment of the other obligations of justice." The maxims of equality and impartiality may, for this reason, be considered as corollaries of the other principles of justice, principles that forbid harm or the withholding of deserved or legitimately expected good.

> If it is a duty to do to each according to his deserts, returning good for good as well as repressing evil by evil, it necessarily follows that we should treat all equally well (when no higher duty forbids) who have deserved equally well of *us*, and that society should treat all equally well who have deserved equally well of *it*. . . . This is the highest abstract standard of social and distributive justice towards which all institutions, and the efforts of all virtuous citizens, should be made in the utmost possible degree to converge. *But this great moral duty rests upon a still deeper foundation, being a direct emanation from the first principle of morals, and not a mere logical corollary from secondary or derivative doctrines. It is involved in the very meaning of Utility, or the Greatest-Happiness principle.* [Final emphasis added.]

In this passage Mill all but expresses the very egalitarian conception of general happiness I have been urging on his behalf.

However, in a footnote, he adds:

> This implication, in the first princple of the utilitarian scheme, of perfect impartiality between persons is regarded by Mr. Herbert Spencer (in his *Social Statics*) as a disproof of the pretensions of utility to be a sufficient guide to right, since (he says), the principle of utility presupposes the anterior principle, that everybody has an equal right to happiness.

Now, on my proposed view, the reply to Spencer that Mill should have given is this: The principle of utility does not presuppose any anterior principle of an equal right to happiness, for this right is incorporated in the very meaning of utility (which point Mill does make); moreover, there is no circularity involved, since this equal right to happiness is not in the first instance a moral right. What Mill in fact says in the remainder of the footnote is:

> If there is any anterior principle implied, it can be no other than this—that the truths of arithmetic are applicable to the valuation of happiness, as of all other measurable quantities.

This comment seems to favor the standard, maximizing account of general happiness. Nevertheless, when we turn from the footnote back to the text, we find:

> The equal claim of everybody to happiness, in the estimation of the moralist and the legislator, involves an equal claim to all the means of happi-

ness, except so far as the inevitable conditions of human life, and the general interest, in which that of every individual is included, set limits to the maxim, and those limits ought to be strictly construed.

This, again, is all but an endorsement of the interpretation I propose.

I remarked at the outset that both the standard maximizing and my egalitarian readings of Mill will meet both congenial and hostile texts. By my intention was not to divine what Mill's own considered view should be taken to be; it was to show that Mill's proof leads to a notion of the general happiness that incorporates strong egalitarian demands on the distribution of happiness from the start.

Notes

1. I have discussed all three stages in "The Proof of Utility and Equity in Mill's Utilitarianism," *Canadian Journal of Philosophy* 3 (1973). In the present essay I argue for a somewhat different account of the third stage than I gave in the earlier paper.

2. Defended most recently by Henry West, this volume.

3. " . . . when I said that the general happiness is a good to the aggregate of all persons I did not mean that every human being's happiness is a good to every other human being; though I think, in a good state of society & education it would be so. I merely meant in this particular sentence to argue that since A's happiness is a good, B's a good, C's a good, &c., the sum of all these goods must be a good." *The Later Letters of John Stuart Mill*, ed. Francis E. Mineka and Dwight N. Lindley, Toronto & London: 1972, p. 1414. Letter to Henry Jones, June 13, 1868.

4. *Methods of Ethics*, London, 1962, p. 388.

5. *Mill's Ethical Writings*, ed. J. B. Schneewind, New York: Collier Books, 1965, p. 166.

6. *A Theory of Justice*, Cambridge: Harvard University Press, 1971, p. 62.

7. *Utilitarianism*, Ch. 5.

8. for some of these details, see two papers by David Lyons: "Mill's Theory of Morality," *Nous* 10 (1976); "Human Rights and the General Welfare," *Philosophy & Public Affairs* 6 (1977).

9. This and all the remaining quotations are from *Utilitarianism*, Ch. 5.

3 Benevolence and Justice in Mill

David Lyons

INTRODUCTION

Mill devotes the last and longest chapter of his essay on *Utilitarianism* to justice.[1] Along with his critics he recognizes that justice creates severe problems for his moral theory. But, whereas he regards justice as important, he does not think it is the whole of morality. In fact, he warns against "merging all morality in justice" by ignoring other moral obligations, such as those of "charity," "generosity," and "beneficence" (*U*, V, 15).

Mill provides no general name for the moral obligations that fall outside the realm of justice; his few comments as well as his utilitarianism suggest the term "benevolence." But we shall find this word misleading, and I shall use instead the neutral expression "nonjustice obligations."

My concern is Mill's division of morality. My aim is to reconstruct for Mill, so far as possible, a coherent set of moral doctrines within the limits of his theories of morality and justice and his version of utilitarianism. Reconstruction is in order, partly because Mill does not address the matter directly, but also because his views need some sympathetic refinement in the process of interpretation.

Mill's division of morality has not attracted much attention, perhaps because he is usually read as morally committed to maximizing happiness, in which case he would seem to have no clear need or even room for a theory of moral obligation, no less a complex, articulated theory. So my first task (which I take up in Section I) is to summarize my general understanding of Mill's theory of morality, built around the idea of obligation.

Work on this paper was supported by a fellowship from the National Endowment for the Humanities during 1977-1978, which I gratefully acknowledge. Earlier versions were presented at the University of British Columbia, the University of California at Davis, and the University of California at San Diego. I am indebted to D. G. Brown, David Copp, Richard Miller, and, most especially, Fred Berger, for helpful comments and suggestions.

Mill's division of morality has two aspects. One is a *conceptual* distinction between justice and other moral obligations. This concerns the idea of justice and by implication, the rest of morality, but does not tell us much about the substance of justice or nonjustice obligations. The other aspect is Mill's *substantive* conception of these two general categories of obligation and their requirements on conduct.

Section II takes up Mill's analytic division of morality; Section III deals with the substantive doctrines in terms of which Mill views that distinction. Both parts of Mill's theory require interpretation—a choice between two primary readings and a defense of one's choice against both textual and philosophical objections. The initial arguments are presented in Sections II and III, but the issues are pursued further in Sections IV-VII.

I argue in Section II that Mill's analytic division of morality turns basically on the notion of a right. Obligations of justice do, but nonjustice obligations do not, correlate with others' rights, according to Mill, so that an injustice is the violation of another person's right whereas other moral wrongs do not necessarily involve the violation of a right. This is Mill's official doctrine, but not the only way he draws the conceptual distinction. I try to show, on philosophical as well as textual grounds, that it is the better reading of Mill. Nevertheless, in at least one passage, Mill threatens to do the very thing he warns against, namely, "merge all morality in justice" (*U*, V, 15). He does so by seeming to assume, in that passage, that any wrong or immoral act involves the violation of another person's right. This difficulty is discussed at length in Section VII. The interpretive hypothesis I finally suggest (with some textual support) is that Mill believes the members of a community generally have a second-order *obligation of reciprocity* towards their fellow members. Although many moral obligations (those falling outside the category of justice) do not *necessarily* correlate with moral rights, when the conditions triggering the obligation of reciprocity are satisfied, an additional, complicating moral factor is introduced into the situation. When one owes it to others to reciprocate their performance of nonjustice (as well as justice) obligations, they also have a right to one's compliance with the same moral principles. So, although rights do not necessarily correlate with nonjustice obligations, rights correlate with the *special* obligation of reciprocity, and these rights are usually at stake when moral principles require us to behave one way rather than another.

I argue in Section III that Mill has, in effect, a negative utilitarian conception of moral obligations. Neither the obligations of justice nor nonjustice obligations require us to promote happiness in any direct way. These categories can be substantively distinguished as follows. Justice requires us to *avoid causing harm* to others, while nonjustice obligations require us to go further in protecting others by *helping to prevent harm*. This reading, too, is defended on both textual and philosophical grounds.

The most direct challenge to this reading of Mill is provided by D. G. Brown's significant discussion of Mill's theories of liberty and morality. On

Brown's reading of Mill, a wrong act causes harm to others. This leaves no room for nonjustice obligations on the interpretation I propose, which sees them as going beyond harm-avoidance to harm-prevention. I discuss these matters in Sections IV and V, in which I argue, first, that a carefully defined principle of liberty does not generate the difficulty; second, that Mill's analysis of morality in terms of sanctions is better read by emphasizing the internal sanctions, such as guilt feelings and self-reproach, rather than external sanctions; and third, that Mill's views about the enforcement of morality must accordingly be more carefully defined.

In Section VI, I try to show why Mill might be inclined to favor a negative utilitarian conception of the basic moral requirements. His apparent argument against paternalism could be extended to yield such a general conclusion, but it could not be so happily contained: Pushed to its logical extreme, it undermines Mill's principles of liberty and utility in general. I offer an alternative argument for Mill—one that seems to harmonize with his primary concerns in *On Liberty*[2] as well as *Utilitarianism*, one that emphasizes the importance of autonomy in Mill's conception of human happiness rather than practical difficulties in knowing others' interests. An essential and important part of living well—or living the best sort of life of which a human being is capable, according to Mill—involves finding one's own way, without help or hindrance from others. At this point in the reconstruction of Mill's doctrines, I am to some extent suggesting a revision more than offering a straight interpretation.

In Section VIII, I question one aspect of Mill's analytic division of morality—a view that is today, I think, quite widely accepted, though it is not associated with Mill. Although it may be held that any injustice involves the violation of a right, I argue that the converse is not plausible: Not every violation of a right is a matter of injustice. Some moral matters that involve rights are not automatically questions of justice. I suggest accordingly that Mill's division of morality needs refinement. The category of nonjustice obligations becomes even more heterogeneous than it first appeared.

This essay has a further theme—that of reconciling Mill's essays *On Liberty* and *Utilitarianism*. Mill's basic conception of morality is presented in *Utilitarianism*, but that work reveals little about his substantive conception of nonjustice obligations. An important source of clues is *On Liberty*, where Mill suggests the range of moral obligations that he recognizes and offers some comments on morality. His general conceptions of morality in these essays, however, appear to clash. My reconstruction of Mill's doctrines seeks to dispel the inconsistency.

I. MILL'S THEORY OF MORALITY

Mill is usually understood to hold a moral theory that expresses the most extreme doctrine of benevolence—a theory known lately as "act utilitarianism." This doctrine says that we must always "maximize utility," that is, promote human happiness or welfare as much as it is possible, on a given occasion, to do. On this view, the failure to maximize utility constitutes wrong or immoral conduct. If that is Mill's position, then his talk of "moral obligations" must be taken with a grain of salt. Rules of thumb may be helpful in reminding us of the usual utilities of certain types of action, but a direct application of the general welfare criterion to individual acts is held *always* to take moral precedence. Obligations have no special moral weight.

As I have tried to show in previous papers,[3] however, this reading of Mill is not the only or the best one. I assume that a moral theory should give special weight to moral obligations (not to speak of moral rights), and I find it possible for Mill to meet this test when one takes him at his word about the nature of morality and utilitarianism. On the one hand, his Principle of Utility says that happiness is the ultimate good, and thus it represents a *theory of value* — not of obligation. As a theory of value, it does not entail any moral requirements, and we are not obliged to understand Mill as making the mistake of assuming that it does — of assuming, in effect, on the act-utilitarian interpretation, that moral requirements are a simple function of instrumental value. On the other hand, Mill appears to hold as a conceptual matter that the rightness and wrongness of conduct is a function of moral duties or obligations, some of which correlate with moral rights. We can understand this so that it does not collapse into act utilitarianism. Wrong conduct consists in the breach of a moral obligation; that is, a breach that cannot be justified by an overriding obligation. A reconstruction of Mill's view points toward the idea that obligations are determined by the utility of internalized standards of conduct. The Principle of Utility thus has *only an indirect* role in moral reasoning; it is not itself a moral principle. It provides the basis for evaluating claims about moral obligations (some of which are also claims about moral rights) in the light of the relevant facts. It does not directly determine the rightness and wrongness of acts. Nor is there an obligation to maximize utility, since there is no satisfactory argument to the effect that it would serve the general welfare, in the long run, if we were to internalize an overriding commitment to maximize utility.

The resulting theory of obligation thus diverges from act utilitarianism and resembles the sort of theory lately called "rule utilitarianism." An important feature of Mill's theory, on my interpretation, however, is that it is based upon his conceptual analysis of moral right and obligation, which tells us how to determine moral rights and obligations by considering the effects of internalized standards of conduct.[4] Mill's ideas about the principles of justice and nonjustice obligations thus assume considerable importance. These principles are the ultimate *moral* guidelines for behavior. They limit the requirements of morality on conduct, and so leave room for supererogation, or meritorious conduct that is not morally required.

II. MILL'S ANALYTIC DIVISION OF MORALITY

Moral rights and the distinction between justice and nonjustice obligations. According to Mill, injustice is a specific type of immorality. It involves "two things:

wrong done, and some assignable person who is wronged." From this Mill seems to infer that "the specific difference between justice and generosity or beneficence" is that, in the former case but not in the latter, there is "a right in some person, correlative to the moral obligation" (*U*, V, 15).

> Justice implies something which it is not only right to do, and wrong not to do, but which some individual can claim from us as his moral right. No one has a moral right to our generosity or beneficence because we are not morally bound to practice those virtues toward any given individual. (*U*, V, 15)

Mill thus distinguishes obligations of justice from other moral obligations in terms of the presence or absence of corresponding rights.

This is Mill's official doctrine—the one he explicitly adopts. But there are two complications here. In the first place, Mill's way of putting the point in the passage quoted tends to run the conceptual and substantive levels of his division of morality together, because he assumes that nonjustice obligations have the content referred to. He assumes, for example, that morality requires us to be generous, which is not a requirement of justice. But it is also clear that his division of morality into justice and nonjustice obligations has two levels—a conceptual level, which is meant to be independent of both utilitarianism and competing doctrines, and a substantive level that, in Mill's case, of course, is predicated on service to the general welfare. That is Mill's avowed approach to moral rights and justice. His theory of nonjustice obligations should, presumably, be understood analogously.

We might use one of Mill's examples in a different way to make his conceptual point. As soon as something may be claimed from me by another person as a matter of his moral right, as something that is owed to or due him, my providing it for him cannot be characterized as generosity, since I would only be giving him what is already his. By the same token, someone who appeals to my generosity cannot be understood as standing on or seeking recognition of his moral right to the desired benefit or service; he is not claiming that benefit or service as something that is owed to or due him, as something that is already his by right.

In the second place, Mill entertains a different way of distinguishing between justice and nonjustice obligations—one that is not equivalent to his distinction in terms of rights.

Perfect and imperfect obligations. Before Mill settles upon his distinction between justice and nonjustice obligations in terms of the presence or absence of corresponding rights, he observes that the same distinction is sometimes drawn in terms of a contrast between

> duties of perfect and of imperfect obligation; the latter being those in which, though the act is obligatory, the particular occasions of performing it are left to our choice, as in the case of charity or beneficence, which we are indeed bound to practice but not toward any definite person, nor at any prescribed time. (*U*, V, 15).

Mill explains the difference between perfect and imperfect obligations in terms of a tight or loose connection between obligations and the rightness or wrongness of conduct. When a tight connection exists, then the breach of the moral obligation constitutes immoral conduct. (This definition requires qualification—but only qualification—to accommodate the possibility of an overriding moral obligation.) But when there is a loose connection, no such judgment about conduct follows (not even "prima facie").

Take the case of charity. Mill appears to assume that one ought to be charitable—one ought to help others by sharing some of one's wealth and resources—but that one is morally free to decide when to "practice" that "virtue." If one rarely performs a charitable act, even though one has had ample opportunity to do so, one may be said to lack that virtue, one's moral character may be said to be deficient, and one's *overall* behavior may be criticized accordingly.

But there is a difficulty here. If charity is obligatory only "imperfectly," in the way Mill suggests, then the connection between such an obligation and the morality of conduct is *too* loose for his purposes. For in that case no particular acts of charity are ever required of any person. Moreover, from one's failing to perform a charitable act on a given occasion, when he has the opportunity to do so and no overriding obligation pertains, we *cannot ever* infer that he has breached his moral obligation to be charitable and has acted wrongly. But it does seem possible for someone to act wrongly by breaching a moral obligation without at the same time acting unjustly. Mill apparently wishes to leave room for this possibility. If so, the distinction between justice and nonjustice obligations drawn in terms of perfect and imperfect obligations, as Mill sketches the contrast, will not do.

Consider the idea of a duty to oneself. This is a good example because, though Mill does not believe that we have such duties (that they are *morally* binding; cf. *OL*, IV, 7), the idea of a duty to oneself does not seem unintelligible and should be allowed for by an *analysis* of moral obligations or an *analytic* division of morality, such as Mill's. That is done by using Mill's primary account of nonjustice obligations as obligations that lack correlative moral rights. Suppose, for example, that one's duties to oneself prohibit one to commit suicide or mutilate oneself (except when such conduct can be justified by an overriding obligation). This means that *(ceteris paribus)* one would act wrongly by committing suicide or mutilating oneself. On the distinction between perfect and imperfect obligations as Mill has drawn it, however, this means that a duty to oneself would qualify as a perfect obligation. If Mill drew the distinction between justice and nonjustice obligations in such terms, then, he would be obliged to classify such a duty to oneself as a duty of justice, which is implausible. This consequence is avoided by Mill's official account, that obligations of justice do whereas other obligations do not, correlate with others' moral rights. For it is implausible to suppose that any person has a moral right that correlates with a duty that he has to himself.

Though Mill expresses dissatisfaction with the terminology of "perfect" and "imperfect" obligation, he does not explicitly reject that way of drawing the distinction. He does not consider the complications I have mentioned. He merely passes on to use the presence or absence of corresponding rights as the basis for his analysis of justice.

But, though Mill does not explicitly reject this second account of the contrast between justice and nonjustice obligations, I propose for the present to ignore it. It would seem unwise to burden Mill, at the outset, with so limited a conception of nonjustice obligations as this second account implies. Later on I shall reopen the question because this way of viewing nonjustice obligations would provide one way of reconciling otherwise clashing aspects of his overall position. But we can postpone these complications until later (see Section VII(b) below).

III. MILL'S SUBSTANTIVE DIVISION OF MORALITY

So far, all we have is a distinction between two types of moral obligations, with no clear notion of what the obligations themselves are supposed to require or allow. Mill tells us very little, especially about nonjustice obligations. Let us consider first what he tells us about justice, and then turn to his examples of moral duties or obligations.

A preliminary interpretation: Justice requires the avoidance of harm and nonjustice obligations require positive benefits. "Justice," Mill says, "is a name for certain classes of moral rules which concern the essentials of human well-being more nearly, and are therefore of more absolute obligation, than any other rules for the guidance of life" (*U*, V, 32). More specifically, "the moralities which protect every individual from being harmed by others, either directly or by being hindered in his freedom of pursuing his own good," are the ones that "primarily . . . compose the obligations of justice." The principles of justice are predicated, in Mill's view, on protecting certain vital interests, such as security, and the chief rules of justice "forbid mankind to hurt one another" (*U*, V, 33).

This suggests a *negative* utilitarian conception of justice, the obligations of which are seen as prohibiting various forms of conduct that harm other persons. Now, since Mill is *some* sort of utilitarian—and thus favors the promotion of human welfare, even if he does not believe that we are always required to act so as to maximize it—it is natural to suppose that his conception of nonjustice obligations complements his conception of justice. Nonjustice obligations may be understood as requiring us to go beyond avoiding harm to others. It is natural to suppose that moral obligations outside of justice require us to act in ways aimed at conferring *positive benefits* and services on other persons, at least to some degree, in some forms, and in some circumstances. If so, "benevolence" would seem a suitable heading for this sector of morality.

Our initial hypothesis, then, is that Mill balances a *positive* utilitarian conception of nonjustice moral obligations against a negative utilitarian conception of justice. Some plausibility is conferred on the positive utilitarian interpretation of Mill's theory of nonjustice obligations by his reference to "charity," "generosity," and "beneficence." Although charity may well be limited to helping individuals in need (and thus might be covered by negative utilitarian considerations), beneficence is traditionally contrasted with "nonmaleficence" and is associated with positively promoting individuals' welfare, beyond mere harm-prevention.

In reviewing the texts of *Utilitarianism* and *On Liberty*, however, one finds no reinforcement of this initial hypothesis. Mill offers no further examples of moral duties or obligations (outside of justice) in *Utilitarianism*, and those he gives in *Liberty* seem limited by the aim of harm-prevention. We do *not* appear to be morally required, in Mill's view, to confer positive benefits or services on others. The only apparent exception would be when one has undertaken to provide a positive benefit or service for another. But this exception is only apparent, for the case is assimilated by Mill to the obligation to keep one's promises; and Mill believes that this obligation has a *negative* utilitarian rationale.

A refined interpretation: Justice requires the avoidance of harm and nonjustice obligations concern harm-prevention more generally. In the essay *On Liberty*, Mill offers two sets of examples of moral duties (or what, for Mill, amounts to the same thing viewed from another standpoint: two sets of examples of immoral actions). Both of these suggest a negative utilitarian conception of moral obligation in general. But these examples nevertheless leave room for nonjustice obligations. For Mill can be understood to hold that, whereas obligations of justice are predicated on avoiding harm to others, nonjustice obligations fall within the further reaches of a negative utilitarian conception of morality. Some of the obligations that Mill acknowledges in *Liberty* and classifies under "beneficence" are clearly predicated on preventing harm to others, even when one's failure to perform them could not be characterized as causing harm to others or as failing to avoid harming others. In other words, Mill believes that we are morally bound, not just to avoid harming others, but also to take positive steps to come to others' aid, and more generally to help prevent harm to others.

Mill's first set of examples appear in his initial presentation of the Principle of Liberty. Mill is concerned throughout the essay *On Liberty* to mark off areas in which coercive intervention cannot be justified. When he first introduces his principle, however, he indicates some cases in which coercive intervention *would* be justified. Some of these examples interest us because they are characterized as cases of moral duty. Thus, Mill says, first, "If anyone does an act hurtful to others, there is a *prima facie* case for punishing him by law or, where legal penalties are not safely applicable, by general disapprobation" (*OL*, I, 11). But Mill does not stop there. He says:

> There are also many positive acts for the benefit of others which [one] may rightfully be compelled to perform, such as to give evidence in a court of justice, to bear his fair share in the common defense or in any other joint work necessary to the interest of the society of which he enjoys the

protection, and to perform certain acts of individual beneficence, such as saving a fellow creature's life or interposing to protect the defenseless against ill-usage — things which whenever it is obviously a man's duty to do he may rightfully be made responsible to society for not doing. (*OL*, I, 11)

One might summarize this passage by saying that Mill believes (a) that we are under obligations to cooperate in some joint undertakings and to act as good samaritans, and (b) that these obligations can legitimately be enforced.

One may be tempted to interpret these examples in either of two extreme and contrary ways. On the one hand, one might suppose that some, at least, are predicated by Mill on the idea of promoting welfare rather than preventing harm. On the other hand, one might suppose that they are all conceived of by Mill only as prohibiting us from acting in ways that would cause harm to others. A consideration of these alternative readings will help explain as well as reinforce the interpretation recommended here.

The former way of looking at the examples focuses on Mill's comment that these duties require "positive acts for the benefit of others." Whereas the good samaritan requirements, such as "saving a fellow creature's life" and "interposing to protect the defenseless against ill-usage" imply harm-prevention rather than the positive promotion of others' welfare, the cooperation requirements might be interpreted in welfare-promotion terms. It is commonly held today that we are under obligations of fairness to cooperate in collective ventures, the benefits of which we have accepted, when our turn comes to do our part, where no condition is laid down that these ventures must be limited to harm-prevention and cannot be aimed at positively promoting welfare.

Various considerations militate against this first alternative reading. For one thing, it would be strange for Mill to approve of the enforcement of obligations predicated on positively promoting welfare in the context of an essay dedicated to the principle "That the only purpose for which power can be rightfully exercised over any member of a civilized community, against his will, is to prevent harm to others" (*OL*, I, 9). If the *enforcement* of such duties can be justified only on harm-prevention grounds, then one would imagine that Mill conceives *the duties themselves* as aimed at preventing harms. Furthermore, the harm-prevention reading I propose is also compatible with Mill's actual language in the passage. For example, "positive acts for the benefit of others" should not be read as "acts for the *positive benefit* of others": It emphasizes *positive acts*, as opposed to the omission of acts that cause harm to others; and "benefits" often refers merely to the prevention or elimination of harm.

My reading of the examples also is reinforced by Mill's reiteration of them later in the essay, when he summarizes his position by saying that

> everyone who receives the protection of society owes a return for the benefit, and the fact of living in society renders it indispensable that each should be bound to observe a certain line of conduct toward the rest. This conduct consists, first, in not injuring the interests of one another, or

rather certain interests which, either by express legal provision or by tacit understanding, ought to be considered as rights; and secondly, in each person's bearing his share (to be fixed on some equitable principle) of the labors and sacrifices incurred for defending the society or its members from injury and molestation. . . . Nor is this all that society may do. The acts of an individual may be hurtful to others or wanting in due consideration for their welfare, without going to the length of violating any of their constituted rights. The offender may then justly be punished by opinion, though not by law. (*OL*, IV, 3)

This passage will require further comment later. For now, it should suffice to say that Mill appears to have in mind only the prevention of harm to others as the basis for these requirements.

At the same time, Mill includes within the range of these examples requirements that he himself places under the heading of "individual beneficence" — acts aimed at preventing harm to other individual persons, such as saving lives or defending those threatened with attack. Although none of his examples suggests that moral obligations require us to confer positive benefits or services on others, they do suggest that nonjustice obligations require us to go beyond merely refraining from harming others by requiring us to take *positive action* (or, at least, to modify our conduct) to prevent harm to others even when, if harm were suffered, it could not be said to have been caused by us.

Thus, in Mill's view, I have a duty to save a drowning man, when I am in a position to do so, even though I may *not* be said to have *caused* the harm he will suffer if I fail to save him (since his plight may be caused by an accident, say, or the action of a third party). Similarly, I am under an obligation to give testimony in court when that is needed, even though my failure to give testimony in many such cases *cannot* be construed as conduct that is harmful or dangerous to others. My being under such an obligation can be explained in negative utilitarian terms — the need for such a rule in the framework of a court system that is ultimately justified on harm prevention grounds. I am under an obligation in such cases, not because I must avoid harming others, but rather because I am required to help *prevent harm*, by giving direct assistance to those I find in need and, somewhat less directly, by cooperating in ventures that prevent harm to others. Lives can be saved and harms to others can be prevented or eliminated by conduct that complies with such obligations.

This brings us to the second alternative way of reading Mill's examples: to conceive of them merely as prohibitions on conduct that causes (or at least threatens to cause) harm to other persons. One may be tempted to interpret them in this way because Mill sometimes suggests that his Principle of Liberty must be understood quite narrowly, as warranting interference *only* with conduct that causes (or at least threatens to cause) harm to other persons, and these examples are all cases in which coercive intervention can be justified under that principle.

But this interpretation is not compelling. Mill's statement of the Principle of Liberty does not demand so narrow an interpretation. And the principle, if so narrowly construed, cannot accommodate these very examples—examples that are given by Mill of interference that would be justified under the principle.[5] Mill says, as we have seen, "That the only purpose for which power can be rightfully exercized over any member of a civilized community, against his will, is to prevent harm to others" (*OL*, I, 9). This principle would justify restrictions on conduct that is harmful or dangerous to others; but it can also justify restrictions on conduct that is neither harmful nor dangerous to others, so long as the restrictions are instrumental in preventing harm to others. Mill's good samaritan and cooperation requirements (limited to preventing harm) illustrate the possibilities. Mill says not only that we are morally bound to act in such ways, but also that these duties may be enforced. The enforcement of such duties cannot be understood as prohibiting conduct that causes (or threatens) harm to others, but it can be predicated more broadly on the prevention of harm to others. These examples seem to show Mill's belief that harm to others can be prevented, not just by prohibiting or otherwise suppressing harmful and dangerous conduct, but also by requiring or otherwise eliciting conduct that contributes directly or indirectly to the prevention of harm to others.

Mill's second set of examples of moral duties are in line with these in the relevant respect: They suggest that Mill's substantive theory of obligation is predicated broadly on the prevention of harm to others. The second set is offered while Mill is clarifying his approach to "self-regarding faults"—conduct that is contrary to the interests of the agent but not others. He says that these faults "are not properly immoralities," and he contrasts them with cases that are (and that are thus counted by Mill as breaching moral duties or obligations). Mill's examples of immoralities are these:

> Encroachment on [others'] rights: infliction on them of any loss or damage not justified by [one's] own rights; falsehood or duplicity in dealing with [others]; unfair or ungenerous use of advantages over them; even selfish abstinence from defending them against injury—these are fit objects of moral reprobation and, in grave cases, of moral retribution and punishment. (*OL*, IV, 6)

Most of these would be classified by Mill (if he follows his own theory of justice as outlined in *Utilitarianism*) as cases of injustice. But the last example seems to fall under Mill's heading of "individual beneficence" (what we are calling good samaritan requirements). Mill's use of this example reinforces my interpretation of his substantive theory of nonjustice obligations, namely, that it goes beyond requiring us to avoid harming others and requires us to help further in preventing harm to other persons. Moreover, Mill's strategic use of "even" at the start of this example implies that he would not go further—that he would not regard as immoral the failure to promote positive benefits for others (save in the performance of voluntary undertakings).

Mill's examples of moral duties and obligations suggest, then, that he conceives of those requirements as predicated on the prevention of harm to others. They go beyond the mere avoidance of harm, and thus beyond the apparent rationale for obligations of justice in Mill's theory, and they extend to the prevention of harm to others, but they do not seem to go any further.

Complications. However, difficulties arise in this reading of Mill—some of them created by Mill himself and springing from apparent inconsistencies among his doctrines. I shall take up the following points:

(1) It has been argued that Mill limits wrongful conduct to acts that cause harm to others. We have already considered this claim to some extent, but a fuller discussion of the issue is in order because it points to the connections between Mill's theories of liberty and morality (Section IV below).

(2) The examples that have guided our interpretation of Mill's substantive theory of moral obligation may appear suspect because they are all cases in which Mill is prepared to endorse the enforcement of morality. One might suppose that Mill believes some moral obligations ought not to be enforced, and it is not implausible to suppose that these would include requirements that go beyond the mere prevention of harm to others. If so, the examples we have considered have been systematically misleading. To deal with this issue, we must consider the relations between liberty and morality in Mill (Section V).

(3) Mill's views about paternalism suggest one possible basis for limiting moral requirements to the prevention of harm to others. One of Mill's arguments, as given, appears unsound, but can be revised in a promising way (Section VI).

(4) Some of the difficulties for Mill's theory of nonjustice obligations arise at the analytic rather than the substantive level. In *Liberty* Mill appears to imply that *all* moral obligations correlate with others' moral rights. This would entail that we have no nonjustice obligations, according to the division of morality laid down in *Utilitarianism.* Several ways of resolving this complication may be advanced: (a) discounting the passage in question; (b) imagining that all nonjustice obligations are modeled by Mill on charity; (c) observing how Mill might find rights linked with some of the obligations that we have assumed he would place outside of justice; (d) taking seriously Mill's suggestion that we are under an obligation of reciprocity to comply with certain useful rules (Section VII).

(5) In trying to reconstruct Mill's division of morality, however, we should not be guided too rigidly by his conception of justice in *Utilitarianism.* For Mill's analysis of justice is incomplete, and the corresponding category of moral requirements is accordingly too broad (Section VIII).

IV. WRONG CONDUCT AND HARM TO OTHERS

Brown's reading of Mill. In an important study of Mill's theories of morality and liberty, D. G. Brown renders Mill's Principle of Liberty as follows:

(L) The liberty of action of the individual ought prima facie to be interfered with if and only if his conduct is harmful to others.[6]

Some comment and qualification is required. The idea that is meant to be expressed here is that there is, in Mill's view, *just one good reason* for interfering with someone's liberty—just one reason capable of justifying social intervention—namely, that his conduct is harmful to others. But this reason is not necessarily conclusive, since good reasons can be given against interfering; to capture this qualification, Brown uses "prima facie." As Brown I think would agree, however, we probably should qualify his formulation to read "harmful or dangerous to others," since Mill evidently meant his principle to license interventions against conduct that is dangerous to others, even though it may not be harmful in all cases, such as reckless driving.

Now, Mill's Principle of Liberty is supposed "to govern absolutely the dealings of society with the individual in the way of compulsion and control, whether the means used be physical force in the form of legal penalties or the moral coercion of public opinion" (*OL*, I, 9). From this passage and others it is evident that Mill's principle directly concerns what he calls "external sanctions" (*U*, III, 4). A striking fact Brown draws to our attention is that Mill *also* links external sanctions to the idea of wrong conduct. In the same section of *Utilitarianism* in which Mill distinguishes justice from other moral obligations, he traces a connection between "the idea of penal sanction" and that of wrong conduct (or the breach of moral obligation). He says, for example, "We do not call anything wrong unless we mean to imply that a person ought to be punished in some way or other for doing it. . . . Duty is a thing which may be *exacted* from a person, as one exacts a debt" (*U*, V, 14). Partly on this basis, Brown attributes to Mill a *Principle of Enforcing Morality,* which he formulates as follows:

> (M) The liberty of action of the individual ought prima facie to be interfered with if and only if his conduct is prima facie morally wrong.[7]

The justification that is referred to here must be qualified as "prima facie" because Mill indicates that coercion may not be employed in all circumstances.[8]

Although Brown formulates the Principle of Enforcing Morality (M) similarly to the Principle of Liberty (L), it must be understood quite differently. For (L) purports to give the *only* good reason for coercive intervention. If (M) were read in a similar way, it too would purport to give the *only* good reason for coercive intervention—but a *different* one; and then the two principles would be inconsistent. Mill makes this clear when he lays down, as a corollary of the Principle of Liberty, that the wrongness of someone's conduct cannot justify interference (*OL*, I, 9).

To avoid needlessly imputing inconsistencies to Mill, without abandoning Brown's main interpretive claim, one must understand that Principle of Enforcing Morality to say (as Brown suggests), not that wrongness itself *gives a reason* for interference, but rather that *there is some reason* for interference when, but only when, conduct is (prima facie) morally wrong. This allows the Principle of Liberty to do what Mill explicitly says it does, namely, state the only justification for interference.

If Mill endorsed both (L) and (M), then he would be committed to the proposition that

(P) Conduct is prima facie morally wrong if and only if it is harmful [or dangerous] to others.[9]

This proposition implies that an act cannot be wrong unless it is harmful (or at least dangerous) to some other person.

One reason this result is significant is that it clashes with the usual reading of Mill as an act utilitarian, according to which he holds that an act is wrong if it simply fails to maximize utility.[10] For one might fail to maximize utility by failing to bring about as much pleasure, joy, happiness, or other positive benefit, either to oneself or to others, as one might have brought about by doing something different under the circumstances, without however harming or endangering another person. So, Mill cannot consistently accept (P) along with act utilitarianism. More precisely, he cannot accept both these doctrines unless he implausibly believes that one cannot fail to maximize utility without harming or endangering other person; but we have no reason for attributing such a belief to Mill.

(P) clashes with my reading of Mill's theory of nonjustice obligations. For reasons presented in Section I, I have no difficulty accepting the idea that Mill is not an act utilitarian. But I perceive a difficulty for Mill if he accepts proposition (P). For reasons developed in Section III, it would appear that his substantive theory of nonjustice obligations rests on the idea that we must sometimes modify our conduct in order to prevent harm to others, even when our unmodified conduct could not be characterized as harmful or dangerous. This would mean that some wrong acts are *neither harmful nor dangerous* to others, but merely fail to help prevent harm to other persons.

If Mill is not inconsistent, then either Brown's reading or our hypothesis about Mill's substantive theory of nonjustice obligations is mistaken. But if our hypothesis is mistaken, then it would seem that Mill leaves no room in his substantive conception of morality for nonjustice obligations, and it is not clear why he makes a special point of acknowledging them.

The refinement of (L) and its consequences. This particular difficulty disappears if we are guided by my reading of Mill's Principle of Liberty. Brown formulates that principle as follows:

(L) The liberty of action of the individual ought prima facie to be interfered with if and only if his conduct is harmful [or dangerous] to others.

But, as I have argued, Mill's principle must be understood more broadly just to accommodate his own examples. This broader reading—which is suggested by

Mill's own official formulation—says that interference may be used, not only to suppress conduct harmful or dangerous to other persons, but more generally to prevent harm to persons other than those whose freedom is restricted. Thus, if my freedom is to be restricted, then the justification for that restriction must include the prevention of harm to others.

We might formulate (just for present purposes) the refined Principle of Liberty as follows:

> (L′) The liberty of action of the individual ought prima facie to be interfered with if and only if interference with it prevents harm to others.

If we combine this principle with the Principle of Enforcing Morality, then we cannot generate proposition (P). We cannot use it to show that Mill is committed to the view that conduct is prima facie morally wrong if and only if it is harmful (or dangerous) to other persons. We can infer only that

> (P′) Conduct is prima facie morally wrong if and only if interference with it prevents harm to others.[11]

Loosely speaking, we might say that the revised correlation of (L′) and (M) imputes to Mill the proposition that wrong conduct *either* harms others *or* fails to help prevent harm to others. But this result accords with our hypothesis about Mill's substantive theory of nonjustice obligations, which is understood as requiring us to take positive action, or otherwise to modify our conduct, in order to prevent harm to others, and not just to avoid harming others.

V. MILL ON THE ENFORCEMENT OF MORALITY

The conceptual link between sanctions and wrong conduct. But we must go further. We cannot rest content with the correlation between the Principle of Liberty and the Principle of Enforcing Morality as presented by Brown, not just because the Principle of Liberty requires qualification. The correlation may be more radically misconceived. If so, it cannot be relied on as a guide to Mill's conception of wrong conduct and, in turn, moral obligation.

So far as the correlation constructed by Brown turns on Mill's analysis of morality in *Utilitarianism*, it assumes that his theory links the idea of wrong conduct (and thus of moral obligation) to the idea of *external* sanctions. For, if it does not, then Mill's analysis of morality does not generate a Principle of Enforcing Morality, it does not overlap with the Principle of Liberty (which is concerned with external sanctions), and it cannot be used to generate a conclusion about the character of wrong conduct. I shall argue here that Mill's analysis of morality should be understood as concerning "internal" rather than external sanctions, and thus that it cannot be used as a basis for interpreting his substantive theory of morality in the way that Brown suggests. I shall go on to argue, however, that a substantive Principle of Enforcing Morality is revealed within Mill's discussion of liberty.

When Mill traces a connection between "the idea of penal sanction" and the concept of wrong conduct, he clearly stretches the former to cover not just external threats and penalties of an informal, extra-legal nature, but even guilt feelings and self-reproach. When he says "We do not call anything wrong unless we mean to imply that a person ought to be punished in some way or other for doing it," he adds, in my view significantly, "if not by law, by the opinion of his fellow creatures; if not by opinion, by the reproaches of his own conscience" (*U*, V, 14). Here "punishment" encompasses self-reproach as well as external sanctions. Furthermore, Mill suggests that self-reproach is not just one among a number of alternative forms of "punishment," the justification of which is connected with the idea of wrong conduct, but rather that it is the minimal, essential sort of "punishment" so linked with the idea of immorality. Mill says that external sanctions may or may not be justified for wrong conduct, but that guilt feelings are always warranted when one acts wrongly.

Brown can accommodate Mill's actual words by qualifying the justification for social intervention that is supposed to be connected with wrong conduct as "prima facie." This allows him to read Mill as saying that external sanctions are not always justified, all things considered, though there is always a presumption in favor of them when conduct is (prima facie) morally wrong.

I do not claim that this reading clashes with the text. I question Brown's reading because it saddles Mill with less plausible contentions than his words, purposes, and conclusions appear to require. One must remember that Mill's enterprise here (*U*, V, 14) is explicitly analytic. He is not laying down substantive principles of punishment, but is trying to display some of the *conceptual* elements of moral obligation and wrong conduct. Mill clearly associates external and internal sanctions very closely, thinking of them all as means of social control and as distinguishable from other devices, such as taxation, by an element of condemnation. But I think we do no favor to Mill if we emphasize his assimilation of internal to external sanctions. Brown's reading represents Mill as extracting from the mere concept of wrong conduct an *analytic* Principle of Enforcing Morality that links wrongness to *external* sanctions; otherwise, the correlation between that Principle and the Principle of Liberty collapses. But the question whether an act is wrong seems logically separate from the question whether others have any warrant for interfering. On my reading, these questions are separate for Mill, whereas on Brown's reading they are not. I understand Mill to claim that wrongness is conceptually connected with justified guilt feelings, but only *synthetically* connected with external sanctions. This seems a more plausible position than the one that Brown attributes to Mill.

To see this point, as well as some reason to believe that Mill in his considered judgment would prefer my version, consider once again the idea of a duty to oneself. Although Mill rejects the claim that we have such duties, he does not have to be read as maintaining that the *mere idea* of a duty to oneself, requiring one to promote one's own welfare or at least to avoid harming oneself, is unintelligible. He can be understood to hold that ascriptions of such duties are false. They are excluded, not by logic, but by considerations of utility (*OL*, IV, 6). Let us combine this idea with another point. Mill holds that others may not interfere with one's purely self-regarding conduct, conduct that would fall within the ambit of a duty to oneself. But he does *not* maintain that the opposite opinion, the acceptance of paternalistic intervention, is unintelligible. I believe that he would furthermore agree that the following position can be held without contradicting oneself: "One has duties to oneself alone, but there is no warrant for interference by others in such matters since they concern oneself alone." If I am right about this—if such a composite claim is not self-contradictory—then the idea that wrongness implies a warrant for others' interference is mistaken; and furthermore Mill would deny such a warrant. If so, we should hesitate to impute the analytic Principle of Enforcing Morality to him when there is room for doubting his acceptance of it.

It follows that we should hesitate to use Brown's correlation of the Principle of Liberty and the Principle of Enforcing Morality as a basis for understanding Mill's conception of wrong conduct and moral obligation.

This does not mean that Mill rejects "the enforcement of morality." He cannot, of course, consistently with the Principle of Liberty, maintain that immorality per se is a ground for intervention, but he can believe that the Principle of Liberty always provides some justification for interfering against wrong conduct. This is because as a matter of fact wrong conduct might have to satisfy a condition that *also* justifies interference under the Principle of Liberty. Such a position follows from our reading of Mill: Conduct is not wrong unless it harms, endangers, or fails to help prevent harm to other persons—which is the condition that warrants intervention under the Principle of Liberty.

Mill's Principle of Enforcing Morality. Mill seems to endorse a Principle of Enforcing Morality in the essay *On Liberty*. It is not objectionable there, in the way it would be if it were incorporated in his analysis of morality, because it can be understood as a derived, *substantive* principle. The context is Mill's claim that purely "self-regarding faults" do not warrant coercive intervention (*OL*, IV,5-7). Mill makes this claim, however, by contrasting them with "immoralities"—"fit objects of moral reprobation." The latter are "acts injurious to others," including, as we have seen, "even selfish abstinence from defending them against injury." The passage clearly implies that "duties to oneself" are not properly enforceable *because* they are not moral duties or obligations. Mill is not committed to the view that morality per se is enforceable. His position is based on utilitarian reasoning, as is the Principle of Liberty itself. One is not accountable to others for the performance of one's "duties to oneself," Mill says, "because for none of them is it for the good of mankind that one be held accountable to them" (*OL*, IV, 6).

It should be observed that Mill does not regard all moral duties and obligations as legitimately enforceable. When speaking of "acts injurious to others," he says that they "are fit objects of moral reprobation and, *in grave cases, of moral retribution and punishment"* (*OL*, IV, 6; emphasis added). This suggests that immoral acts satisfy *a* condition that also must be satisfied by conduct that legitimately may be interfered with, but that they do not automatically satisfy *all* such conditions. They do so only "in grave cases."

Mill leads us to believe, then, that there is a convergence between his substantive theory of moral obligation and his doctrine of liberty. If that is so, then we have no reason to suspect that his examples of moral duties and obligations in the essay *On Liberty* are misleading, just because they are regarded by Mill as properly enforceable. Some moral requirements are properly enforced and others are not, but they are all predicated on the prevention of harm to others.

A new difficulty. So far, perhaps, so good. But Mill goes further. He contrasts "the loss of consideration which a person may rightly incur by defect of prudence or of personal dignity, and the reprobation which is due him for an offense against the rights of others" (*OL*, IV, 7). In context, this statement implies that *all* immoralities are violations of others' rights, which appears to commit Mill to the view that all moral duties and obligations correlate with others' rights. Mill thus seems to make the mistake he warns against in *Utilitarianism:* He "merges all morality in justice" by implying (according to the analysis given there) that all moral obligations are obligations of justice.

This formulation poses a different problem for Mill than the one we have been considering. We have been worrying about the negative utilitarian basis for his substantive theory of obligation. At first this might have seemed to rule out nonjustice obligations, but we have come to see how the prevention of harm to others, when it extends beyond the mere avoidance of harm, leaves room for some limited forms of "beneficence." Now, however, it appears that in *On Liberty* Mill may be excluding at the conceptual level all nonjustice obligations.

We will turn to this matter in a moment. First, I wish to suggest one reason why Mill might wish to place moral obligations within the confines of preventing harm to others.

VI. PATERNALISM AND BENEVOLENCE

Mill's rejection of paternalistic intervention (that is, coercive interference aimed at benefiting those whose liberty is restricted) follows formally from the Principle of Liberty. But this may be misleading. Mill actually offers no general argument for the principle, though he does give arguments for its chief corollaries, such as the rejection of paternalism. One of Mill's arguments against paternalism may be used to explain his rejection of positive benevolence as a moral obligation. But we shall find it unsatisfactory.

The argument from ignorance and risk. Mill's actual argument against paternalism may be summarized as follows (*OL*, IV, 4, 12): We know our own interests well, because we naturally care about them; but we do not have reliable knowledge of others' interests, because we do not concern ourselves nearly so much about them. We are likely to be right in judging whether others' actions will adversely affect *us*, and so the use of coercion for the purpose of "self-protection" can, at least in some cases, be justified. But our judgments about the effects of others' actions on *their* own interests are so unreliable as to make paternalistic intervention counterproductive.

One might imagine Mill extending this argument as follows: If we are such poor judges of others' interests, then benevolence is just as pointless as paternalism is counterproductive. To conceive of benevolence as an obligation is to conceive of sound moral requirements that we confer positive benefits on others independently of mutual arrangements. But, given our ignorance of others' interests, any disposition to benefit others is unlikely to be really helpful. It will often be positively harmful. Such internalized dispositions cannot be justified on utilitarianism grounds; so moral obligations are quite properly predicated on, and generally limited to, the prevention of harm.

There are several difficulties with these arguments—both the original one against paternalistic intervention and the suggested extension of it against obligations of positive beneficence. It will suffice, for our purposes, if I show how they conflict with Mill's intentions: The given argument against paternalism is far too sweeping, since its premises would undermine much more than paternalism if they were effective against it.

Mill apparently believes that some coercive intervention can be justified, that is, for the purpose of preventing harm to others. But if paternalism were misconceived because we simply do not have reliable knowledge of others' interests, then we would presumably be ignorant not just of what benefits others but also of what harms them. We would be incapable of usefully directing any sort of coercive intervention. The argument would extend not only against positive benevolence, but also against nonmaleficence: We would have no moral obligations to avoid harming others, either. Indeed, by such reasoning, we would be incapable of making any judgments about the general welfare!

Mill appears to miss these implications of his argument against paternalism because he characterizes the restrictions that would be licensed by the Principle of Liberty as "self-protection." His metaphor leads him to imagine that we need merely know our own individual interests when evaluating coercive intervention, and need not know others'. But that is a mistake, as Mill himself should recognize. For he often envisages coercive intervention on the model of legislation and its enforcement, and these assume judgments about the interest of persons other than those who initially set the rules or later apply them. Under the Principle of Liberty, we do not merely restrict persons other than ourselves who threaten to act contrary to our own personal interests. More typically, we restrict persons who threaten to act contrary to someone else's interests. Under Mill's own principle, coercion typically would be used by one party to protect a second from a third. For such intervention to be well-grounded, the first party must have reliable knowledge of the second party's interests.

An alternative argument against paternalism and positive beneficence. It does not follow that Mill must reject the idea that we do not know others' interests well enough to act on such knowledge, and consequently must accept paternalistic intervention. An alternative is possible—one that seems implicit in his acceptance of action based on harm-prevention, along with his qualms about paternalistic intervention and positive requirements of positive benevolence. Mill can distinguish between our knowledge of what harms persons and other knowledge of their interests. It is clear that he wishes to do this anyway; for his doctrines of liberty and justice both plainly assume that we have knowledge of the vital interests of human beings and of the major harms that one can suffer, and that such knowledge is a sound basis for both private conduct and public action. Furthermore, without some such general knowledge, the Principle of Utility itself could not be put to any useful work.

Mill believes that certain conditions must be satisfied if one is to have a reasonable chance of living well as a human being. He believes, for example, that we all require certain biological conditions, such as physical nutriment; security in our persons and in others' undertakings to us; freedom from others' interference and from oppressive customs; even a variety of experiences and of opportunities for self-development. One might suppose that it is the lack or deprivation of such things that Mill chiefly refers to as "harm." The sort of view Mill suggests is this: Human beings have certain fundamental interests in common; beyond this, they vary a great deal. Because they vary, they have a special interest in being left alone as much as possible, to find their own ways, to develop their own judgment, to experiment with their own lives. Most important, engaging in such activities is an *essential* part of what it is, in Mill's view, for a human being to live well and thus be "happy." In this respect, human happiness cannot be understood in terms of the satisfaction of existing preferences. That is clearly not what Mill has in mind when he discusses happiness most carefully and at length. For, as he well understands, acting on existing preferences and for maximum gratification can be contrary to living well as a human being and thus contrary to one's best, long-term interest (see, e.g., *OL*, III, and *U*, II, 4-8).

If we understand Mill in this way, we might help him salvage his argument against paternalistic intervention. Since we have reliable knowledge of certain universal, vital human interests, coercive intervention can be predicated on preventing harm, which is constituted by the undermining of these interests. Beyond this, however, coercive intervention is most likely to be counterproductive. This is *partly* because people vary a great deal in their further interests, so that living well will be different for different persons. But living well also involves *finding one's own way.* An added factor, of course, is the clear costs of "compulsion and control." Coercive rules can be justified only when the stakes are comparatively high, the interests to be protected are not speculative but uncontroversial, and the interests themselves do not militate against intervention. Intervention can therefore be justified only when it is predicated on serving a limited range of common, basic interests, or in other words, on preventing the corresponding range of unproblematic harms. To put this another way: Mill suggests an argument for identifying a limited class of "primary goods," the service of which is the only acceptable basis for social intervention. It is not that we lack other interests or cannot be harmed in other ways, but rather that, given a full view of human interests, it appears wisest to limit public policy by reference to these interests and harms.

Such an argument would allow Mill to reject so-called "strong paternalism," which permits interference with others' conduct not only to prevent them from harming themselves but also to make them serve their own positive interests better. This is because Mill would be committed by the foregoing argument to grounding intervention on the prevention of a certain class of primary harms. It follows, however, that Mill may have to accept a "weak" version of paternalism, one that allows interference in order to prevent a person from harming himself, though his version need only be based on protecting those uncontroversial, unproblematic, shared interests, or primary goods.

But this would seem, in turn, a welcome modification of Mill's position on paternalism. For he appears to condemn weak as well as strong paternalism (except in special circumstances), and thus seems to go too far. The idea of a primary good involving the preservation of freedom might show how to account for Mill's obscure condemnation of contracts into slavery (*OL*, V, 11). On the revised version of weak paternalism suggested here, Mill can also accept various social schemes that are sometimes urgently needed to prevent harm, even though the beneficiaries might actually reject them, such as mandatory pension plans and medical insurance.

The revision of Mill's approach to paternalism has, of course, another consequence more directly relevant to our purpose here. It suggests how Mill might reject any moral requirements of positive beneficence. His argument would rest in part on variations among individuals and our lack of reliable knowledge of others' interests beyond certain primary goods, as well as the costs of guilt feelings and self-reproach when obligation is put to this additional use. Furthermore, what people need most from us, Mill seems to say, is the secure establishment of certain conditions necessary for a good human life, and beyond that benevolent tolerance or neglect.

We thus have some reason to believe that Mill wishes to limit the range of moral obligations—that he would require us to avoid and help prevent and eliminate harms to others, but would not generally require us to confer positive benefits or services on others. This accords with all the information we can extract from *On Liberty* and *Utilitarianism* about the duties Mill actually recognizes and with the chief doctrines of those works.

VII. RIGHTS AND LIMITED BENEFICENCE

Now we must return to the problem we deferred at the end of Section V: Mill's suggestion that all our moral obligations correlate with others' moral rights. This position was suggested in his contrast of self-regarding faults with immoralities, because Mill treated immoralities as violating others' rights. How can this idea be reconciled with Mill's acknowledgment of nonjustice obligations, when the latter are defined as obligations that do *not* correlate with others' rights?

(a) *Discounting Liberty*. One possibility would be simply to discount the troublesome passage. The only basis that we might have for doing so, I think, is this: *On Liberty* was composed earlier than *Utilitarianism* and does not address itself directly to analytical questions such as those dealt with in the latter work. It seems reasonable to suppose that Mill's concern with identifying the nature of justice led him to appreciate the distinct character of nonjustice obligations and that the analysis of morality in *Utilitarianism* expresses his more considered judgment of these matters.

There may be an element of truth in this way of treating Mill's difficulty, but it is important to observe that alternative accounts are possible.

(b) *Nonjustice obligations as imperfect*. In Section II we considered Mill's account of the "imperfect" obligation of charity. Such an obligation is incapable of determining the wrongness of particular actions. If all of the nonjustice obligations that Mill recognizes were like charity, then all wrong actions would be breaches of justice obligations and, accordingly, violations of another's right. This could explain Mill's suggestion that all immoralities violate others' moral rights.

The trouble with this explanation is that it does not account for some of Mill's own examples of nonjustice obligations. Take the case of "individual beneficence," violation of which is instantiated as "selfish abstinence from defending [others] against injury." The latter would seem to count as wrong conduct—and so be unlike the lack of charity—and yet fall outside injustice. One's moral obligation to be a good samaritan cannot be modeled on the imperfect obligation of charity, but it does not seem to be (in our or Mill's view) an obligation of justice either.

(c) *Perfect obligations and rights*. Mill's good samaritan requirements are not like charity because they do *not* allow free choice about whether or not to confer one's services on potential beneficiaries. When someone is drowning or is under attack and I am in a position to help, Mill believes, I am under a moral obligation to come to that person's aid. If I fail to do so, I may be condemned accordingly, not just as an uncharitable person.

Let us take this further. If I perform only as duty requires, gratitude may be an appropriate response on the part of the person I have helped—but it is the gratitude of someone who also could feel resentment and even indignation at my failing to help him. If he needs my help and I am morally bound to help him, then he may rightfully demand it. He may furthermore assume all those attitudes that one may rightfully hold about another who is on the verge of respecting or failing to respect one's right to another person's assistance. That is to say, in such cases, it is not implausible to suggest that the individuals we are *morally bound to help* may be said to *have a right* to our assistance—not just a right in the weak sense that they would do no wrong in accepting it, but in the much stronger sense that they would individually be *wronged* if denied it. Thus, Mill might hold that one has a right to help from others when the others are in a position to help prevent harm to one in such a situation. This idea would partly account for Mill's suggestion that rights are violated whenever moral obligations are breached. It would, at least, account for good samaritan requirements.

It might be objected, however, that this way of reconciling Mill's doctrines in *Utilitarianism* and *On Liberty* is unacceptable, because it requires Mill's category of justice to encompass far too much. All "perfect" obligations, all obligations with a direct bearing on the rightness and wrongness of particular actions, would be included. To avoid this result, one might resist the argument that the beneficiaries of good samaritanism be considered as having moral rights to others' help. One might argue, for example, that terms like "moral right" should be limited to cases in which one individual has a certain "limited sovereignty" over another — a claim on the other that he can press or waive at his option, either insisting on the other's performance or releasing the other from the obligation generally or else from its immediate demands. Hart observes that when terms like "right" and "obligation" are limited to such cases, they have distinctive linguistic functions to perform. They are not needed to characterize cases in which one person simply ought or ought not to behave in a certain way and the applicable requirement cannot be waived by the potential beneficiary.[12]

This line of reasoning should not affect our interpretation of Mill's doctrines. In the first place, it is not clear that in the relevant cases the potential beneficiary cannot waive his rights and release the other person from his obligation to help. In the second place, Hart sees "right" and "obligation" as tied together. He would object, for example, not only to the suggested use of "moral right" in good samaritan cases, but also to Mill's broad use of "moral obligation" (even when restricted to "perfect" requirements). In the third place, and most important, Hart's strictures are not based on the actual limits of these concepts but amount to recommendations. Hart urges that we refine our use of "right" and "obligation" by reserving them for distinctive purposes. But he recognizes that these terms are not normally so restricted, and thus he cannot claim that Mill's use of "obligation" or the suggested use of "moral right" is conceptually defective. Hart's argument therefore cannot show that Mill would err if he held that all moral duties and obligations that we actually have, including good samaritan requirements, correlate with others' moral rights.

However, other difficulties occur with this way of accounting for Mill's claim that all wrong actions violate others' rights. In the first place, one's moral obligation to act as a good samaritan does not seem to be an obligation of justice. One trouble with this approach then, is that it tends to overpopulate the category of justice. In the second place, it would render Mill's expressed concern about "merging all morality in justice" misleading, at best, justified only by his recognition of imperfect obligations such as charity. The result would not be satisfying.

It should be observed that Mill's category of justice is already overpopulated, for related reasons. As I shall argue later, Mill is too liberal in classifying obligations under justice merely because they correlate with rights. The category of justice is accordingly too full, independently of good samaritan requirements, and must be thinned out by refining Mill's analysis. Before we take on that topic, however, we should consider one last way in which Mill might account for the moral rights that he believes are violated when we act wrongly.

(d) *Reciprocity.* In both *Liberty* and *Utilitarianism,* Mill appears to hold that those who benefit in a social setting from protective rules that correspond with principles of moral obligation acquire special debts of obligation to those whose compliance with the rules enables the harm-prevention. We *owe* it to those others to do our part in supporting these mutually beneficial arrangements.

In *Liberty,* as we have seen, Mill says that "everyone who receives the protection of society owes a return for the benefit, and the fact of living in society renders it indispensable that each should be bound to observe a certain line of conduct toward the rest." One is required, *first,* to respect those interests of others "which, either by express legal provision or by tacit understanding, ought to be considered as rights"; *second,* to bear one's fair share "of the labors and sacrifices incurred for defending the society or its members from injury and molestation"; and *third,* to refrain from conduct that "may be hurtful to others or wanting in due consideration of their welfare," even if it does not violate "any of their constituted rights" (*OL*, IV, 3).

Mill thus recognizes *three sets of justified requirements.* He goes on to imply that these three categories exhaust the sphere of conduct that is properly subject to coercive social control, just as his earlier discussion of self-regarding faults implied, as we have seen, that they also exhaust the realm of ("perfect") moral requirements. The general picture conveyed here is that of minimal requirements predicated on the prevention of harm to others, reinforced by considerations of reciprocity.

(i) *Justice.* Some of the rules are described in terms that place them under the heading of justice (according to Mill's account in *Utilitarianism*). The first set, for example, protects interests that "ought to be considered as rights" (Mill means, presumably, that a sound argument is available to support the corresponding ascriptions of moral rights). The second and third sets do not involve rights so directly. (ii) *Fair shares of burdens.* The second is explicitly concerned with harm prevention; rights enter in primarily because Mill requires that the burdens be distributed equitably.[13] (iii) *Individual beneficence.* The third set is likewise concerned with harm avoidance and prevention: These are presumably the rules under which one is required to aid those in distress. On the view I am sketching here, Mill would *not* claim that rights correlate *directly* with the obligations covered by the second and third categories. This reading therefore clashes with the one suggested in (c) above.

Mill presumably holds that one who has indeed "received the protection of society" by virtue of others' compliance with rules in these three categories "owes a return for the benefit" because that protection must have been secured at some cost. The cost is borne by those who have modified their behavior in order to comply with the rules. As a consequence, those others *have a right* to one's compliance in return. Failure to comply with such rules not only harms, endangers, or fails to help prevent harm to others; it also violates others' rights to one's reciprocal performance.

Mill's argument thus resembles recent invocations of the duty of fair play.[14] But note the following points. First, it is limited to requirements that are predicated on preventing harms to others; it does not go as far as those who invoke fairness in otherwise similar cases to show that one is under an obligation to others for positive benefits. Mill's use of fairness is narrower and presumably less controversial. Second, qualifications can readily be added. Such a right presumably would be forfeited, or perhaps never held, by one who ignores the rules and fails to support them. Third, this line of reasoning obliges Mill to defend a duty of fair play, which presumably must be predicated on the prevention of harm to others. I shall not attempt a reconstruction of that here.[15]

Even if Mill is too sanguine about the likelihood of giving such a duty a utilitarian foundation, there seems little doubt that he appeals to it. Somewhat similar ideas are suggested in Utilitarianism; for example, where Mill says:

> He who accepts benefits and denies a return of them when needed inflicts a real hurt by disappointing one of the most natural and reasonable of expectations, and one which he must at least tacitly have encouraged, otherwise the benefits would seldom have been incurred. (U, V, 34).

Mill's emphasis is different here. He seems to assimilate reciprocity to fidelity, by referring to tacit undertakings that commit one to returning "good for good." rather than fairness. Otherwise, his positions in the two essays seem similar: The benefits in question may be linked to prevention of harm, and the potential beneficiaries can be said to acquire a right to one's help, or compliance, not just as beneficiaries of a moral requirement, but by virtue of one's tacit undertaking to cooperate and comply with such rules in return for the benefits one has received and can expect to continue to receive as a consequence of others' compliance.

In these passages, then, Mill recognizes a *second-order obligation of reciprocity,* incumbent on one who benefits from an effective system of rules predicated on preventing harm to others, which correlates with others' rights to one's compliance, rights belonging to those who have themselves contributed to the harm-prevention efforts by complying with the rules.

One special virtue of this line of reasoning is that it promises to restore a distinction between justice and nonjustice obligations. On the account I am suggesting here, not all the obligations that correspond to the three categories of justified requirements themselves correlate with others' rights. Some of them do, such as the obligations aimed at protecting interests that "ought to be considered as rights." But we need not think of the other sets of rules in the same way. When those rules are violated, the corresponding moral obligations are breached, but no rights correlate with them per se. Rather, when such rules exist and one has benefited from others' compliance, a further obligation of reciprocity is established, and others accordingly have a right to one's corresponding compliance.

It seems to me that this last account of Mill's suggestion that all immoralities involve the violation of another's right is to be preferred. It accommodates Mill's clear commitment to an obligation of reciprocity while securing his substantive division of morality. For Mill can hold that obligations to cooperate in harm-preventive practices, to act as a good samaritan, and otherwise to avoid harming others (even when the harm would not constitute an injustice) fall outside of justice.

On this account, moral phenomena are not simple in such circumstances. But it would undoubtedly be a mistake to imagine that they were. Mill's theory has at least the virtue of reflecting this complexity within morality.

VIII. JUSTICE AND RIGHTS

I have already suggested that Mill's cateogry of nonjustice obligations breaks down into two significantly different parts, one containing perfect obligations, such as the obligation to cooperate in joint harm-prevention efforts and the obligation to act as a good samaritan, and the other containing imperfect obligations, such as charity, which do not help determine the rightness or wrongness of particular actions. Now I wish to suggest that Mill's category of justice obligations breaks down too. My main point is that the justice-nonjustice distinction does not correspond, as Mill claims, to the distinction between obligations that do and those that do not correlate with others' moral rights.

Justice and rights. When he surveys the field of justice, Mill finds that it chiefly and most directly concerns, besides rights, matters of desert, impartiality, equality, and voluntary undertakings. By analyzing justice (so far as it affects the rightness and wrongness of conduct) in terms of rights correlative to obligations, Mill claims, in effect, that these other concerns of justice (so far as they affect the rightness and wrongness of conduct) can be analyzed in such terms too.

On the surface, at least, of the matters listed, desert would seem least amenable to analysis in terms of rights. For voluntary undertakings, such as promises, are commonly assumed to create correlative rights and obligations, and it is not implausible to suppose that the relevant considerations of equality and impartiality also can be glossed in such terms. But desert is another matter. For, as Mill recognizes, one can deserve ill as well as good, and the idea of a right to bad treatment appears paradoxical. So, if claims about desert must be translated into claims about rights, it would seem that a simple substitution of "has a right to" for "deserves" will not work. Mill provides no gloss of these other claims in terms of rights, but I believe that we might help him here.

When what is deserved is good, then "has a right to" can do in place of "deserves." When what is deserved is bad treatment, the translation must be indirect. Let us assume that one *ordinarily* has a right to decent treatment by others, under, say, the three types of rules listed by Mill in *Liberty*—that questions of desert affecting the rightness and wrongness of conduct arise only in this context. Then we can have recourse to the idea of *forfeiting* one's right to such decent treatment. To deserve bad treatment by others, in view of one's prior bad treatment of them (which is clearly what Mill has in mind), is to forfeit one's antecedent right to certain forms of good treatment by others. If something like this formulation will do, then I think it plausible to say, along with Mill, that all questions of justice concerning right and wrong conduct can be understood in terms of rights and their correlative obligations.

Rights and justice. But, even if this is granted, it does not follow that all questions involving rights and correlative obligations are matters of justice. Mill's general position implies that all violations of rights (all breaches of the corresponding perfect obligations) are injustices. Now, this principle is often assumed; but it strikes me as implausible. In some cases, it seems perfectly natural to say that a person has been wronged and her rights violated although no injustice has been done. By this I do not mean that the wrong done or the injury suffered is morally trivial or otherwise unimportant. I mean simply that we would not normally classify some cases as injustices. Rape, torture, cruelty, and unwarranted assault are important wrongs that can, I think, be said to violate the victims' rights, but they would not normally be characterized as injustices.[16] I see no incoherence in refusing to so characterize them, which suggests that the term "justice" is sometimes stretched, rather than applied rigorously, to cover such cases. So Mill appears mistaken in supposing, in effect, that it is analytically true that all violations of rights are injustices.

One might try to save Mill some embarrassment here by invoking Hart's argument against applying terms like "right" and "obligation" to such cases, because they appeal to blanket prohibitions that cannot be waived, as rights can be, by those they are supposed to protect. One may say it is "wrong" to rape, torture, etc., but should not speak of a "duty" or "obligation" not to rape, torture, etc., or of a corresponding "right." It may be observed, however, that Hart's argument has problematic application to such cases, because willing acceptance of the relevant treatment by the person acted on would (from a moral point of view at least) remove these cases entirely from such categories (e.g., rape) or would eliminate at least some objections to them, which seems functionally equivalent to the waiving of one's rights. In any case, as I noted before, Hart's linguistic point is more a recommendation than a report of existing logical limits on these terms, so Mill's use of "right" and "obligation" in such cases cannot be excluded as incorrect. Partly for this reason, Mill's overpopulating of the category of justice cannot be avoided or even minimized by correcting his application of "right" and "obligation."

It should also be observed, however, that Mill's problems are not limited to cases in which Hart would prefer us not to use terms like "right" and "obligation." Consider, for example, promises and other voluntary undertakings, which, for the sake of argument, we shall assume give rise to rights and correlative obligations (at least when they may be said to be morally binding). Suppose that I accept an invitation to a party. It then becomes incumbent on me to offer an appropriate excuse if I should fail to attend. How weighty the excuse must be, and whether it should be offered in advance of the event, are matters that depend on further facts about the particular circumstances. Suppose that I know my attendance is important to others who, relying on my word, are reasonably assured they need make no further provision to meet the needs I am to serve. In such a case, we might well say that I would not only breach an obligation but would also violate others' rights should I fail to attend without warning others of my impending absence. But it does not follow, nor does it seem to be true, that I would in such a case do anyone an injustice. In failing to live up to one's word, one wrongs those who rely on it. But infidelity is one thing and injustice appears to be another. Of course, we might have special reason to characterize a broken promise as an injustice—if, say, one not only broke his word but did so to cheat or otherwise take advantage of those to whom one gave it— but such features are not inevitable accompaniments of infidelity. It does not seem incoherent to distinguish between breaking one's word and treating another person unjustly, and it seems arbitrarily to widen the ambit of justice to classify infidelities under injustices.

If my suspicions are sound, then Mill's analytic division of morality (as it concerns the rightness and wrongness of conduct) needs revision because he falls into the trap of linking rights too closely with justice. It may be the case that injustice always involves the violation of a right; but it does not follow, nor does it seem to be true, that all violations of moral rights (even when such violations are unjustified) are injustices. If so, justice cannot be analyzed so simply in terms of rights as Mill believes, and issues concerning justice require further differentiation. Mill may be on the right track, but he has not yet got to his destination.

This gives us another reason to refrain from placing Mill's nonjustice obligations under the heading of benevolence. Mill needs to refine his theory of justice with the consequence that some obligations correlating with rights will pass into the category of nonjustice obligations. Promising may be useful, but it is hardly a case of benevolence.

Mill's category of nonjustice obligations finally must be a mixed collection of distinctly different moral factors. Then it will more faithfully reflect the complexity of moral phenomena beyond justice.

CONCLUSION

I have argued for the following understanding of Mill's theory of morality: Right and wrong are functions of moral rights and obligations. The obligations of justice do, whereas nonjustice obligations do not, correlate with others' rights. Mill believes, furthermore, that obligations of justice require us to avoid acts that cause harm to other persons, whereas nonjustice obligations require us to go further and to act in ways calculated to help prevent harm to others. Mill thus maintains a negative utilitarian conception of our moral obligations.

In the course of the discussion, I suggested how an argument against paternalism that accords with Mill's basic doctrines might be extended to account for this negative utilitarianism. I tried to show how recalcitrant examples could be accounted for once we incorporate within Mill's theory his commitment to an obligation and corresponding right of reciprocity. Finally, I argued, independently of problems that may attach to Mill's utilitarianism, that his analytic division of morality needs refinement, since not every matter concerning moral rights is an issue of justice.

Notes

1. John Stuart Mill, *Utilitarianism* (first published 1861), Chap. V. Hereafter, references to this work will be given in the text, within parentheses, in the following form: "*U*," the chapter number, then the number of the paragraph in that chapter.

2. John Stuart Mill, *On Liberty* (first published 1859). Hereafter, references to this work will be given in the text, within parentheses, in the following form: "*OL*," the chapter number, then the number of the paragraph in that chapter.

3. "Mill's Theory of Morality," *Nous* 10 (1976):101-120; "Human Rights and the General Welfare," *Philosophy & Public Affairs* 6 (1977):113-129; and "Mill's Theory of Justice," in *Values and Morals: Essays in Honor of William Frankena, Charles Stevenson, and Richard Brandt*, ed. A. I. Goldman and J. Kim (Dordrecht: Reidel, 1978), pp. 1-20.

For alternative readings of Mill, see David Copp, "The Interated-Utilitarianism of J. S. Mill," in *New Essays on John Stuart Mill and Utilitarianism*, ed. Cooper, Nielsen, and Patten (*Canadian Journal of Philosophy* Supplementary Volume V [1979]), pp. 75-98, and works cited there. For a discussion of some of the issues involved in interpreting Mill, see L. W. Sumner, "The Good and the Right," in *New Essays on John Stuart Mill and Utilitarianism, op. cit.*, pp. 99-114.

4. This allows Mill's indirect form of utilitarianism to appear nonarbitrary. Acts, rules, etc., have general utility, but the moral concepts tell us, in effect, *how* such values as general utility are relevant to claims of right and obligation and, through them, to judgments of right and wrong conduct. (Note that Mill makes no distinction between moral duties and obligations.)

5. I discuss these examples and their bearing on Mill's Principle of Liberty more fully in "Liberty and Harm to Others," in *New Essays on John Stuart Mill and Utilitarianism, op. cit.*, pp. 1-19.

6. "Mill on Liberty and Morality," *Philosophical Review* 81 (1972):135.

7. *Ibid.*, 148.

8. It is unclear why Brown thinks it necessary to add the second "prima facie."

9. Brown, *op. cit.*, 150.

10. *Ibid.*, 150ff.

11. Some problems arise with this result, as Fred Berger has pointed out to me. It suggests, for example, that an act is (at least prima facie) wrong if it would be prohibited by a coercive rule that could be justified on grounds of harm prevention—even when there is no such rule. I do not discuss these complications here since I go on to question the correlation that generates such a consequence. Analogous problems may well accrue, however, to the reading of Mill that I suggest in "Mill's Theory of Morality," *op. cit.*

12. "Are There Any Natural Rights?", *Philosophical Review* 64 (1955):180f.

13. For a fuller discussion of this point, see "Liberty and Harm to Others," *op. cit.*

14. See, e.g., Hart, *op. cit.*, 185f., and John Rawls, "Justice as Fairness," *Philosophical Review* 67 (1958):179-183.

15. For an account, see Fred R. Berger, "John Stuart Mill on Justice and Fairness," in *New Essays on John Stuart Mill and Utilitarianism, op. cit.*, pp. 115-136. Berger's work first led me to appreciate the facet of Mill that I discuss here under (d).

16. Here I follow H. L. A. Hart, *The Concept of Law* (Oxford: Clarendon Press, 1961), pp. 153f.

4 Inchoately Utilitarian Common Sense: The Bearing of a Thesis of Sidgwick's on Moral Theory

Allan Gibbard

One of the central theses of Sidgwick's *Methods of Ethics* is that the morality of common sense is "inchoately and imperfectly utilitarian" (IV.iii.2, p. 427).[1] This is an intriguing thesis, and part of what I want to do in this paper is to ask what the content of the thesis might be. What I principally want to do is to explore the normative implications of the thesis: to ask whether the thesis, if true, would give us any reason to be utilitarian.

I

Sidgwick's claim is not that the morality of common sense is precisely utilitarian.

> Utilitarians are rather called upon to show a natural transition from the morality of Common Sense to Utilitarianism, somewhat like the transition in special branches of practice from trained instinct and empirical rules to the technical method that embodies and applies the conclusions of science: so that Utilitarianism may be presented as the scientifically complete and systematically reflective form of that regulation of conduct, which through the whole course of human history has always tended substantially in the same direction. (IV.iii.1, p. 425)

The thesis here concerns the sociology and psychology of the formation of moral convictions. How are we to interpret what Sidgwick says? He draws an analogy between, on the one hand, the relation of utilitarianism to the morality of common sense, and on the other hand, the relation of scientific technology to the lore of skilled artisans—to "trained instinct and empirical rules" in the "special branches of practice." What this analogy means depends crucially on the way we are to understand traditional craftsmanship. I suggest the following picture.

The community of artisans often comes to regard the maxims of the craft with a reverence that is detached from any consciousness of the ends to which those maxims conduce. An artisan may adhere to principles, then, not only without being able to say how they achieve his purposes, but even without being able to say what purpose they achieve. Adhering to the principles of his mystery becomes an end in itself. Nevertheless, if following a principle leads often to spoiled work, the principle will begin to lose its mystique in the community of artisans, and other principles may take its place. Artisans, in short, do not draw on their tradition for consciously teleological reasons; they are genuinely conservative. Nevertheless, a rule becomes discredited if it often fails the test of practice, and new rules become enshrined if they generally pass that test.

Part of what is involved, then, in the shift from traditional practice to scientific technology, is a growing consciousness of the goals of the manufacture. Reverence for the mystery of the craft is replaced by a propensity to examine techniques for their effectiveness in reaching conscious goals.

With the special branches of practice understood in this way, Sidgwick's analogy becomes this: The morality of common sense is not consciously utilitarian, because people attach an importance to things like keeping promises that is not consciously utilitarian. That is to say, for example, people regard promise-keeping as morally binding, and would not give as their reason for so regarding it that keeping promises tends to avoid unhappy long-term results. Indeed, for some classes of promises, a person may believe that such promises ought to be kept without believing that keeping promises in that class does lead to happier results than breaking them. (Cf. IV.iv.1, pp. 466-7.) But if *in fact*, the analogy tells us, keeping promises in that class generally led to unhappy results, the moral aura that attached to keeping promises of that sort would fade, and the class would come to be regarded as an exception to the rule enjoining promise-keeping.

The role of utilitarianism as an ethical first principle, on this reading of the analogy, is to make conscious the goal that shaped the development of common-sense morality unconsciously. The advantage of substituting utilitarianism for the old rule-worship is that systematic techniques then can be applied to moral issues: With the end explicit, we can now apply a technology of universal happiness maximization. Economics yields cases in point: Once an end is explicit, arguments can be directed against the corn laws, cost-benefit analysis can be used to guide decisions on public works, and survey research techniques can be used to assess the impact of policy. Shifting from unconscious utilitarianism to conscious utilitarianism allows us to apply scientific techniques of felicific assessment to further the achievement of the old, unconscious goal.

I shall refer to this theory of the morality of common sense as *Sidgwick's thesis*. Sidgwick's thesis, then, is a sociological and psychological thesis about the development of common-sense moral convictions. We might put the thesis as follows: First, the thesis denies that the morality of common sense is consciously utilitarian. Even so, according to the thesis, the morality of common sense is utilitarian unconsciously, in that widespread experience with cases in which obeying a rule has unhappy consequences will lead, through a complicated sociopsychological process, to the rule's ceasing to be held in respect. On the other hand, a rule that is not held to constitute a moral requirement may come to be so. That will happen — again through a complicated sociopsychological process — after widespread experience of acts with unhappy consequences, where, it is perceived, obeying that rule would have had happier consequences. Finally, distortions, both random and systematic, will occur in the process, and so the coincidence between the morality of common sense and the morality utilitarianism would recommend, extensive though it will be, will be far from complete.

When is a departure from utilitarianism a "distortion"? Sidgwick himself does not use the term "distortion"; he speaks rather of "what, from the utilitarian point of view, appear to be partial aberrations of the moral sense." (IV.iii.7, p. 455) To express his thesis, though, he seems to need a notion of "partial aberration" or "distortion" not from the utilitarian point of view, but from a point of view neutral among moral theories. What Sidgwick claims of utilitarianism, as I am construing him, is not only that it coincides with the morality of common sense in a multitude of ways and to a remarkable degree.[2] A systematic rival to utilitarianism might do so as well, for its specific consequences for action might roughly coincide both with those of utilitarianism and with the judgments of common sense.[3] When Sidgwick claims that the morality of common sense is unconsciously utilitarian, though, he suggests not only a complex coincidence but guidance: that utilitarian considerations guide the development of the morality of common sense in a way that other morally relevant considerations do not. If that indeed is what Sidgwick wants to claim, then he must be committed to the view that discrepancies between utilitarianism and common-sense morality are a result of partial failures of a system of guidance. Thus in some sense neutral among moral theories, they constitute distortions of the common moral consciousness.

What account of this sense can we offer Sidgwick?[4] He himself gives examples of what we need to capture:

> The aberration is often only an exaggeration of an obviously useful sentiment, or the extension of it by mistaken analogy to cases to which it does not properly apply, or perhaps the survival of a sentiment which once was useful but has now ceased to be so. (IV,iii.7, p. 456)

I propose the following explication: A feature of the morality of common sense is a *distortion* if common-sense morality came to have that feature by responding to considerations that, on reflection, we would regard as morally irrelevant. Cultural lags, for instance, constitute distortions according to this explication, since if we are sure that in our society, acts of a certain kind do not now, on the whole, have unhappy consequences, that they formerly had unhappy consequences in our society would not strike us as a consideration against performing such acts now.

With a rough account of the term "distortion" in hand, I shall proceed to use it as if we understood it.

II

Even with Sidgwick's thesis in the rough form I have presented, we may be able to explore whether it has any bearing on normative issues. Sidgwick's thesis, as I have said, is sociological and psychological rather than normative, whereas utilitarianism is a normative theory. If we accepted Sidgwick's thesis, I want to ask, would that give us any reason for or against being utilitarians?[5]

I am interested in this question not because I believe Sidgwick's thesis to be correct, but because I think that any account of the formation of moral convictions will raise the same kinds of questions as does Sidgwick's thesis. Once we have grounds for accepting any such account, we will need to ask whether it bears on normative issues and issues of moral epistemology, and if so, how. In the absence of a well-supported sociopsychological theory of the formation of moral convictions, it may be useful to see what we would conclude if a particular theory *were* well supported. That is what I shall attempt to do.

Implicit in Sidgwick's thesis may be a kind of equilibrium. Call a rule *felicitous for* a society to the degree that its being widely held in respect in that society would on balance have happy consequences, and *infelicitous for* a society to the degree that its being widely held in respect in that society would on balance have unhappy consequences. According to the thesis, infelicitous rules tend to be abandoned, felicitous rules to be adopted, and more felicitous rules to replace less felicitous alternatives. In the limit of this process, we might expect, members of a society will hold in respect a set of rules most felicitous for their society, and the forces that work for moral change will be in equilibrium.

This is not an equilibrium that is normally reached, according to the thesis, for distortions prevent its realization. Cultural lags, false beliefs, fixations on analogies, exaggeration of sentiments useful in moderation, and the like will keep the common moral consciousness of a society from embracing precisely those rules that are most felicitous for that society. The equilibrium in question is ideal: It is the equilibrium that would be reached without distortions.

In what follows, I shall speak of *Sidgwickian equilibrium:* the state members of a society would reach in their moral thinking were that thinking subject to no distortions.[6] My use of this term will not presuppose that the equilibrium is in any sense utilitarian; rather, the term will be used to express the claim that it is. My use of the term does presuppose that some kind of sociopsychological process determines the content of ordinary moral thought, that a distinction can be made between aspects of that process that constitute distortions and aspects that do not, and that there is a unique state of moral opinion that would be the outcome of the process without its distortions.

What precisely "most felicitous" means will not much matter for what I have to say. Perhaps we should say the *most felicitous* rules are those whose recognition as morally binding would produce more total happiness than would recognition of any alternatives. Refine the formulation as you wish, but note and preserve an important feature: It is only with respect to a given society that rules can be said to be most felicitous or not. The rules whose recognition would produce the most happiness in one set of social circumstances may not be the ones whose recognition would produce the most happiness in another. We must speak, then, of rules as most felicitous *for* a given society.

In the vague language now at our disposal, Sidgwick's thesis is that in Sidgwickian equilibrium, members of a society take as morally binding those rules that are most felicitous for their society. That, as I have said, is a thesis of moral sociology and psychology. The same vague terminology allows us to formulate a normative thesis that is a version of rule utilitarianism: An act is right if and only if it is permitted by those rules that are most felicitous for the society of its agent.[7] I shall appropriate the term "rule utilitarianism" for this version, and acts that are right according to rule utilitarianism in this sense I shall call *RU-right*.

I have put "Sidgwick's thesis" and "rule utilitarianism" in terms of two other vaguely defined technical terms, "Sidgwickian equilibrium" and "most felicitous." The resulting vagueness, deplorable though it may be, is no disaster. For when the same vague term enters formulations of distinct theses, some logical relations among the formulations will hold however that vagueness is resolved. What will matter in the formulations I have given is the following: (1) The common-sense morality of a society tends to approach a unique equilibrium, called *Sidgwickian equilibrium,* which somehow depends on the happy and unhappy consequences that various kinds of acts are prone to have in that society, and (2) rule utilitarianism is formulated in such a way that for any society S, as rule utilitarianism so formulated applies to acts within S, it coincides with the equilibrium common-sense morality of S.

Here and throughout the paper, let me note, I confine myself to the case of homogeneous societies that do not interact. Thus the society of the agent and the society within which the act is performed is always the same. Problems concerning intersocietal relations, the duties of immigrants, expatriates, and travellers, diverse moral subcultures within the same geographical area, and the like will be ignored.

Now according to Sidgwick's thesis, in Sidgwickian equilibrium we are what might be called "domestic rule utilitarians." For suppose Sidgwick's thesis holds and we are in Sidgwickian equilibrium. Then we judge an act right if and only if it is permitted by the rules that are most felicitous for our own society. That holds whether the act we judge be domestic or foreign. The act is RU-right, though, if and only if it is permitted by the rules that are most felicitous for the society of its agent. For domestic actions, it follows that we judge an act right if and only if it is RU-right; our domestic moral judgments coincide with rule utilitarianism. In the case of foreign agents, no such conclusion may be drawn. The rules most felicitous for the agent's society may permit an act that the rules most felicitous for our society forbid: In that case the act will be RU-right but we will judge it wrong. Likewise when the agent is foreign, we may judge an act right that is not RU-right. In short, then, if Sidgwick's thesis holds, then in Sidgwickian equilibrium, we will judge a domestic act to be right if and only if it is RU-right, whereas we may judge a foreign act to be wrong when it is RU-right or right when it is RU-wrong.[8]

III

A chief method of attacking utilitarianism has been what I shall call the *method of counterexample*. The method is to find a case in which a consequence of utilitarianism conflicts with our considered moral convictions. The only kind of support an ethical theory could have, it is then argued, is its agreement with our considered moral convictions, and so utilitarianism fails to meet the one appropriate test for an ethical theory.

The method of counterexample has been used chiefly against act utilitarianism. Ross gives as a counterexample a case in which keeping a promise would produce slightly more good than would breaking it; in that case, he says, our considered moral convictions prescribe keeping the promise whereas utilitarianism prescribes breaking it.[9] Alan Donagan has used the method of counterexample to attack a version of rule utilitarianism as well.[10] I shall discuss the method both as applied to act utilitarianism and as applied to rule utilitarianism.

Now a striking aspect of Sidgwick's thesis is that if we accept the thesis, then we should expect utilitarianism — both act and rule — to be subject to counterexamples of this kind. Suppose in what follows that Sidgwick's thesis is true, and consider first act utilitarianism.

An act may, in exceptional circumstances, have maximally happy consequences, even though it violates the rules most felicitous for the society of its agent. In such cases, according to Sidgwick's thesis, our judgment in Sidgwickian equilibrium is that the act is wrong, even though according to act utilitarianism it is right. Such cases, then, will constitute counterexamples to act utilitarianism.

For rule utilitarianism, such cases may not constitute counterexamples. Suppose we have reached Sidgwickian equilibrium. Then for any act performed by a member of our society, we will judge it to be wrong if and only if it is RU-wrong. We should, though, expect rule utilitarianism to be subject to counterexamples of other kinds. In the first place, an act may violate the rules most felicitous for our society, but not the rules most felicitous for the society of the agent. In such a case, the act will be RU-right, but in Sidgwickian equilibrium we will judge the act to be wrong. For like reasons, we may sometimes judge an act of a foreign agent right when it is not RU-right. Such cases may be drawn both from societies other than our own and from hypothetical societies; in either case they will constitute counterexamples to rule utilitarianism. In the second place, according to Sidgwick's thesis, the morality of common sense is only imperfectly utilitarian: Our considered moral judgments may suffer from cultural lag, excesses of enthusiasm for principles that lead to happiness when applied in moderation, and other systematic and chancy distortions. Even our considered moral judgments of acts in our own society, then, may not accord with rule utilitarianism, for they may not be judgments in Sidgwickian equilibrium. Thus if Sidgwick's thesis is correct, we may well find counterexamples to rule utilitarianism even within our own society.

IV

If we accept Sidgwick's thesis, we have seen, then we should expect counterexamples both to act and to rule utilitarianism. Does that mean that we should reject utilitarianism in both forms? The method of counterexample, after all, is widely thought to provide decisive reasons for rejecting those ethical theories against which it can be brought to bear. Perhaps, then, since Sidgwick's thesis leads us to expect counterexamples to utilitarianism, it tells against utilitarianism.

The "counterexamples" Sidgwick's thesis would lead us to expect, though, have a strange feature that perhaps ought to make us distrust them. An expectable counterexample, we have seen, will be of one of these three kinds: (a) a counterexample to act utilitarianism that is not a counterexample to rule utilitarianism, (b) an act that violates the rules most felicitous for our society, but not the rules most felicitous for the society of the agent, or *vice versa*, (c) an act that we judge to be wrong because our considered moral judgments differ from our judgments in Sidgwickian equilibrium.

Suppose an act violates the rules most felicitous for our society but not those most felicitous for the agent's. Whereas the act is RU-right, we judge in Sidgwickian equilibrium that it is wrong. That act is thus a counterexample to rule utilitarianism as I have been using the term "counterexample." The counterexample has the strange feature, though, that were we members of the agent's society, and his society were in Sidgwickian equilibrium, we would not find it to be a counterexample. For since the act does not violate the rules most felicitous for his society, were we members of his society, we would judge his act not to be wrong. We have counterexamples of this kind, then, only in cases where our judgments in Sidgwickian equilibrium are a result of cultural contingencies. Such purported counterexamples look suspicious.

Counterexamples to act utilitarianism are more difficult to evaluate. If an act is right according to act utilitarianism but is not RU-right, then our opinion in Sidgwickian equilibrium will be that the act is wrong. That, whether we realize it or not, is because the act violates the rules most felicitous for our society. Once we realize the source of our judgments in Sidgwickian equilibrium, perhaps we will regard our deviations from act utilitarianism as ill-founded. For they result, we may then think, from an irrational social tendency to embrace rules rather than look at special features of individual acts. Reflection, in other words, may move a person from Sidgwickian equilibrium. The code toward which the morality of common sense moves may not be the code a person accepts when he considers all the possible arguments on the matter. For Sidgwickian equilibrium is the equilibrium of a social process by which moral views common to a community are generated. It involves only that degree of systematic philosophical investigation of moral questions that normally occurs in a society. It may not be reflective equilibrium in Rawls's sense[11] – the equilibrium reached by an individual in the limit as he subjects his moral views to an arbitrarily high degree of philosophical scrutiny. Perhaps, then, as regards domestic affairs, we are rule utilitarians in Sidgwickian equilibrium but act utilitarians in reflective equilibrium. If so, then so long as our considered moral beliefs are those of our society in Sidgwickian equilibrium, we will find counterexamples to act utilitarianism among acts in our own society, but those counterexamples will not survive the most careful reflection. Whether in reflective equilibrium we would indeed be act utilitarians I shall not attempt to say in this paper.

V

Still supposing Sidgwick's thesis to be correct, let me now confine myself to counterexamples on one pattern: that of an act that violates the rules most felicitous for our society but not the rules most felicitous for the society of the agent. Such an act provides an apparent counterexample to rule utilitarianism. In the last section, I voiced suspicion of such apparent counterexamples, but the grounds I cited were vague. Its appearing to be a counterexample, I argued, is a result of contingencies of our culture; once we realize that, we ought no longer to regard the purported counterexample as providing grounds for rejecting rule utilitarianism.

What, more precisely, is wrong with such counterexamples? Any account of what is wrong with them must depend on the theory of justification that is used to back the method of counterexample. One prominent theory is that of Ross, and I propose first to discuss his theory.

Ross speaks of "our actual apprehension of what is right and what is wrong," and says, "I would maintain, in fact, that what we are apt to describe as 'what we think' about moral questions contains a considerable amount that we do not think but know."[12] Ross's intuitionism may strike the reader as being too dated for it to be worthwhile to explore its consequences. A similar epistemology, however, that of mathematical Platonism, has been accepted by many philosophers of mathematics as the only satisfactory account of mathematical knowledge. How does Ross's claim of moral apprehensions fare if Sidgwick's thesis is correct?

It seems to me that we cannot reconcile Ross's epistemological view – that our considered moral judgments often constitute apprehensions – with both Sidgwick's thesis and a nonutilitarian normative theory. Assume all these, and suppose I apprehend a moral truth that is incompatible with rule utilitarianism. Suppose it is a case of the kind I have discussed, in which my considered moral judgment is in Sidgwickian equilibrium, and I judge as wrong an act that is RU-right. That, we have seen, can only be because the act is forbidden by the rules most felicitous for my society but permitted by the rules most felicitous for the society of the agent. If the act is indeed wrong, I come to have a true judgment of it only because I happen to be a member of a society of a certain sort: of a society with the property that the rules most felicitous for it forbid that act. I might have been a member of a different sort of society, and so if I judge truly about the act, I do so only by happenstance. A fortuitous true judgment is not an apprehension.

To what principle am I here appealing? Apprehension is a kind of knowledge, and it looks as if the consideration I am invoking is one that applies to knowledge in general. The situation is this: I seem to apprehend that an act is wrong, but someone else would seem to apprehend that it is not wrong, and his epistemic situation is no worse than mine. That, I have concluded, is grounds for denying that my seeming apprehension constitutes knowledge. The general principle I am invoking, then, must be something like this: In order for me reasonably to maintain, in the face of contrary opinion, that I have knowledge, I must have reason to believe that those who disagree with me are in some way in a worse epistemic position than am I.

My reason for so believing will in some cases be grounded simply in what those others believe. For I may think of a proposition, "Anyone who believes *that* must be in a poor position to judge," and that may be my only reason for supposing the epistemic position of those who believe it to be worse than mine. Such reasoning on my part may be cogent enough if, apart from it, I have better evidence that my own epistemic position is good than that their epistemic position is good. What can I say, though, if I accept Sidgwick's thesis?

My talk of "epistemically better" positions here has been vague, and I shall leave it so. It could be argued plausibly, though, that the best of epistemic positions for morally judging acts involves, perhaps among other things, being a member of a society in Sidgwickian equilibrium and judging an act of a member of one's own society. For in Sidgwickian equilibrium, a society is free of cultural lags and other distortions of the process that shapes moral judgments. If our moral judgments are shaped in the way Sidgwick thinks they are, then they respond to features that kinds of acts typically have in our own society, not to circumstances in other societies. Thus, it would seem, if common-sense moral judgments ever give ethical knowledge, they must do so most reliably when a person judges an act in his own society, where that society is in Sidgwickian equilibrium. The best of epistemic positions for making moral judgments may have other features — it may, for instance, require reflective equilibrium — but it seems that at least it will have these.

Now suppose that at least when we are in the best of epistemic positions, our common-sense moral judgments indeed constitute apprehension.[13] We have seen that in a society in Sidgwickian equilibrium, common-sense moral judgments are rule utilitarian as regards acts in that society. Thus, we may conclude, our moral apprehensions in the best of epistemic circumstances are rule utilitarian.

For some acts, on the suppositions we have made, no one is in the best of epistemic circumstances. If a society is not in Sidgwickian equilibrium, then no one satisfies both the requirement of being from that society and the requirement of being from a society in Sidgwickian equilibrium, and so on the suppositions we have made, no one is in an ideal epistemic position to judge acts in that society. Without further assumptions, we can conclude nothing about what is right in such a society.

One further assumption that might seem plausible on examination is this: The factors that determine whether anyone is in an epistemically ideal position to judge acts in a society are irrelevant to whether rule utilitarianism is true for that society—that is, whether in that society, all and only RU-wrong acts are wrong. If the assumption withstands scrutiny, then we can conclude that rule utilitarianism is true without restriction. For any act that anyone is in an epistemically ideal position to judge, rule utilitarianism truly applies, in the sense that the act is wrong if and only if it is RU-wrong. The factors that determine whether anyone is in an epistemically ideal position to judge an act, we are supposing, make no difference to whether rule utilitarianism truly applies to the act. Hence, we may conclude, rule utilitarianism truly applies to all acts, or in other words, rule utilitarianism is the correct theory of moral rightness and wrongness.

VI

So far, I have relied on Ross's theory that our common-sense moral judgments at least sometimes constitute apprehensions of moral truths. It is perhaps more common to back the method of counterexample with a metaethical theory of a different kind. On the theories I now want to address, moral convictions are, or are intimately associated with, moral attitudes. Moral attitudes, though, can be justified or unjustified. The test of a normative theory is whether its consequences agree with our justified attitudes. Thus any conflict between a consequence of a normative theory and a justified attitude gives us reason to reject the normative theory, and so constitutes a counterexample to the theory.

What justifies an attitude? The requirements for justification include impartiality, full and vivid awareness of the relevant nonethical facts, and being in a normal frame of mind. It also may be required that the attitude survive certain kinds of reflection—for instance, an attempt to match attitudes with general normative principles.[14] What, if anything, then, unites these requirements? They seem to be chosen for their similarity to requirements for being in a good position to judge matters of fact. They are the requirements that would be met by an ideal jury if the jury were to judge not only particular matters of fact but general facts. Rawls puts this last point quite explicitly (though perhaps his metaethical theory does not fit the sketch I have given).

> And once we regard the sense of justice as a mental capacity, as involving the exercise of thought, the relevant judgments are those given under conditions favorable for deliberation and judgment in general.[15]

Suppose, then, that a moral attitude is justified as fully as moral attitudes ever can be, or *ideally justified*, when it is formed under conditions that are ideal for judgment in general. Then the same considerations that apply to Ross's theory of moral apprehension should apply to theories of justified attitudes. For the same reasons as were given earlier, we may again suppose that ideal epistemic circumstances include being a member of a society in Sidgwickian equilibrium and judging an act in one's own society. For it is under those circumstances that relevant social experience has had its fullest effects on our judgment. Thus again it will follow from Sidgwick's thesis that attitudes formed in epistemically ideal circumstances are rule-utilitarian.

What can we say of epistemic circumstances that are not ideal? The answer will depend on our second-order attitudes. Morally serious people have attitudes toward their moral attitudes; we can think of the special status we give to moral attitudes formed under epistemically ideal circumstances as representing such a second-order attitude. We can also say, roughly, that in circumstances that are not epistemically ideal, morally serious people favor adopting the kinds of attitudes they would have in epistemically ideal circumstances, if they know what those attitudes are. With near success, then, we could argue as follows: From Sidgwick's thesis and the other assumptions we have made, it follows that in epistemically ideal circumstances, our moral attitudes accord with rule utilitarianism. Thus a morally serious person who accepts Sidgwick's thesis, the other assumptions, and their implications will favor having attitudes that accord with rule utilitarianism in all circumstances.

There is one catch to this argument: A person might regard the differences between a society in Sidgwickian equilibrium and one not in Sidgwickian equilibrium as making a difference as to whether attitudes in accord with rule utilitarianism toward acts in the respective societies were warranted. These judgments of what makes a difference to the applicability of rule utilitarianism are themselves a matter of second-order attitudes. What we can say is this: Suppose we accept Sidgwick's thesis and other assumptions from which it follows that in ideal epistemic circumstances, moral attitudes accord with rule utilitarianism. Suppose we think further that the differences between (1) any society such that there exist ideal epistemic circumstances for judging acts performed within it and (2) any society such that there do not—are irrelevant to the validity of rule utilitarianism for acts in those respective societies. Then we will conclude that rule utilitarianism is valid in general.

Sidgwick's thesis, I have argued, may well bear on normative issues. For I have suggested a kind of reflection by means of which accepting Sidgwick's thesis could turn us into rule utilitarians. Whether the assumptions on which I have depended will withstand scrutiny, I do not pretend to have shown. I do want to suggest that our moral judgments may respond to considerations about the sociopsychological process that generates moral convictions, because that process has epistemological implications. I have tried to sketch a way in which such reflection might procede.

VII

So far I have said nothing of the truth of Sidgwick's thesis. The question is a broad and difficult one, and I can say very little on the subject.

Something approximating what Sidgwick claims does seem to happen: As Sidgwick says, "The remarkable discrepancies found in comparing the moral codes of different ages and countries are for the most part strikingly correlated to differences in the effects of actions on happiness, or in men's foresight of, or concern for such effects" (IV.iii.1, p. 426). After reading Sidgwick's argument (IV.iii), we can, I think, agree that there is a complex approximate coincidence between utilitarianism and the morality of common sense, and an approximate coincidence is all that could be expected on the basis of Sidgwick's thesis. An approximate coincidence alone, though, will not support utilitarianism against any rival theory that gives like prescriptions in most common situations. If it supports one normative theory against another, where the two theories approximate each other in their prescriptions, it must be because the morality of common sense deviates from one of them in some coherent, identifiable way.

What about the sociopsychological process by which our moral convictions arise? Anything we say must be highly speculative, but speculation can be valuable if we recognize it as speculation.

Our innate dispositions to form moral convictions presumably evolved in small bands of hunter-gatherers, and what we have seen in the last few millenia is the response of human culture to economic changes that resulted in societies on a large scale.[16] Here I shall venture two brief speculations about what may have happened to our moral code.

We may expect that a propensity to altruism, at least toward close associates, evolved in the hunting-gathering society. This might take the form of a propensity unconsciously to shape one's moral code according to the effects of kinds of acts on the happiness of oneself and one's associates, where the moral code is maintained by the mutual influence of people's moral responses on each other.[17] In complex societies, though, some people are in socially dominant positions and some are in subservient positions. Those in socially dominant positions have more influence, and if they respond chiefly to the happiness and unhappiness of their associates, who are from the same social group, the happiness and unhappiness of the socially dominant will have a disproportionate effect on the moral code of the society. In complex, inegalitarian societies, then, if a common moral code exists, it is likely to approximate rule utilitarianism with a class bias, with each person's happiness to count according to the *per capita* influence of his social class.

Would Sidgwick's thesis in this version support rule utilitarianism with a class bias as a normative theory? I think it would not. To accept this version of Sidgwick's thesis is to accept that our common-sense morality has been shaped by a consideration that strikes us as morally irrelevant: the social influence of those whose happiness is at stake. The class bias thus constitutes a "distortion" in the sense I earlier offered to Sidgwick. The reasonable response is to correct for the bias, and adopt rule utilitarianism without class bias.

A second kind of systematic deviation of the morality of common sense from utilitarianism can be explained as follows. In a hunting-gathering society, an enormous survival advantage accrues to cooperation and the avoidance of conflict. Now people in such a society often would face *bargaining situations*: situations in which benefits are to be gained from cooperation as opposed to conflict, and there are a variety of ways in which these benefits can be divided. Shelling argues that agreement in bargaining situations is facilitated by like mutual expectations of how the benefits will be divided: then each person thinks he can successfully hold out for the expected amount but for nothing more, and so each will readily agree to the expected outcome.[18] Now expectations of a particular outcome will be buttressed if a moral significance is attached to it, so that each person feels that he would be cheated if he received less, and that he is entitled to no more. For each person to attach moral significance to the same outcome, the outcome must have a special prominence. In symmetrical situations, equal division has that prominence. In other situations, salience attaches to traditional divisions of benefits, possession, and the like. Hence there is an evolutionary advantage to a strong tendency to demand equal, traditional, or otherwise prominent distribution of benefits—of a strong sense of "to each his due." There is a strong evolutionary advantage to being disposed to reach a small group consensus on what is due each person.[19] What is striking about this sense is, on the one hand, its strength, and on the other hand, outside highly traditional societies, the diversity of distributive schemes to which it attaches: We agree much more on the importance of giving each his due than we do on what is due to whom.

If what I am saying is true, the morality of common sense will deviate from rule utilitarianism in a marked and systematic way. We will have what Hume called a sentiment of justice, and in societies where change is slow enough for genuine conservativism to be possible, this sentiment will be conservative: It will demand that each person be given his traditional due, regardless of whether the traditional scheme distributes the means to happiness in the way that will produce the most happiness.

What effect believing this should have on our normative views I find puzzling.

Notes

1. All page, chapter, and section references, unless otherwise noted, are to Henry Sidgwick, *The Methods of Ethics*, 7th edition (London: Macmillan, 1907). I use capital Roman numerals for the Books, lower case Roman numerals for the Chapter, and Arabic numerals for the section. The definitive study of Sidgwick and the *Methods of Ethics* is J. B. Schneewind, *Sidgwick's Ethics and Victorian Moral Philosophy* (Oxford: Clarendon Press, 1977). Schneewind's superb discussion of Sidgwick's theory of the common moral consciousness is mostly in Chapter 1 and Chapter 12, especially Section ii.

2. Sidgwick's summary of "the complex character of the coincidence" between utilitarianism and common sense is in IV.iii.1, pp. 425-426. An exposition in some detail occupies IV.iii.2-6.

3. John Simmons developed this point in his comments on the version of this paper I presented in May of 1978. In revising this paper for publication, I have been helped at many points by the insightful and careful comments he gave on that occasion, of which he gave me a copy.

4. This may not be a problem for Sidgwick because he finds only two "methods of ethics" to yield coherent and systematic moral theories: egoism and utilitarianism. Considerations of afterlife put aside, egoism departs substantially from the morality of common sense, and so utilitarianism's status as a systematic moral theory remarkably coincident with common sense is unique. Here I am trying to develop a version of Sidgwick's thesis that at least makes sense to someone who thinks utilitarianism to have systematic rivals apart from egoism.

5. Sidgwick's own use of the thesis depends on a moral epistemology that is a refined version of Cartesian rationalism. For the epistemology, see III.xi.2 and Schneewind, Ch. 9 Sec. ii, and for Sidgwick's chief use of what I am calling "Sidgwick's thesis" in support of utilitarianism, see IV.iii and Schneewind, Ch. 12.

6. In what follows I assume that if Sidgwick's thesis is correct, this equilibrium will be unique: that there is a unique set of rules most felicitous for a society, and in the absence of distortions, common-sense morality settles on those rules. Even if one accepts Sidgwick's thesis as I put it in Section 1 above, one may well doubt this further assumption of unique equilibrium. In the first place, no unique set of rules may be most felicitous for a society. More important, the sociopsychological process that results in less felicitous rules' being dropped and more felicitous rules' being accepted might work no changes once the rules accepted are felicitous enough, even though alternative rules were slightly more felicitous. Simmons developed this point in his comments. I shall try to cope with its implications in note 8 below, and assume unique equilibrium in the text.

7. For a theory along these lines worked out in great detail, see Richard B. Brandt, "Toward a Credible Utilitarianism," in *Morality and the Language of Conduct*, ed. H. N. Castaneda and G. Nakhnikian (Detroit: Wayne State University Press, 1963); Richard B. Brandt, "Some Merits of One Form of Rule-Utilitarianism," *University of Colorado Studies, Series in Philosophy*, No. 3 (1967):39-65.

8. With respect to a rule utilitarianism of a somewhat different kind, the same point could be made for a version of Sidgwick's thesis without a claim of a unique possible equilibrium for a given society. The modified thesis is that, in the absence of distortions, the common moral consciousness of a society will be in equilibrium whenever the rules accepted in S are highly felicitous for S. Call such an equilibrium a *satisficing equilibrium* The modified rule utilitarianism states that if a society of S has a common morality and the rules of that common morality are highly felicitous for S, then an act performed in S is right if and only if it conforms to those rules. Call this *satisficing RU*. Then members of a society in satisficing equilibrium will judge an act performed in their society to be right if and only if it is right according to satisficing RU. Note that satisficing RU is not a complete theory of rightness and wrongness, for it says nothing of acts performed in a society with no commonly accepted morality, or with a commonly accepted morality the rules of which are not highly felicitous for that society.

9. W. D. Ross, *The Right and the Good* (Oxford: Oxford U. Pr., 1930), p. 38.

10. "Is There a Credible Form of Utilitarianism?" M. D. Bayles (ed.), *Contemporary Utilitarianism* (Garden City, N.J.: Doubleday, 1968), pp. 194-196.

11. John Rawls, *A Theory of Justice*, (Cambridge, Mass.: Harvard U. Pr., 1971), pp. 48-50.

12. *Op cit.*, p. 40.

13. This is to suppose, among other things, that moral apprehension does not require a kind of reflective equilibrium in which even members of a society in Sidgwickian equilibrium would reject their common-sense moral judgments.

14. A prime example of the sort of theory I have in mind here is Brandt's qualified attitude method [Richard B. Brandt, *Ethical Theory* (Englewood Cliffs, N.J.: Prentice-Hall, 1959)]. Firth's ideal observer [Roderick Firth, "Ethical Absolutism and the Ideal Observer," *Philosophy and Phenomenological Research* 12 (1952):317-345] satisfies the conditions of impartiality and awareness of nonethical facts, but does not try to match his attitudes with general principles. Rawls [*op. cit.*, pp. 46-53] speaks of "considered judgments"; they are "those judgments in which our moral capacities are most likely to be displayed without distortion" (p. 47). They are (perhaps among other things) judgments we make without hesitation when we are impartial and in a frame of mind that is normal in various ways.

15. *Op. cit.*, p. 48.

16. For an extensive and impressive study of human mores from this point of view, see Gerhard E. Lensky, *Power and Privilege: A Theory of Social Stratification* (New York: McGraw Hill, 1966).

17. For a bibliography of writings on sociobiology, see Richard D. Alexander, *Darwinism and Human Affairs* (Seattle: University of Washington Press, 1979).

18. Thomas Schelling, *The Strategy of Conflict* (Cambridge, Mass.: Harvard U. Pr., 1960), Ch. 2.

19. John Maynard Smith ["Evolution and the Theory of Games," *American Scientist* 64 (1976): 41-45] discusses the application of the theory of games to evolution, and in particular, the evolutionary stability of a "convention" of recognizing ownership (pp. 44-45).

5 Utilitarianism and Unconscious Utilitarianism

A. John Simmons

I

The most prominent claim in Book IV of Sidgwick's *The Methods of Ethics* is that "the Morality of Common Sense may be truly represented as at least unconsciously Utilitarian."[1] Sidgwick presents this claim as an important step in the only possible "proof" of utilitarianism, and hence as having considerably more significance than one might normally attribute to an observation about "positive morality." Similarly, Mill's *Utilitarianism* suggests in several places that a convincing defense of utilitarianism relies in part on showing that common-sense morality is at heart utilitarian. In Chapter V, for instance, Mill undertakes to demonstrate that the demands made by "the various popular acceptations of justice" can all be understood as disguised utilitarian demands, and consequently that justice, as it is commonly understood, is "only a particular kind or branch of general utility."[2] That demonstration, Mill thinks, will remove "one of the strongest obstacles" to the acceptance of the principle of utility. And this, of course, merely extends Mill's more general view (advanced in Chapter II) that the "rules of morality for the multitude" are really rules designed to advance the general happiness. The position being defended by Sidgwick and Mill is not just that the actions required by common sense and utilitarianism are (more or less) the same in ordinary circumstances; both authors make it clear that this view is not (or is not the whole of) what they intend to convey. Although their claims differ in some respects, for both Mill and Sidgwick the important further point is that the rules of common-sense morality are at heart utilitarian, are inspired by utilitarian reasoning on some level. Why this point is important needs to be examined.

One obvious consideration is this. The most common kind of attack aimed at utilitarianism involves accusing utilitarianism of yielding counterintuitive results, of sanctioning actions condemned by widely shared moral standards. Now the utilitarian can respond to such attacks in a variety of ways. He can, on a case by case basis, try to show that the demands of common sense and utilitarianism are not "disjoined in fact" (to use Mill's phrase); contemporary literature on utilitarianism abounds with demonstrations that apparent conflicts between utility maximization and intuitively right action are apparent only. This "finger in the dike" approach, however, seems ill-designed to resolve any disagreements on fundamental questions of theory. On the other hand, the utilitarian can directly assault the platform from which the attacks are launched, by denying the authority of common-sense morality. That common-sense morality in some cases condemns utility maximization should in no way influence our conclusions about what ought to be done; to argue otherwise is to adopt a "milk and water approach."[3] Although I am sympathetic to these sentiments, the difficulties involved in persuading others share them are admittedly severe.

Ideally, perhaps, the utilitarian wants to dispose of objections from common sense en masse without having to deny the authority of common sense in moral matters, especially if he is not, in the first place, inclined to deny its authority (as many utilitarians are not). And it seems that the utilitarian can take this middle road precisely by arguing that the morality of common sense is at heart utilitarian. If the widely shared standards appealed to in the objections can be shown to be themselves utilitarian in inspiration, it seems they could hardly serve to support arguments against utilitarianism. This position allows the utilitarian to either concede the authority of common sense, or circumvent the problem altogether, while still disposing of the objections. Both Mill and Sidgwick, I will suggest, had some such argument in mind when they claimed If that is so, then if Sidgwick's thesis is correct, our judgments in ideal epistemic circumstances will be made in accordance with rule utilitarianism. Parallel have made the availability of such a line of argument almost painfully obvious). Whether the positions defended by Mill and Sidgwick could or were intended to support utilitarianism in any more positive fashion seems less clear. As we proceed, I will try to clarify the arguments to be found in Mill and Sidgwick (though this will involve, admittedly, characterizing them in fairly general terms), to see whether it is reasonable to claim that the morality of common sense is at heart utilitarian, and what the consequences of such a claim might be for a defense of utilitarianism.

II

Mill's views on the morality of common sense are not clearly defined in *Utilitarianism*, nor are all of his remarks on the subject obviously consistent. Mill clearly believes at least that the maxims of common-sense morality require behavior that is characteristically justifiable as well in utilitarian terms; large portions of *Utilitarianism* are spent defending the theory against misguided accusations that originate in the moral beliefs of the masses. But it seems to be necessary for Mill's argument to progress beyond this limited claim. Chapter V, "On the Connection between Justice and Utility," begins with the assumption (undoubtedly false) that we will all agree "that objectively the dictates of Justice coincide with a part of the field of General Expediency" (U:Ch.V, para. 2). What Mill wants to defend is the further claim that "the Just" does not exist "as something absolute, generically distinct from every variety of the Expedient, and, in idea opposed to it, though (as commonly acknowledged) never, in the long run, disjoined from it in fact" (U:Ch.V, para. 1).

The argument to this conclusion begins with an examination of the common-sense rules of justice in an attempt to find "the mental link which holds them together." Mill discovers that "in our survey of the various popular acceptations of justice, the term appeared generally to involve the idea of a personal right" (U:Ch. V, para. 15). From this point Mill proceeds, through a bit of moral psychology and an analysis of the idea of a right, to the claim that our views of justice originate in "considerations of general expediency." We distinguish the Just from the Expedient not (as we suppose) because they are fundamentally different in kind, but because the rules of justice "concern the essentials of human well-being more nearly, and are therefore of more absolute obligation, than any other rules for the guidance of life" (U:Ch. V, Para. 32). A distinction we have made based on a difference in degree has come to seem to us to be based on a difference in kind. Those useful rules set aside from the others for being more important in the promotion of happiness, seem to common sense to be both more imperative than the other useful rules (which, in fact, they are) and opposed to them "in idea" (which they are not). The "maxims of justice current in the world, and commonly appealed to in its transactions," are simply "instruments" for promoting the general happiness in certain crucial areas of our lives (U: Ch. V, para. 35). Of course, these maxims may yield conflicting demands when more than one maxim applies to our situation (when our action is of more than one type, these types having conflicting felicific tendencies). The "complicated nature of human affairs" guarantees that "hardly any kind of action can safely be laid down as either always obligatory or always condemnable" (U: Ch. II, para. 25). Where these maxims do yield conflicting results, the only possible solution is a direct appeal to the principle of utility, for this principle is "the ultimate source of moral obligations," the source from which each of the conflicting rules of common-sense morality was initially derived (U:Ch. II, para. 25).

The argument sketched above suggests a certain view of the morality of common sense. Specifically, it suggests that the morality of common sense is at least in part unconsciously utilitarian; that though we consciously regard certain of our shared moral standards as having independent force, we in fact (though unconsciously) support these standards because they are instrumental in the promotion of the general happiness. This is true, on Mill's view, at least in the realm of "duties of perfect obligation" (duties that correlate with rights), since it is this area of morality that constitutes "the province of Justice." If I seem here to be stressing a rather obvious implication of Chapter V of *Utilitarianism*, I do so only by way of defending Mill from what is, I think, a common interpretation of his views on common-sense morality. According to this version, Mill holds the (almost incredible) view that the morality of common sense is *consciously* utilitarian. This reading is based on Mill's remarks on "secondary principles" in Chapter II of *Utilitarianism,* where, admittedly, much that he says is at best unclear. We are told that "all rational creatures go out upon the sea of life with their minds made up on the common questions of right and wrong" and that "mankind must by this time have acquired positive beliefs as to the effects of some actions on their happiness; and the beliefs which have thus come down are the rules of morality for the multitude" (U:Ch. II, para. 24). The effect of such remarks is the creation of a very misleading impression: that ordinary men regard the moral rules they accept as "summary rules" (to use Rawls's terminology) as merely effective instruments for the promotion of their consciously shared goal of utility maximization. The picture is one of men accepting the rules of traditional morality on the understanding that these rules represent an accumulation of man's knowledge about how best to proceed in increasing the general happiness. The rules are taught and understood in these terms, and each generation is engaged in the conscious pursuit of still better instruments for advancing the utilitarian end.

Such a picture is, of course, far indeed from being an accurate portrayal of the role of common-sense morality in our lives (as Sidgwick notes, ME:456); nor do I think it is the picture Mill wishes to paint. As we have seen, Mill's discussion of justice makes clear that he recognizes that we standardly attach a significance to moral rules that is in no way consciously utilitarian (indeed, it is hard to believe that anyone could overlook such a fact). We must, I think, take Mill's remarks on secondary principles to indicate only that the rules of common-sense morality are at heart utilitarian. They tend to conform to utilitarian demands, and are properly regarded as being derived from utilitarian calculations, but not as a result of widespread conscious effort. None of Mill's remarks really asserts anything different, the main point of the passages cited being only the recommendation of the rules of common-sense morality as a reasonably good set of subordinate principles by which the principle of utility can be applied. Common-sense morality, then, is for Mill only unconsciously utilitarian, in that our "real reasons" for accepting its maxims are utilitarian ones. That these are our real reasons can be shown, Mill's remarks suggest, in several ways. First, there is the remarkable tendency of the rules supported by common sense to be precisely those that would best serve as utilitarian secondary principles. Second, elementary speculations in moral psychology support this view. Finally, the way we conduct moral arguments, settle problems of distribution, and so on, reveals our unconscious utilitarian outlook; for we tend naturally, in such contexts, to fall into utilitarian modes of reasoning, even when trying to avoid them (U: Ch. I, para. 4, Ch. V).

Assuming, then, that this is in fact Mill's view, we may ask how he thinks his project will be furthered by it, understanding here by "his project" the presenting of considerations "capable of determining the intellect to give its assent" to the principle of utility. In what ways could the claim that common-sense morality is unconsciously utilitarian advance the case for utilitarianism? Combined with a defense of the authority of the deliverances of common sense, of course, the claim's significance would be obvious; for if the deliverances of common sense were authoritative in moral matters, certainly the principle that guided them (albeit unconsciously) would have to be accepted as valid. But Mill attempts no such defense of common sense in moral matters. He rejects intuitionism and moral sense theory in Chapter I, and there and elsewhere (for example, U:Ch. V, para. 2) it is made clear that ordinary moral beliefs enjoy no special privileges or presumptions. We have already seen, of course, a way in which Mill's thesis of unconscious utilitarianism could support his theory without deciding this question of the authority of common sense. The support is purely negative, in that it consists in eliminating possible alternative theories or countering certain objections. But negative arguments are not without weight when obvious alternatives are limited. (Indeed, Bentham's overt case for the principle of utility was almost entirely negative.) The general strategy again operates against those who insist on the authority of common-sense moral judgments, by granting arguendo the soundness of their position. They are then forced either to accept the authority of the principle that guides common sense (and is consequently of a higher order than the derivative rules of traditional morality), or to reject the authority of common sense. Any suggested conflicts between the requirements of the principle of utility can be dismissed either as inevitable distortions in an otherwise determinedly utilitarian process, or as the result of common sense's habitual adherence to rules of thumb. The argument of Chapter V of *Utilitarianism*, I maintain, is in part an application by Mill of this general strategy, and, if successful, would serve as strong (negative) support for the utilitarian principle.

It is, however, advisable to characterize the point of Mill's argument in a slightly different way as well. One need not have a general view about the import of common-sense moral rules to respect the deliverances of one's own conscience. Mill's argument can be understood as well as an attempt to persuade ordinary men who are sincere in their moral beliefs to become utilitarians. We should become utilitarians because, in a sense, we are utilitarians already. If Mill convinces us that the morality of common sense is unconsciously utilitarian (and if our moral convictions are widely shared), it is irrational for us to accept the deliverances of conscience while rejecting the principle under which they are issued. In these ways Mill's suggestion that common-sense morality is unconsciously utilitarian seems to play an important role in his promotion and defense of utilitarianism. And it seems fair to say that his views in some ways anticipate the later development of the position in Sidgwick.

III

Sidgwick makes explicit much that I have had to read into Mill. His points are naturally subtler, better developed and defended, and more clearly integrated into a systematic defense of utilitarianism than those attributable to Mill. When Sidgwick maintains the thesis of unconscious utilitarianism, for instance, this follows on a detailed and insightful examination of the maxims of common-sense morality, no semblance of which is to be found in Mill. But in spite of its superior development, some difficulties are involved in understanding the intended point of Sidgwick's claim as well.

Initial problems are caused by the stated purpose of *The Methods of Ethics*, which seems not at all in line with its conclusions. Sidgwick's object, he tells us, is only "to expound as clearly and as fully as my limits will allow the different methods of Ethics that I find implicit in our common moral reasoning; to point out their mutual relations; and where they seem to conflict, to define the issue as much as possible," but not to attempt any "complete and final solution of the chief ethical difficulties and controversies" (ME:14, 13). This object would seem to rule out a defense of utilitarianism of the sort to be found in Mill. Yet it would be impossible to deny that Sidgwick's *Methods* appears to contain a spirited defense of utilitarianism, as well as a clear rejection of intuitionism.[4] When Sidgwick describes his position as utilitarian "on an Intuitional basis" (ME:xx), this statement should not be taken to indicate a genuine reconciliation of the two methods; all of the methods are "intuitional" in this very broad sense of the term (ME:98, 201). But intuitionism as it is commonly understood ("dogmatic intuitionism") is unconditionally dispatched in Chapter XI of Book III.

The details of the "proof" of utilitarianism are presented by Sidgwick in Book IV, Chapter II, where the role of his thesis of unconscious utilitarianism is discussed. In fact, however, Sidgwick already has argued for utilitarianism in Book III on what appear to be completely independent (if not completely satisfying) grounds. There, in his efforts "to throw the Morality of Common Sense into scientific form," Sidgwick rates the maxims of positive morality in terms of their clarity, true self-evidence, consistency, and degree of acceptance. The content of the evaluation is that these maxims fail to satisfy the conditions necessary to "elevate [them] into a system of Intuitional Ethics" (ME:361). But Sidgwick does eventually find elsewhere "clear and certain ethical intuitions": he arrives, in fact, "at the fundamental principle of utilitarianism" (ME:361). I will not comment on this part of the argument beyond noting that the appeals to self-evidence involved in it are not, in my view, overly persuasive. Sidgwick has another side to the argument, however, which he calls "a more positive treatment of Common-sense Morality, in its relation to Utilitarianism" (ME:361, Note 1). It is in this part of Sidgwick's argument for utilitarianism that we are interested.

Like Bentham and Mill, Sidgwick rejects the possibility of providing a "strict proof" of the principle of utility (or of any other ethical first principle).

The "proof" of utilitarianism he discusses is an argument ad hominem, designed to force "a man who already holds some other moral principles" to embrace utilitarianism, whether that man be an intuitionist or an egoist (ME:419). In fact, Sidgwick is able to provide no such proof for the egoist, so the "proof" of utilitarianism cannot, on his view, be completed; Sidgwick settles instead for a practical "reconciliation between the two principles" of Universal and Egoistic Hedonism (ME:420). But he does attempt to prove utilitarianism to the intuitionist, and his strategy at first appears to follow the general lines of that which we found in Mill's *Utilitarianism*. The argument must again be viewed as purely negative, being designed only to show that intuitionism cannot stand as a viable option to utilitarianism, that the intuitionist must either become a utilitarian or reverse his stance on the authority of common sense. The positive version of the argument, which would include a defense of the authority of common sense in moral matters, is not directly suggested by Sidgwick, though he is obviously far more willing than Mill to grant at least provisional authority to common sense (see, e.g., ME:77, 213, 373). (It is of course quite possible, in light of Sidgwick's apparent view that the business of ethics is to systematize and make rational ordinary moral views [ME:77], that he has in mind here a positive form of the argument we will consider.[5] I will confine my attention, however, to Sidgwick's actual presentation of the argument in Book IV, which is undeniably ad hominem and negative.)

Sidgwick's actual argument is "addressed" directly to the intuitionist, and "allows the validity, to a certain extent" of the maxims of common-sense morality that the intuitionist regards as self-evident (this allowance being made solely to permit us to engage the intuitionist in argument, or so Sidgwick's remarks suggest). He then attempts to show

> how Utilitarianism sustains the general validity of the current moral judgments, and thus supplements the defects which reflection finds in the intuitive recognition of their stringency; and at the same time affords a principle of synthesis, and a method for binding the unconnected and occasionally conflicting principles of common moral reasoning into a complete and harmonious system. If systematic reflection upon the morality of Common Sense thus exhibits the Utilitarian principle as that to which Common Sense naturally appeals for that further development of its system which this same reflection shows to be necessary, the proof of Utilitarianism seems as complete as it can be made (ME:422).

We can see now an argument rather different from the one we discussed in connection with Mill. When we examine the maxims of common-sense morality carefully, as Sidgwick does in Book III, we find a loose, unconnected, internally inconsistent set of rules with no organizing principle. The rules often conflict, but they recognize no higher principle of decision and display no determinate priority. In short, "the principles of common sense moral reasoning" cry out for "a principle of synthesis" that settles conflicts by defining the boundaries of the lower principles and unifies them in a coherent system. The collection of unrelated principles needs to be bound into a "scientifically complete and systematically reflective form" (ME:425) before it can claim to constitute a rational process for determining behavior. The ideal "principle of synthesis," then, is one that is broadly consistent with all of the principles it organizes, but that clarifies and unifies them in a way consistent with their spirit. By arguing that the morality of common sense approximates utilitarian morality, Sidgwick can claim that the principle of utility constitutes an ideal principle of synthesis for the collection of common-sense rules. Because of this object, he does not want to demonstrate "an exact coincidence between Utilitarian inferences and the intuitions of Common Sense." Sidgwick wants to characterize common-sense morality as only "inchoately and imperfectly Utilitarian"; he can then show "a natural transition from the Morality of Common Sense to Utilitarianism, somewhat like the transition in special branches of practice from trained instinct and empirical rules to the technical method that embodies and applies the conclusions of science" (ME:427, 425).

Now this "proof" has a different basic premise than the argument we attributed to Mill. Sidgwick seems to be relying only on the claim of approximate coincidence between the demands of common sense and utilitarianism, whereas Mill clearly needed the further explanatory thesis of unconscious utilitarianism. Mill's argument, remember, turned on the claim that it would be irrational for a person to accept as authoritative the deliverances of common sense while refusing to accept the principle that unconsciously guides common sense to its conclusions. Here the thesis of unconscious utilitarianism is used in such a way that its explanatory force is essential. If it is not true that some person's common-sense judgments are guided by an unconscious commitment to the principle of utility, then that person is given no compelling reasons to seriously consider utilitarianism. All that he will have to consider is the close coincidence between the results of utilitarianism and those of his common sense. But, this, by itself, gives a person no reason to choose utilitarianism. It is only insofar as an individual is himself an unconscious utilitarian in the principles he practices or advocates that Mill's argument will persuade that individual. Sidgwick's version of argument, on the other hand, does not obviously even require the explanatory force of the thesis of unconscious utilitarianism. If an approximate coincidence could be shown between the demands of common sense and utilitarianism, and if common-sense morality could be shown to be badly in need of a principle of synthesis, it would be at least initially plausible to argue for utilitarianism on these grounds alone. There is no obvious need for evidence that common-sense moral rules derive from the (unconscious) application of a principle of utility, or for establishing, e.g., that changes in common-sense morality during the course of human history have been changes in a utilitarian direction. The mere synthesizing power of the principle of utility, independent of any psychological or historical explanations of the character of common-sense morality, could well be taken as a strong reason for its acceptance by anyone who accepts the authority of common sense. The two versions of the argument, as thus far characterized, proceed to the same conclusion (the elimination of intuitionism as an option), but seem to differ in the kinds of factual support required to make them plausible. Because this second "synthesis argument" apparently requires less in the way of factual support that would be difficult to find, it may seem the preferable line to take.

This is not, of course, to say that any obvious bar exists to using both versions of the argument in conjunction, or the main point of one to support the other. Although Sidgwick stresses the "synthesis argument," he goes to great lengths as well to defend the thesis of unconscious utilitarianism (in Book IV, Chapter III); why he does so is not yet clear. And Mill is certainly not oblivious to the role of the principle of utility as a possible synthesizing principle for common-sense morality (U:Ch. I, para. 2, Ch. II, para. 25, Ch. V, paras 26-31). Nonetheless, a certain tension is apparent between the two versions of the argument, as I suggested above. The principle of utility is an appealing principle of synthesis when the coincidence between the demands of common sense and utilitarianism is only rough and approximate. As Sidgwick notes:

> Utilitarianism is not concerned to prove the absolute coincidence in results of the Intuitional and Utilitarian methods. Indeed, if it could succeed in proving as much as this, its success would be almost fatal to its practical claims; as the adoption of the Utilitarian principle would then become a matter of complete indifference (ME:425).

The thesis of unconscious utilitarianism, however, seems to be better supported and more persuasive the more exact the coincidence between the demands of common sense and utilitarianism can be shown to be. The wider the gap between these demands, the less plausible our attribution of unconscious guidance of common sense by the principle of utility. In individual cases, for instances, we are disinclined to attribute to an individual an unconscious urge or desire unless we can see a very close coincidence between his behavior and what we suppose he would do if he were consciously pursuing the end in question. Now Sidgwick does argue, quite convincingly that we should expect various kinds of deviations by common sense from the utilitarian path in a society of unconscious utilitarians (Book IV, Chapter IV). This argument, however, will not alter the fact that the greater the deviation from the utilitarian path in real life, the greater the difficulty will be in convincing a neutral party to accept an ascription of unconscious utilitarian motivation. In this respect, then, the principle of utility will tend to seem a more appealing principle of synthesis for common-sense morality as the thesis of unconscious utilitarianism seems less convincing.

Why, then, given these difficulties and the apparent superfluity of the thesis of unconscious utilitarianism for the purposes of his synthesis argument, does Sidgwick even bother to defend the thesis of unconscious utilitarianism? I believe he has good reason, for, as we have presented it, at least, the "synthesis argument" requires additional support to be at all persuasive. In the first place, whereas conventionalism must always threaten such arguments, the present form of the synthesis argument seems conventionalist in the most rigid way. It needs at least to be shown that common-sense morality has "through the whole course of human history . . . always tended substantially in the same direction"

(ME:425), for this impression to be in any way modified. But second, a principle of synthesis will only strike us as obviously preferable to a collection of unconnected and even conflicting rules which we accept, where it isolates something implicit in that collection. It is not enough that the synthesizing principle be broadly consistent with those rules and capable of resolving conflicts; it must somehow capture the spirit of the rules. Otherwise it will not seem to synthesize and unify, but merely to impose an arbitrary form for form's sake. The thesis of unconscious utilitarianism, of course, assures us that the principle of utility will be the ideal principle of synthesis for common-sense morality, since it simply reflects the derivation of the common-sense rules. Some such thesis, I suggest, is requisite to support Sidgwick's synthesis argument. The thesis of unconscious utilitarianism, then, is quite as necessary to Sidgwick's argument as it is to Mill's. And if that thesis can be called into question, the kinds of support for utilitarianism suggested by Sidgwick and Mill will be undermined. In spite of Sidgwick's careful defense of the thesis there are, I think, good reasons to doubt its truth, reasons that can, I hope, be advanced without the presentation of a detailed analysis of the theses of common-sense morality. Let me try to briefly present the sketch of an argument that utilizes these reasons.[6]

IV

The difficulties involved in arguing either for or against the thesis of unconscious utilitarianism are obvious from the start. In the first place, the thesis ascribes to common-sense morality only an imperfect tendency to conform to utilitarian guidelines. This is certainly all that the facts could hope to support; and Sidgwick's argument, as we have seen, cannot accommodate a stronger thesis of perfect or near perfect conformity anyway, making any attempt to support the stronger thesis superfluous for his purposes. But the ascription to common sense of only an imperfect conformity to the demands of utilitarianism entails that the factual evidence supporting the thesis must include all sorts of common-sense moral rules that do not serve to advance the general happiness as effectively as possible. Some of the rules might be positively pernicious, with none of them being maximally useful, and the thesis of unconscious utilitarianism would still not be contradicted. Sidgwick, in fact, undertakes only to show that existing moral rules possess "some manifest felicific tendency," not that the rules are "*more* conducive to the general happiness than any others" (ME:425). But unless we are viewing the character of common-sense moral rules as supporting a thesis whose truth is simply presupposed, it is hard to see how the mere usefulness of these rules should incline us to see common-sense morality as unconsciously guided by a maximizing principle of utility. I will try momentarily to show that as a thesis competing on fair terms with alternatives, the thesis of unconscious utilitarianism looks seriously undersupported.

Sidgwick, as we have seen, needs to defend the thesis to complete his argument, yet his evaluations of common-sense morality often seem to be such that they would only convince one predisposed to accept the thesis of unconscious utilitarianism. Evidence of nonutilitarian tendencies in common-sense morality, for instance, is covered by Sidgwick's careful explanation of how such distortions might naturally arise in a society of unconscious utilitarians. But to show how such deviations might arise is not to show that they do arise, and Sidgwick makes no real effort to demonstrate the superiority of his hypotheses to alternative possible explanations of these nonutilitarian tendencies in common-sense morality. Indeed, one sometimes feels that it is simply being taken for granted that such tendencies are anomalous and irrational, and that in the presence of recalcitrant but rational nonutilitarian tendencies in the morality of common sense, no effort would be made to determine that they were not mere distortions.

To approach the question from neutral ground, we might begin by asking what evidence we in general accept as establishing that an individual is unconsciously pursuing some end (if, indeed, we think any evidence would establish such a claim). We commonly attribute an unconscious desire to a person on the basis of a close coincidence between that individual's behavior and what he would do if he were consciously pursuing the end, conjoined with the absence of other facts that would seem adequate to explain the behavior. We are also impressed when, as a result of reflection, cross-examination, analysis, or whatever, the individual comes to recognize the unconscious desire as his own, as providing the correct explanation of his behavior.

Now the thesis of unconscious utilitarianism cannot obviously claim these kinds of support. Although we may be convinced by Sidgwick's argument that a close coincidence does exist between common-sense moral judgments and what common sense would dictate if it were consciously utilitarian, Sidgwick does very little by way of showing us that no plausible alternative explanations of common sense's deliverances are available. Indeed, there are myriad alternative psychological theories purporting to explain the same data, all with at least some degree of plausibility. Nor does it seem likely, given the simple facts of moral training, that the thesis of unconscious utilitarianism will be supported by ordinary men coming to recognize the principle of utility as that which has in fact guided their moral views. Whereas the average man might well recognize on reflection that his common-sense moral judgments fitted neatly with the demands of utilitarianism, if he has been trained to regard certain kinds of acts as wrong regardless of their felicific tendencies, and recognizes that he judges as he does because of this training, he will not accept the claim that he is an unconscious utilitarian (nor should he). We may, of course, claim that most men are not utilitarians, conscious or unconsciously, without denying that the development of common-sense morality has been influenced by the efforts of those who did seek (consciously or unconsciously) to maximize (or at least increase) the general happiness. But to admit this much is not to admit that common-sense morality is unconsciously utilitarian.

What may, however, seem convincing support for the thesis of unconscious utilitarianism is Sidgwick's argument that the rules of common-sense morality can be perceived to change, and be accepted and rejected by society, according to utilitarian demands. Common sense, Sidgwick seems to suggest, has responded to utilitarian demands roughly as follows:[7] Where obeying a standing moral rule of a society has had consistently unhappy consequences, that rule has ceased to be held in respect; and where society could, by following some rule, avoid unhappy consequences, that rule has tended to be accepted as constituting a moral requirement. Similarly, exceptions to the rules, and the like, have been roughly controlled by utilitarian considerations, of course with the inevitable distortions.

Whether or not these claims about common-sense are true, I don't know, though I suspect they are not. But even if they were true, they would not, as far as I can see, favor the thesis of unconscious utilitarianism over certain competing claims that the morality of common sense unconsciously tended in some nonutilitarian direction, or had no coherent tendency at all. In Sidgwick's discussion, as we have seen, it is not maintained that common-sense moral rules are maximally useful rules (that is, rules, general adherence to which would have the best possible consequences). We must assume, then, that Sidgwick would not suggest that common-sense rules tend to lose their hold on society when they cease to be maximally useful. Common-sense moral rules presumably would tend to lose their hold on society when they cease to be merely useful, when unhappy consequences begin to flow from obedience to them. This is all that Sidgwick's discussion supports, and surely all that could reasonably be maintained about common-sense morality.

But now suppose that common-sense morality includes a set of rules obedience to which has good but not ideal consequences. These rules are not, however, the product of utilitarian considerations, but stem, say, from considerations about the sanctity or dignity of human beings—they may consist in absolute, or virtually absolute, prohibitions, where the ideal utilitarian rules would require exceptions of various sorts. And suppose that the conditions of human life were such that these rules continued to be highly useful, sometimes more so, sometimes less so, but never ideally so. Now the fact that the body of common-sense moral rules was changed, accepted and rejected according to its promotion of happiness, leaving this special set of rules untouched, would not seem to support the thesis of unconscious utilitarianism. It would be natural to conclude in such a case that if common-sense morality tends to be unconsciously utilitarian, it does so only in part; that it tends to recognize the promotion of the general happiness as one good end among others.

Something like this seems to me to be true of common-sense morality, and, as a result, it seems that the evidence adduced in favor of the thesis of unconscious utilitarianism is perfectly compatible with common-sense morality's tending in nonutilitarian directions, or better, perhaps, in no coherent direction at all. I suspect that the rules to which I have referred would continue to be held in respect by common sense even in the face of changing conditions that rendered the consequences of obedience to them significantly less happy. They might, of course, be given up in the face of extremely unhappy consequences of continued obedience. But this result would show only that common-sense morality did not regard any good end as having absolute weight with respect to the others; it would not show that the morality of common sense was unconsciously utilitarian.

Surprisingly, perhaps, Sidgwick often makes observations about common-sense morality very similar to those which I have made above. But we have seen that if common-sense morality does not display an underlying coherent tendency of the sort suggested by the thesis of unconscious utilitarianism, Sidgwick's "synthesis argument" will be unconvincing. We can conclude, then, that if the main points urged here are correct, and the thesis of unconscious utilitarianism is therefore inconclusively supported (and very likely false), the defense of utilitarianism will not be furthered by the examination of common-sense morality. We may, of course, believe that insofar as common-sense morality is not unconsciously guided by any principle capable of being used as its "principle of synthesis," that we ought not to respect its dictates as even provisionally authoritative. In such a case, however, I would not share with Sidgwick any sense of loss.

Notes

1. Henry Sidgwick, *The Methods of Ethics*, 7th Edition (Dover, 1966), p. 24. Future references will be to this edition, indicated by ME and followed by page numbers.

2. J. S. Mill, *Utilitarianism*, Chapter V, paragraph 2. Future references will be indicated by U, followed by chapter and paragraph number.

3. J. J. C. Smart, "Extreme and Restricted Utilitarianism," *Philosophical Quarterly* 6 (1956).

4. Peter Singer has defended the view that Sidgwick is not in fact attempting to argue for utilitarianism. As my characterization of Sidgwick's claims will suggest, I am at least partially sympathetic with his reading. See Singer, "Sidgwick and Reflective Equilibrium," *The Monist* 58 (July 1974). For an opposing view, see J. B. Schneewind, "First Principles and Common Sense Morality in Sidgwick's Ethics," *Archiv für Geschichte der Philosophie*, Bd. 45 (1963).

5. Sidgwick seems to me to have beeen undecided about the availability of such an argument, considering it without actually presenting it. Singer (in "Sidgwick and Reflective Equilibrium") urges us to view Sidgwick's appeals to common sense as mere rough "confirmations" of positions to be defended in other ways. The passages noted above show that such a reading of Sidgwick must ignore at least some of his remarks to attribute to him a firm position on this subject.

6. A large portion of Section IV of this essay was presented as part of a reply to Allan Gibbard's paper, "If the Morality of Common Sense is Unconsciously Utilitarian, Does That Give Us Any Reason to be Utilitarians?" (at the May 1978 conference on Utilitarianism at V.P.I. & S.U.) [in this volume as "Inchoately Utilitarian Common Sense: The Bearing of a Thesis of Sidgwick's on Moral Theory"]. Gibbard clarified my views on this problem in many ways and the ways in which I approach the subject in Section IV are influenced by his characterizations of it. For different approaches to the thesis of unconscious utilitarianism, see Gertrude Ezorsky, "Unconscious Utilitarianism" and D. D. Raphael, "Sidgwick on Intuitionism," both in *The Monist* 58 (1974).

7. Here I follow the main lines of Gibbard's discussion of this point.

Section II: Utilitarianism and Contractarianism

The most significant challenge to utilitarianism in recent years has come from theorists who can be termed "contractarians" or "contractualists" because of their use of the metaphor or theoretical construct of a contract to provide a systematic, integrated theory of right action, purporting to match utilitarian theories in that respect. According to them, the correctness of moral rules turns not on the maximization of happiness or other good, but on the voluntary acceptance of these rules by rational persons, under conditions of fair choice or (as on Gauthier's account) as the outcome of an ideal bargain. Such a choice or bargain reflects the impartial regard for individual persons that is the spirit of morality. Contractualist thinkers deny that utilitarian principles would be agreed to as its outcome. Persons would not choose a scheme for the maximization of aggregate happiness, they contend, but one assuring equal respect for their partially conflicting interests.

The contractualist viewpoints represented here by Diggs, Fuchs, and Gauthier are supported by different lines of argument (with different degrees of formality) reflecting different (and in the case of Fuchs [or Rawls] and Gauthier) conflicting models of rationality in ethics.

Utilitarians have defended themselves against contractualist competitors in part by accepting the constructs of morality from which the competing theories are purportedly drawn and by claiming to show that these devices both incorporate utilitarian modes of reasoning and yield utilitarian principles—or, at least, ones not inconsistent with utilitarianism. This kind of utilitarian defense is exemplified here by Narveson and by Harsanyi as represented in Gauthier's essay.

In this section, then, we are concerned once more with the justification of utilitarianism and also with its relation to more specific rules of conduct. The critical question here is whether or not any contractualist approach captures essential features of morality and rationality ignored or excluded by every form of utilitarianism. If it does, and it is otherwise correct, then even if some form of utilitarianism should give, by chance, the same appraisals of particular actions, the latter will fail as an account of right action.

6 Utilitarianism and Contractarianism

B. J. Diggs

Until recently contractarianism was not widely regarded as a moral philosophy although traditional contract theorists often discussed morality more than government. The early parts of Rousseau's *Social Contract,* for example, read better as moral than as political philosophy, not that the two should be wholly separated. Contractarianism in moral philosophy is a kind of ethical formalism; as such, it is theoretically compatible with a number of other views, including some kinds of utilitarianism. Rawls says as much when he mentions the possibility of using some form of contract theory to defend utilitarianism.

A form of contractarianism will be developed here that is simpler and more traditional than Rawls's theory—although it *may* be close to what Rawls calls "the Kantian interpretation of justice as fairness." Part I outlines this "contractualism," as it will be called. Part II considers how much support some forms of utilitarianism obtain from contractualism and, in the process, tries to illuminate differences between them.[1]

I

The contractualism to be developed here begins by regarding a social morality, or the morality of a society, primarily as a system of voluntary social control that "governs" the way a society's members act toward one another—a view of morality that an anthropologist or sociologist might take. However, the contractualism is normative; it will be generated by pointing out certain conditions, drawn from commonly accepted ideas in our moral tradition, that must be satisfied for a social morality, taken in the descriptive sense, to be moral, in a nor-

---

Both the positive and critical parts of this paper have greatly benefited from comments of Louis Werner in earlier versions. His untimely loss is keenly felt by the author.
Some of the research in this paper was made possible by the grant of a Senior Fellowship (1972-3) from the National Endowment for the Humanities. The author is much indebted to the Endowment.

mative sense. This approach should at least have the advantage of relating normative moral requirements to social moralities as we find them in this world. One can follow our procedure simply by asking oneself: What conditions must a social morality satisfy to deserve our moral support? At the outset three conditions will be emphasized, only the latter two of which are normative.

(1) First, a social morality is constituted of moral views and dispositions shared by a society's members; to the degree to which members of a society do not hold the same moral views, it is improper to speak of *the* morality of their society. A morality may be expressed verbally most often in statements of the society's leaders, in the operation of its legal system, in the teaching of the young, etc. But one should not overlook the practical character of a morality; it is apt to be expressed at least in a loose sense, more often in the way persons treat one another than in words, and it is more accurately conceived as commonly extolled dispositions to act than as some set of principles, rules, or other articles to which allegiance is sworn. We shall speak of a social morality as if it were constituted of either moral articles or moral ways of acting; let us think of persons subscribing to the former primarily by acting on them and being disposed to act on them.

(2) Second, although the moralities of actual societies often seem to be sustained by social pressures, if a social morality is to be given our full-fledged moral support, it is reasonable to require it to be consistent with one's having a freedom, a "moral freedom" as we shall refer to it, to develop one's own view of how one ought to live, and to live accordingly, insofar as this is consistent with every other person having a like freedom. Two reasons for this requirement are traditional. If the unexamined life *is* worth living, it is not worth what it might be; although one's choices are inevitably limited by the institutions of one's society, as well as by human nature, a freedom to examine one's life, including how persons should act toward one another, and to govern one's life is essential to one's humanity. And, since a social morality itself is constituted of the shared moral views of individuals, it is only as good as the moral thoughtfulness of the society's members; personal moral reflection is essential if a social morality is to be accepted critically, rather than passively, and to be subject to reform. But how is it possible for a social morality, which is a system of social control, to be consistent with the moral freedom of persons? Clearly it can be entirely consistent with this freedom only if each and every person, in the course of self-government, without threats or coercion, freely accepts its restrictions. This means that the individual members of a society must freely subscribe to a common morality right. The same conclusion is evident from the fact that if persons, living together, are to treat one another in ways that each regards as morally right or all right, and not to coerce one another, then they must govern their lives with one another according to the same morality, however different their moral views and ideas may be in other respects. Moral freedom does not allow unbridled liberty; if one is mindful of human nature, and the radical dependence

of human beings on one another, it is quite clear that persons, to develop and exercise this freedom, must accept many restrictions, including those of a social morality. Not every social morality will do; a worthy one, of such a kind that each person can freely subscribe to it, cannot be achieved in a day.

(3) Third, although articles of social moralities often appear to be sustained by false beliefs and irrationalities, any social morality that deserves our moral support must be such that good and decisive reasons exist for each person to whom it applies freely to subscribe to and act on it. Persons often have difficulty in stating the reasons for the morality they support, but they commonly suppose both that good reasons do exist, whether or not people can state them, and further that these reasons are decisive in the sense that when all things are considered, people ought to act on that morality. One may have qualifications about some directive, of course, but these would argue against the directive being included in the morality. The presupposition of the reasonableness of morality is perhaps most evident when moral articles are recommended or taught; it does not seem proper to tell someone that he ought to act as morality directs unless one thinks there are decisively good reasons for him to do so. And in one's own case, it seems quite odd to think that one morally ought to do something and at the same time wonder whether there are decisive reasons for doing it. Sometimes one may think that the morality of one's society requires something that one should not do, but then that individual does not subscribe to the morality as a practical guide in this instance; in such a case one seems committed to the belief that the morality is defective, in the sense that it requires something that it should not require.

What are the decisively good reasons for subscribing to articles of a worthy morality? This large issue, which involves the whole character of practical reason, cannot be discussed here. However, these reasons surely derive from the social character of human life and the necessities related thereto; in view of them, "the social facts of life," it should hardly be surprising to discover that some ways of human beings living with one another are more reasonable than others—of which more as we proceed.

One point needs to be made without delay. When it is said that there are decisively good reasons for each person freely to subscribe to a worthy social morality, it is not being said that these reasons are independent of how other persons act. It may be theoretically possible for an entire social morality to result from the accidental intersections of persons acting according to independent ideals, but this is most unlikely. The good and decisive reasons for one's acting on a morality are usually reasons only when others act on it, or can be persuaded to do so. Since the benefits it affords, as with rules of a game, derive from a common acceptance, the reasons for it are reasons for each person subscribing to it *together with others* (although they may also be good reasons for one's trying, up to a point, to get others to do so). Moreover, moral ways of acting often result from compromise. They often do not constitute the *best* solution of a moral problem from *anyone's* own point of view even though, when all things are considered, there are decisively good reasons for each person to act in these ways. Thus, what is reasonable to one person may well be partly a function of what is reasonable to others. Actually this is what we find in many "social forms," for example, in a marriage, and it is what we should naturally expect of a social morality.

A morality that satisfies the aforementioned conditions is clearly an ideal, which actual social moralities only partly realize. We might like to have a morality that meets these conditions govern all human beings, or, if that is not possible, all members of our own society. In either case, to the degree to which such a morality is realized, persons act toward one another in ways that each, together with others, freely and for good reasons subscribe to as moral. Doubts may arise immediately about whether there are such ways of acting, when each person is free to develop his own view of how he should live—we shall return to these doubts shortly. But there are a number of indications that this sort of ideal morality is not vacuous and that we do indeed often try to live up to it.

One such indication is to be found in the teaching of articles of our own social morality, or some of them, to children; when we do so, we surely think that good reasons exist for them to accept these articles, in learning to govern themselves and that they can do so without seriously abridging their freedom to form reasoned ideals of their own. We seem to assume that these moral restrictions can be freely accepted partly because their common acceptance helps secure the conditions in which individual freedom can be exercised. Moreover, we commonly assume that it is reasonable for all persons in our condition to subscribe to such basic moral requirements as respecting another's life and person, keeping promises, caring for one's children, helping those in need, etc. What a mess there is when people fail to do so! Furthermore, in our daily life with others, when we want to act morally but have no moral article to guide us, we usually try to act in a way that others as well as we ourselves find reasonable, and we also hesitate to impose a solution on others, even when this is possible. It is as if we acknowledge that a moral way of acting must be reasonable to all parties, and as if we are trying to realize our ideal in this instance.

Certainly if this ideal is not empty, it has considerable normative consequences. Although the line of argument can only be suggested here, the traditional requirement "to respect persons" can be explained and clarified in terms of the ideal. If such a morality is to be *realized*, each person must join others in acting in ways that each, together with others, can reasonably and freely subscribe to as a common moral standard. Moreover, each person must treat every other in ways that allow the other freely to exercise his capacity to govern himself, insofar as this is consistent with every other doing the same. Thus, to realize the ideal, each must be concerned to live in moral ways that are reasonable to others as well as to oneself; and further, each must be concerned not to coerce or deceive others but to have them freely adopt these ways for the reasons that make it reasonable to do so. This fits the traditional idea of respect for persons, which is commonly thought to include both a consideration of each person's well-being, and also an acknowledgment of the freedom of each to govern himself or herself. Moreover, each person who respects others, and thereby "does his or her part" in the moral community, may be regarded as having a valid claim, and thus a right, to the respect of others—and perhaps one would do well to extend this right more widely.

This moral ideal may be thought of as a "practical regulative ideal." We have given some indications that the ideal, although formal, at least for our society, has some "material content"—or, in other words, that some moral articles (for example, one should keep one's promises) *are* reasonable to all. Nevertheless, it is often more illuminating to regard this ideal, not primarily as generating a set of moral articles or directives, but as a fundamental procedural guide. To respect others, one must act in ways that are reasonable to them as well as to oneself. But how is one to determine what is reasonable to others? With or without the other's help, one must both "put oneself in another's shoes" and "look at the matter in question through the other's eyes." And this is only the beginning. Having done this, and also "argued the case" of the other, one must then adopt the position of a kind of "moral judge" and try to decide the matter in a way that is fair to others and to oneself. If one is confident that one has found a reasonable way of acting, moreover, one must not shove it down the other's throat but, if at all possible, treat the other as a person capable of appreciating the reasons for it and governing himself. These procedures, which the ideal morality requires, are purely formal but of fundamental importance. Achieving moral solutions is an endless process, and the moral relations between persons are constantly being put to the test. Often the problem is not so much getting persons to act according to a commonly accepted morality but achieving a morality that will offer common direction. If persons could count on one another to follow the basic procedures, a large part of the moral problem would be solved. On this view, ideal morality consists not so much in a set of fixed principles (or other moral articles) as in the basic procedures that serve as an operational guide.

It should be readily acknowledged, however, that in some cases it is impossible in fact to achieve a morality, or moral solutions, reasonable to all parties. In the past, this has been true of the Nazi and the Jew, and surely in many other cases. But what do facts of this sort show? They show only that there is little or no hope of achieving a common morality when people hold fundamentally opposed views, which no one wishes to deny; they certainly fail to show that there are no moral ways of acting reasonable to all parties. If persons hold unreasonable views, it should not be surprising that no reasonable solutions are available. There are many ways of being unreasonable; at this point we are concerned with only one of them. If a person acts toward others in ways that are inconsistent with their having an equal moral freedom, then this way of acting, although it may be advantageous to that one person in certain respects, is not one that can be defended as a reasonable way for them all to live with one another. Why? Because even though the others may be cajoled into being treated in this way, to the extent to which it is inconsistent with their freedom, it deprives them of something that is essential to their living as human beings, and to their being accorded the respect due to them as fellow members of the moral community. On this account *they* cannot *freely* and *reasonably* agree to being treated in this way, or subscribe to action of this kind as moral, whether they do so in fact or not. But granted that it is unreasonable to them in this respect, if it is advantageous to the person so acting, how can it be said to be unreasonable to him? In order for him to get the advantages, he *must* live with them, *and* in ways that he and they together could not freely and reasonably agree to—in ways that are not reasonable to them all together. If there are not good reasons for others freely to act in these ways, to get them to do so he must give them reasons in the form of threats, coercion, or the like, or else he must hoodwink or propagandize them in some way, and he may even have to "dispose" of some of them. The costs incurred and the benefits lost are apt to be considerable and lasting; one's own character, one's relations with others, the character of one's society, all are at stake. The question here is large, but the presumption of morality, that the advantages gained do not outweigh the disadvantages, and that it is impossible wholly to live in this way, even though vicious people think otherwise, surely has much to be said for it.

A related point is of equal importance. As the foregoing account shows, on some occasions if a moral social morality is to be realized, persons must change their views and adopt more reasonable ones. This means that in trying to determine ways of acting or articles that can be reasonably and freely accepted by each person together with others, we cannot take individuals' views, tastes, preferences, ideals, and so on as simply given, or as the bedrock on which a morality must be built; if we were to do so, a morality might be impossible. At the same time, it is part of the conception of a moral social morality that decisively good reasons exist for each person to join others in subscribing to it. This implies that on some occasions decisively good reasons exist for a person to change his views, dispositions, and actions, in certain respects—for example, when one's opinions are unreasonably in the way of his joining others. This principle in turn suggests that when decisively good reasons exist for persons to change their views, etc., the views to be changed are in some way incompatible with those that are retained—so that when a person holds views that are inconsistent with the requirements of ideal morality, the practical views he holds are internally inconsistent. But perhaps this is not necessarily the case. An ideal morality may be valuable, and adopted for good reasons, not only because it enables persons to attain goals they already have (for example, peace) but also because it affords a different and better kind of life, with new goals and effective ways of attaining them (for example, a life of mutual respect). Sometimes one acts for good reasons that one only dimly perceives.

So that the foregoing very abstract account of an ideal morality will not make it seem too ethereal or other-worldly, we would do well to remind ourselves that, as noted above, the basic moral procedures this morality requires are not infrequently followed. In some quarters, they are an everyday guide. Furthermore, some grand examples may be given of morally successful outcomes to which they have substantially contributed. One of the most notable is religious toleration; another is the partly voluntary elimination of slavery; another is the partly voluntary elimination of discrimination. In cases of this kind, people have discarded unreasonable views and have come gradually to accept a more moral way of life, sometimes for moral reasons.

II

We come now to utilitarianism; how is it related to the contractualism outlined above? On the contractualist view, any social morality that deserves our unqualified moral support must satisfy the conditions of a moral or ideal social morality; and consequently, if some kind of utilitarianism is to be endorsed, then the moral articles it proposes must be such that decisively good reasons exist for each person together with others freely to subscribe to them. First let us ask: Can utilitarians agree with this general, formal requirement?

The answer to this question depends largely on the kind of utilitarianism espoused. The utilitarianism that derives morality from benevolence has attached no special importance to the moral freedom of persons, and it has not been much concerned to find forms of social organization that protect or promote this freedom. It does not regard morality, primarily, as a kind of social institution or "form of social life." On its view, morally right acts are simply those that promote the good of persons generally. The most natural examples of morally right acts are acts of simple beneficence, not acts that either respect persons' rights or accord with a commonly accepted morality. To be sure, if the general good is to be promoted, rules and conventions are needed, and thus some morally right acts are conventional or rule governed. But these rules or conventions, however they may be conceived in other respects, are only intermediaries; they lack any independent moral authority; persons should follow them only when doing so can be expected to have the best overall consequences. To many utilitarians it has seemed entirely proper to say that the only fundamental moral requirement is expressed by the utilitarian principle that one should act in the way that one can reasonably expect to maximize the good of all. To them, this is the only principle that a true benevolence, from which morality originates, can unqualifiedly endorse.

By contrast, on the contractualist view outlined above, a social morality is a response to personal and social needs—it arises when persons, faced with the problem of "governing" their social life, voluntarily accept certain ways of acting as a "morality" and voluntarily restrict the pursuit of their individual goals and ideals within its bounds. However, on this view, a social morality cannot be fully moral, or perform its functions with complete success, unless each one (a) acts toward others in ways that are reasonable to them as well as to oneself—first putting oneself in their places and then trying to render "fair and reasonable judgments" ("fairness" will get its content and its meaning, in part, from persons making such judgments), and (b) uses reasons rather than threats or propaganda to get others freely to accept reasonable judgments. In short, the moral person must treat others with a respect *due* them as fellow members of the moral community, and must accord those who do their parts a *right* to respect. In acting in this way, one may think that all would be better off if all acted in this way, but one need not take the utilitarian principle to be a moral article that there are good reasons for everyone to accept. One does not regard oneself as morally required to respect others *because* this would maximally promote the good of everyone, but, rather, because not to do so would be to treat them in ways that are inconsistent with persons living together morally.

Although "benevolent utilitarians" may accept some features of this view, they can be expected, first, to criticize it. They may have noted that the exercise of moral freedom often does not lead people to become benevolent, and on this account may form a low opinion of it. They may argue that the contractualist requirement, that moral ways of acting must be such that each person together with others can reasonably and freely accept them, is deceptive and inadequate. What persons can reasonably subscribe to, a "benevolent utilitarian" may rightly point out, depends on their goals, ideals, and well-being; and until they become perfectly benevolent, what they subscribe to will not be moral. From this point of view, the contractualist requires only some sort of congruity in the desires of different people; beyond that, anything goes.

But no one, not even a perfectly benevolent person, has any "moral authority" to say or lay down for others what is morally right and wrong. Why should people accept the act-utilitarian principle?—especially if a utilitarian has so little regard for moral freedom that he says it is best to keep the principle hidden from people?

Before considering the reasonableness of the act-utilitarian principle itself, notice that the "benevolent utilitarian," to defend his position, may interpret the principle in a special way. He may interpret it not as a moral guide to be regularly followed in practice, but as the first principle of a moral theory, whose job is to organize, and give "the best philosophical account" of the moral articles that *do* serve as practical moral guides. This fits with the occasional utilitarian suggestion that common moral directives are more useful practical guides than the act-utilitarian principle itself. Since this principle will be the theory's keystone, if benevolence really is the source of morality in human life, the theory should be basically sound. But if one takes this line, and advocates an "educated or enlightened benevolence," is there not much to be said for the theory allowing each one to "pursue one's own good in one's own way" so long as one's pursuit is restricted by moral articles that grant every other a like freedom? Can one be of much benefit to others if one is not given the freedom to do well by oneself? As suggested above, a benevolent utilitarian may want to include within his theory the contractualist contribution. He may say that moral freedom is an important human good, that one ought to respect persons because doing so most promotes the general good, and he may go on to adopt other features of contractualism. If so, he could have some problems in reconciling his utilitarianism with what he is trying to include. To take one example, many people probably neither give thought to moral freedom nor value it, and thus it may not appear in some lists of preferences. (Perhaps one should think of the desire for this freedom as "naturally emerging" in conditions that have to be achieved to satisfy other desires that everyone has.) There will be other problems, but before considering them, we turn to a different kind of utilitarianism.

Many utilitarians seem to think that the source of morality is not benevolence but desire, not the affective but the appetitive part of human nature. On their view, each one has desires the satisfaction of which is one's goal and good. Each person seeks his or her own good, the good of all is the goal of the aggregate of persons; morality's job is to promote the attainment of this goal and, in this sense, this goal is the "standard of morality." In brief, the morally right act is the act that one can expect to be "optimific" relative to the utilitarian goal, and moral articles are those "the observance of which" can be expected most efficiently to lead us to it.

The much-noted tension between one's alleged desire for one's own satisfaction and the moral demand that one maximize the general good is particularly strong in this kind of utilitarianism although not peculiar to it. When confronted with this tension, several moves are open to utilitarians. They may possibly argue that persons will have the greatest success in attaining their individual goals by simply following the act-utilitarian principle. Or they may defend the act-utilitarian principle, not as a practical moral guide, but in the manner indicated, as the fundamental principle of a moral theory, which contains a number of subordinate practical principles (as before, they may include a number of contractualist principles in their theory). And, in either case, they may come to regard the contractualism outlined above not as a threat but as something they can use the better to make their case; they may positively embrace it. On their view, the utilitarian principle is eminently reasonable, and people do not have to be threatened or hoodwinked to have good reasons for accepting it. Since each person seeks his or her own good, what goal can persons more reasonably and naturally agree to pursue than the good of all? And what moral standard can persons *together* more reasonably subscribe to than one that prescribes the act, and/or the following of secondary principles, that can be reasonably expected most to promote the attainment of this goal?

How strong is the case for the act-utilitarian principle when it is defended in this way? When all things are considered, can either happiness seekers or a society of benevolent persons, each together with others, freely and reasonably subscribe to it as the first principle of morals? This question primarily involves two issues. The first, which is well known, concerns the relation of the principle to more specific directives. The second concerns the utilitarian goal and the kind of consideration that utilitarianism gives to the individual person.

If the act-utilitarian principle itself is meant to be the basic guide of persons' acts, many will object that there are *not* good reasons for persons to subscribe to it. Why? Because it is so very difficult to determine what act maximizes utility. Each person can be presumed to discover this difficulty, and to realize that others are no better off, and to conclude that it is unwise to try to act together with others on such an unclear directive. But as Mill suggested in his reply to a similar objection, acknowledgment of the first principle is consistent with the acceptance of secondary principles. What we need minimally (and, according to Mill, what we have) is a set of moral rules or directives that give more concrete guidance and, when generally accepted, fix expectations sufficiently to permit persons to count on one another to act in certain ways and to plan ahead with confidence. (If it be thought that nonmoral, for example legal, institutions are adequate to do this job, one need only be reminded of how easily confidence can be shaken when the moral habits of a people do not support their institutions.)

However, this "solution" immediately raises the central difficulty: How do these more specific "moral rules" jibe with act utilitarianism? There would be no problem on this score if, as Mill said in one passage, they are simply "landmarks along the way" or "intermediate generalizations" from experience; but if they were *no more* than this, it is very doubtful that expectations would be sufficiently determinate. If Mill interpreted them in this way, he seems to have taken a significant step backward. However, even if we follow Hume's much more penetrating view of these rules, or current act-utilitarian accounts of Humean conventions, we run into trouble. It may be highly beneficial for a person to join others in subscribing to conventional rules of property, for example, but unlike one of Hume's rowers, who might never reach his destination if he broke with his rowing convention, one can violate property rules on some occasions to one's considerable advantage—or if one is an act utilitarian, to the advantage of everyone. Hume recognized this sort of case as a practical problem and proposed government and legal sanctions as its solution, but he seems never to have noticed how great a problem it is for his utilitarianism. Granted that following conventional rules is highly beneficial on the whole, if the point in having these rules and conventions is to promote the public good, and if one can do this better by violating the rules, then why on earth should they not be violated? Who will pretend that government is fully effective in preventing violations or in punishing violators? Following a contemporary trend, one can extend Hume's device by saying that, on the utilitarian view, "socialization" should be undertaken to supplement legal sanctions both with social sanctions and the internal sanction of conscience. But moves of this sort, although they narrow the difficulty (by altering the application of the act-utilitarian principle), do not remove it. The act utilitarian cannot have it both ways. Because he acknowledges that unless sanctions exist, his utilitarian principle is an unreliable guide to the public good, he can advocate adding sanctions, thus artificially increasing the costs of using the principle when it conflicts with commonly accepted rules and conscience, until its use in such cases no longer conflicts with ordinary moral judgments. Or, on the other hand, notwithstanding the conflict, the act utilitarian can stand firm (at some point) and say that when an opportunity to promote the public good clearly presents itself, one should recognize sanctions for what they are, seize the opportunity, do the morally right thing, and refuse to bow either to law, public opinion, or qualms of conscience. This is what we expect of a moral person. Although one may make use of the first option, in the end the good act utilitarian will choose the second, and thereby condone *some* acts, such as instances of punishment of the innocent, some cases of theft, and so on that ordinary moral judgment finds repugnant.

Whether one chooses the first or the second, ordinary folk will not find it reasonable to subscribe to the act-utilitarian principle as an article of their social morality. They require effective guides to action, thus publicly accepted articles and procedures. It is always possible that a moral hero might do something in the public interest that later they will recognize as right. But they will be distrustful of anyone who violates their moral articles in the name of their good — this is too much like one's "taking the law into one's own hands." On the contractualist view, if one wants morally to violate a moral article, one must appeal, in principle, not to the greatest good but to the "reasoned judgment of the moral community." That is where the moral authority to make articles and to grant excuses ultimately lies. The contractualist will resolve the problem of moral exceptions to accepted rules by noting, for example, that a proposed case of theft or cheating, if approved by all the parties involved, is no longer theft or cheating.

Now let us consider whether or not utilitarianism has a proper regard for the individual person. As pointed out, contractualism requires one (a) to put oneself in another's place and to assume the position of an impartial judge — to determine what can be freely and reasonably accepted; and (b) not to impose even a reasonable solution on another but to try to get the other to accept it because it is reasonable.

With respect to the first part of this requirement, the utilitarian can point out that he requires the good of each and every person to be considered. To make the proper calculation of utilitarian consequences, it is necessary for one to put oneself in each person's place and to estimate the consequences from that person's point of view. Furthermore, one must impartially consider the preferences of each and every person in making the calculation of total consequences. What more could ont want?

The essential point to notice is that if everyone's good could be attained and if everyone could be rationally persuaded to accept whatever measures are necessary to achieve this goal, persons obviously would have no grounds for complaint. The problem arises because this goal is unattainable and choices have to be made, and because the utilitarian chooses the greatest *attainable total* or *average* happiness as the best compromise goal and the standard of right action.

What is wrong with taking one or the other of these as the standard? Trouble arises because happiness exists only as the happiness of individuals; the total or average happiness is an abstraction — the reality behind an "increase in the total or average" is that some are happier and a few, or many, or even a majority may be less happy. Thus on what ground or in whose shoes is one standing when one says that increasing the total is better? In the shoes of a benevolent person? This does not seem right: A benevolent person may be not only distressed but regretful, even though the total is greater, because some are worse off. One might say that his benevolence is too confined, that the benevolent (as well as the self-interested person) should take more joy in the net increase of happiness and in those who have benefited. But we should not ask a greater benevolence of those who suffer than of those who benefit. Are those who benefit to be called benevolent if they manage to increase the total by increasing their own happiness by more than others lose? (If the captain of a lifeboat threw out the feeble to save the rest, would we call him "benevolent"?) The "general benevolence" of the utilitarians is as abstract an idea as the "total happiness." The only *genuine* benevolence that can serve the utilitarian cause is a "benevolence for mankind," and often it does not allow tradeoffs. Why not? Primarily because benevolence, as we usually think of it, is *toward individual persons,* not a maximum of happiness. If to serve the latter, one sacrificed some persons, one may be sorry without feeling sorry for *them,* and certainly one will not have been beneficent toward them—one will not have done well by them. In these significant respects, having a disposition to weigh a person's happiness in the balance and to promote it *if and only if* the total or average will be increased is consistent with a lack of benevolence toward that person; the act utilitarian treatment of persons, even of those who are helped, is that of a social engineer and, unless something is added, a parody of benevolence. But act utilitarians are as good hearted as anyone else; thus, to the disposition to promote the utilitarian goal, let us add the virtue of benevolence toward all. If one wishes everyone well, and at least tries to be beneficient toward all, is not the act-utilitarian principle the only rational guide for allocating scarce resources? This leaves us with the problem we had before: What more exactly does the principle prescribe? Who is interpreting it? In view of the dangers to the individual of social engineers, even a benevolent people cannot reasonably subscribe to the principle until general agreement is reached on secondary principles that state its practical meaning and give safeguards of justice against its misinterpretation and its misuse. Once these secondary principles are accepted, it is very doubtful that the act-utilitarian principle will have much moral use. It will seldom be allowed as a reason for violating principles designed to protect against its misuse, and most benevolent people will find it too deceptive and too obscure to serve as a guide. Even if they want to do "as much good as they can," ordinarily they will not systematically neglect (groups of) persons in order to "maximize happiness." (However, perhaps utilitarians can point out some illuminating applications under secondary principles that all can reasonably accept.)

If benevolence does not direct us to promote the "total happiness," justice often positively forbids it. The arguments are well known, and utilitarian devices to counter them have been unsuccessful. On matters as important to oneself as one's own well-being and that of other particular persons, it is misguided and imprudent to have fundamental guarantees of just treatment rest on fallible judgments of such often obscure items as comparative utilities and diminishing marginal utility. To the ordinary way of thinking, these factors usually are not even *relevant* to questions of justice — a sign that something is fundamentally wrong. On the contractualist view, the most basic right of a person, the right to moral respect, derives from conditions that must be satisfied if persons are to live morally with one another. In an advanced society such as ours, once this "formal" right is acknowledged, to make it more effective, persons can be expected to seek guarantees that each person's voice will be heard and the point of view of each, considered. In other words, persons would then find it reasonable, as many do now, to subscribe to certain material principles of justice, which give rise to more specific personal and political rights, such as freedom of expression, some degree of "social security," and so on. In this derivation, which is simple and direct, a reference to comparative utilities and diminishing marginal utility is out of place. To make a person's basic rights contingent on such factors is to refuse to accept a person's being a willing and able participant in the moral community as sufficient grounds for granting him basic rights. An appeal to such factors to establish the basic moral rights of persons is an affront to them and their moral worth.

Furthermore, although some utilitarians, like Mill, have emphasized the importance of moral freedom, it would seem to be insecure if the case for it rested on the utilitarian principle. It is a fact that a person's exercise of moral freedom often does *not* promote his or anyone else's good; this freedom is a condition of living as a human, not a guarantee of success.

There is another reason why persons will not regard the act utilitarian's consideration of them as reasonable, a reason that is obscured as long as one simply talks about preferences, utilities, and the like and fails to consider their complexity. What is reasonable to persons depends on their desires, ideals and well-being. And often their goals and ideals, some of which they may think others would do well to share, are at odds with those of others. Since utilitarianism is supposed to supply the proper *social* ideal, the utilitarian, in weighing individual preferences, may try to eliminate personal preferences of social ideals from consideration. But this may not be easy; for example, one's social ideal may be a part of one's ideal of oneself. Moreover, one's preferences are so dependent on, and so much involve the institutions of one's society that it appears impossible to use preferences as a utilitarian guide to the good society without presuming the acceptance of certain institutions. And persons with minority preferences are apt to be highly critical of majority institutions; will it be reasonable for them to accept the greatest total or average happiness as the standard of morality? For example, will it be reasonable for a free thinker in a religious country or a cultured person in an illiterate country to have social institutions set by what maximizes total or average utility? How can one give proper consideration to a person while burying the goals and ideals of that person under institutions that "maximize happiness"? Benevolence on one's part does not require a regular subordination of one's goals and ideals to those of others.

The utilitarian may be able to expand his view and counter objections of this sort, but only if he takes the good of each and every person as his goal and as the standard of morality, and refuses to accept "the greatest total or average happiness" as a substitute. If he foregoes *ad hoc* devices, such as appeals to marginal utility, and includes the contributions of other approaches in his general view, he *may* be able to develop it in an interesting and illuminating way. The most important contribution of contractualism for him to consider is the manner in which it jealously guards a freedom of each person to pursue his own goals and ideals in his own way, and at the same time substitutes "a moral and legal equality for that physical [psychological, etc.] inequality which nature placed among men" (Rousseau). On its view, the point in having a social morality is, partly, to have an "established, settled, known law [so to speak] received and allowed by common consent to be the standard of right and wrong" (Locke). If there were some set of moral articles that benefited each and every one to the greatest degree, it undoubtedly would be the most reasonable for all to adopt. But from this it does not follow that the best morality is like the rules of an individual or communal enterprise designed to attain so un-ideal a goal as the "maximization of individual satisfaction," at least as this has usually been interpreted. (Such a goal is too unholy a compromise with the ideal.) A morality is best, if it is, because it enables persons, in pursuing their own distinctive goals, to count on one another to act within bounds that all together, following the procedures outlined earlier, and without making any blunders, at a given time, etc., *accept* as the most reasonable. Since this is an ideal, and what is reasonable is ever changing, respect for individual persons is the first moral duty. If the utilitarian can include in his theory views of this sort, and others, the end result may not look so much like utilitarianism; but as Mill conclusively showed, it is better to be an imaginative than a doctrinaire utilitarian.

Notes

1. The contractualism outlined in Part I is more fully developed in "A Contractarian Ground of Respect for Persons," read at the Oberlin Colloquium, April 1978. A version of this will appear in *The American Philosophical Quarterly*.

7 Fairness to "Justice as Fairness"

Alan E. Fuchs

John Rawls's *A Theory of Justice*[1] expounds a potentially viable and certainly influential contemporary alternative to utilitarianism. Rawls confesses, moreover, that his desire to present just such an alternative ethical system motivates his exposition and defense of a contractarian normative theory (viii), and his attempt to demonstrate the preferability of "justice as fairness" vis-à-vis classical utilitarianism informs many of the central arguments of his book.[2] I therefore propose to look at one central feature of Rawls's work in the light of this overall objective. I shall argue that, as they are articulated and applied in his theory, Rawls's distinctive views on the justification of moral precepts actually vitiate rather than support his principles of justice in their confrontation with those of utilitarianism. Fortunately, however, for those who would march with Rawls in his antiutilitarian campaign, we can suggest a modification of his contractarian theory of justification that not only remedies the suggested deficiencies of the original presentation but that actually enhances the normative cogency of the resulting antiutilitarian system.

One of the most distinctive features of *A Theory of Justice* is the manner in which Rawls attempts to justify his substantive normative principles. The two principles of justice (as well as the other precepts that make up the theory of the right) are, he contends, supported by a synergistic union of several considerations. Most important, they are claimed to present both an accurate explication of our "considered judgments" in reflective equilibrium *and* to constitute the outcome of a deductive derivation from an explanatory model, the theoretical fiction of the "original position." The former, Socratic procedure purportedly reveals the principles that implicitly underlie and account for our actual moral faculties; hence, they are tested by their congruence with our actual moral intuitions, or, more precisely, by their coherence with the judgments that we would most firmly hold under suitable conditions of rational deliberation and theoretical reflection. The latter, Kantian method attempts to present a theoretical representation of the concept of morality and to derive, *a priori*, the substantive principles that are allegedly uniquely entailed by that model. The analogy here to geometry is obvious and intended. True to its Euclidean proto-type, the theory postulates acceptable, intuitively plausible premises that, in turn, rationally entail substantive theorems. The presumed logical validity of the derivation forces every rational disputant who has consented to the theory's weak, noncontroversial, axiomlike presuppositions to accept its strong prescriptive conclusions. A critic may no more deny the normative import of these principles than may the mathematician, having accepted the Euclidean postulates, deny that the sum of the internal angles of a triangle equals one hundred eighty degrees.

It is reasonable to argue, I believe, that if Rawls did actually demonstrate the soundness of his proposed normative principles by means of these two independent modes of argumentation, he might properly claim that their resultant justifactory force was greater than that of the sum of their individual contributions. But Rawls denies them their independence. On the one hand, we are told that the process of reflective equilibrium is to be continually influenced by reflection on the theoretical models that support alternative conceptions of the right, and participants in the process are supposed to revise or abandon their considered judgments when and if they fail to conform to the results of particularly attractive theories. More problematically, Rawls sometimes suggests that we may alter the content of his theoretical model, that is to say, we may revise the description of the contract situation itself, so as to ensure a perfect fit between the conclusions of the contract argument and the principles already established by their congruence with our considered judgments. "We want to define the original position," he tells us, "so that we get the desired solution" (141). This, I believe, is a serious mistake, one which significantly weakens the *normative* import of Rawls's entire theory. In this paper I shall therefore discuss some of the deleterious consequences of this aspect of his methodology, though not so much to bury Rawls as to praise him. For I want to contend that the error I attribute to his justifactory procedures obscures certain significant philosophical insights and blunts other potentially powerful moral arguments that his contractarian theory, freed from this needless burden, would otherwise suggest and support. I shall therefore propose that we declare the independence of the Kantian argument from its reliance on considerations of reflective equilibrium. The resulting purified theory will, as a consequence, more clearly and legitimately accomplish Rawls's main philosophical goal, the rational justification of particular normative moral principles. In particular I shall argue that the proposed theory would more persuasively support Rawls's contention that the principles of "justice as fairness," rather than those of utilitarianism, constitute a sound normative ethical theory or conception of the right. Moreover, the argument for the proposed modification of the contractarian argument reveals that the revised theory possibly offers important insights into the concept of morality itself, an issue I unfortunately cannot explore in the present paper. Rawls's theory, I therefore claim, offers formidable contributions to two of the most significant issues facing contemporary moral philosophy, the rational adjudication of disputes between alternative conceptions of justice and the proper analysis of the concept of morality. But our appreciation of these insights has been vitiated by Rawls's own methodology. The proposed revisions are needed, I contend, to do justice to *A Theory of Justice,* to show fairness to "justice as fairness."

My first concern is with Rawls's suggestion of a "moral geometry" (121), for in this exciting proposal lies the possibility of a rational procedure for the resolution of conflicts among competing normative theories, especially the one between "justice as fairness" and utilitarianism. The argument is at once simple and attractive. We propose a theoretical model for the concept of morality, a model that is sufficiently weak and neutral with regard to competing moral conceptions such that all parties are willing to accept it as a common point of agreement. The argument then ideally proceeds deductively according to commonly accepted principles of inference, such that any conclusions of the theory become rationally binding on all who have accepted the premises. (In practice, alas, we have few noncontroversial rules of practical reasoning, and conscientious practitioners of the method may therefore fail to agree finally on the principles that are in fact entailed by their mutually acceptable premises when and if they hold alternative theories of rational choice. But even when this occurs we are left with a case of *rational* ethical discourse. The dispute between, say, utilitarians and contractarians would no longer consist solely in comparing unsupportable intuitions, appealing to local mores, or trading charges of moral blindness, but rather in presenting and defending competing claims for alternative outcomes to a specifically defined rational choice problem.)

Such a proposed moral methodology, if successful, would of course deliver a fatal blow to ethical relativism, particularly the methodological version that explicitly denies the possibility of any rational procedure for resolving disputes among alternative normative views. It is therefore not surprising (though nevertheless regrettable) that this dimension of Rawls's thought has been by and large slighted by his sympathetic and hostile commentators alike as they fix on the inherently relativistic implications of the method of congruence.[3] More regrettable still is that Rawls himself aids and abets this interpretation of his work, both in the book and in his subsequent articles, thereby inviting the charge (that didn't need any invitation before it was offered) that his work is nothing but the philosophical apologia for the contemporary liberal welfare state, a useful study in normative self-examination ("value-clarification" as it is faddishly called in some circles), but devoid of any normative force as compared with alternative value systems. Although such an enterprise would not completely lack value (it might serve, for example, to make Rawls's values more attractive to someone who is attempting to make a fully informed choice in the fullness of his wisdom),[4] the possibility of providing a nonrelativistic framework for rational ethical argumentation should not be forsaken until its possibilities have been fully explored. Let us therefore take a preliminary look at the Rawlsian contract theory freed from the requirements of reflective equilibrium and see to what extent it can serve as a moral geometry in the above-described sense.

A perceptive relativist will immediately note an apparent fallacy in our attempt to establish the objectivity and normative inescapability of Rawls's particular conceptions of justice and social morality. "You draw an analogy between moral theory and deductive geometry," the relativist protests, "but any sophisticated high-school sophomore knows that Euclidean geometry and its kindred mathematical disciplines are nothing more than *formal* systems. From their assumed axioms they can indeed demonstrate numerous conclusions. But the resulting theorems do not necessarily describe the real world; their truth values remain relative to the self-contained, internally consistent sets of signs and operational rules that constitute the formal systems. The theorems are therefore 'truths' only for those naive enough to take the apparent self-evidence of the postulates as warrants for their descriptive truth." "We," he continues, "recognize many possible geometries. They are as numerous as the consistent sets of postulates that imaginative geometers can formulate; and no one of them can claim to actually model the real physical world without begging what remains a disputed scientific question." (He is a *very* sophisticated sophomore!) "Therefore," he concludes, "even if Rawls's principles of justice did methodologically resemble the theorems of Euclid in that they logically followed from some axiomlike assumptions, they would nevertheless remain fundamentally subjectivistic, relative now to the idea-system of Rawls and his fellow-travelers, but devoid of any reasoned claim to objective truth and therefore normatively nugatory against the utilitarians, or any proponents of alternative conceptions of justice, who simply do not accept the so-called 'axioms' of this inherently liberal contract theory."

Now, it is indeed true that the conclusions of a valid deductive argument have prescriptive force only for those who have either voluntarily granted the premises of the argument or who are rationally obligated to accept them because they are either logically or empirically demonstrable. Let us therefore see whether any of these three conditions holds for possible critics of Rawls's normative principles. That is, can we demonstrate to them that the basic grounds of the contractarian theory are (1) self-evident, (2) empirically true, or (3) that other factors should lead to their ready acceptance.

Examining each possibility in turn, we can dismiss the first alternative with the observation that Rawls's theory never claims analytical or logical certitude for its premises. Indeed Rawls explicitly repudiates the Cartesian methodoligcal model because a theory using it would have to presuppose some self-evident starting point, a moral equivalent of the Cartesian *cogito*. Similarly, Rawls denounces all reliance on definition or the analytical determination of the meaning of words, procedures that some other contemporary philosophers have extensively employed to provide apodictic foundations for their moral theories.

What of the next possibility? If the bases of the contractarian theory lack *a priority*, are they possibly true *a posteriori*? Are there, perhaps, indisputable *facts* that all must recognize and thereby acknowledge as the appropriate grounds for a theory of justice? We cannot as easily answer this part of the question. To do so, something must at last be said concerning the content of the theory I have been defending in absentia as the bearer of objective moral truth. In particular, we must take note of several features of the so-called "original position," the state-of-nature-like situation that functions as the premises for Rawls's demonstrative argument. Rawls contends that the principles of the right are the basic social rules that free, rational, and basically equal persons would unanimously choose in a situation that was fundamentally fair. But this situation, the "original position," clearly does not purport to describe empirically the context in which principles of justice actually function, nor does it attempt to literally characterize the manner in which societies adopt (if they ever do adopt) such principles. Similarly, when Rawls describes the parties in the original position as basically equal, free, rational, mutually disinterested, and knowledgeable about general truths (though quite fantastically ignorant of any facts that would enable them to identify who they are or to determine their particular places in society), he is certainly not describing the character or the epistemological status of actual moral agents in the real world. It is surely obvious that no such beings under such conditions ever did, now do, or ever will exist, and that no philosopher, especially one as wise and as learned as John Rawls, would ever have us believe that they could. But since critics have faulted Rawls's characterization of the original position as somehow empirically unrealistic (suggesting, for example, that it either exaggerates or deprecates the actual moral capabilities of man), we must clearly restate the obvious and stress that the original position is designed solely as a theoretical construct. It is a position from which specially characterized agents are imagined to make a hypothetical contract. We are asked to speculate as to the principles people would have agreed to if, contrary to obvious fact, they really had to face such a choice in such a situation. Therefore, since the actual nature of reality does not directly determine the specification of the theoretical basis of justice as fairness, we clearly cannot use the demonstrable truth of any such purported "facts" to coerce the unwilling critic to accept the premises of the contract theory, and therefore its deductive argument cannot yet even begin. But before turning to the third possible mode of agreement on premises, we should note one sense in which empirical knowledge *is* pertinent to Rawls's argument, especially since this factor tends to inject some degree of relativism into the resulting principles. The parties to the hypothetical social contract are imagined to possess all relevant general knowledge. Like ideal products of a good liberal arts and sciences curriculum, they choose the principles of justice with full awareness of the general laws of economics, history, political science, psychology, and sociology. This verifiable body of knowledge—Rawls stresses that any data utilized must be established by commonly and widely acknowledged methods of scientific proof—will naturally limit the possibilities of rational agreement and disagreement. Principles may be rejected, for example, when and if they clash with known social theories. Thus, for example, the parties would not choose a set of rules if economic and psychological theory predicted the destabilization of any society that attempted to follow them. Our current state of general factual knowledge will determine to some degree the conceptions of justice and the right that are rationally defensible, thus relativizing them somewhat to the known state of the world. (The principles of justice are not inscribed in stone in some Platonic heaven, but are inevitably dependent on which one of the many logically possible worlds God actually created.)

But the acknowledgment that the principles of justice and morality are to some degree dependent on the truth of certain general facts about the world does not constitute any major concession to relativism. If the nature of man or the condition of the world in which he lives were to change fundamentally, we might indeed have to revise our normative theories. But the body of general knowledge then available to the contractees would still (ideally) uniquely determine a choice of a set of new moral principles and, pace the relativists, there would remain a rational method for the justification of this new normative theory. Moreover, the general facts that are relevant to the choice of moral principles are sufficiently characteristic of the human condition as we have known or could imagine it that it is difficult to conceive of a world in which they did not basically hold. (I have in mind general features of the human condition such as the limited altruism of people and the limited affluence of the world, features that Hume emphasized in his account of the necessary background conditions for the operation of principles of justice.[5] And that theorists as diverse as Thomas Aquinas and H. L. A. Hart[6] have both given characterizations of these facts that are essentially equivalent to Hume's account corroborates my claim that these conditions have tended to and shall continue to remain fundamentally constant through changes of time and place.)

We should therefore proceed with our third alternative. Can we bring forth any other positive grounds or, to paraphrase Mill, considerations capable of influencing the intellect that will persuade everyone to acknowledge the postulates of our revised contract theory? Here Rawls tends to use two arguments. The first contends that all reasonable parties actually *are* committed to the assumptions of his theory, or at least that they would come to be so after a modicum of reflection on the entire theoretical edifice that they support. Since this unaided claim is patently vulnerable, — Rawls has not, for example, even persuaded his own departmental colleague, Robert Nozick, let alone his utilitarian and other critics from further afield, — let us turn to his other more plausible and more profitable suggestion, namely, that we liken the use of the original position in contract theory to the role of *theoretical constructs* in some other more familiar types of theories.

Scientists, we may observe, oblige us to accept proposed theoretical entities or models when they can show that these hypothetical constructs successfully perform certain theoretical functions. For example, one is rationally committed to the deep structures and transformational rules of the modern grammarian, the drives and complexes of the clinical psychologist, and the fields, forces, and photons of the nuclear physicist, to the extent that each of these theorists demonstrates that his/her theoretical entities and the theories that incorporate them adequately explain the phenomena of meaningful speech, neurotic behavior, and atomic events, respectively. Using this notion of a theoretical postulate or model, Rawls, as I interpret him, argues that anyone committed to any conception of justice whatsoever is implicitly committed to the assumptions of his contract theory because the deduction of the principles of justice from the original position provides a *theoretical model* for the concept of justice or for the role or function of the principles of justice in a society. Since all of the parties to our usual moral disputes, utilitarians, libertarians, liberals, and Marxists like, advocate some one *conception* of justice or another and since they coherently debate with one another about which is the correct conception, we can claim that they each use and understand a common *concept*, "justice."

The use, here, of the terms-of-art "concept of justice" and "conception of justice" may require clarification. The Socratic inquiry "What is justice?" is ambiguous, for at least two different sorts of questions are possibly being asked. First, one may be inquiring about the nature or essence of the "concept" of justice itself or, eschewing questions of definition or meaning, one may be seeking an analysis of the role or function that justice performs in our lives.[7] Alternatively, one may already understand the concept of justice or clearly see what role it performs in society, but wish to determine which states of affairs actually are just. Is it just, for example, to maximize the greatest average good for the aggregate of persons or, perhaps, to distribute all social values "equally unless an unequal distribution of any, or all, of (such) values is to everyone's advantage?" I shall follow Rawls's usage and designate such particular answers to the second sort of questions as alternative "conceptions" of justice. Rawls marks the distinction between concepts and conceptions as follows:

> In existing societies . . . what is just and unjust is usually in dispute. Men disagree about which principles should define the basic terms of their association. Yet we may still say, despite this disagreement, that they each have a *conception* of justice. That is, they understand the need for, and they are prepared to affirm, a characteristic set of principles for assigning basic rights and duties and for determining what they take to be the proper distribution of the benefits and burdens of social cooperation. Thus it seems natural to think of the *concept* of justice as distinct from the various *conceptions* of justice and as being specified by the *role* which these different sets of principles, these different conceptions, have in common. (p. 5)

Using this concept/conception distinction, our argument proceeds as follows. First we note that all of the parties to each of our imagined disputes (the utilitarian as well as the Rawlsian) actually employ a common *concept* of justice when they propose their different accounts of which states of affairs are "just," in that each suggests principles that are allegedly appropriate for the regulation of our social lives. Next we show that the theoretical model of justice as fairness accurately represents this essential role or function of justice in society, thereby providing a theoretical explication of that common concept of justice. We will thereby have shown that our normative opponents (for example, the utilitarians) actually do accept the basis of the contract theory and the preliminary battle is won! Complete victory requires only the deductive demonstration that the Rawlsian *conception* of justice follows uniquely from the contractarian model.

Although the complete development of this line of argument would surely exceed the limits of the present paper, I shall present at least a cursory sketch of the proposed battle plan (thereby beating a weary metaphor to its timely death!).

Rawls assumes that society is a roughly "self-sufficient association of persons who in their relations to one another recognize certain rules of conduct as binding and who for the most part act in accordance with them" (p. 4). This rule-governed social activity is a mutually advantageous cooperative venture, for like Hobbes and Hume, Rawls believes that life in society contributes to every person's well-being, at least when compared with any hypothetically nonsocial "state-of-nature." Despite these benefits of civil order, though, the interests of individuals inevitably conflict with one another, for people are not indifferent about how the advantages and disadvantages of social living are allocated. Moreover, since the resources of the world are limited, some division of the stock of socially regulated goods is necessary, for the finitude of our collected wealth clearly precludes the complete satisfaction of everyone's desires.

It is within the foregoing characterization of the nature of social life that Rawls imbeds his analysis of the *function* of justice.

> A set of principles is required for choosing among the various social arrangements which determine (the) division of advantages and for underwriting an agreement on the proper distributive shares. These principles are the principles of social justice: they provide a way of assigning rights and duties in the basic institutions of society and they define the *appropriate* distribution of the benefits and burdens of social cooperation. (p. 4)

This is, of course, his analysis of the *concept* of justice. Particular *conceptions* will naturally differ about which distributions are deemed "appropriate." Since it is also this notion of the essential role or function of social justice that Rawls attempts to depict in his characterization of the original position, the various elements of that model must together present an explanatory representation of the social role of justice and each feature of the theoretical construction must manifest some aspect of that function. In our proposed version of Rawls's theory, that modeling role constitutes the sole grounds for inclusion of a possible element in the theory. (No moral epicycles will be permitted, in order to save the phenomena of our considered judgments!) Let us therefore examine several controversial features of the original position, paying special regard to their explanatory force as basic parts of a theoretical model for the concept of justice.

First, the so-called motivational assumption. Rawls states that the contracting parties are mutually disinterested; they take no special interest in the interests of others. He clearly does not claim here, we must note once again, that psychological egoism is a true description of the human condition. Rather, he attributes this self-interested motivation to his hypothetical contractors merely to represent theoretically one aspect of the social role of justice, namely, the principled resolution of the conflicts among interests that inevitably arise owing to the almost universally present conditions of "limited affluence" and "limited altruism." That is, given what Rawls calls "moderate scarcity," individuals' conceptions of their own good regrettably interfere with those of their fellow citizens. Our conflicts, moreover, are not merely those of Hobbesian egoists seeking self-benefit at all costs. Some of our most heated disputes reflect differing aesthetic, moral, ideological, nationalistic, political, and even religious interests. In all such cases, however, a well-ordered society appeals to shared standards of justice and morality to settle these potential or actual disputes in a rational and often mutually acceptable manner. Rawls abstracts these occasions of conflict from the complexities of our ordinary life and represents them in his model by the motivational assumption. That is, by characterizing the parties in the original position as rational egoists, persons seeking to further their own ends, aesthetic, religious, political, intellectual, sexual, or whatever, he captures those situations in which our interests are in conflict and in which justice performs its required function of assigning rights and determining the proper distribution of goods.[8]

No feature of the contractarian model is more controversial than Rawls's characterization of the "veil-of-ignorance," so we must therefore look to its theoretical role. The veil is, first of all, partially justified as "reasonable" and "natural," because given their above-described purposes, all would surely consider it unfair for the ultimate moral principles of a society to arbitrarily reflect the perceived interests of any one individual or group. Rawls's model automatically eliminates any such arbitrary bias from the chosen rules by forbidding to the parties in the original position any knowledge of special interests that could influence them in their choice of principles. But this elimination of bias, however significant, constitutes only part of the explanatory and justificatory function of the analytical device of the veil of ignorance. Critics have correctly noted that a relatively "thin" veil would equally ensure impartiality. Why require, they ask, contractors who know absolutely nothing at all about themselves? Why are they forbidden, for example, even the knowledge of their own values and moral ideals?[9]

Rawls replies that this criticism is based on an incomplete understanding of the theoretical purpose of his intentionally "thick" veil of ignorance. Besides the elimination of arbitrary bias from the resulting normative rules, the choice of principles from behind an almost totally opaque veil is designed to incorporate two further closely related aspects of all moral rules, features that were most effectively emphasized in the moral philosophy of Immanuel Kant. Moral rules, Kant insisted, must be viewed as the autonomous choices of free and equal rational beings and they must be recognized as fundamentally "categorical" (as opposed to "hypothetical") imperatives. Kant formulates these notions within the framework and in the terminology of his complex metaphysical system. Rawls attempts to explicate them in terms of a more readily conceivable, de-metaphysicalized theory. Rawls, first of all, represents the notion of the autonomous or self-legislative nature of moral beings by the straightforward device of having free and equal rational persons unanimously contracting with one another to obey rules of their own choosing. The contractors are imagined as purely rational beings who try to preserve their essential autonomy in a moral world that they are creating by their own choices. Thus, the denial to the parties in the original position of all specific information except the knowledge that they shall all be members of this moral community models this aspect of the nature of all moral principles. This also leads directly to the second dimension of the Kantian moral perspective. Contrary to the doubts of his critics, Rawls feels that his problem is not so much to account for the depth of the parties' ignorance of specifics as to justify the extent of their knowledge of general facts; for the preservation of the categorical quality of the principles accepted by the parties in the original position requires that their choices be free from consideration of any of the *contingent*, that is, nonnecessary *particularities* of the actual (phenomenal) world. Rawls thus interprets Kant's analysis of morality as constituted by categorical imperatives as the requirement that moral principles be regarded as the autonomous choices of rational agents who do not act from any such *contingent* particular inclinations, and whose wills are therefore not determined by any *accidental* natural or social conditions. Since the "thick" veil of ignorance effectively prevents any such particular accidental aims or desires from influencing the wills of the choosing parties, forcing them to choose merely qua rational beings, it thereby incorporates into the design of the theoretical construction this essential categorical quality of moral rules.[10]

The veil of ignorance also serves the further theoretical function of establishing the essential fairness of the choice situation. This allows Rawls to use the notion of "pure procedural justice" in the derivation of his principles of justice and morality. The basic idea of pure procedural justice is that the outcome of a perfectly fair procedure is necessarily just when there is no other appropriate independent standard for the justice of the outcome. The results of certain games of chance are just, for example, no matter who wins what, if the games were truly fair to all players. The outcome of some fair selection procedures or the allocations of suitably constrained market economies might likewise yield just results because their procedures may establish what constitutes just outcomes for those cases. In applying this notion of pure procedural justice to the selection of the principles of justice themselves, Rawls must assert, as he of course does, that the choice situation represented by the model of the original position is essentially fair to all persons, for if it were not, the results of their agreements could not be claimed to constitute the principles of justice. Rawls contends that the major threat to the fairness of this fundamental choice in the contract situation is that the motives and interests of some parties, and therefore their choice of principles, might be unduly influenced by their particular social or natural conditions, all of which are ultimately fortuitous and undeserved. This threat to the fairness of the contract is of course eliminated by the imposition of the veil of ignorance, which further justifies its inclusion in the characterization of the original position. However, we must remember that processes exemplifying pure procedural justice establish the justice of their results only if there are no independent criteria for the justice of their outcomes. The results of even a fair game of chance would not always be just if one player somehow possessed a valid independent claim to the winnings, nor would the result of any voluntarily agreed on transfer constitute a just outcome if any party got other than what he or she somehow deserved. But if that is the case, Rawls's *own* use of pure procedural justice is undermined by his methodological reliance on reflective equilibrium. If his design of the choice procedure is allowed to be influenced by the necessity of matching principles independently established by their coherence with our actual moral judgments, rather than, as I have urged, purely by consideration of the inherent fairness of that situation and by consideration of the basic concept of justice itself, then the powerful justificatory argument of pure procedural justice cannot be utilized. For then the preestablished principles supported by reflective equilibrium would in effect constitute the independent standard of justice, the absence of which pure procedural justice presupposes. Therefore, since this notion of pure procedural justice plays an absolutely essential role in any contract theory (especially one that takes "justice as fairness" as its motto) the independence and primacy of the deductive argument must be maintained, and we see further grounds for our proposed reinterpretation of Rawls's theory.[11]

I have argued in the main part of this paper that a contract theory based on Rawls's "justice as fairness" but one that renounced his methodological reliance on reflective equilibrium would constitute a rational, nonrelativistic procedure for the resolution of value conflicts, especially the fundamental one between Rawls and the utilitarians. Since the proposed argument essentially portrays the contract situation as an acceptable theoretical model for the concept of justice (and of the morally right in general), it presupposes that all who use that concept can be persuaded to accept the theory as a common basis for their rational moral discourse.

The success of the entire enterprise therefore rests on the widest possible acceptance of the theory's premises, and that, in turn, requires their formulation in the weakest possible noncontroversial terms. Rawls at times recognizes this, as when he claims that each of the characteristics of the original position should seem "innocuous or even trivial" and that his theoretical assumptions should be as "weak" as possible. "At the base of the theory," he states, "one tries to assume as little as possible (129)," and throughout his discussion of the original position he contends that his assumptions are "natural," "reasonable," "intuitive," "plausible," and so on. It is therefore distressing that even after rather fully describing the basic original position, Rawls asserts that five additional conditions, the so-called "formal constraints of the concept of right," are to be imposed on all suggested choices in the contract situation. The parties are to choose only those principles that are simultaneously (1) general, (2) universal in application, (3) public, (4) ordering of conflicting claims, and (5) final (130-136). Since several of these conditions are clearly controversial issues in contemporary moral theory, requiring everyone to accept them as formal constraints on their choice of moral principles would demolish the chances of wide general acceptance of the theory's theoretical premises, and it would probably eradicate the prospects for our proposed rational ethical system. Fortunately, however, a Rawls-like contractarian argument need not presuppose the acceptance of these five formal conditions, for they are superfluous as constraints even in Rawls's own argument. That is, they exclude no principles that would otherwise have been chosen without them. We can therefore dispense with them as constraints without in any way affecting the content of the moral precepts derived from and justified by the contract argument, and I therefore recommend their elimination from the contract model as a further revision of Rawls's views. The resulting simplified theory is clearly more elegant in that it demonstrates identical conclusions from weaker assumptions. (All theories become more attractive after a shave with Occam's razor!) But the significance of this refinement of justice as fairness extends beyond considerations of mere formal elegance. For I believe that we can prove that each of the five formal criteria is derivable directly from our pared-down contract model. Since, as we have already shown, that model essentially captures the concept of a social morality itself, we could then claim to have demonstrated that generality, universality, publicity, ordering, and, most important of all, finality, are necessary features of the concept of morality itself, thereby clarifying one of the most fundamental ongoing controversies in ethical theory.[12] Our analysis would likewise illuminate another significant controversy in this area, the purported need for a material content requirement in the concept of morality, for I believe that we could similarly deduce this condition from our theoretical model. Unfortunately, we must leave these projects for another occasion, resting content with our more limited revision of Rawls's contractarianism and our claim that it significantly strengthens Rawls's forces in his antiutilitarian crusade.

Notes

1. John Rawls, *A Theory of Justice* (Cambridge, Mass.: Harvard University Press, 1971). Page numbers in the text are references to this book.

2. See, for example, *A Theory of Justice*, pp. 167-175, 177-183, 320-324, 449-451, 499-504, and 572-573.

3. See, as an example of the former, Ronald Dworkin, "The Original Position," *University of Chicago Law Review* 40 (1973):500-533. R. M. Hare epitomizes the latter group. See, for example, his excoriating review, "Rawls' Theory of Justice," *Philosophical Quarterly* 23 (1973):152 and 248.

4. W. D. Falk and William Frankena, among others, have held such a choice to be the explication of the notion of rationally choosing a morality. See, for example, Frankena, "The Concept of Morality," *Journal of Philosophy* 63 (1966):696.

5. For Hume's account of the circumstances of justice, see *A Treatise of Human Nature*, Bk. III, Pt. II, Sec. ii, and *An Enquiry Concerning the Principles of Morals*, Sec. III, Pt. I.

6. H. L. A. Hart, *The Concept of Law* (Oxford: The Clarendon Press, 1961), pp. 189-195.

7. For an explication of the notion of the "function" of an ethical system see Richard Brandt, *Ethical Theory* (Englewood Cliffs, N.J., Prentice-Hall, Inc., 1959), pp. 257-258.

8. Rawls elaborates this explanation of the motivational assumption in "Fairness to Goodness," *Philosophical Review* 84 (1975):542-543.

9. See Hare, *ibid.*, and Thomas Nagel, "Rawls on Justice," *Philosophical Review* 82 (1973):224-229, for the argument that depriving the parties knowledge of their own conception of the good is unfair to some of them.

10. Rawls has developed this Kantian interpretation of the role of the original position in his most recent papers. See especially "The Kantian Conception of Equality," *Cambridge Review*, (1975):98-99; "The Basic Structure as Subject" *American Philosophical Quarterly* 14 (1977):161; and, most recently, "Kantian Constructivism in Moral Theory," *Journal of Philosophy* 77 (1980):515-572.

11. The congruence argument might still play some minor justificatory role even in our proposed theory, but only if it could be used to present an independent confirmation of the results of the basic contractarian derivation.

12. I argued that the five formal constraints are superfluous and that they can be derived from the pared-down model of the original position in my 1975 paper to the Eastern Division of the American Philosophical Association, "The Role of the Formal Constraints of the Concept of Right in Rawls' Theory."

8 Rawls and Utilitarianism

Jan Narveson

The major polemical concern of John Rawls's by now celebrated *A Theory of Justice* (Cambridge, Mass.: Harvard, 1971) is utilitarianism. On the very first pages of the preface (vii-viii; henceforth all numbers in parentheses in this essay refer to pages or sections of that book), he observes that in modern times the "predominant systematic theory" of justice has been "some form of utilitarianism," whereas his own theory offers an "alternative systematic account of justice that is superior, or so I argue, to the dominant utilitarianism of the tradition." Many pages and whole sections of the book are devoted to working out this comparison and arguing for the superiority of his account. Obviously, these comparisons presuppose that utilitarianism really is an *alternative* to his own account, and certainly most of his critics have accepted this presupposition. Indeed, with a few important exceptions,[1] most critics appear to have accepted his claim that the Two Principles with their supporting framework offer the superior account, whatever may be their detailed criticisms of his own theory. It is more or less a commonplace among many that, whatever else he may or may not have done, Rawls has at any rate succeeded in laying to rest for good and all the ghost of utilitarianism.

In the present paper, it will be my concern to dispute this presupposition of incompatibility. *A fortiori*, I dispute the alleged superiority of the Two Principles. I will argue, in the first section, that it is by no means clear and certainly not demonstrated by Rawls that utilitarianism really is an alternative to the Two Principles. In Part Two, I will show that it is quite possible to argue for the Two Principles from the utilitarian position, construed as Rawls construes it and not in some exotic way. Finally, in Part Three, I will argue that on what seems to be the most plausible reading of Rawls's own arguments for his Two Principles, they appear to be arguments of that very same type themselves;

that is, they are arguments that, if true, would show that the net utility of society would be maximized by adoption of the Two Principles—though of course Rawls does not recognize this.

If these claims are satisfactorily made out, of course a question will arise as to just what further implications they have, either for Rawls's program or for social philosophy in general. I will, however, have little to say about these. That little will be found in some concluding remarks.

1. RAWLS'S CHARACTERIZATIONS OF THE CONTRASTS

Utilitarianism is a theory that reaches, in principle, much wider than the area of justice as conceived by Rawls, and therefore than the Two Principles, which are meant to apply only to that area. According to Rawls, justice is but one, if the major, virtue of institutions. A conception of social justice "is to be regarded as providing in the first instance a standard whereby the distributive aspects of the basic structure of society are to be assessed" (p. 9). Just how one distinguishes the "basic structure" from the rest of society, or whether the proposed distinction between justice and everything else is tenable or accurate, are matters we need not go into here. What is important for our purposes is that this is intended to be a narrowing of the subject matter of justice to a particular sphere, and it has the consequence that some of the traditional questions about utilitarianism are irrelevant to the present subject. For example, it is meant to rule out appeals to very small-scale cases, those involving, say, two persons (Cf. pp. 87-88, for example): We are to confine ourselves to considering general (and presumably large) classes of people, and representative persons from those classes, rather than individuals as such. Further, it is only their long-term, life prospects that are relevant. Consequently, implications of utilitarianism for such small-scale cases are beside the point here. If utilitarianism is to be an alternative to the Two Principles, it must be shown that its implications *for this sphere* are contrary to the Two Principles. It is worth mentioning, for example, that such intramural disputes among utilitarians as the question of "act" versus "rule" utilitarianism are beside the point for the subject Rawls takes justice to be concerned with. (Rawls has also said that his theory represents an alternative to "utilitarian thought generally and so to all of these different versions of it" (p. 22).)[2]

There are other aspects of the framework of Rawls's theory, which, it is important to realize, also are not in dispute (or not necessarily so) between Rawls and utilitarians. Most important, the basic idea of justice as fairness, that the principles of justice are those that would be chosen by rational and self-interested men from behind a "veil of ignorance" is one that utilitarians could accept. Rawls himself observes that given this conception, it is "an open question whether the principle of utility would be acknowledged" (p. 14), though he thinks it would not in fact be. Similarly for Rawls's list of "formal constraints of the concept of right" (pp. 130-136): obviously, utilitarians can accept that moral principles must be general, must be universal in application, must impose an ordering condition on conflicting claims, and must provide final decisions. (As to the remaining one, about publicity, it is not perfectly clear whether either theory would always meet it, in all circumstances. This still may leave no difference between them, therefore; but the point cannot be discussed here.)[3]

There is one alleged contrast, however, on which we cannot be so brief, especially since it sheds important light on the present issue. This is the claim that utilitarianism is, whereas justice as fairness is not, a "teleological" theory (p. 30). Since it may be thought that this is an obvious and elementary point of contrast, we had best set matters straight right here.

To start with, it is not clear whether Rawls thinks that this represents a contrast between the whole idea of justice as what would be agreed to in the initial position, on the one hand, and utilitarianism on the other, or whether it is only supposed to contrast the Two Principles and the Principle of Utility. It cannot coherently be thought to be either one, however. It cannot be the former, since, as Rawls agrees, the principle of utility might itself be chosen from the initial position. Might it, then, be the second? Let us consider.

A teleological theory, on Rawls's understanding of that expression, is one in which (a) the good is defined independently from the right, and (b) the right is that which maximizes the good (p. 24). Is utilitarianism such a theory, and the two principles not? It is easy to see why this might be thought to be so, since the principle of utility would seem to meet the two conditions, whereas the Two Principles do not come right out and say anything about maximizing the, or any, good. But it is sheer confusion to invoke the contrast at this point. In the first place, this is because we don't as yet know whether the Two Principles do or do not promote, or even maximize, "the good": not saying that they do it doesn't show that they don't, nor that that isn't their *raison d'être*. In the second place, and more important, there is the question of exactly what "independently from the right" means here. Does it mean "antecedently to any moral considerations whatever"? In that case, utilitarianism is quite clearly *not* a "teleological" theory. The moral good, in utilitarian theory, is the general good. But there is no reason to expect, and much reason not to expect, that individuals will acknowledge such a good antecedently to moral considerations of some kind. Utilitarians have generally assumed that men are by nature egoists, acknowledging initially only their *own* good, just like Rawls's "self-interested" men. And if we ask such "natural" men why they might acknowledge the principle of utility, it will not be replied that they want to acknowledge the general good in order to maximize their own good, the only "good" that is "antecedently" recognized. If there is a reason for doing this, it cannot, evidently, be a purposive, teleological, reason at all. It will have to be some sort of intuition, or some feeling, or whatever, to the effect that it is *right* to treat others' good equally with one's own. And if we shift to Rawls's general conception, we get the same answer. Why should we do what we would agree behind a veil of ignorance that we ought to do? Not, I take it, because doing so will maximize our own interests. It may not. Some similar move to what is needed in order to acknowledge the claims of general utility will be needed, and it will not be teleological. In short, the teleological-deontological contrast in this context is a red herring. It does *not* constitute a deep contrast between the Principle of Utility and the Two Principles.

Another quite different kind of purported difference has to do with the matter of interpersonal comparisons of utility. What is claimed by Rawls is that whereas the utilitarian needs to make such comparisons, the user of the Two Principles does not. He can confine himself, it is thought, to making only ordinal comparisons of amounts of "primary goods," the things that it is supposed "a rational man wants whatever he wants" (p. 92). Further, Rawls says that in justice as fairness, one does not inquire into the actual use made by individuals of their primary goods, nor into the real value for themselves or others of such use. "Once the whole arrangement is set up and going, no questions are asked about the totals of satisfaction or perfection" (p. 94).

It is a mistake to take these claims at their face value. From the fact that cardinal comparisons of utility are not needed to apply the Two Principles, it does not follow that they are not aimed at maximizing utility. As we shall see later, Rawls seems to make precisely such cardinal comparisons when he tries to justify use of the Two Principles. And from the statement that the Two Principles do not call for making detailed inquiry into the use of primary goods once "the system gets going," nothing pertinent to our subject follows at all. For one thing, utilitarians can argue that it works out best on the whole to have a system in which such inquiries are not made or even permitted; and for another, Rawls has defined the subject matter of justice in such a way that such inquiries simply do not come into the subject. This leaves open, in principle, the question whether such detailed inquiries should not be made for *some* purposes or whether, when made, they may not be more important than considerations of "justice" as defined by Rawls. Nothing in Rawls's system prevents a father, for instance, from maximizing the welfare of his children rather than maximizing the worst-off children, nor from using maximax or arbitrary preferences or what-have-you. The higher-level inquiry of just how the theory of what Rawls calls "justice" fits in with all the rest of moral theory is not gone into in Rawls. It is an open question what might be said about the rest of the field, and in particular whether what would be said about it is the same as what a dedicated utilitarian should say.

Having devoted considerable space to the exclusion of what is not relevant to the comparison between utilitarianism and the Two Principles, we should now consider the point that Rawls believes to be the essential one. In brief, this is that utilitarianism in any form permits distributive injustices because it permits the system to depress the lot of some in order to improve that of others (p. 178). A rational man, he says, "would not agree to a principle which may require lesser prospects for some simply for the sake of a greater sum of advantages enjoyed by others" (p. 14). Rawls goes on to develop a sort of corollary of this idea, namely that utilitarianism "does not take seriously the differences among persons" (p. 27), because its theoretical basis is in effect the conflation of all parties into one agent, so that one adopts "for society as a whole the principle of rational choice for one man" (pp. 26-27). Further, when addressing himself to the choice at the initial position, Rawls claims that utilitarianism would require "gambling" in ways that the Two Principles do not (Sect. #28, for example).

We will consider the claim about gambling below. But it is important here to address ourselves to the central claim, that a rational man would not be willing to accept an enduring loss simply that others may gain. What is important about this central claim is not merely that it is quite obviously false to fact, though it surely is—people do, obviously, make such sacrifices for such reasons, frequently and not obviously irrationally. Far more important is that in the context of his own theory, this claim of Rawls's must be either exaggerated, or misstated, or else bafflingly preposterous. In the first place, it is surely obvious that in any even modestly plausible theory of justice, people will be required to accept the possibility of an enduring loss that must, and especially so on Rawls's theory, be (in effect) in order to improve the lot of others. Thus on Rawls's "difference principle," it is perfectly clear that those in the upper classes are required to accept losses, positions inferior to what they might have had in the system of "natural liberty" for instance (p. 72, for example), and they must endure these substantial, life-long losses for the sake of others, viz., the bottom classes.[4] On his first principle of equal liberty, everyone is required to forgo possible advantages, some of which might be enduring, *in order to enable others* to enjoy equal freedom. These obvious considerations must surely raise a question about the meaning of this fundamental claim about utilitarianism.

It is no good to reply, for instance, that those choosing principles behind the veil of ignorance are doing so out of self-interest, so that in effect we are losing nothing because we impose all rules on ourselves. As others have noted,[5] it is pretty misleading to talk about "self-interest" when you don't know who you are, which interests are those of *your* self as opposed to others'. To claim that because we would have chosen a principle to be governed by if we had no idea who we were, we have therefore in fact chosen it ourselves, is not far from sophistical. To go on to infer that we therefore are not actually required to endure any losses for others is to cross the line into sophistry.

I suspect that such initial plausibility as Rawls's claims on this head have evidently had for many readers is due to Rawls's tendency to talk of "enduring losses" and losses of "basic liberties," etc., versus "advantages" and "satisfactions" for others. Thus it is subtly suggested that the difference between the Two Principles and utilitarianism is that utilitarianism permits some to have to endure serious and weighty sacrifices merely to promote the frivolities and whims of others, thus implicitly identifying utilitarianism with the *ancien régime*, and the Two Principles with some sober egalitarian society such as that of contemporary Sweden. The inappropriateness of such comparisons will, I hope, be sufficiently demonstrated below. Meanwhile, it is easy enough to see that Rawls *could* have an important point here. It is, of course, of the essence of utilitarianism that it calls for maximization of utility whether this results in equality or inequality, whether it favors the upper or the lower classes (or none), whether it is at the expense of "liberty," and so on. At this point, I am merely reminding the reader that the particular fundamental point of contrast Rawls says there is simply cannot be there. And, of course, that utilitarianism calls for the maximization of utility, not of the Gross National Product, for instance (or of American military security, or of deterrence without regard to liberty in criminal law, and so on).

One small final point may also be mentioned here. Rawls speaks, perhaps in an unguarded moment, of the Two Principles "guaranteeing a satisfactory minimum" (p. 156). Were they genuinely to do this, of course, there would be a contrast between them and utilitarianism; but in fact they cannot do any such thing.[6] That the bottom classes are to get as much as they can, subject to the constraints of equal liberty, proves nothing at all about whether the amount they thus get is, in all circumstances, "satisfactory." That will depend on variables, such as the weather, which no theory of justice can do anything about. Whether utilitarianism might sanction a Rawlsian shoring up of the bottom classes, on the other hand, remains to be seen. There is no reason in principle why it could not do so.

Indeed, the whole tendency to argue about what utilitarianism might "in principle" permit is largely misleading and nearly useless, as we shall also see. As Rawls, to his credit, insists, we cannot disentangle concrete social principles from factual considerations. In the end, what we shall see is that everything depends on what further factual assumptions one makes. So far I have been concerned only to show that none of the usual things said by way of contrasting utilitarianism and the Two Principles actually succeed in establishing the contrast. We shall turn now to sharpening up the comparison by showing how a utilitarian might argue for Rawls's Two Principles.

2. UTILITARIAN DEFENSE OF RAWLS'S TWO PRINCIPLES

To defend the Two Principles on utilitarian grounds is to argue that the basic, concretely described institutions of society will be so arranged as to maximize utility if they are rigged as specified by the Two Principles. (This is the characterization given also by Rawls (p. 22).) To see what is required here, let us recall the content of the Two Principles. They are a specification of what Rawls calls the "General Conception," which says:

> All social primary goods—liberty and opportunity, income and wealth, and the bases of self-respect—are to be distributed equally unless an unequal distribution of any or all of these goods is to the advantage of the least favored. (p. 303)

The specific conception is incorporated in the familiar Two Principles. The first of these says that everyone has a right to the highest possible level of equal basic liberty. The second says that other primary goods are to be distributed equally unless an unequal distribution would maximize the primary-goods allocation of the least favored class, and provided that the advantageous unequal positions are open to all under conditions of fair equal opportunity. (Summarized from pp. 302-3.)

The first problem to deal with arises from the supposed "lexical ordering" of the principles. According to this idea, we are to realize the first principle before we even take up the second one[7] (Sect. #39, for example). Similarly, we are to observe the equal opportunity clause of the second before we turn to its main body (p. 89). Now, it may be thought that the lexical ordering presents an insuperable obstacle to the utilitarian here, for on utilitarian principles, to claim that one sort of good should be strictly lexically ordered relative to another, it would have to be the case that the first sort of good had infinite utility compared with the second, for otherwise there would surely be *some* quantity of the first which one would rationally trade for some quantity of the second. And even if we think that liberty is to be valued for its utility rather than for some other reason, it is surely implausible to think that no amount of improvement in the economic situation could ever have more utility than would be lost by any decrease of social liberty. This is true, and the appearance, in Rawls's principles, of denying it has occasioned understandable doubts about the rationality of the lexical ordering. However, it turns out that the lexical ordering simply isn't what it at first sight appears. The lexical ordering is only an ideal, to be realized in "conditions favorable to liberty" (pp. 244-45; 542). At some point, not specified by Rawls, the claim is that it will no longer be just to pursue economic justice at any cost at all in equal liberty. And when one recalls that we are concerned only with appraising the broad outlines of institutions rather than their detailed workings in individual cases, it becomes reasonable to suppose that there might be two such broad-scale goods so related to each other in "favorable circumstances"; the specifics on the point will be found below.

As we have seen, the Two Principles are, so to speak, on a different level from the Principle of Utility. The latter is stated in terms of utility, the former in terms of primary goods. To compare them with respect to their implications, we therefore need to have some information, some assumptions and/or empirically based beliefs, about how they are related. Although Rawls seems to be aware of this difference, it is nevertheless possible to get the impression that he thinks that utilitarianism would call for maximization *of primary goods*—maximizing, so to say, the G.N.P. of primary goods. But nothing in the theory inherently requires this interpretation. What it all depends on is whether utility is linearly related to primary goods or not. Until we have assumptions about this matter, we can make *no* inferences about what utilitarianism does or doesn't say concerning the Two Principles.

Now, as it happens, it has been commonplace among theorists of utilitarian leanings to assume that this relationship is not linear, but rather that it characteristically obeys a law of declining marginal utility: As amounts of money, for instance, increase, the utility of a given increment decreases. Now, Rawls is not unaware of these possibilities (Sect. #30 and #49, for example), but he does seem curiously insensitive to them. He even argues that the difficulties in using notions of utility precisely versus the relative manageability of the Two Principles counts in the latter's favor (p. 321, for example). Nevertheless, he claims that even if they could be solved, utilitarianism would still give demonstrably the wrong kind of results; this despite the following striking passage:

> Utilitarians seek to account for the claims of liberty and equality by making certain standard assumptions, as I shall refer to them. Thus they suppose that persons have similar utility functions which satisfy the condition of diminishing marginal utility. It follows from these stipulations that, given a fixed amount of income say, the distribution should be equal, once we leave aside effects on future production. For so long as some have more than others, total utility can be increased by transfers to those who have less. The assignment of rights and liberties can be regarded in much the same way. There is nothing wrong with this procedure provided the assumptions are sound. (p. 159)

This is a strange passage, in view of the many other things Rawls has said which suggest that utilitarianism, in *any* form, gives the *wrong results*. For now it seems that what is wrong may be only the "standard assumptions." And yet, as we shall see below, Rawls seems to share the assumptions in question. Before getting to that, however, let us amplify somewhat the case described.

Starting with the general conception behind the Two Principles, we get this by making two assumptions. First, we assume that marginal utility of increments of all primary goods taken together decreases as the quantity already enjoyed increases. Second, we assume that the shape of the curve illustrating this tendency is essentially the same for all persons. Given these two assumptions, it will be clear that we get a prima facie norm or "benchmark" of equalities as Rawls refers to it (pp. 150-51), any departures from which would need to be justified. If such departures are justified, it would have to be because they improved the lot of some without significantly worsening the lot of others. If any choice was possible about how to distribute gains made by introducing inequalities, one would obviously turn first to the worst off, since a unit increment in their primary goods allotment would yield the greatest gain in utility, other things being equal. We do not in this way get a definite limit on the size of the gap that separates such social extremes as exist; but we get a case for redistribution that gets stronger as the gap gets larger. This seems to be the gist of Rawls's General Conception, which similarly puts no positive limit on permissable inequality, but does make the case for distributing from the bottom up the prima facie indicated policy, and makes gaps less easy to justify as they get larger (since the larger they are, the less plausible it is that the bottom class could not be better off).

Turning to the special conception, what must we assume about liberty to give some sort of priority to high levels of equal liberty as distinct from other goods? Obviously, that liberty is more valuable, has more utility, for any typical individual. Or more precisely, and more plausibly, that beyond some very minimal state of economic well-being this is so, since of course one must eat and enjoy some other minimal material goods to live at all. Just where the turnover point is, the point in increasing economic well being beyond which no sacrifice of civil liberties would be worthwhile in order to improve one's economic conditions, is of course hard to say. But let us conjecture that one such does exist; or, more reasonably, that there is a zone at the upper limit of which losses in liberty would have to be infinitesimally small to justify even quite substantial economic gains. Given this sort of assumption, we get a case for the two principles as stated. In favorable economic circumstances, incursions on civil liberties for any citizens would not be justified by the prospect of economic gain. As an idealization, in one sense, and as a practical rule, in another, such trade-offs simply would not be permitted.

It is perhaps scarcely necessary to mention the clause in the Second Principle that calls for equal opportunity. After all, this clause is not construed in such a way that we must equalize the probability of getting the job for all applicants regardless of ability. It says rather that no one is to be excluded because of his or her sex, color, and so on—factors irrelevant to the merit of the applicant in nearly all cases; and where they are relevant, it does not seem Rawls's intention that they must still be ignored. If so, then the obvious justification of the clause is that the justification of inequality is a contribution to the well-being of the worst-off, and not the sex, race, etc., of persons in unequal positions. Thus a tendency to allow such factors to subvert the relevant one could not be justified on utilitarian grounds. Considered as a broad rule for governing large-scale classes of cases, the equality of opportunity proviso is obviously called for.

3. RAWLS'S ARGUMENTS FOR THE TWO PRINCIPLES

Rawls at many places says that the above sort of derivation is unsatisfactorily indirect and rests on shaky assumptions. The crucial question is this: Is it that the assumptions are *shaky*, or that they are *false*? Does he mean that it would be better to dispense with any assumptions on these subjects? So much is suggested in the following passage:

> From the standpoint of the original position it may be unreasonable to rely upon these hypotheses and therefore far more sensible to embody

the ideal more expressly in the principles chosen. Thus it seems that the parties would prefer to secure their liberties straightway rather than have them depend upon what may be uncertain and speculative actuarial calculations. (pp. 160-61)

As usual when reading these statements, one must discount a bit for overstatement. For example, the Two Principles do *not* secure peoples' "liberties": They secure a mix of liberty and economic security, the latter to some extent at the expense of the former. Bearing such things in mind, what then is the meaning of "straightway" in the statement above? It really ought to mean something like, "without making any assumptions of the kind that a utilitarian derivation would rely on," viz., assumptions about the probable gains and losses of alternative possible principles. Does Rawls's argument for the choice of the Two Principles make no such assumptions? Let us consider.

The kingpin in Rawls's derivation of the Two Principles is his insistence that in the original position, a rational chooser would use the "maximin" strategy, that is, would pick the alternative with the best worst outcome. In the present case, this would mean picking the social principles that, if properly followed, would give the largest allotment of primary goods to those in the worst positions in society as compared with other possible societies, those determined by properly applying other possible principles. Now, Rawls himself notes that maximin is not the strategy that is generally preferred in choice situations. A strategy that would lead to the choice of the utilitarian principle would, on the usual principles of rational choice, be the generally indicated one. Considerable discussion of this preference for maximin in the initial position has animated the critical literature. What does not seem to have been noticed is that we may not have to take our choice. A maximizer will, in some circumstances, use maximin. Why does everyone assume that we must use either the maximizing strategy *or* maximin? Even to decide whether such a choice has been made we will need to look at the character of the justification for using maximin provided by Rawls.

As is well known, Rawls offers three reasons for using maximin in the special circumstances of the original position. They are as follows:

(1) On a straight maximizing strategy, we would take the probability of ending up in a given position, multiply it times the utility of being in that position, and then choose the principle which would maximize expectations. But we can have no reliable information about probabilities in the initial position. Such knowledge is "impossible, or at best extremely insecure" (p. 154).

(2) "The person choosing has a conception of the good such that he cares very little, if anything, for what he might gain above the minimum stipend that he can, in fact, be sure of by following the maximin rule" (p. 154).

(3) "The rejected alternatives have outcomes that one can hardly accept" (p. 154).

Elsewhere he goes so far as to say the following:

> Any further advantages that might be won by the principle of utility, or whatever, are highly problematical, whereas the hardships if things turn out badly are intolerable. . . . In view of the serious nature of the possible consequences, the question of the burden of commitment is especially acute. . . . In this respect, the two principles have a definite advantage. Not only do the parties protect their basic rights but they insure themselves against the worst eventualities. They run no chance of having to acquiesce in a loss of freedom over the course of their life for the sake of a greater good enjoyed by others, an undertaking that in actual circumstances they might not be able to keep. Indeed, we might wonder whether such an agreement can be made in good faith at all. Compacts of this sort exceed the capacity of human nature (pp. 175-76).

We have already seen reason to reject some of the implicit claims made in these last statements. However, what is of interest at present is the character of these arguments for using maximin, rather than their plausibility. Let us consider them in order.

There has been considerable controversy about the first claim, understandably, since it is an unclear one.[8] Rawls says that the argument for choosing the principle of utility in the initial position requires the assumption of the "principle of indifference," according to which if one knows no reason for not giving different probabilities to distinct possibilities, then one should assume that those probabilities are equal (p. 168). However, "there seems to be no objective grounds in the initial situation for assuming that one has an equal chance of turning out to be anybody" (p. 168), and hence the choice is, in the decision-theoretic sense, a "choice under uncertainty," that is, one where one simply has no idea what the probabilities of the alternatives are. Now, if this really were the case, it still wouldn't follow that one ought to opt for maximin (p. 153). But besides this, it seems strange for Rawls to talk as if it were somehow a matter for conjecture or investigation whether those choosing behind the veil of ignorance are or are not to assume that their chances of being any particular actual person are equal or not.[9] For after all, the whole thing is Rawls's idea: Either he specifies that this is the condition, or that it isn't and something else is. Why the business about there being "no objective grounds"?

Perhaps the point is that our intuitions about fairness ought to guide us in our decision on this sort of point. If so, though, surely the overwhelming case is in favor of the equiprobability assumption (which should *not* be confused with the principle of indifference. There is *no* need for assuming that principle). The reason is simple. No other condition would be fair. Our ordinary intuitions about fairness do not declare rules to be fair when they load the dice in favor of the poor, or the rich, or anybody: They are fair when they do not load the dice at all. We will see in a moment why Rawls wants to do this, and also why he does not have to do it in the present case. Meanwhile, I wish to argue that in addition to being the only fair condition to suppose to obtain in the initial position, it is also the only rationally defensible one. For consider: It is essential to the idea of the initial situation that people are to choose the rules under which they themselves as well as everyone else will henceforth live (pp. 11-13). It follows that for each real person in history, there is one person behind the veil of ignorance—who, however, doesn't know which historical person he will turn out to be. It could not, therefore, be reasonable for people behind the veil to assume that there was an unusually *high* probability of their being in, say, the unlucky classes historically. For it is logically impossible for them all to be correct in such an assumption. Yet as Rawls says, the initial position is one that erases all distinctions among the parties: All must make the *same* assumption. The only rational one to make is that one's chances of being any given person are the same as those of being any other person.

The interesting thing, however, is that in objecting to equiprobability at this point, Rawls is simply barking up the wrong tree. For now let us consider the second and third conditions. According to them, people are alleged not to "care" very much about the advantages available in the advantageous positions, as compared with the disadvantageousness of being in the disadvantaged positions. What they can gain in the better positions doesn't matter as much as what they could lose by being in the worse positions. What's more, some of these worse positions are actually "intolerable" and thus "unacceptable." But what do such things mean? Clearly, something about values is being assumed here—something about the basic values of every rational person. Yet Rawls's theory of value is entirely consonant with that of the utilitarians: The good is the satisfaction of rational desire, getting what you want out of life as a whole, an idea "following an idea of Sidgwick's" (p. 416). What's wrong with utilitarianism in Rawls's eyes is not its value theory but the illegitimate employment of that theory in the case of society as a whole. Thus we are driven to the conclusion that these value assumptions are in fact assumptions about the marginal utility curves for primary goods. In saying that the good positions (those with more primary goods above a certain [vague] minimum) don't matter as much as the bad ones (those with inadequate primary goods, goods below this minimum), he must be saying that utility, that is, degree of satisfaction of (rational) desire, diminishes for unit increases of primary goods above this hypothetical minimum, whereas it is very high for the first few units of such goods, those below the line. And in saying that some positions are "intolerable," what could possibly be meant but that the satisfaction available in such positions is extremely low or nonexistent (that is, that the dissatisfaction, the negative utility, of such positions is very high)?[10]

Perhaps some will still think that his value theory is basically different from that of the utilitarians. For instance, it might be thought that his predilection for what he calls the "Aristotelian principle" and his denial of hedonism are relevant at this point. But this is a mistake. Both of these tendencies are irrelevant. Rawls has defined utility as "the satisfaction of desire, or better, rational desire" (p. 25), a definition that makes it presumably an open question whether hedonism is correct. And the "Aristotelian principle" is not even on this subject. According to it

> other things equal, human beings enjoy the exercise of their realized capacities (their innate or trained abilities), and this enjoyment increases the more the capacity is realized, or the greater its complexity. (p. 426)

Obviously, the principle is psychological (as Rawls sees, p. 432) and not a definition of value, as the thesis that value is utility clearly is. Utilitarians could accept or reject the Aristotelian principle without in the least affecting their utilitarianism.

There is, then, simply no other reasonable interpretation of the assumptions used to support maximin than that they are assumptions about marginal utility. Now we need merely note that if these assumptions are correct, they do not require us to modify the assumption of equiprobability in the initial position. The reason for rigging your institutions in such a way that the size of the impoverished or oppressed classes is minimized is that you maximize utility that way as compared with what would happen if you instead had larger poor or oppressed classes but very great wealth and freedom for a few. What makes this so are the stated assumptions about how utility is correlated with amounts of primary goods. But these assumptions do *not* lead one to use maximin with respect to *utility*, thus leading us to reject the principle of utility; on the contrary, they lead us to use maximin with respect to *quantities of primary goods*, which in fact is precisely what Rawls does on those pages. But they would lead us to do that, having *accepted* the principle of utility. It is difficult to see how Rawls could have thought that he was rejecting the principle of utility here unless he had temporarily confused that principle with the principle of maximizing gross primary goods in the society. Despite the several passages in which, as we have seen, he is evidently aware of the differences, it is difficult to avoid the conclusion that he makes the confusion in other passages, especially in this one (the section, #26, on "The Reasoning for the Two Principles").

To complete our case, let us now consider the passage in which Rawls defends the priority of liberty:

> as the conditions of civilization improve, the marginal significance for our good of further economic and social advantages diminishes relative to the interests of liberty, which become stronger as the conditions for the exercise of the equal freedoms are more fully realized. Beyond some point it becomes and then remains irrational from the standpoint of the original position to acknowledge a lesser liberty for the sake of greater material means and amenities of office. . . . (p. 542)

To be sure, it is not the case that when the priority of liberty holds, all material wants are satisfied. Rather these desires are not so compelling as to make it rational for the persons in the original position to agree to satisfy them by accepting a less than equal freedom. (p. 543)

Here again Rawls is obviously making marginal-utility assumptions of precisely the kind that a utilitarian setting out to defend the Two Principles would make. I suppose some could again object that Rawls is only talking about what the rational person wants, or what he wants in the original position, rather than what ordinary human beings want. But this sort of objection would be completely misguided. It would either raise doubts about the utility of the whole idea, doubts that as we have seen arise for Rawls anyway and that we would not have space to discuss in this inquiry; or it would reflect a misunderstanding. If ordinary people don't have utility curves anything like this, then people in the original position who know that they themselves are going to be ordinary people when they get on the other side of the veil had better take that into account, if they are rational; it would be foolhardy not to.[11]

4. CONCLUSIONS

What I have tried to establish in this paper is only that Rawls's numerous criticisms of utilitarianism from the perspective of his theory are wholly misconceived, since within the framework of that system it is not only possible to argue for utilitarianism as the basis for his Two Principles, but in fact he appears to rely on the very arguments that the utilitarian would use in doing so. In view of the apparently widespread acceptance of Rawls's purported criticisms of utilitarianism, it seems high time to set the record straight on this matter.[12] If I am right in the foregoing arguments, then whatever Rawls has done, he most certainly has not constructed an "alternative" to utilitarianism, and only confusion could make one think so.

It would be somewhat misleading to infer from these arguments that Rawls simply is a utilitarian, since the actual conformity between his theory and utilitarianism is at least unintended. But it would probably, on the whole, be less misleading to say that than to continue talking as though there is a basic and radical opposition between his theory and utilitarianism. Further, I am of course not arguing that the Two Principles could not be defended from a nonutilitarian perspective, nor that Rawls would not do so upon reconsideration.

Additionally, it should be very clear that Rawls's theory is not a special variant of utilitarianism, for example a new species of rule utilitarianism.[13] It is impossible to decide this matter on the available evidence, since it depends not only on whether there is any such thing as "rule-utilitarianism" as opposed to other kinds, but also on how one proposes to treat the rules embodied in the Two Principles. Are they always to override all else? Are they to be allowed to be set aside in individual cases? One cannot say just what Rawls's attitude toward such questions is. Further, either side on both questions can be defended by utilitarians, depending on their assessment of other utilities and various other questions of fact.

Most important of all, I have not argued for (or against) the plausibility of the assumptions on which, as we have seen, Rawls's defense of the Two

Principles depends. These assumptions, which amount to a normative theory of human nature, are interesting and certainly not to be dismissed out of hand. But it must be admitted that they do seem extremely implausible on the whole. They certainly have all of the dubiousness that Rawls attributes to their utilitarian counterparts. As Rawls says, for instance,

> it seems impossible to justify the assumption that the social utility of a shift from one level to another is the same for all individuals. (p. 321)

But of course, the assumptions Rawls makes do have precisely this implication if they are taken strictly. After all, Rawls is talking about Everyman when he assumes a preference for liberty over other primary goods once society reaches a certain stage of material advancement, and so on. If these assumptions fail for actual indiviuals, as we know they do, then how can it be sensible nevertheless to design social systems around them? Or if real individuals' preferences do not matter, then why should we bother about principles that have been framed from so unrealistic a perspective? But to pursue these and other reservations in the present paper would be out of place. What is important here is that we realize where the problems lie: not in the Principle of Utility, but rather in the particular assumptions about the utility of such things as Rawls's primary goods. Rawls may not be a utilitarian: But the theory of *A Theory of Justice* is.[14]

Notes

1. Most important, perhaps, Barry (Brian Barry, *The Liberal Theory of Justice* [Oxford: Oxford University Press, 1973]) whose important work came to my attention after earlier versions of this paper were completed, has come closest to anticipating my conclusions. As an example of the majority view there is, for instance, the otherwise quite perceptive and trenchant review by A. M. MacLeod (Critical Notice of Rawls' *A Theory of Justice, Dialogue* 13 [1974]: 139-159) who finds "faults, some of them major," but accounts it a prime merit of Rawls's work that "He succeeds brilliantly in displaying the inadequacy of a utilitarian theory of justice" (p. 158).

2. However, I will assume throughout that utilitarianism is "average" rather than "total" so far as the issue of expanding population is concerned. It would require a separate discussion to consider Rawls's account of the derivation of "classical" (total) utilitarianism.

3. According to Rawls, the condition of publicity "arises naturally from a contractarian standpoint. The parties assume that they are choosing principles for a public conception of justice" (p. 133). If this is an argument for the naturalness of this condition, it is simply wrong. It does not follow that because the parties know which principles they are choosing they will want to know what they are once they are out from under the veil; that would be a discussable issue. And it cannot be proven that, for instance, the difference principle is in perfect harmony with publicity. Perhaps people would only go along with it if they didn't know that's what was being done. If this seems fantastic, then bear in mind that alleged refutations of utilitarianism along these lines require equally bizarre suppositions, if, as here, one is thinking of large-scale cases. Those who have supposed that utilitarianism is self-refuting because it could only work if people didn't know that it was being used are surely making weird assumptions about the way rational people work.

4. On this point, see especially the powerful arguments of Robert Nozick (*Anarchy, State, and Utopia* [New York: Basic Books, 1974]) especially pp. 189-197.

5. It is somewhat seen by MacLeod, p. 144, and better by Gauthier (David Gauthier, "Justice and Natural Endowment: Toward a Critique of Rawls' Ideological Framework," *Social Theory and Practice* 3 [1974]:3-26). Really, though, the point ought to be bawled from the rooftops. Once seen, it surely makes havoc of Rawls's complaints that utilitarianism somehow eliminates the difference between persons, or doesn't take it "seriously" (p. 27).

6. This point is well appreciated by Barry, pp. 104-105.

7. Independently of the present issue, the lexical ordering of the liberty principle creates a special and, I think, very grave problem for Rawls. This is discussed in my "A Puzzle About Economic Justice in Rawls' Theory", *Social Theory and Practice*, Fall 1976 (also in a different version, "Rawls on Equal Distribution of Wealth," *Philosophia*, June 1978).

8. See, again, Barry, Ch. 9 especially.

9. Since this was written, Robert Paul Wolff's *Understanding Rawls* came out (Princeton, 1977); Wolff notes this tendency in Rawls—cf. p. 58. See also my critical notice of Wolff's book, *Social Theory and Practice*, Spring 1978, esp. pp. 493-494.

10. Here, again, Barry has seen the point very clearly, p. 103.

11. Of course, the further and really fundamental question arises of how those in the initial position will react to the eventuality that when they become real people, they will be self-interested in the proper sense of the word. The importance of this consideration is emphasized and elaborated most perceptively in Gauthier.

12. The original version of this article was written in 1973; the present version, apart from minor changes of wording, in 1975. Five years later, the time is still "high": I have not seen general recognition of the point.

13. I do not, for instance, go along with Braybrooke in classifying Rawls as a utilitarian of one kind among others, defined by various constraints they impose on the matter of whose utilities and when are to be promoted. See David Braybrooke, "Utilitarianism with a Difference: Rawls' Position in Ethics," *Canadian Journal of Philosophy* 3 (1973): 303-331, especially pp. 304-308 and 331.

14. Thanks are expressed to the members of many, many colloquia and meetings for discussion of this paper. By and large, the discussion has left my assessment intact.

9 On the Refutation of Utilitarianism

David Gauthier

1.

Modern normative social thought treats ethics as part of the general theory of rational behavior.[1] It has been argued by thinkers from Bentham to Harsanyi that the *only* theory of ethics consistent with acceptable conceptions of value and reason is utilitarianism.[2] I hold that on the contrary, utilitarian ethical theory is *incompatible* with the accounts of value and rationality characteristic of modern economic and social thought. This claim is too large to demonstrate in the present paper. Rather, I hope to establish a much more modest thesis — that the most subtle and sophisticated defense of utilitarianism as uniquely rational, that offered by John Harsanyi, fails. But I shall use this thesis as support for my larger antiutilitarian claim.

I shall characterize a theory of behavior as *ethical* only if the choice set that it defines over the set of possible actions in any situation is determined, at least in part, by an impartial and positive consideration of the values of all those persons interacting in the situation. Now I shall introduce conceptions of value, reason, and utilitarianism in the next section, but it is evident that, however these conceptions are characterized, one of four possibilities must hold:

(i) No ethical theory is compatible with the general theory of rational behavior;

(ii) Only a utilitarian ethical theory is compatible with the general theory;

(iii) Both utilitarian and nonutilitarian ethical theories are compatible with the general theory;

(iv) Only a nonutilitarian ethical theory is compatible with the general theory.

Some of the ideas developed in the paper were originally formulated in my critical notice of Harsanyi's Essays . . . , in *Dialogue* 17 (1978):696-706. The original version of this paper was presented at Virginia Polytechnic Institute and State University, Blacksburg, Virginia, in May, 1978.

After providing the necessary conceptual groundwork, I shall reject an argument for (i) (sec. 3). Then I shall show the inadequacy of Harsanyi's defense of (ii) (secs. 4 and 5). Finally, I shall urge that the considerations advanced against (i) and (ii) offer support for (iv) (sec. 6).

2.1

The conceptions of value and reason that are to be related to utilitarianism cannot be fully explicated, much less defended, here. A few commonplace remarks must suffice. But the paucity of these remarks must not conceal their importance to my argument. Harsanyi and I are not in significant disagreement about the utility-maximizing implications of the received accounts of value and reason that are at the core of our general theory of rational behavior. But it is open to another utilitarian to rescue his position by rejecting that general theory. However, in so doing, he would cut himself off from the conceptual framework within which utilitarian ethical theory was developed, and which alone affords it apparent—albeit, in my view, spurious—plausibility.

Value, as understood here, is identical with *utility*. The primary objects to which utilities are assigned are *prospects*, or possible states of affairs, and each prospect is, or may be, assigned a utility. The value of any entity is thus to be understood contextually, in relation to some prospect or set of prospects in which it figures.

Utilities are assigned to prospects by, or from the standpoint of, some person or other sentient being, as a measure of his preferences. Thus one prospect x has greater value for some person a than another prospect y, if and only if a prefers x to y. I shall assume that the preferences involved are *true* preferences, based on or arising out of adequate experience, information, and reflection. Preferences are therefore not strictly behavioral; the actual choice of x over y need not exhibit a (true) preference for x over y, if the choice is inadequately informed.

Since utilities are assigned from the standpoint of some person, the value of a prospect is always the value *for some valuer*. A prospect cannot meaningfully be said to have value in itself, where this is intended to exclude reference to any sentient being, and the value of a prospect for any one sentient being is logically, and often factually, entirely independent of its value for some other sentient being.

The assignment of utilities to prospects leaves open the question of their interpersonal comparability. But this question need not be resolved here, since my argument does not depend on the answer. What is essential is to note that if such comparisons are meaningful, so that some normalization of each person's utility function brings all utilities to a common measure, this measure concerns only *values-for-persons*. To say that a prospect x has greater value overall than a prospect y, is to say only that the sum of values-for-persons attaching to x is greater than the sum attaching to y. Although this statement implies that for some person x must have greater value than y, it does not imply that x has greater value for most persons, or for any randomly selected person.

Given this conception of value, we may say that a person is *rational* as a *valuer* if and only if, for each set of prospects that he faces, a von Neumann-Morgenstern (vNM) utility function can be defined representing his (true) preferences over the members of the set. A person is then a rational *agent* if and only if, given that he is a rational valuer, his choice set defined over all possible strategies—that is, over all probability distributions over the alternative courses of action available to him—is determined by principles of *utility-maximization*. In particular, for situations not involving interpersonal interaction, a rational agent chooses among his strategies in accordance with the principle of expected utility-maximization formulated in Bayesian decision theory. The principles of utility-maximization appropriate to situations involving interpersonal interaction are in part the province of (normative) game theory, in part the province of ethical theory. Thus we must determine whether utilitarianism, and utilitarianism alone, adequately formulates these principles.

Reason, as understood here, is adequately characterized by Harsanyi when he says that "rational behavior is simply behavior consistently pursuing some well-defined goals, and pursuing them according to some well-defined set of preferences or priorities."[3] This conception is, in a large sense, instrumental; goals and preferences are themselves ultimately neither rational nor irrational. Thus Hume rightly insisted that it is not contrary to reason to choose the destruction of the world rather than the moving of one's finger, but wrongly claimed that it is equally not contrary to reason to choose one's acknowledged lesser good to one's greater—a claim that is inconsistent if "good" is used as a synonym for "utility."[4]

2.2

A utilitarian ethical theory may be characterized as one that introduces a quantity, which we shall call *welfare*, as a linear, increasing function of individual *utilities*, and then applies the maximizing conception of *rationality* to establish, as its basic prescriptive principle, the *maximization of welfare*. The definition of welfare induces an interpersonal comparison of individual utilities. All utilitarian theories assume a linear relationship among these utilities. However, theories may differ on the grounding of such a relationship.

For convenience we may set the welfare (W) of a prospect x, $W(x) = 0$, if the utility (U) of each individual i for that prospect, $U_i(x) = 0$. Welfare may then be represented as a weighted sum of utilities, the weights all being positive, so that the family of utilitarian theories is represented by the set of functions $W = \Sigma a_i \cdot U_i$, each particular theory involving a particular specification of the weights a_i.

If we suppose that these weights are specified by the theory in a manner unconstrained by extra-theoretic considerations, then we shall term the theory *weak*. A weak utilitarian theory is thus characterized by a set of *weights* to be assigned to individual utilities. If, on the other hand, we suppose that there is an objective basis, independent of the theory, for comparing the utilities of different persons, then we shall term the theory *strong*. Such a comparison provides an objective normalization of the utilities of different persons, so that all the normalized utilities are expressed in the same unit of preference measure. A strong theory presupposes such a normalization, and is then represented by the function $W = \Sigma U_i$, where each U_i is antecedently normalized. This distinction, between weak and strong forms of utilitarian theory, will prove helpful in our analysis of Harsanyi's arguments in sections 4 and 5.

3.

If utilitarianism is part of the general theory of rational behavior, then that theory contains two maximizing requirements: the maximization of individual utility and the maximization of welfare. Now it is in general impossible simultaneously to satisfy two such requirements, and if we were to suppose that both are to be understood as constraining an individual's choice among his possible strategies, then they would easily be proved incompatible. The argument requires use only of a weak form of utilitarianism.

Let there be two persons with utility functions U_1 and U_2, and suppose that a proposed weak utilitarian theory assigns positive weights, a_1 and a_2, to these functions. The first person is thus required simultaneously to maximize the values of U_1 and $(a_1 U_1 + a_2 U_2)$, and the second person is required to maximize the values of U_2 and $(a_1 U_1 + a_2 U_2)$. Consider the situation with utility matrix:

	s_2	s'_2
s_1	0 , 0	$1+a_2$, $-a_1$
s'_1	$-a_2$, $1+a_1$	1 , 1

and so with welfare matrix:

	s_2	s'_2
s_1	0	a_1
s'_1	a_2	$a_1 + a_2$

Given independent choices of strategy, s_1 and s_2 are strongly dominant with respect to utility-maximization, but s'_1 and s'_2 are strongly dominant with respect to welfare-maximization. Thus in this situation utility-maximization and welfare-maximization are not compatible requirements, and so they can not be compatible as constraints on all possible choices among strategies.

This argument makes use of the well-known characteristics of Prisoners' Dilemma-type situations. Our concern is with its significance in an analysis of the rationality of utilitarianism. Since individual utility-maximization is a requirement of the general theory of rational behavior, then superficially this argument seems to establish the incompatibility of utilitarianism with this theory. Indeed, it would seem that this argument could be extended to every proposed ethical theory that satisfied the requirement of affording impartial and positive consideration to the utilities of every person, and that prescribed a maximizing principle based on such consideration. And this would lend support to the view that no ethical theory is compatible with the general theory of rational behavior.

But this conclusion would be only superficial. Harsanyi, who is of course well aware that the maximization of welfare may conflict with the maximization of individual utility, holds that utilitarianism simply prescribes what "anybody who wants to serve our common human interests in a rational manner must" do.[5] My concern in the next section will be to show that his view is mistaken. But even were it not mistaken, it would be an insufficient defense of utilitarianism as part of the theory of rational behavior. This general theory would be completely trivialized were we to suppose it to include every principle that specifies the form of the choice set for any conceivable constraint on preferences. Rather, we must surely restrict the theory of rational behavior to those principles that specify the form of the choice set for each *rational* constraint on preferences. In other words, if ethics is part of the general theory of rational behavior, then we must show that it is rational, at least in some contexts, to constrain preferences so that we extend impartial, positive consideration to the utilities of every interacting agent. Harsanyi ignores this problem.

Now an argument defending such a constraint can be based on the kind of situation I have used to show the superficial incompatibility of utilitarianism with rational behavior. In Prisoners' Dilemma-type situations, persons who make direct application of the tenets of Bayesian decision theory, so that they choose strategies strongly dominant with respect to the maximization of individual utility, find that the outcome of their interaction is suboptimal. Greater utility is available to each person, at no cost in utility to the other or others. Greater utility would indeed be secured were each to maximize welfare rather than utility.[6] The utilitarian principle of welfare-maximization ensures individual utility-optimization; each person secures the greatest utility compatible with that received by others. Hence one may suggest that, far from being incompatible with the general theory of rational behavior, the utilitarian ethical theory establishes the principles of rational conduct in situations involving interpersonal interaction. Bayesian decision theory and utilitarian ethical theory would then be complementary, the one applying to situations not involving any interaction among rational agents, the other applying to situations involving such interaction.

This suggestion is open to two interpretations. One, suggested by Jeremy Bentham's famous title, *An Introduction to the Principles of Morals and Legislation*, is to claim that the welfare-maximizing requirement of ethical theory is not to be understood as a direct constraint on choices by individuals among possible strategies. Rather, welfare-maximization constrains the choice of a framework within which these individual choices occur. Each individual rationally seeks to maximize his own utility, but it is rational for each to do this within a framework that will ensure that in maximizing his own utility, he also maximizes welfare. The utilitarian principle is thus to be understood as the requirement of the general theory of rational behavior, for the design and evaluation of social institutions.

Furthermore, it may be urged, still following his first interpretation, the utilitarian principle should guide the design of educational as well as economic institutions, so that each individual is socialized to identify his own utility with the welfare of society. John Stuart Mill's conception of social progress centers on the emergence of individuals whose preference orderings over prospects define utility functions identical with the welfare function.[7] Thus, although welfare-maximization and utility-maximization remain incompatible in theory as constraints on individual strategy choices, the design of social institutions may ensure that in practice they prove compatible. In this way the principle of welfare-maximization may guide individual action, even if each person seeks to maximize his own utility.

A second, and in some ways more interesting, interpretation of utilitarianism denies that in situations involving interaction among rational agents, each person should be guided by the requirement of individual utility-maximization. Given that directly maximizing principles suggested by Bayesian decision theory lead, in certain situations, to suboptimal outcomes, this second interpretation urges that individuals have good reason to commit themselves, conditionally on similar commitment by others, not to act on such principles, but rather to aim directly at optimal outcomes, whether or not the framework of interaction ensures the coincidence of individual maximization with optimization. And this commitment, it is urged, is best assured by the adoption of the utilitarian principle as determining each individual's choice set over possible strategies.[8]

I shall not be concerned here with the respective merits of these two interpretations of the place of utilitarianism within the general theory of rational behavior. Whether welfare-maximization should be a principle of *social* choice, or a principle to which persons *mutually commit* themselves for *individual* choice, does not affect the subsequent argument. In any case, these interpretations have been sketched only in a rhetorical manner. They suggest an answer to the charge that no ethical theory is part of the general theory of rational behavior, but they do not demonstrate that the charge can be met.

Let us then, for the sake of argument, grant that the suboptimal outcome of individual utility-maximization, in Prisoners' Dilemma-type contexts, affords a place for a rational ethics the principles of which prescribe optimizing behavior. We have supposed that an ethical theory, whether viewed as prescribing the design of social institutions, or as determining the mutual commitments of individuals, must base its principles on a positive and impartial consideration of the utilities of all interacting agents. We shall now examine two arguments advanced by Harsanyi, either of which, if successful, would suffice to establish utilitarianism as the sole ethical theory compatible with our conceptions of value and reason.

4.1

John Harsanyi defines ethics as "a theory of rational behavior in the service of the common interests of society as a whole."[9] Rational behavior, he argues, is defined "either by some set of axioms or by a constructive decision model," and from this primary definition "a secondary definition of rationality" is derived, which in the case of ethics "is in terms of *maximizing the average utility level* of all individuals in the society."

If the average utility level is to have objective significance, then a strong form of utilitarian theory is needed. The welfare of any prospect is then the sum of the interpersonally comparable individual utilities for that prospect, divided by the number of persons. But the significance to be given to interpersonal comparisons of utility need not be considered in assessing the first of the defenses Harsanyi offers for utilitarianism, since that defense leaves undetermined the assignment of weights to individual utilities, and so establishes, if successful, only the weak form of utilitarian theory as rationally *required*.

Harsanyi distinguishes "between two classes of preferences by any given individual. One class comprises his *personal* preferences, based on his personal taste and his personal interests (as well as on the interests of those individuals, if any, whose well-being is a matter of personal concern for him). The other class comprises his *moral* or *social* preferences, which express his views about the general interests of society as a whole, defined in terms of impersonal and impartial criteria."[10] Utility is the measure of personal preferences; welfare is the measure of moral preferences. For a rational moral valuer, a welfare function, possessing all of the characteristics of a vNM utility function, can be defined as representing his moral preferences.

In Harsanyi's argument, the demand for a positive and impartial linkage between moral preference and the personal preferences of all individuals is reduced to the very weak requirement that a prospect x be morally preferred to a prospect y, if some individual personally prefers x to y, and no individual personally prefers y to x. From this, and the requirements that both personal and moral preferences be capable of representation by vNM utility functions, Harsanyi proves the surprisingly strong theorem that each person's welfare function, representing his moral preferences, must be a weighted sum of all the individual utility functions representing personal preferences, and that all weights must be positive.[11] But this is the conception of welfare required by a weak form of utilitarian theory. Hence only utilitarian theories can be impartial, optimizing with respect to individual utility, and consistent with the maximizing conception of rationality.

ON THE REFUTATION OF UTILITARIANISM 151

This is a stunning demonstration. The importance of Harsanyi's result for ethical theory can be compared only to the importance of Arrow's impossibility theorem on constitutions for social choice theory.[12] I shall not discuss the formalization of Harsanyi's argument, since it occasions no difficulties; validity is not at issue. If one grants Harsanyi's very weak premises, then one is committed to utilitarianism as the only ethical theory that can be part of the general theory of rational behavior.

Since I do not accept the conclusion, which of the premises do I reject? Not the requirement that the personal preferences of a rational valuer be capable of representation by a vNM utility function. Not the Pareto requirement that a prospect x be morally preferred to a prospect y if some person prefers x to y and no person prefers y to x. Hence I must reject the remaining requirement, that moral preferences parallel personal preferences in being capable of representation by a vNM utility function.

Let us begin our critical discussion of this requirement by drawing an interesting parallel between the views of Harsanyi and Arrow. Both are concerned with the rationality of preference aggregation. Arrow assumes that personal preferences determine, not a vNM utility function, but only a weak ordering of all possible prospects. He then requires that a preference-based constitution, or social welfare function, determine a weak ordering of all prospects as a function of the individual orderings. He demonstrates that no such constitutional function is compatible with weak requirements for a positive and impartial link between personal and constitutional preferences.[13] Harsanyi assumes, as we have seen, that personal preferences determine a cardinal measure (with arbitrary unit and zero-point) over all possible prospects. He then requires that an ethical function also establish a cardinal measure of all possible prospects as a function of the individual measures. He demonstrates that only a utilitarian measure is compatible with requirements for a positive and impartial link between personal and moral preferences.

We may refer neutrally to Arrow's constitutional preferences and Harsanyi's moral preferences as *social* preferences. Then we may say that both require that social preference parallel personal preference, that social preference must induce the same kind of ordering on prospects as that induced by personal preferences. This requirement seems to me clearly suspect.

Given personal preferences over prospects, the role of either an Arrovian constitutional function or a Harsanyian ethical function is to determine a social choice. Thus a non-empty *choice set* is required for each set of prospects and each set of individual orderings over those prospects. This choice set contains the *socially best prospects*, given the individual orderings. Now a social ordering of the prospects, although sufficient for the existence of a non-empty choice set, is not necessary for the existence of such a set.[14] Hence we may suggest that both Arrow and Harsanyi have imposed too rigid a requirement for passing from individual preferences to social choice. We need not determine social choice *via* an ordering of social preferences comparable to orderings of individual preferences, but instead we may determine social choice directly. We shall of course require that the social choice set be based in a positive and impartial manner on all individual preference orderings, but this condition does not in itself give rise to the results established by Arrow and Harsanyi.[15]

It is not my intention to introduce a theorem on choice sets comparable to Harsanyi's theorem on orderings—that is, a theorem exhibiting the range of admissable ethical theories, given that personal preferences be capable of representation by vNM utility functions, that there be a non-empty moral choice set for every configuration of personal preferences, and that a prospect y not be a member of the choice set if there is a prospect x such that some individual prefers x to y and no individual prefers y to x. One *example* of an admissible nonutilitarian theory is obtained by generalizing Rawls's difference principle so that it requires maximization of the utility of the least advantaged, breaking ties by maximizing the utility of the next least advantaged, and so on.[16] This shows the *formal* inadequacy of Harsanyi's argument, but he and I would agree that the principle is not plausible. Hence this example does not show that any interesting alternative to utilitarianism is admitted by requiring only a moral choice set and not a moral preference ordering.

Another example will show what I consider an interesting alternative. But before introducing it, we should consider Harsanyi's reply to my rejection of the requirement that moral choice rest on a moral preference ordering. In a written comment on an earlier version of this paper, Harsanyi states: "when Mr. Carter acts as a private individual then rationality requires that his behavior should be guided by a set of preferences that amount to a consistent weak ordering over all alternatives. Does not rationality equally require that, when he acts as President, then his behavior should be likewise guided by a consistent weak ordering over all alternatives? . . .

"Of course, when I am making a moral decision or a moral value judgment, I am not acting as a public official, as a President does when he acts in his official capacity. But the *logical problem* I will have to solve is essentially the same as a public official has to face: It is to act *rationally* (i.e., in accordance with the rationality requirements appropriate for *individual* behavior), and at the same time to act *impartially, impersonally*, and *sympathetically* to the human interests of all individuals in society."[17]

I fully agree with Harsanyi that rationality should guide the conduct of a public official, or of an individual making a moral judgment, so that he "should surely follow at least as high standards of rationality as we follow . . . in looking after our own personal interests."[18] What I deny is that a public official, or a moral agent, does this by following the rationality requirements appropriate for individual, private behavior. Rather, I suggest that one acts impartially, impersonally, and sympathetically to the interests of all, insofar as once acts as an *arbitrator* among those interests—or in other words, insofar as one's judgment expresses a *fair compromise* among the preferences of different individuals, when their preferences do not agree in ordering all prospects in the same way. I suggest that the appropriate model for ethical theory is the *theory of rational bargaining*.[19] In bargaining theory the choice set is defined over the vNM utility functions of all interacting agents, and satisfies a Pareto requirement. The theory of bargaining, rather than the generalization of Rawls's difference principle, offers what I consider the interesting alternative to Harsanyi's utilitarian ethical theory.

An arbitrator who conforms to an acceptable theory of bargaining exhibits standards of rationality equal to those of an individual who follows Bayesian decision theory in the conduct of his private affairs. A rational arbitrator meets the ethical requirements of impartiality and positive concern for the preferences of all. By requiring only a moral choice set and not a moral preference ordering, we thus allow a model of moral judgments that focuses, not primarily on the production of as much individual utility as possible, but rather on the distribution of utility among persons, given that no one shall receive less than he might compatibly with the utilities received by others. And this seems a properly ethical concern.

4.2

Harsanyi, however, objects to consideration of the distribution of utility among persons, for he treats this as an instance of concern with utility dispersion, contrary to the tenets of Bayesian rationality.[20] If there are three prospects, x, y, and z, with utility for me of 0, 1, and 2 units respectively, then on the Bayesian view I *must* be indifferent between y, and an equiprobable mix of x and z, since the utility of that mix is determined by summing the probability-weighted utilities of each prospect it contains, and so is $(.5 \times 0) + (.5 \times 2)$, or 1, equal to the utility of y. As Harsanyi correctly reminds us, objections to the Bayesian prohibition on considering utility dispersion are based on mistaken identifications of utility with other measures of value, which are themselves not linear in terms of utility.[21]

But must we extend this prohibition on the consideration of utility dispersion to situations involving the utilities of different persons? Let us assume some way, whether subjectively or objectively based, of relating the utilities of different persons, and two prospects, x, with utility to a of 0 and to b of 2, and y, with utility to each of 1. Harsanyi insists that we *must* be rationally and morally indifferent between these prospects. If we say that an ethical function assigns *ethical value* or *ethical worth* to prospects, then ethical worth can only be identical with welfare.

Harsanyi argues that to suppose dispersion ethically relevant is to make "an illegitimate transfer of a mathematical relationship from money amounts, for which it does hold, to utility levels, for which it does not hold. . . . even if social welfare is a nonlinear function of individual *incomes*, it does not follow at all that it is a nonlinear function also of individual *utilities*. . . . It makes very good sense to assume a law of decreasing marginal utility for *money* . . . ;

but it would make no sense whatever to assume a law of decreasing marginal utility for *utility*."[22]

The last clause, which is crucial to the argument, begs the point. In dealing with the utilities of a single person, it clearly makes no sense to assume a law of decreasing marginal utility for utility. But it does not follow that, when dealing with the utilities of different persons, it makes no sense to assume a law of decreasing *ethical worth* for utilities. Unless we *assume*, what we must *prove*, that ethical worth is welfare, defined as a sum of utilities, we cannot show that increases in ethical worth must be *linear* with increases in each individual's utility. We may grant that ethical worth is an increasing function of individual utilities, but it need not therefore be a linear function. The relationship between ethical worth and individual utility remains to be established.

But Harsanyi does not rest his case on a purely formal appeal to the violation of allegedly relevant constraints of Bayesian rationality. He argues: "When we are assigning the same quantitative measure to utility changes affecting two different individuals . . . , then we are implicitly asserting that these utility changes for both individuals involve human needs of *equal urgency*. But, this being so, it would be highly unfair . . . discrimination to claim that, as a matter of principle, satisfaction of one man's needs should have a lower social priority than satisfaction of the other man's needs should have."[23] In other words, adherence to the tenets of Bayesian rationality is necessary if our ethical function is to rest on an impartial consideration of individual preferences.

This argument also begs the question. To speak of "equal urgency" is to presuppose what must be shown—that only the magnitude of the concern (expressed in utility) is of ethical significance. Let needs be ever so equal, it is still not evident that they should receive equal treatment. In considering the preferences of a single person, we employ a single quantitative measure, because what is at stake is the satisfaction of that person—his preferences do not represent independent claims each of which demands its share of satisfaction. But in dealing with the preferences of several persons, we are dealing with independent claims. Satisfaction accrues, not to the persons collectively, but to each individually. A single quantitative measure obscures the difference among persons. And although this may not be of ethical significance, we cannot simply *assume* that it is not relevant. That ethics requires the maximization of a single quantitative measure must be the utilitarian's conclusion, and not his premise.

If we ignore the distribution of utilities among persons, then we invite the very charge of unfairness that Harsanyi advances against those who consider interpersonal utility dispersion. The basis of this charge is that some persons may not receive their fair share of utility, however much total utility, or welfare, may be produced. Someone might reply that the belief that shares are unfair is itself a source of disutility, which should be taken into account in determining the individual utilities involved. But this reply is incoherent.

For if what is being objected to is the *distribution of utilities*, then any disutility occasioned thereby cannot be included in those utilities involved in the distribution.

Harsanyi suggests that if we are determined to take the distribution of utilities into account, we should nevertheless base our moral choices on a preference ordering that satisfies the requirements of Bayesian rationality, by introducing, into the set of orderings over which moral preference is defined, an ordering of *egalitarian preferences*, which is assigned some weight in relation to the orderings of personal preferences. In this way, equal utility distributions would be favored over unequal ones, even though the total quantity of welfare would not be affected.[24]

I agree with Harsanyi in finding this suggestion unsatisfactory, for, as he recognizes, it sacrifices the Pareto requirement of optimality with respect to personal preferences. Distributive considerations should not override optimality in determining the ethical worth of prospects. If we must choose between a prospect x that affords a and b each one unit of utility, and a prospect y that affords a one unit and b 10^6 units, it seems to me evident that we should choose y, despite the extreme inequality of the distribution. We have no reason to reject optimality; it is always morally better to increase one person's utility at no *utility* cost to others, whatever the distributive effect. To suppose otherwise is to make an illegitimate transfer from money amounts to utility amounts.

I conclude that Harsanyi offers no valid objection to ethical functions that provide only non-empty choice sets, rather than moral preference orderings, defined impartially and positively over all sets of individual preference orderings of prospects, and that may allow the relevance of utility dispersion, or the distribution of utilities among different individuals, in determining ethical worth, provided optimality is not sacrificed. I suggest that the model of reasoning appropriate for moral judgment is not that of the individual following the requirements of Bayesian decision theory, but that of the arbitrator following the requirements of bargaining theory. But Harsanyi has a second argument that, if successful, would short-circuit my objections and alternatives. For this second argument purports to show that the requirements of impartial and positive consideration for individual preferences enable and require us to represent ethical choice directly as the choice of a single rational individual, based on the maximization of a vNM utility function. The particular function, of course, turns out to be a member of the utilitarian family.

5.1

A moral judgment, or choice, must reflect a positive and impartial concern with the preferences of all interacting individuals. How is this concern to be operationalized? Harsanyi's second argument presents a direct operationalization of impartiality in individual choice. He states that "this requirement of impersonality and impartiality would always be satisfied if he [the individual expressing an ethical choice] had to choose between the . . . alternatives on the assumption that he had the *same probability* of occupying any of the existing social positions, from the very highest to the very lowest. (This model I shall call the *equiprobability model* of moral value judgments.)

"According to moden decision theory, a rational individual placed in this hypothetical choice situation would always choose the alternative yielding him the higher *expected utility*—which, under this model, would mean choosing the alternative yielding the higher *average utility level* to the individual members of society. Thus . . . making a moral value judgment involves trying to maximize the arithmetic mean of all individual utilities."[25]

Each individual, in making a moral judgment or choice, must appeal to an interpersonal measure of utility; thus Harsanyi's argument leads to a strong form of utilitarian theory. In his moral choice, each individual seeks to maximize, not strictly the *sum* of all individual utilities, but the *average* of such utilities. Operationally, maximizing the average differs from maximizing the sum only when choice is among alternatives involving groups of different size. The welfare function thus takes the form $W = 1/n(\Sigma U_i)$. Harsanyi's claim, then, is that an impartial choice, affording positive consideration to each individual's utility, is necessarily choice based on the average-utilitarian principle.[26]

This argument, if sound, would seem to meet the objections raised to utilitarianism in the preceding section. One cannot reasonably complain about unfairness in the distribution of utilities, if that distribution results from one's own choice among prospects made in circumstances that ensure impartiality. We have agreed that ethical principles must be linked positively and impartially with individual preferences; Harsanyi's equiprobability model seems to establish that link. If by assuming rationality and impartiality, we can show that individual choice must maximize expected average utility, then rationality and impartiality are *sufficient* to determine a utilitarian theory of behavior. And so utilitarianism, and only utilitarianism, can be acceptable as that part of the general theory of rational behavior which applies when it is indeed rational to be impartial.

But the argument is not sound. Consider the type of choice envisaged. Each of the prospects among which one is to choose may be characterized as an assignment of equal probabilities to the members of a set of ordered pairs, each pair specifying a *person*, and a *situation* for that person, such that the situations are mutually compatible. The total prospect then represents the society comprising all of the persons in their respective situations, and the choice is operationally impartial since equal probability has been given to being each of the persons.

Now we may assign, to each pair in any prospect, a number, representing the utility, by hypothesis interpersonally comparable, of the situation to the person. Let (a,s) represent person *a* in situation *x*; we assign it the value of $U_a(x)$. Harsanyi supposes that for any person *i*, the expected utility of the prospect will be determined by summing the utilities so assigned to the pairs, and then dividing by the number of persons. But this is obviously false. When person i considers the pair (a,x), the utility he will assign to it will be, not the value of $U_a(x)$, but the value of $U_i(a,x)$—that is, the utility, *to himself*, of *being* person a in situation x. The expected utility of the entire prospect to him is the sum of these utilities, divided by the number of persons.

If Harsanyi's argument is to survive, it requires the assumption that, whenever utilities are interpersonally comparable, the value of $U_a(x)$ must equal the value of $U_i(a,x)$ for all i. But this need not be so. $U_a(x)$ is greater than $U_b(y)$ if and only if person a in situation x receives more utility than person b in situation y—or person a's preference for being in situation x is greater than b's preference for being in y. $U_i(a,x)$ is greater than $U_i(b,y)$ if and only if person i prefers being person a in situation x to being person b in situation y. Now if the value of $U_a(x)$ must equal the value of $U_i(a,x)$, and the value of $U_b(y)$ must equal the value of $U_i(b,y)$, then person i's preference between *being* a in x and *being* b in y must depend *solely* on the utilities received by a and b. But person i's preferences need not depend solely on these utilities—or on the strength of the preferences of a and b; his preferences may also depend on the personal characteristics of a and b.

Consider, to take an example made famous by John Stuart Mill, Socrates dissatisfied and the fool satisfied.[27] Socrates' dissatisfaction reflects the low ranking his situation receives in terms of his "wise" preferences; the fool's satisfaction reflects the high ranking his situation receives in terms of his "foolish" preferences. But wise or foolish, we may not incorporate into our interpersonal measure of utility any evaluation of the preferences on which utilities rest; if they are the *true* preferences of the individuals concerned, they must be taken at face-value to conform to our assumptions about value and reason. Hence we must assign greater utility to the fool in his situation than to Socrates in his situation. But it does not follow that we should prefer to be the fool in his situation than to be Socrates in his. Our preference will reflect, not just a comparison of their utilities, but also a comparison of them as persons. We may not include this latter comparison in determining *their* utilities, but we may not exclude it in determining *our own* utilities for being them. And so the utility to some person i, of being Socrates dissatisfied, may exceed the utility, to i, of being the fool satisfied, even though i is fully aware that the utility to Socrates of being dissatisfied is less than the utility to the fool of being satisfied.

As a second example, consider two prospects, x and y, such that average utility is the same in both, the average utility of philosophers is the same in both, the average utility of baseball players is the same in both, and the average utilities of philosophers and baseball players are equal. But let the probability of being a philosopher be greater in x, and the probability of being a baseball player greater in y. Now consider two persons: a would prefer to be suited to and living the philosophic life rather than to be suited to and living the life of a baseball player, and b would prefer the opposite. *Ceteris paribus, a* will prefer prospect x to y, and b will prefer y to x. Persons need not agree in choosing among prospects, even though they do not know who they will be or what role they will play.

In choosing among prospects without knowing what one's characteristics and circumstances will be, one will rationally maximize, *not* the average utility to be received by the various persons in their situations, but the average of one's own utilities for being each of those persons. Since these averages need not be identical, Harsanyi's proposed operationalization of rational and impartial individual choice does not require that such choice be based on the utilitarian principle. And indeed, since each individual will choose in accordance with his own preferences, we may deny that true impartiality has been achieved. Harsanyi's operationalization is therefore *irrelevant* to ethical choice.

5.2

It will be objected that this last conclusion shows that Harsanyi's argument has been misconceived. The requirement of impartiality, it will be urged, must extend to the basis of choice. It is not enough that an individual not know *who he will be*, that is, what characteristics he will have and what role he will play in the prospect selected. He must also not know *who he is*, that is, what characteristics he now has, determining his preference ordering over the various pairs of persons and situations in the possible prospects.

How then is one to choose among prospects? One knows neither who one is, as chooser, nor who one will be, in the chosen prospect. But it seems appropriate to assume that one is the person one will be. Hence if in prospect x, person a_1 is in the situation x_1, person a_2 in situation x_2, and so on, then one supposes that either one is person a_1, for whom the utility of x is the value of $U_{a_1}(x_1)$, or one is person a_2, for whom the utility of x is the value of $U_{a_2}(x_2)$, and so on. Thus the expected utility of x, it would seem, is given by the value of $1/n[\Sigma U_{ai}(x_i)]$, which is the average of the expected utilities of x to the various individuals involved in the prospect. And so in choosing among prospects in ignorance of who one is, one maximizes expected utility by employing the average-utilitarian principle. Thus Harsanyi's argument seems to be vindicated.

But this description of choice is fundamentally mistaken. To understand why, consider the question: *For whom* is the expected utility of x equal to the average of its expected utilities to the individuals concerned? If person j is making the choice, then the answer must be: for person j. In other words, the value of $U_j(x)$ must be equal to the value of $1/n[\Sigma U_{ai}(x_i)]$. But the function U_j is a measure of person j's preferences. The alleged value of $U_j(x)$ is not a measure of j's preference for x, since by hypothesis j does not know *who he is*. Lacking this information, person j is not able to express *any preference* concerning x. He is able to calculate the average value of the preferences for x expressed by those persons a_i involved in x, but he cannot identify this value with *his preference*, since he cannot identify *himself*.

Harsanyi supposes that moral judgments are a subclass of decisions made under *uncertainty*.[28] But in choices made under uncertainty, the chooser knows who he is, and so is able to express a *single set of preferences*, which may then be represented by a single utility function. The prospects among which he expresses preferences may, of course, involve his coming to possess different personal characteristics, as well as his coming to be in radically different circumstances, and he may be uncertain about the likelihood both of characteristics and of circumstances. But he still has a single, unified standpoint from which to establish a prefereence ordering.

In the kind of choice required by Harsanyi's argument, as we have now reformulated it, the chooser does not know who he is, and so cannot express a single set of preferences, to be represented by a single utility function. Not only do the prospects among which he expresses preferences involve his coming to possess different personal characteristics; he is required to express each preference from the standpoint of the person with those characteristics. He does not have a single, unified standpoint from which to establish a preference ordering. The ordering that can be derived from calculating the average expected utility for each prospect is not the preference ordering of any individual chooser. The existence of a single interpersonal utility measure does not entail the existence of a single preference ordering.

Now I want to insist that the conditions for individual choice are not properly satisfied if the supposed chooser is denied any knowledge of his own identity, so that he must take different identities from the characteristics of the persons in the prospects among which he is to choose. I agree here with Rawls's criticism that the expectations of someone denied such knowledge of his identity are not "as expectations should be, founded on one system of aims."[29] Given that one has no knowledge of one's own identity, one can function as an arbitrator, selecting an outcome that is a fair compromise among the preferences of the individuals involved. But without preferences of one's own, and so without a utility function to maximize, one cannot act as an individual chooser. The formula $1/n[\Sigma U_{ai}(x_i)]$ cannot serve as a surrogate for an individual utility function in problems of moral choice.

If it be agreed that the conditions for individual choice are violated by the chooser's ignorance of his own identity, and so of his own preferences, then Harsanyi's argument fails, because it ensures impartiality in choice only by violating individuality. Average-utilitarianism is not shown to be the principle to which a person would conform in any circumstances appropriate for individual choice. But I do not want to rest my case entirely on this formal contention. Suppose, then, we allow an individual to choose, in ignorance of his identity, and agree that he would then choose in accordance with the average-utilitarian principle. Would this establish Harsanyi's case for utilitarianism?

To answer this question, let us reflect again on fairness. I suggested at the beginning of this section that one cannot reasonably complain about unfairness if the outcome is determined by one's own impartial choice among prospects.

But does this hold if impartiality is secured only by attenuating the sense in which choice is one's own to the point at which one chooses in ignorance of one's identity and one's preferences? Is fairness secured by a choice reflecting no point of view, but which is made by giving equal probability to each point of view?

Here we must draw an important distinction between an impartial bargain and an impartial choice. An impartial bargain reflects every point of view; its outcome is rational and fair for each fully imformed bargainer. An impartial choice reflects no point of view; its outcome need be considered rational and fair by no chooser aware of his own identity. A rational bargain reconciles impartiality and individuality. An impartial choice secures its impartiality only by suppressing individuality, so that once individuality is reinstated, impartiality vanishes. Harsanyi's argument owes its plausibility, I suggest, to the assumption that impartial choice is properly akin to decision-making under uncertainty. Once we recognize that impartial choice prevents any individual from identifying with the chooser, Harsanyi's equiprobability model of moral value judgments loses both ethical and rational appeal.

6.

Although utilitarianism developed as the ethical partner of modern economic and social theories that assume a subjective, preference-based conception of value, and an instrumental, maximizing conception of rationality, it must appear, on full reflection, an unlikely partner. We saw in section 3 the *prima facie* incompatibility between utility-maximization and welfare-maximization. The failure of utility-maximization to secure optimality in Prisoners' Dilemma-type situations led us to treat this incompatibility as superficial, and to recognize the need for some principles of ethical conduct that would constrain or override utility-maximization to ensure mutually advantageous, optimal outcomes. This opened the door for the consideration of utilitarianism as a possible part of the general theory of rational behavior. But no positive argument was offered to support welfare-maximization as the appropriate constraint on utility-maximization.

Both Harsani's arguments for utilitarianism turn on representing ethical choice as subject to the rationality constraints appropriate to individual choice. His first, axiomatic argument turns on basing ethical choice on a single set of preferences; his second, decision-theoretic argument turns on treating ethical choice as that instance of decision-making under uncertainty that results from imposing impartiality on the decision-maker. Our objections to these arguments depend on rejecting the parallels Harsanyi draws between ethical choice and individual choice. Rational choice based impartially on everyone's preferences, I have suggested, may parallel the outcome of a bargain, or the decision of an arbitrator.

Brief reflection on the relationship between the principles of utilitarian ethics and the theory of the free, perfectly competitive market may reinforce the plausibility of this alternative. In general, the application of any utilitarian principle in a market situation will determine a unique point on the utility possibility frontier as the welfare maximum. But this point usually will not coincide with the market optimum achieved under conditions of perfect competition. And since this optimum depends, *ceteris paribus*, on the initial factor endowments of the persons in the market, any coincidence between market optimum and welfare maximum must be accidental, unless we suppose some connection more mysterious than the Invisible Hand that relates the weights assigned to individual utilities (or the basis for comparison among them) to the initial factor distribution.

Why would rational persons accept utilitarianism as a guide to the design and evaluation of their economic institutions? To do this would be to impose either a particular distribution of initial factors dictated by the requirement that market optimum and welfare maximum coincide, or a final redistribution of goods and services from the market optimum to the welfare maximum. Leaving aside the practical problems inherent in either policy, it is suficient to note that either an imposed distribution of factors or an imposed redistribution of goods and services must be regarded as *strictly redistributive* in its effects—as affording greater utility to some at the price of lesser utility to others. Neither policy would result in a move from a nonoptimal point of equilibrium to a mutually superior outcome on the utility possibility frontier, but rather in a move along that frontier from one optimal point to another. Neither policy could be justified by an appeal to mutual advantage.

But it is by considerations of mutual advantage that ethics may be brought within the framework of the general theory of rational behavior. The mutual disadvantageousness of direct utility-maximization in Prisoners' Dilemma-type situations, or more generally in situations characterized by external inefficiencies, grounds a theory constraining directly maximizing behavior in the interest of optimality.[30] But with such grounding, ethical theory cannot override the principles of direct utility-maximization in contexts such as the free, perfectly competitive market, in which adherence to maximizing principles suffices for optimality. Rather, the task of ethical theory must be to provide principles that ensure a mutually acceptable distribution of the surplus utility that cooperation to overcome external inefficiencies can provide. Each individual's concern will be, not with maximizing the total surplus utility, but with maximizing the share accruing to himself. Each person's share is secured at the expense of others. Hence the impartiality appropriate to ethical choice is surely the impartiality of an ideal bargain, in which the outcome reflects equally the partially conflicting preferences of the several bargainers.

The ethical theory to be developed is, I should argue, contractarian rather than utilitarian in its basic structure. It may yield results equivalent to utilitarianism in particular circumstances. Such equivalence will not always be accidental; if production of utility is independent of distribution, then maximizing the size of the utility pie will be part of any rational bargain. But production need not be independent of distribution; and when it is not, then each person's concern with the size of his slice of the pie may lead to outcomes that impartially reflect each person's preferences but do not satisfy the utilitarian principle. Neither the bargaining optimum of an agreement to achieve public goods or avoid public bads nor the competitive optimum of a perfect market need be the welfare maximum.

Noting that in the perfect market, individual utility-maximizing behavior leads to an optimum, our forefathers in normative social theory assumed this optimum to be the welfare maximum, and leaped to the conclusion that maximizing individual utility and maximizing social welfare are, or should be, mutually compatible. They embraced the utilitarian creed as part of their theory of rational behavior.

When this naive faith was dissipated, and the divergence between welfare maximum and market optimum became evident, those who had been converted to the utilitarian gospel abandoned the free market for the welfare state, little realizing that in so doing, they had also abandoned the framework of value and reason that alone conferred on utilitarianism its aura of plausibility. With a clearer conception of the general theory of rational behavior, we must begin anew, this time to develop an ethics that will meet the demands of optimality, while focusing on those distributive problems not solved by the free market — the endowment of initial factors that requires the guarantee of the protective state, and the division of public goods that requires the activity of the productive state.[31] To this task, the refutation of utilitarianism is but a negative preliminary — an exercise in clearing our minds in readiness for the conceptual construction ahead.

Notes

1. Cf. John C. Harsanyi, "Morality and the Theory of Rational Behavior," *Social Research* 44 (1977):625-656, and "Advances in Understanding Rational Behavior," *Essays on Ethics, Social Behavior, and Scientific Explanation* (Dordrecht & Boston:Reidel, 1976), pp. 96-98.

2. Jeremy Bentham, *An Introduction to the Principles of Morals and Legislation*, ch. I; John C. Harsanyi, "Cardinal Welfare, Individualistic Ethics, and Interpersonal Comparisons of Utility," in *Essays*, and "Morality and the Theory of Rational Behavior."

3. "Morality and the Theory of Rational Behavior," pp. 627-628.

4. David Hume, *A Treatise of Human Nature*, Bk. II, Pt. III, Sec. III.

5. "Morality and the Theory of Rational Behavior," p. 655.

6. In the example above, the outcome of individual utility-maximization affords each person a utility of 0; the outcome of welfare-maximization affords each a utility of 1.

7. John Stuart Mill, *Utilitarianism*, Chs. II, III.

8. Part of the argument for this interpretation of ethical theory — although not offered in defense of a utilitarian theory — is found in my paper "Reason and Maximization," *Canadian Journal of Philosophy* 4 (1975); especially pp. 424-430.

9. "Morality and the Theory of Rational Behavior," pp. 629-630.
10. John C. Harsanyi, "Nonlinear Social Welfare Functions: Do Welfare Economists Have a Special Exemption from Bayesian Rationality?," in *Essays*, pp. 65-66.
11. See, for example, the proof in "Morality and the Theory of Rational Behavior," pp. 636-637.
12. The Theorem is proved, using the terminology of constitutions, in Kenneth J. Arrow, "Values and Collective Decision-Making," in Peter Laslett and W. F. Runciman (eds.), *Philosophy, Politics and Society*, Third Series (Oxford: Basil Blackwell, 1967) pp. 215-232.
13. *Ibid*.
14. See Amartya K. Sen, *Collective Choice and Social Welfare* (San Francisco: Holden-Day, 1970), pp. 14-16.
15. See *Ibid*., Ch. 4.
16. The generalized difference principle is found in John Rawls, *A Theory of Justice* (Cambridge: Harvard University Press, 1971), pp. 82-83.
17. Quotation from a letter from John C. Harsanyi to Professor Gordon Tullock, May 1, 1978.
18. "Morality and the Theory of Rational Behavior," p. 637.
19. See my papers, "The Social Contract: Individual Decision or Collective Bargain?," in C. A. Hooker, J. J. Leach, and E. F. McClennen (eds.), *Foundations and Applications of Decision Theory* 2 (Dordrecht & Boston: Reidel, 1978), especially pp. 66-67, and "Economic Rationality and Moral Constraints," *Midwest Studies in Philosophy* 3 (1978):90-93. Note that I argue that the theory of rational bargaining has limitations as a model for ethical theory. But these limitations are irrelevant in the present context.
20. "Nonlinear Social Welfare Functions: . . . ," pp. 73-77.
21. *Ibid*., pp. 73-74.
22. *Ibid*., pp. 74-75.
23. *Ibid*., p. 75.
24. *Ibid*., pp. 80-81.
25. John C. Harsanyi, "Rule Utilitarianism and Decision Theory," *Erkenntnis* 11 (1977): 28.
26. I shall not explore here the differences between *classical* utilitarian theories (where welfare is the *sum* of individual utilities) and *average* theories. Harsanyi and I agree in finding average-utilitarianism more plausible.
27. Mill, *Utilitarianism*, Ch. II.
28. "Cardinal Welfare, Individualistic Ethics, and Interpersonal Comparisons of Utility," p. 14.
29. Rawls, *A Theory of Justice*, p. 175.
30. See "Reason and Maximization," pp. 421-433; "Economic Rationality and Moral Constraints," pp. 88-95.
31. See James N. Buchanan, *The Limits of Liberty: Between Anarchy and Leviathan* (Chicago: University of Chicago Press, 1975), pp. 68-70, for explanation of the terminology used here.

Section III: Welfare

Since utilitarianism prescribes the maximization, in some sense, of welfare, its significance and its usefulness as a guide for action turn in part on what notion of welfare it uses. The most widely accepted notion of welfare in recent times is that of the satisfaction of desires. It is not clear, however, that utilitarianism can provide a plausible or even coherent account of morality if it is formulated in terms of the maximization of desire-satisfaction. First of all, getting what one wants does not always make one happier or, in any recognizable way, better off. Second, if getting what one desires were of itself to count as one's being better off, then whatever one were to seek to bring about for others would seem to count as being in one's interest, even if, paradoxically, it were to constitute what we should all recognize as self-sacrifice. Moreover, the seemingly substantive thesis of psychological egoism, that one always seeks to advance one's own interests, would on this conception appear to beome trivially true. Third, it is doubtful that one can formulate a coherent program for maximizing desire-satisfaction that is at the same time plausible. The chief problem is that anyone's desires, or the intensities of his desires, alter over time, so that it is unclear which of his desires we should seek to satisfy, or satisfy first, were we to undertake maximizing his desire-satisfaction.

The first difficulty may be met in part by restricting the notion of welfare to the satisfaction of "corrected" desires. However, although it may be more likely, no guarantee exists that the satisfaction of these will be enjoyed or constitute a benefit.

It may be possible to distinguish between those satisfactions of desire that constitute enhancement of one's interests and those that do not, so as to allow for the conceptual possibility of self-sacrifice and of the disconfirmation of psychological egoism. Mark Overvold offers such a proposal.

Finally, a "flexible" program of desire-satisfaction that aims at each moment of decision to maximize the satisfaction of the desires of the beneficiary at that moment may be a coherent program, though Richard Brandt raises doubts concerning its plausibility as a program of *welfare* maximization as well as concerning its implementation by utilitarians who aim to maximize the aggregate welfare of all members of society.

Brandt recommends a happiness concept of welfare as one that clearly permits (given the possibility of interpersonal comparisons of utility) a coherent program of maximization. He also holds that happiness is more plausibly put forward as that which benevolent persons seek for others. Although he defines welfare as happiness in terms of desire—that in one's current experience the continuation of which one desires for its own sake—Brandt is at pains to argue its important difference from the concept of welfare as the satisfaction of desires.

There may be insuperable difficulties with any account of welfare defined in terms of desire, including Brandt's happiness conception. That is because our desires can be defective in so many ways. The attempt to formulate a concept in terms of "corrected" desires may be thwarted by the necessity of incorporating the very notion to be defined in any sufficiently powerful account of correction. This view is advanced by Thomas Schwartz. One may wonder, on the other hand, how any plausible account of welfare (one in terms of need, for example) can be formulated in complete abstraction from motivation or desire.

10 Two Concepts of Utility

Richard B. Brandt

1

Utilitarians have agreed that acts, laws, and institutions should be appraised by their actual or expectable consequences, in one way or another, more particularly by whether they maximize the utility or welfare of sentient creatures. The various kinds of act utilitarians, utilitarian generalizers, and rule utilitarians agree on this, however much they disagree about whether it is total or average utility, actual or expectable utility, the individual act or the acceptance of a moral rule that counts, and so on.

Utilitarians of all these kinds have a decision to make: how to define "utility" or "welfare," that is, what it is that is to be maximized. In what follows I consider the comparative virtues of two views: the hedonist view, which I shall call the "happiness" theory, and the currently popular "desire" theory. My main conclusion will be that when we spell out the latter theory in its several possible specific forms, we find none to be very attractive.

Of these two, historically the happiness theory came first among utilitarians. Among philosophers generally, the desire theory may have priority, since it was often assumed among the early Greeks that what persons seek or strive for is good. But, if we confine attention to early utilitarianism, which seems to have begun in the writings of Richard Cumberland in 1672 (if not in Epicurus), it was happiness that was thought to be what is to be maximized and to be the sole intrinsic good; indeed Cumberland seems to equate "good" with "happiness." The theological utilitarians generally thought that God aims to maximize the happiness of his creatures.

A desire theory of good or of utility is widely held today among philosophers, and not only among utilitarians but among nonutilitarians. It was urged by R. B. Perry. Recently a form of it has had the support of Rawls. It is

---

I wish to thank James Griffin for allowing me to use the manuscript of an unpublished lecture "Utility as Satisfaction of Desire," given in 1974, for discussions with him, and for his criticism of a remote ancestor of this paper. Griffin, in his lecture, favored a qualified form of desire theory.

defended by R. M. Hare, Jan Narveson, and, essentially, Rolf Sartorius; and it is defended by James Griffin, in an unpublished paper, "Utility as Satisfaction of Desire." I once defended it myself.[1] It appears to be supported by many economists. One contemporary writer on price-theory (Jack Hirshleifer) says: "What modern economists call 'utility' reflects nothing more than rank ordering of preference. The statement 'Basket A is preferred to basket B' and the statement 'Basket A has higher utility than B' are equivalent."[2] He goes on to write that "the economic utilitarians generally . . . [say] that it is the satisfaction of factually observable wants, whether sensate or 'higher,' that should govern policy." (p. 442). Or, as two other economists[3] put it, "Utility means want-satisfying power. It is some property common to all commodities wanted by a person. . . . A commodity does not have to be useful in the ordinary sense of that word; the commodity might satisfy a frivolous desire or even one that some people would consider immoral" (p. 66). John Harsanyi[4] proposes that we "follow the economists in defining social utility in terms of the preferences (and, therefore, the utility functions) of the individual members of society," with some qualifications, as we shall see.

Utilitarians have sometimes adopted *neither* of these theories: They have thought, sometimes, that the good is not identical either with happiness or with the satisfaction of desire. G. E. Moore and Hastings Rashdall, for instance, held that good is an indefinable supervenient quality that belongs to various things like pleasure, virtuous action, knowledge, aesthetic appreciation, friendship, and a distribution of happiness in accordance with merit. What we are to maximize, then, is just the good, and we are to bring about bearers of goodness like states of pleasure or knowledge, in view of the amount of goodness each bears. An emotivist might hold a variant of this view: He might call various things "good," meaning thereby to express his favoring them, and then say that acts are "obligatory morally," thereby expressing a moral kind of favoring, when they promise to maximize the good in his sense. I propose to ignore all views of this sort.

2

We must begin by getting as clear as we can what might be meant by a "desire theory" and a "happiness theory." We begin with the desire theory.

To begin at the bottom, let us note what it is for a person to have a *desire* at a time. To have a desire is not for some introspectible event, like an itch, to occur, but is roughly to have a dispositional property, as follows:[5] Let us suppose a person at a time t has a desire for a state of affairs S to occur. Then we can suppose there is a disposition at t to *tend more* to perform an action A, if the person judges that doing A will make the occurrence of S more likely; to tend to be pleased, if he learns that S is going to be the case when he has been supposing it would not be the case; to tend to be disappointed, if he hears that S is not going to be the case when he has been supposing it would be the case; and so on, possibly with a *ceteris paribus* clause inserted in each of the hypotheticals. We can then say that a person wants S more than he wants S', or prefers S to S', if and only if, other things being equal, he would tend more to perform A . . . and so on.

It is convenient to consider only the "intrinsically desired" in the sense of what is desired at least partly for itself,[6] that is to say, the disposition at t to tend more to perform an action A, if the person judges that doing A would make the occurrence of S more likely even when the judgment that S is made more likely does not include reference to any prospective consequences of the occurrence of S or to any properties of the obtaining of the state of affairs S beyond what is included in the definition or conception of "S." (The same for the other dispositions constituting desire.)

When "desire" is explained in this way, it is obvious that a person can have many desires at the same time. At the present moment, for instance, I would rather like to have something to eat, to be watching a basketball game on television, to get away for a vacation next week, and so on. Desires need not be future-oriented. I can want it to be the case that my friend in India received a letter from me last week; and I can want it to be the case that I spoke more diplomatically yesterday than in fact I did. If I thought I could do something to effect these changes, I would tend more to do it.

We should note that it does not follow, from the fact that one desires at t that S occur—even desires that S be the case at t—that one feels frustrated or disappointed at t even if one knows at t that S is not occurring and probably will not occur. A necessary condition for feelings of disappointment (etc.) is that one thinks consciously, at the time, that S is not occurring and probably will not occur. No unhappiness is caused at t by the failure of a desire to be satisfied unless one thinks about the matter.

Aversions can be explained correspondingly. To say a person has an aversion to a state of affairs S is to say that, if he judges that doing A will make S more likely, he will tend less to perform A than he otherwise would; and so on, *mutatis mutandis*, for the rest of the explanation.

3

If "utility" is defined as "satisfaction of desire," we need to know what is meant not merely by "desire" but by "satisfaction." One, and the simplest, account is this: What it is for a desire for S to be satisfied is for S to occur, or to obtain.[7] According to this account it is not necessary for a person to *know* that S occurred. (Of course, what one might want is for S to occur, *and* to know that it occurred; that is a different desire.) Again, for a desire to be satisfied in this sense is not for the person to be *pleased* that S has occurred, at least in the sense of having been given some pleasure by S or by the thought that S has occurred.

It follows, provided we adopt this conception of "satisfaction," that a person who defines "utility" in terms of desire-satisfaction must say that we put a person on a higher level of welfare at t if we bring it about that there obtains one of the states of affairs that he desires at t. (We shall return to the question whether it is just something he desires at t, or whether desires earlier or later are also relevant.) We put a person on a lower level at t if we bring it about that there obtains one of the states of affairs to which he is aversive at t.

In the case of many desires, satisfaction of them in the foregoing sense brings about a reduction in intensity in the desire, along with various other desires in the same "family."[8] For instance, suppose I want to eat a steak. When I have done so, I normally do not want another steak; my desire for a steak has been reduced to zero. Indeed, I am also likely to be less interested in eating peanuts, or fish—although my desire for drinking something may have been increased. One *could* define "desire-satisfaction" so that it occurs only in this syndrome. But it is not necessary, and it is inconvenient to do so. For one thing, aversions hardly occur in families in quite this way. And some normal-looking desires appear not to belong to a family. Suppose I want to help feed hungry people, and I do so on one occasion; it is doubtful whether that reduces my desire to do so again. Or I want to solve philosophical problems; solving one probably does not reduce the desire to solve more. Again, sometimes when I have had a desire satisfied I am glad that it was—I still want it to *have* happened. It looks, then, as though we do not wish to define "desire-satisfaction" generally so as to require reduction in desire-strength, or to occur only when the relevant desire is a member of a "family."

4

The above conception, that what it is for a desire for S to be satisfied is just for S to occur or obtain, is not sacrosanct, and a person who wants to explain "utility" or "welfare" in terms of desire-satisfaction might wish to add some restrictions. (a) We might say that we add to a person's utility at t by bringing about a desired S at t only if the person is alive at t. Some philosophers would not accept this restriction and therefore consider that we are creating utility if we satisfy the past desires of the dead, even those dead long ago. (b) Another possibility is to say that utility is increased for a person with respect to his or her desire for S, only if both S obtains at some t *and* if the person *believes* at t that S has come about or obtains. If a man desires his wife's loyalty, does she add to his welfare-utility if she is loyal, or if she ensures that he *believes* she is, or only if both conditions obtain? (c) Still another possibility would be to add the stipulation that utility is increased with respect to a person's desire for S only if both S occurs or obtains at some t *and* either the occurrence of S at t or the belief that S obtains or occurs at t brings pleasure to the person.[9]

(d) There is another restriction we shall certainly want to introduce, in one form or another, into any desire-satisfaction theory of "welfare" or "utility." For consider altruistic desires, or the aversion to doing anything immoral, or the desire to be a morally ideal person. If I satisfy one of these desires, for example, if I make a contribution to CARE, it is far from obvious that so doing adds to *my* welfare or utility, as distinct from the welfare or utility of the recipients. Perhaps, as Bishop Butler suggested, I may derive some enjoyment from the satisfaction of this desire, just as from that of any other "particular" desire. But, as Professor Mark Overvold points out in a recent paper,[10] if we are to make a distinction between self-interest and self-sacrifice, I must have some desires that it is not in my self-interest to satisfy, and hence desires the satisfaction of which does not, as such, add to *my* welfare or utility. Every action is motivated by desires/aversions and hence, if we do not make this distinction, every successful intentional act, at least unless the motivating desires fail of being "ideal" in some way (see below), must make a contribution to the agent's own welfare—a result certainly at odds with our ordinary concept of a person's welfare. Bringing about my own death for the sake of a moral principle would have to count as adding to my utility or welfare. I shall not attempt to suggest how this stipulation ought to go; Overvold's suggestion is roughly that producing S adds to a person's utility or welfare only if the person "intentionally" or "ideally" wants (wanted) S and the state of affairs S entails that the person is alive.

5

A further class of possible variations is important in desire-satisfaction theories of utility. One might say that utility consists in the satisfaction of just *any* desire, as foolish as you please. Harsanyi, however, holds that only satisfaction of certain qualified desires constitutes an increase of utility. He says:

> It is well known that a person's preferences may be distorted by factual errors, ignorance, careless thinking, rash judgments, or strong emotions hindering rational choice, etc. Therefore, we may distinguish between a person's *explicit* preferences, i.e., his preferences as they actually *are*, possibly distorted by factual and logical errors—and his "true" preferences, i.e., his preferences as they *would be* under "ideal conditions" and, in particular, after careful reflection and in possession of all the relevant information. In order to exclude the influence of irrational preferences, all we have to do is to define social utility in terms of the various individuals' "true" preferences, rather than in terms of their explicit preferences.[11]

Harsanyi would also exclude preferences based on sadism, resentment, or malice, but let us pass that. Now there is some doubt whether the conditions he describes distinguish "foolish" desires for *things for themselves*, as distinct from "foolish" desires for *means* to things wanted for themselves. But since I believe that some rational criticism can be directed at what we may call "intrinsic" desires, I believe we can follow him in supposing we can distinguish between *actual* and *corrected* or *ideal* intrinsic desires. If we do that, then we might say that one has raised a person's level of utility/welfare only if one has satisfied one of his corrected desires, and not if one has satisfied just any actual desire. For our purposes we can leave the decision between these possibilities open; we shall see later some of the implications of one choice rather than the other.

Thus far I have said nothing at all about what seems a serious problem for the desire-satisfaction theory of "utility," what must be the *date* of the relevant occurrent desire for S, and what are we to say if the person's desire for S varies in intensity from one time to another — and if at some times the person *wants* S and at other times is *averse* to the occurrence of S. I shall come back to this. First let us review the happiness theory.

6

Let us begin with the *concept* of enjoyment or happiness. I am supposing that a person is enjoying (liking) a certain experience if and only if the experience is making him want to continue it (or repeat it) for itself. For instance, I am enjoying a dish of ice cream if the taste is making me want to finish the dish or even order another — for itself, not just to please the person who served it to me. If it is not making me want to eat more, I am not enjoying it. (For very young children, those too young to want continuation of an experience in the sense of "want" explained earlier, it may be more proper to say that what it is to enjoy something is for the experience of it to instigate maintenance activities; for instance, if a child is enjoying an ice cream cone, he will hang onto it hard if someone tries to tug it away.) The definition does not restrict pleasures to so-called sensate ones; a person can perfectly well enjoy reading, or even writing, a paper or book, if the experience makes him want to do that for itself.

This conception differs somewhat from that of Robert McNaughton, who suggested[12] roughly that "x is happier than y" means "x and y are both moments of experience, and x is preferred to y for its own sake," where "prefers" means "one would act to bring about the first experience rather than the second." According to this view, which does not specify the time of the preferring, one could prefer a certain experience at t_1 to a different experience at t_2, with the preference itself obtaining later or even before (if one *imagined* a kind of experience at some time), at t_3. McNaughton assumes that a person can make up his mind permanently about which experience he prefers; the one so preferred is the more pleasant. (Mill might have had something similar in mind in his discussion of qualities of pleasure.) In contrast, I have said that the degree of pleasantness of an experience is fixed by the magnitude of the wanting to continue it for itself, which the experience *causes at the time*. So, on this view, an experience E at t_1 is more pleasant than E' at t_2 if and only if at t_1 E is making the person want more intensely to continue E beyond t_1 than E' at t_2

makes him want to continue the quality of E' beyond t^2. (Whether, at other times, he would prefer another experience like E to one like E' is a wholly different matter, although not causally unrelated.) One might ask how we may know about such matters. To which the answer is that sometimes we can make such comparisons fairly directly, since a person can enjoy various experiences at the same time. For instance, a person may be eating a steak, conversing with a friend, and hearing music; if any of these came to a halt he could know that he wants to continue it. If all came to a halt he could, apparently, know which one he wants to continue the most. If, however, the experiences occur at different times, he would need to rely on memory—recall the intensity of frustration, or remember how much he was willing to pay for a continuation. A main problem with McNaughton's view is that in fact there is not a stable preference-ordering off experiences. In some cases there is stability: The experience of reading a certain novel always is rated above a certain bad toothache. But repititions of an experience make the idea of the earler experience seems less attractive (also less aversive); acquired associations can change its rating; and the same for the dimming of recollection—a feeling of seasickness is less aversive when we are deciding on the rationality of another ocean voyage. I shall follow my account.

It is worth noticing that, just as we distinguished between actual and ideal desires, we can distinguish between actual and ideal enjoyments. For instance, a person might be enjoying talking with another under the impression that the other person respected and liked him, whereas if he believed the truth, he would not be enjoying himself. If one is moved by this point, one will view the happiness theory of utility sketched below as only a first approximation, although I think, quite a near one.

It is theoretically simple to identify the act that will maximize utility in the happiness interpretation of "utility." To reduce the problem to the bare essentials, let us consider just the case of one person X who can do either A or B at t, and who wishes to maximize the welfare of another person Y, over Y's lifetime. Let us ignore the fact that we can know only with probability what will happen; let us suppose we can talk freely just of what *will* happen to Y if A is done, as compared with what will happen if B is done. (To know this, we might have to know what Y will want, or be averse to, at various moments of his life, since this will affect how happy he will be as a result of what happens to him.) We suppose, then, that for every future moment of time we can know what difference it will make to Y's experience whether A or B is done, and hence can decide how much happier (assuming we can measure the happiness of the different expected experiences) Y is at that moment given one act occurred, than he would have been had the other occurred. Let us represent these results by a broken curve, plotting the moments at which he is happier if A is done above the X-axis, the distance above the axis fixed by how much happier he is than he would have been had B been done; and similarly plotting points below the X-axis representing how much happier he is at some moments if B is done than he would have been had A been done. This operation will give us curve-segments probably both above and below the X-axis. Let us then compute the area under these curves; when we know whether the area above the curve is larger or smaller than that under the curve, we know which act will contribute more to Y's happiness over his lifetime. Whatever the practical difficulties in measurement, this conception is clear.

If we want to maximize welfare in general, on this view, we simply construct curves for the happiness-level of everyone concerned, and sum. I anticipate the objection that this summing across persons requires interpersonal comparisons. I happen to think such comparisons are possible, albeit only rough ones; therefore this fact is not an objection to the happiness theory.[13]

7

It could be that an act that maximized utility$_H$ would always be the same act as one that maximized utility$_{DS}$, or that, with a given resource available, what one would do to increase another person's utility$_H$ maximally would be the same as one would do to increase his utility$_{DS}$. We cannot yet be precise on this, pending a discussion of what would count as maximizing utility$_{DS}$. But it will be helpful to consider whether doing what would maximally satisfy a person's desires at t would also produce maximal happiness from t on to the end of his life. Do we know anything about the relation of desires and pleasures that makes at least this coextensiveness plausible or implausible?

Several facts tend to produce a correlation between maximizing satisfaction as defined by desires at t and maximizing utility$_H$. First, since enjoying an experience is wanting it to be continued, giving a person an experience he enjoys is (roughly) satisfying a desire. Second, people generally just want enjoyment; as Bishop Butler pointed out, you can motivate a person by promising him something nice, without telling him what it is. So, when you produce enjoyments, you satisfy that want. Third, when a person has been wanting something for some time he is to some extent pleased by its occurrence just because it is what he wanted. (One may have been looking forward to an opera at Covent Garden for years and be thrilled by the thought, when one finally gets there, that "Here I am at an opera at Covent Garden!" even though subsequently one is bored by a substandard performance.) Fourth, normally a positive correlation exists between strength of desire and pleasure produced, because of the way we get our desires. Normally, we want things because and to the degree that we have enjoyed them in the past (but there are complicating factors, for example, the frequency of past enjoyments); we want to hear Rampal to the degree to which we have liked his music-making in the past. And, since likings are fairly stable, what we have enjoyed in the past is a good clue to what we shall enjoy in the future (not a perfect clue: tastes do change). Psychologists like P. T.

Young, L. T. Troland, and David McClelland have emphasized the role past enjoyments or disasters play in molding present wants and aversions by a process of conditioning.

There are, however, also some notable exceptions to this correlation. It has long been part of the lore of hedonism that some things people want strongly are poor avenues to enjoyment: honor or social status, achievement or success (especially posthumous fame). Desires for these things (or aversions to their absence) often do not come in the normal way, from past enjoyments of them; they arise in the process of "socialization" or "culture transmission." We hear our parents expressing pity for the neighbors whose son has opted to take up motorcycle repair as a life-work; then we associate negative feelings with that occupation. Or a person comes to aspire toward achievement because his middle-class parents rewarded him generously for good marks in school, with embraces and ice cream, and treated him coldly when he came home with poor marks. An aversion to a low-prestige occupation can be very counterproductive as far as hedonic consequences are concerned: One can work hard to avoid this occupation, find little enjoyment in having succeeded in avoiding it, and in fact deprive one's self of what might have been just the happy career for one.

When one reviews these latter facts, it seems doubtful whether maximizing utility$_H$ is necessarily, or perhaps even normally, accomplished by placing a person in the optimal position as fixed by his own preference-ordering at the time of action. The person might even prefer a "successful" life to a happy life, and be quite right that the two are not identical. (Matters might be different if we defined "maximize utility$_{DS}$" in one of the other possible ways, described below.)

We have seen, however, that some advocates of a desire-satisfaction theory would argue that "utility" should be defined not in terms of actual but of "ideal" desires. And it could be that desires/aversions acquired from parental preachments (and similar contingencies) are to be ruled out as not "ideal." In that case, maximizing utility$_H$ and maximizing utility$_{DS}$ might correlate much more closely. To become clear on this point, we require an account of how to identify "ideal" desires. It is not *obvious* that satisfaction of these is going to produce happiness to an extent that maximizing utility$_H$ will *exactly* coincide with maximizing utility$_{DS}$. In any event, if we define "utility$_{DS}$" this way, economists in particular should be put on notice that determining utility-maximizing courses of action is getting complicated and we are moving far away from a simple behavioral test for "ideal" preference-ordering.

The foregoing remarks show that it is at least doubtful whether a program of action that will maximize utility$_{DS}$ will maximize utility$_H$. If the argument is well taken, however, it does not show that either of these programs is *mistaken*; it merely shows that they may be different—that the program of maximizing utility$_{DS}$ will likely comprise different actions from the program of maximizing utility$_H$.

8

I come now to the main argument of this paper: I shall show that the desire-satisfaction conception suffers from a puzzling defect, when we try to work it out in detail.

In Section 6 I explained how in principle to decide, given ideal information, which of two courses of action will maximize utility$_H$ for a person. What we must now do is consider whether we can similarly explain in principle how to decide, given ideal information, which of two courses of action will maximize utility$_{DS}$. I shall argue that there is no plausible way of doing this.

For the sake of simplicity let us set aside the conception of "ideal" desires, and confine ourselves to actual desires.

We can see the problem by looking at a simple example.

Let us suppose I am considering what to do, to maximize utility$_{DS}$ with the funds at my disposal, for my son on his 20th birthday next week. I am considering two courses of action. He has recently manifested a strong desire to learn Greek, and has avowed a wish to possess a Greek lexicon. So one course of action is to order a Liddell and Scott. I am also considering contributing to his nonintellectual life, specifically by purchasing a ten-speed bicycle. We assume the costs of the options are substantially the same. Which will maximize his utility$_{DS}$?

What sort of information may we assume to be available? To parallel the generous information assumed when we discussed the theoretical question of how to maximize utility$_H$, let us suppose that we have a profile of all his intrinsic desires for each moment of his lifetime, and all the consequences of an act we might perform (as compared with an alternative) that would satisfy some one of these desires (aversions). (There is a complication, because a projected action may *change* his desires, for example, if we start a person on a career of morphine addiction. Should we consider his desires as they would be if we performed an action rather than an alternative, or if we performed the alternative, which of course might be *in*action? Presumably the former. But we must remember to count the change of desires as a consequence, and there may well be "second-order" desires/aversions directed at the having/not-having of these desires.) We assume that each of these desires is for some state of affairs to obtain, at some particular time or stretch of time, or perhaps at some indefinite time. We may assume also that to each desire we can assign a number, unique up to a linear transformation, measuring its strength at the time of measurement, determined by some procedure such as that suggested by von Neumann and Morgenstern or more recent writers. If we have these numbers, for any moment, we can rank-order alternative biographies for a person or the world by means of them, for *any particular moment* t_1, if we think of these biographies as combinations of occurrences or states of affairs in which the desires are gratified or frustrated.

It would seem, then, that my project in deciding what to do for my son is to scan all the desires he may have at some time over his lifetime, and take the course of action that will satisfy the strongest set of these desires. But when we scrutinize this conception in detail, it becomes elusive. Let us see why.

The fundamental difficulty for the desire-satisfaction theory is that desires change over time: Some occurrence I now want to have happen may be something I did not want to have happen in the past, and will wish had not happened, if it does happen, in the future. Desires for something may also vary in intensity.

We should not underestimate the extent of such changes. Notice that one acquires some desires and loses others as one matures: One loses one's desire to be an airline pilot, and gains the desire to have a family or at least to provide for it after it arrives. There are temporary fancies: A person suddenly wants to learn Greek, works at it, and then loses interest before achieving mastery. Most obviously, some desires are cyclical, in the sense that after satiation there is a period of no desire for a whole family of events, after which interest is recovered. Some desires, as in morphine addiction, are a result of an earlier sequence of activities. Again, as a person grows older and realizes he has only a finite amount of time to live, he may lose many of his hedonistic interests, acquire a stronger desire to achieve something and make some contribution to the world, and perhaps a desire to have done things differently in the past. (Of course, an equal variety exists in the sources of a person's happiness; and to know what will give him happiness, we need to know, among other things, what his desires are at any given time. But, if the earlier account was correct, this raises no difficulty in principle for deciding which of two courses of action will maximize utility$_H$.)

To see the problem of principle in this situation, let us revert to the example of a choice between ordering a Greek lexicon or a ten-speed bicycle for my son. Let us suppose, for simplicity, that we can lump together his intrinsic desires for getting/having the lexicon, and for the consequent ability to look up words conveniently when occasion arises; and, in the case of the bicycle, the desires to own it and for the consequent ability to go places rapidly. We suppose that we have a picture of the intensity of these desires at every moment over his lifetime. Certain segments of this time span are of special interest: (1) the period before the time t_1 when I make my decision and order the present; (2) the desires he has at the time t_1; (3) the desires he has at the time t_2, his birthday, when he receives the present; and (4) the desires posterior to t_2. Now suppose some change occurs in these desires. For instance, let us say that from age 6 to 18 his desire for a bicycle is to be assigned the number 10, compared with 0 for the Greek lexicon, on his von-Neumann-Morgenstern scale. Then, from 19 until some time after 20, his desire for a Greek lexicon is 15 and the interest in a bicycle down to 5; and thereafter the interest in a Greek lexicon declines to 1, with the desire for the bicycle remaining stationary. How do we decide whether we maximize utility$_{DS}$ by giving the lexicon or bicycle?

(a) One possible procedure is to identify the utility number for having the lexicon for each day (or hour?) of the person's whole life — past, present, and future—sum the numbers, and then compare with the like sum for the bicycle. This procedure is complicated. It is also artificial. For the relative utility of something will depend on how long one wanted something (even though no frustrating experiences occurred, since the matter did not cross the person's mind) before getting it, and on how long one was glad retrospectively to have had it, afterward, even though again one never gave thought to the matter and was not pleased by the thought. (It is true, of course, that we think the gift of the lexicon better justified if the gladness to have had it stands up for five years rather than one day, and this procedure gives place to that conviction.)[14]

There are two somewhat more simple procedures. The first (b) is to proceed as in (a) except that all desires before the time t_1 are to be ignored. The second (c) is the same except that now all desires before t_2 are to be ignored. In favor of these alternative procedures is their relative simplicity as compared with (a)—although one is still committed to thinking of desire-levels for the rest of the person's life after either t_1 or t_2. Also, we think that what a person didn't want at age 8 is no clue to what it is rational to give him at age 20. If a person is deciding what to do for himself, we should think it strange for him to decide on the basis partly of what he wanted or did not want ten years ago (unless he thinks this is evidence for what he does want now or will want later.)[15] Nevertheless, it is not obvious why there should be this asymmetry in the treatment of past versus future desires, on the desire theory. If satisfaction of a desire is for the desired event to occur, whether the person knows about it or not, why has a desire not been satisfied even if it occurred some time ago? (The justification of the asymmetry is clear enough on the happiness theory. For past happiness is irrelevant to action at t_1, since it is beyond change at t_1. But past desires *can* be satisfied by action at t_1.) Moreover, for some cases it does not seem plausible, or at least definitively convincing, to ignore past desires altogether. Consider the following example (for which I am indebted to Derek Parfit and James Griffin): A convinced sceptic who has rebelled against a religious background wants, most of his life, that no priest be called in when he is about to die. But, when he is on his deathbed he weakens as he feared he would, and asks for a priest. Do we maximize his welfare$_{DS}$ by summoning a priest, or not? If we ignore his desires before t_1, we shall send for the priest. (This may be what a person would do who was aiming at utility$_H$.) Some persons will not feel comfortable about this—although one can avoid this consequence (also on the happiness theory) by claiming that the present desire is not "ideal" and hence should be ignored.

The reasons that favor procedure (b) as compared with (a) are also reasons for preferring (c) over (b). Of course, in practice, a person's information about another's desires at the time t_2, available to him at the time of action t_1, will normally be the person's avowals of desire at t_1. So in practice the procedures usually amount to the same, although there can be differences if the interval between the two times is great, as there usually is when one is writing a will.

(d) Both the two preceding programs are somewhat simpler than procedure (a), since there is a large segment of times, with associated utility-numbers, that they propose to ignore. But they are still complicated, and face much the same problem of artificiality as procedure (a). These problems are largely resolved if we decide to ignore *future* desires along with past desires. One can do this by making decisions *solely* on the basis of desires at some particular time, either t_1 (call this program dt_1) or t_2 (call this program dt_2). We have discussed whether it is plausible to ignore *past* desires; the question now is whether it is plausible to ignore *future* desires. If it is, then we might opt for one of these (d) programs.

The first point to notice is that a complication arises about the date t_2. Consider the proposed gift of a Greek lexicon. What is desired is not only the *getting* of the lexicon, but the having of it, and the ability, over a period of time, to look up words conveniently. If we take this fact into account, then "t_2" should refer not to a point of time, but to a stretch of time, and what we should perhaps be considering is not the utility number of the lexicon at the moment of receiving it, but the average utility number over the whole period of its possession (as compared with the average utility number of the bicycle over the same period.) This process gets complicated, but of course much of it can be avoided for a relatively durationless event like an expensive wedding. Suppose that a person at t_2 (and at t_1) wants an expensive wedding badly, but thereafter wishes very much that the money had been spent on some durable goods. Our question is whether it is convincing to adopt a procedure that ignores these latter desires, which were relatively weaker (than the desire for the wedding) earlier, and relatively stronger later.

Some philosophers would certainly hold that the later desires (the regrets, the being glad in retrospect) are not to be ignored. We may recall that some philosophers have thought it irrational to expend effort for pleasure, since the pleasure lasts only a moment and then is gone; they presumably also would be moved to agree that a wedding that lasts one hour and is intensely wanted during that hour (and at the time the decision to have it was being made) is worthless, at least if the parties are not glad it occurred for some period of later time. Indeed, it is possible to think that preference among alternative biographies, at the very end of life, is important for assessing choices, if not decisive. This last proposal, if taken as affirming that utility is fixed *solely* by preferences among possible biographies, just before one's death, is unconvincing. Suppose we provide a person with something that he likes very much and is glad to have over a long period of time; but toward the end of his life he wishes intensely that he had not had it, but had lived a spartan life of sheer intellectual achievement. I do not believe we want to say that we made a mistake in giving him this thing. Utility, viewed as what a rational person would want to maximize, apparently should be defined so as not to leave desires after the event (t_2) matters of indifference, or so as to make all other desires matters of indifference except the preference-ordering just before death.

If we had to make a choice between dt_1 and dt_2, it appears that the reasons for which program (c) is preferable to program (b) could be adduced in support of dt_2. An implication of dt_2 is that a person's utility is not enhanced by what happens after his death; the same holds for program (c).

From a practical point of view, the desire-theory program that would, I think, arouse most sympathy is dt_1. The idea, of course, is that, at the time of decision between two courses A and B, I adopt the recipient's set of priorities at the time (or, alternatively, his set of corrected or ideal priorities). To the extent to which he ignores his own past desires, I ignore them. To the extent to which he ignores his own future desires (or would do so, if his present desires were corrected), I do so. Of course, if we are to consider "corrected" desires, we need to decide how much information we are to require the ideal other person to have and other corrections that should be made; and if we find that he has a second-order desire to maximize his own utility$_{DS}$, *he* will have to be considered as facing the very problem we have been discussing.

It might be argued that this program is practically the most likely or efficient way of maximizing utility$_{DS}$ as defined by one of the other methods, (a), (b), or (c). But it has to be made plausible that this is so, and these other methods themselves we have seen to have serious shortcomings.

Given all these options, how are we to define—and justify defining—"utility$_{DS}$" for any contemplated event S? When choosing between two courses of action, what is it we want to maximize? Perhaps the despised happiness theory is not so bad after all.

9

There is an interesting puzzle that the desire-theorist might pose, as a rejoinder against the happiness theory, at least as framed above. He might say: "You take a motivational, or reduction-to-desire, view of the nature of pleasure, so that in the end the happiness theory of utility reduces to a variety of desire-theory. The difference is that the happiness theory assigns utility only to *moments of experience*, with a degree of utility depending on how intensely the experience is wanted (or its continuation wanted) for itself at the time (of course, with summing over relevant periods of time). So does not this proposal have to be justified by showing that it is somehow preferable to the other desire-analyses that have been proposed? Why should we want to maximize happiness as compared with utility defined in some of these other ways?" Of course, since in fact everyone wants moments of happiness, happiness does have utility according to the other theories.

Is the happiness theory a form of desire theory? Strictly not: for utility is assigned to an experience E at t not on the ground that it is wanted at t (or some other time), but on the ground that its *continuation* is wanted. The point is a fine one, however, and it would seem mistaken to place weight on it.

How may the theory be compared with some of the other desire theories already considered? (1) It is like plan (c) in considering no desires for the occurrence S at any time before t_2, the moment at which S occurs. (There might be added any pleasures of anticipation.) (2) Later desires for the event S are taken into account only to the extent to which they play a role in moments of pleasant retrospection about S; and what is taken into account is not the intensity of the desire for S, but only the intensity of the pleasantness of the reflection about S. Thus no latent regrets, but only actual pangs of regret (and the same for being-glad-that) are taken into account, so that if a person is the type who never looks back, the event that one would regret if one did look back is not made worse by the mere "aversion after the event." In this respect the happiness theory is rather like desire-theory dt_2. (3) The theory is unlike the desire theories in confining utility to moments of experience.

Why might the happiness theory be thought superior to the desire theories?

(1) It is consistent with the intuitions of the many philosophers who have thought that only experience can be intrinsically worthwhile. (2) Pleasure is motivationally basic, in the sense that all our intrinsic desires for a state of affairs S owe their existence to an experience of S having been pleasant, or to something similar to S having been pleasant, or to the association of an experience of S with something else that was pleasant. In that sense Bentham was right that pleasure and pain are on the throne.[16] (3) If the preceding discussions have been correct, the happiness theory is clear and relatively simple; and it does not suffer from the artificial and implausible features of the various desire theories. We might, then, be moved to go along with Sidgwick's statement (made, however, for a slightly different context): "If we are not to systematise human activities by taking Universal Happiness as their common end, on what other principles are we to systematise them? . . . I have failed to find—and am unable to contruct—any systematic answer to this question that appears to be deserving of serious consideration."[17]

10

There is, however, another option for desire-theorists. They might take a pragmatic line and simply abandon the ideal of applying the theory to *all* types of case. They might concede that the theory can be applied plausibly only in case the relevant desire is approximately stable (so that the artificial multiplying of moments by utility-numbers is unnecessary). They might argue that these special situations are the most frequent and most important, and that the application of the notion of maximizing utility$_{DS}$ to them is all, or almost all, we need for practice. Or at any rate, if that is not all we need, it is all that it is possible to get, and we have to learn to live with no more. A person who is thus willing to cut his suit to fit the cloth might then go on to say that program dt_1 is a reasonably good guide to the action that will maximize utility$_{DS}$, for the cases to which that concept is applicable. Incidentally, it might be argued with some force that this program is not a bad rule of thumb for maximizing utility$_H$, especially if the desires are "corrected."

Some philosophers and economists appear to think that some form of desire definition of "utility" is much simpler than any form of the more traditional hedonist theory. An implication of the above reflections surely is that this confidence is misplaced.

Notes

1. In "The Concept of Welfare," S. R. Krupp, ed., *The Structure of Economic Science* (Englewood Cliffs: Prentice-Hall, 1966).
2. Jack Hirshleifer, *Price Theory and Applications* (Englewood Cliffs: Prentice-Hall, 1976), p. 85.
3. D. S. Watson and M. A. Holman, *Price Theory* (Boston: Houghton Mifflin, 1977).
4. "Rule-utilitarianism and decision theory," *Erkenntnis* 11 (1977), 25-53, especially p. 27.
5. The conceptions of "desire" and "pleasure" are discussed much more fully in Chapter 2 of my *A Theory of the Good and the Right* (Oxford: Clarendon Press, 1979).
6. Notice that if we are appraising two courses of action and do not confine utility-assignments to consequences that are desired for themselves, we are apt to get misleading duplications. Suppose we intrinsically want an outcome Z, and we want, because each is an instrument for getting Z, each of Y, X, and W. Suppose also we intrinsically want U, which we can obtain by direct action. Suppose then we are deciding which act will maximize utility, A, which will bring about W, X, Y and Z, or B, which will produce U directly. Now if we want U more than Z, manifestly we should favor course of action B. But if we counted in all the instrumental desires, we might well favor action A. Obviously we should assign utilities only to the extent something is wanted for itself.
7. J. J. C. Smart, in a recent discussion of "satisfaction utilitarianism," in "Hedonistic and Ideal Utilitarianism," *Midwest Studies in Philosophy* 3 (1978):249, writes: "The principle of maximizing satisfaction of desire uses 'satisfy' in a sense related to that in which Tarski says that a predicate is satisfied by a sequence of entities. A person's desire that p (or his desiring-true 'p') is satisfied if 'p' turns out to be true. Presumably Sir Edmund Hillary desired-true the proposition 'Hillary climbs Mt. Everest.'"
8. For the concept of a "family," see my *A Theory of the Good and the Right*, Chapter 2.
9. The first of the above stipulations was suggested in a lecture by James Griffin in 1974.
10. Marc C. Overwold, "Self-Interest and the Concepts of Self-Sacrifice," *Canadian Journal of Philosophy* 10 (1980), 105-118.
11. In his 1977 paper, cited above.
12. "A Metrical Concept of Happiness," *Philosophy and Phenomenological Research* 14 (1953):172-183, especially 172-174.
13. I discuss such comparisons in *A Theory of the Good and the Right*, Chapter 13.
14. This procedure sets no limit on the date on which the desired state of affairs is brought about; thus it is consistent with saying that an event a deceased person wanted during his lifetime adds to his utility—a view held by some. Since I personally do not feel inclined to maximize "utility" in this sense, I hasten to point out two facts. First, it is consistent to deny that one adds to welfare/utility of a deceased person by what one does after his death, and at the same time to concede that the law possibly ought to take account of the known wishes of the decedent at certain points, say in construing his will. But the

reason for this is to give living individuals ability to control the disposition of their estates. Second, much the same is true about morality. It may be that people ought to pay some attention to the wishes of a deceased person, again for the reason that it is a good thing for living people to control the execution of their desires after their death. But this point about morality does not show that we are adding to a person's welfare or utility, after his death, by paying attention to his living wishes. My attention was drawn to these two points by W. K. Frankena.

15. I think we happen to know that a person's actions are a function of his desires and beliefs at the time of action (t_1), so the question whether his act should be determined to some extent by past (or future) desires does not arise — except for second-order desires to be "rational" in some sense, or to satisfy past or future desires.

16. I have surveyed the evidence for this thesis in *A Theory of the Good and the Right*, Chapter 5.

17. Henry Sidgwick, *The Methods of Ethics*, 1907, p. 406.

11 Self-Interest and Getting What You Want

Mark Carl Overvold

I

When we think about a person's self-interest, there is usually little doubt about the kinds of things that enhance welfare. Insofar as one gains happiness, develops abilities, maintains good health, and has a life marked with significant achievement, one will have enhanced one's welfare. On the other hand, pain, misery, failure, frustration, ill health, untimely death, or lack of friends all jeopardize a person's welfare. If we consider the elements on our list, however, they appear to be a motley collection, including elements of health, success, development, and satisfaction. Why are all of these things important? How do they contribute to a person's welfare?

Contemporary analyses of self-interest have usually identified it with some aspect of what the person wants. In "Rationality, Egoism, and Morality," for example, Richard Brandt defines the agent's welfare or utility as what that agent would most want to do if one were fully aware of all the relevant information concerning the act and one's wants and aversions were themselves rational.[1] The important feature of this characterization for our purposes is that it treats the satisfaction of any of the person's wants and aversions as constitutive of an individual's welfare. In this respect the analysis is similar to Von Wright's account of "the good man" in *Varieties of Goodness*, that of most welfare economists, who use indifference curves as a measure of individual utility, and possibly that of Rawls, if we extrapolate from his account of primary goods in *A Theory of Justice*.

Despite its popularity, there are difficulties with the prevailing account. The problems emerge when we reflect on the place of the concept of self-interest in a wider range of concepts including the concepts of self-sacrifice and selfishness. Consider an apparent case of self-sacrifice: An individual dies

---

This paper incorporates substantial portions of my "Individual Welfare and Getting What you Want," which received the 1980 Richard M. Griffith Memorial Award in Philosophy at the Southern Society For Philosophy and Psychology. I am indebted to William Frankena and Richard Brandt for helpful discussions on the topic.

in an effort to save another. Now it seems to me that it would be not only incorrect, but unintelligible, to describe such a case as both a genuine instance of self-sacrifice and an act that enhances the individual's welfare. Let this be our first constraint on the concept of self-interest: The account of self-interest must not be so broad as to allow us to describe the same act as a self-sacrifice and as an act that promotes the agent's self-interest.

At the same time, however, for something to count as self-sacrifice, it must be voluntary and cannot be the result of a blunder. If one is coerced or has absolutely no idea that one's action is likely to harm oneself, we would not describe it as a case of self-sacrifice. But now it appears that any act we might describe as a case of self-sacrifice because it was voluntary and the harm was anticipated will also satisfy the prevailing definition of self-interest, for the agent did choose to perform the act and was not mistaken about the harmful consequences. If self-interest and self-sacrifice are genuinely incompatible, it then becomes impossible for any act to be a self-sacrifice given an account of self-interest that identifies an individual's welfare with the satisfaction of the totality of the agent's desires and aversions. In this way, the prevailing account of self-interest or personal welfare renders the concept of self-sacrifice incoherent.[2]

But we must be careful not to restrict the concept of self-interest too narrowly. In this respect, the concept of selfishness is instructive. It provides our second constraint: For an account of self-interest to be adequate, the following proposition must be intelligible: Action A is unselfish, and action A maximizes my self-interest. This stipulation resists any attempt to restrict a person's self-interest to the class of actions that are performed for selfish motives. It has often been argued, most forcefully by Bishop Butler, that a life of caring for others, i.e., acting at least sometimes from unselfish motives, can in the long run maximize an individual's welfare. Although this need not be true, it does pose an intelligible possibility. An adequate analysis of the concept of self-interest must not make such an alternative conceptually impossible.

The problem, then, is to find a way of specifying the wants and aversions that it promotes an agent's self-interest to satisfy or avoid.[3] An agent's desires might include a desire to help another, a desire to serve a social cause, or a desire to harm another. What would make satisfying such desires an enhancement of an individual's welfare? That they are all *his* desires does not seem sufficient for saying that satisfying one or all of them would promote his welfare. Anything a person does is something for which he has a motive or in some sense wants to do. Yet we would not want to conclude from this that everything a person does is designed to promote his welfare. We can all think of cases in which individuals act contrary to their self-interest. But if some wants and aversions are to be singled out as constitutive of an agent's self-interest and others to be excluded, we need a rationale for the classification, a rationale within the limits set by the relations between the concept of self-interest and the concepts of self-sacrifice and selfishness.

II

In determining which desires and aversions are logically relevant to a person's self-interest, we are interested in those that directly affect, involve, or concern the individual. I suggest that the only desires and aversions that are relevant to the determination of an individual's, S's, self-interest are S's desires and aversions for states of affairs in which S is an essential constituent. An act maximizes S's self-interest if it is the act (or one of them) that S would most want performed if he were fully informed of all the relevant facts, but choosing only on the basis of his rational desires and aversions for features and outcomes of the act that are such that S's existence at t is a logically necessary condition of the proposition asserting that the outcome or feature obtains at t.

What features or outcomes meet this condition? Clearly, any outcomes that involve S's having various types of experiences will be included. It is a logically necessary condition of the proposition that S is in pain at t, that S exist at t. But outcomes or features like S knowing or believing that p, S being a person of a certain kind, or S performing an action of a certain type also meet the condition.

What the proposed restriction excludes are one's desires for the welfare of others, one's desires that others be harmed, that a social cause succeed, and so on, at least when these desires are considered in isolation. Often, however, if what an individual most wants to do, all things considered, is to provide for another's welfare, then performing that act will enhance one's self-interest. But if so, it is not because one's desire for another's welfare is satisfied, in the minimal sense that the agent gets what he wants. Rather, for certain psychological reasons, that he has that desire means that he will also derive feelings of satisfaction as another outcome of performing the act, and it is this outcome, since it is one of his experiences, that makes the act an enhancement of his welfare. In the extreme case, however, where a person suffers great pain and personal loss, possibly even death, for the sake of another, we need not say that he has promoted his self-interest—even if he did perform the act he most wanted to perform, all things considered. If his primary motive was the welfare of another, the strength of that desire does not automatically transfer to the determination of his self-interest. For if his deliberations had been confined to the features and outcomes of the act for which his existence at the time was a necessary condition, then he might have chosen some other alternative. If so, then that alternative, not the act he actually did perform, was the act that would have maximized his welfare.

Intuitively, the restriction seems to give us what we want. The only outcomes or features of the actions that are logically relevant to a person's self-interest on this view are those in which the individual is an essential constituent. All such outcomes or features directly concern one, and insofar as one wants them to obtain, getting what one wants would clearly be relevant to one's personal welfare. The features excluded, on the other hand, are such that they can obtain whether or not the individual exists, and thus appear to be logically irrelevant to one's welfare. One's welfare may be affected by the occurrence or nonoccurrence of such features, but if so, it is due to causal factors that make such features necessary for the individual to be happy, successful, miserable, and so on. When this is the case, presumably there are desires and aversions for these consequences, desires and aversions that do meet the condition that the person exist at the time. It is in virtue of such features that the act that maximizes one's self-interest is determined.

But as it stands, the proposed restriction is inadequate. The purpose of the restriction is to exclude a person's desires for the welfare of others or for the success of a social cause from the class of desires and aversions that are logically relevant to a determination of one's self-interest. Thus, we want to be able to exclude, for example, S's desire for his wife's welfare from the determination of S's self-interest. As stated, the desire would be excluded since it is not logically necessary that S exist at t for his wife to be happy, sad, or successful at t. But now consider the following: S's desire that the present wife of S be happy. If we read "present wife" in such a way that S must be living at the time to have a present wife (otherwise she would be his widow), then S's existence at the time is a logically necessary condition of this outcome obtaining, and thus on the present account would be relevant to a determination of S's welfare.[4] This is not an isolated case, but part of a general problem that threatens to produce a description for any desire whatsoever, such that under that description, S's existence at the time is a necessary condition of the object of his desire obtaining, and thus, the proposed restriction would become vacuous. For any outcome or feature, we can begin the description with "S bringing it about that . . . ," where the stress is on S's active agency, or "S living in a world such that . . . ," placing the feature or outcome in the blank, but with the result that under this description, S's existence at t is a logically necessary condition of the object of his desire obtaining at t. Armed with such devices, it looks as if the totality of an individual's desires and aversions can be made relevant to the determination of an individual's self-interest, despite the proposed restriction. If so, the restriction fails in practice, since there will be no difference between what a person most wants to do, all things considered, and the act that satisfies the proposed definition.

To handle this objection, let us introduce the notion of the *reason* that a person desires that a particular state of affairs obtain. In determining an individual's self-interest, we are not interested in states of affairs where the individual only happens to be an essential constituent, that is, where one's essential involvement plays no role in one's desire that the state of affairs obtain. For the desire to be relevant to one's welfare, the reason that one wants the state of affairs to obtain must be due to one's essential involvement in that state of affairs. Consider, for example, S's desire that he bring it about that his wife is happy. If the only reason for this desire is an independent desire that the person who happens to be his wife be happy, then the desire does not seem to be logically relevant to the determination of his welfare. If he lacked an independent desire for his wife's happiness, his essential involvement in the more complex state of affairs would not give him any motivation to perform an act that would have this outcome. For this reason, the desire should be excluded from the determination of his self-interest. Conversely, if the primary reason for his desire is his essential involvment in that state of affairs, so that he has virtually no interest in his wife's happiness apart from his being the one to bring it about, then it does not seem strange to include this desire in the determination of his self-interest; for in this case, his primary concern is with himself and his involvement in the complex state of affairs.[5]

In general, the only desires and aversions that are logically relevant to the determination of an individual's self-interest are those in which (1) it is logically necessary that the individual exist at t for the object of one's desire or aversion to obtain at t, and (2) the reason for this desire is due to one's essential involvement in the state of affairs. But this formulation seems to presuppose that *the* reason for the individual's desire will be either one's essential involvement or something else. What of cases in which the desire is partly due to one's essential involvement and partly due to other considerations?

Surely, it is only insofar as a person's wanting the state of affairs to obtain is due to or a product of one's essential involvement in that state of affairs that the desire is relevant to the determination of one's self-interest. Insofar as the person wants the state of affairs to obtain for reasons other than one's essential involvement, the desire is not logically relevant to the determination of one's welfare. Thus, in cases in which a person's essential involvement is only part of the reason one wants the state of affairs to obtain, only part of one's desire for that state of affairs will be relevant. But how is this to be determined?

Our original proposal offers us the means of guaranteeing that this will be the case. Basically, the proposal states that an act maximizes an individual's self-interest if and only if it is the act (or one of the acts) that he would most want to have performed if he were fully informed and his choice were motivated only by his desires and aversions for features or outcomes of the act in which he is an essential constituent. We can interpret "if his choice were motivated only by" as being equivalent to "if his choice were motivated as it would be if he did not have any desires or aversions for features or outcomes of the act in which he is not an essential constituent."[6] Thus, the act (or one of the acts) that maximizes an individual's self-interest is the act that he would most want to perform (1) if he were fully informed, and (2) had only those desires or aversions for features or outcomes of the act in which the individual is an essential constituent. This guarantees that when the condition has been met, a person's desire that he be bringing it about that . . . , or his desire that his present wife be happy, depends only on his essential involvement in that state of affairs, and hence the desire is relevant to the determination of his welfare.

Consider, for example, S's desire that his present wife be happy. S is an essential constituent of the object of this desire. But since his desires for states of affairs in which he is not an essential constituent have already been eliminated, such desires could not be the reason for his desire that his present wife be happy. That is, the choice situation that determines the act that maximizes S's welfare is one in which is he choosing without the independent desires for the happiness or welfare of the person who just happens to be his wife, and thus such desires cannot be the reason for his desire that his present wife be happy in the choice situation. The only desires that could be the reason are those for features of the act in which he is an essential constituent, and thus the desire is relevant to the determination of his welfare.

It should be clear how the restriction on the desires and aversions relevant to a determination of an individual's self-interest makes it possible to speak coherently about self-sacrifice. Since some of the desires and aversions are eliminated from the determination of a person's self-interest, it is possible that what he most wants to do, all things considered, is not the same as the act that maximizes his welfare. If so, the person could voluntarily and knowingly pass up an alternative that would have been to his advantage to perform another act that he knows will cost him great personal loss. We can explain the person's choice by citing his desires for the welfare of another, to see justice done, etc. But since these desires do not figure in the determination of his self-interest, it is entirely possible that had such desires not been present, he would have chosen another act. If so, then that alternative was the act that would have maximized his welfare, and in knowingly and voluntarily passing it up, the agent has performed an act of self-sacrifice.

The restriction also enables us to meet the second constraint on the concept of self-interest: A person can perform an act with altruistic motives, but still succeed in enhancing his personal welfare. Our analysis of self-interest says nothing about the agent's actual motive in performing the act. All that is required is that the act coincide with the act that would be chosen when the restriction is imposed. Thus a person could act with no thought of himself, thinking only of what would make another happy. But if this also gives him great feelings of satisfaction and wins praise, even though this is not his motive, it could be that given such considerations, the act he would most want to perform, given full information, but choosing only on the basis of the desires and aversions that satisfy the restriction, is the same as the act that he did choose to perform. If so, he has maximized his self-interest by acting on an altruistic or unselfish motive. In such cases, we can say of the same act that it was unselfish (primarily a question of the actual motive) and maximized the agent's welfare.

III

A number of questions remain. The requirement of full information and the restriction to rational desires and aversions are designed to eliminate problems arising from ill-informed, irrational, and malconditioned desires.[7] But how much information is required for full information? What facts are relevant? How do we characterize rational desires without surreptitiously invoking the concept of welfare? How do we handle the individual whose basic desires change radically over time?[8] These are important questions, but cannot be taken up here.

My concern in this paper has been to argue that if we are to talk about self-interest in terms of satisfying a person's desires, i.e., getting one what one wants, we must restrict our attention to the satisfaction of one's self-regarding desires and aversions. In the space remaining, I would like to explain why the proposed analysis is preferable to the prevailing account.

First, we have seen that unlike a view that identifies self-interest with what a person most wants, all thing considered, the proposed account enables us to speak coherently about self-sacrifice. Moralists have often argued that much of what is admirable and worthy of praise in the moral life involves self-sacrifice, or at least a willingness to sacrifice one's own welfare for the sake of others, if that is what the situation requires. This claim may be open to challenge, but it does present a significant and seemingly intelligible alternative. That the proposed account enables us to speak coherently about self-sacrifice is certainly a powerful reason for preferring that account to one which renders all talk of self-sacrifice incoherent.

A second virtue of the proposed account is that is makes the thesis of psychological egoism a significant claim, rather than trivially true. Unlike the prevailing view, the proposed account restricts the concept of self-interest to the satisfaction of a distinctive and significant class of human desires. Hence, the claim that people are interested only in promoting their welfare, that we are all self-interested, is not compatible with all possible human motives. If individuals sometimes act with the ultimate purpose of making others happy, or seeing that a social cause succeeds, the thesis of psychological egoism is false. This makes it difficult for the defender of psychological egoism to establish his thesis. He will have to show that ultimately all human actions are aimed at providing for the agent, either bringing about states of affairs in which the agent is an essential constituent and which the agent desires or else avoiding states of affairs in which the agent is an essential constituent and to which the agent is averse.

But the increased difficulty has its reward. For if the thesis of psychological egoism can be established on the basis of such an account, this reveals a startling and significant fact about human motivation: Ultimately people are always seeking things like personal health, personal happiness, a certain kind of character, various experiences, and so on. They are never ultimately motivated by a concern for the welfare of others or a desire to see a social cause succeed. And this is just what we would have expected the egoist's claim to involve. The motives included (a desire for happiness, health, success, knowledge, etc.) are all plausible candidates for self-interested motives. The motives excluded (concern for the welfare of others, interest in the success of a social cause, etc.) are those that we suppose the egoist wants to deny a status as ultimate springs of human action.

Thus, unlike accounts of self-interest that identify an individual's welfare with what one most wants done, all things considered, the proposed account makes the thesis of psychological egoism both interesting and significant. The restriction picks out motives that have good claim to being egoistic while it excludes the motives that the psychological egoist is concerned to deny. In doing so, the proposed account provides a sound logical framework for assessing the thesis of psychological egoism.

Finally, the proposed account provides a way of answering the question: "Why should I be moral?" It has often been argued that this question is unintelligible. The standard argument runs as follows: We are most interested in justifying morality in cases where morality conflicts with prudence. But morality and prudence are both ultimate reasons for action, and the only ultimate reasons. When they conflict, there is no third perspective for resolving the conflict, and thus it is in principle impossible to provide a satisfactory answer.[9]

Now it seems to me that the prevailing account of self-interest is a plausible account of the rational act. That is, the rational act is the act which an individual would most want to perform, all things considered. If the argument in this paper is correct, the rational act need not be the same as the act that maximizes a person's self-interest, since the latter is what that person would most want when choosing *subject to certain special restrictions*. The rational act also need not be the same as the moral act. Thus the rational act, on this approach, does provide a third perspective for resolving conflicts between morality and prudence. If the agent has strong altruistic or principled desires, desires excluded from the determination of self-interest on the proposed account, it may be that what one most wants, all things considered, is to perform the moral act at some cost to oneself. If so, it is rational for one to do so.

The above only sketches the argument. But it does show how one could answer the query: "Why should I be moral?" It is a final virtue of the proposed account that it makes this an intelligible question.

Notes

1. Richard B. Brandt, "Rationality, Egoism, and Morality," *Journal of Philosophy* 69 (1972):681-697. Brandt no longer holds this view. For a statement of his present view see his "Two Concepts of Utility," this volume, Chapter 10.

2. For a much fuller development of this argument, see my "Self-Interest and the Concept of Self-Sacrifice," *Canadian Journal of Philosophy* x (1980):105-118. See also Thomas Schwartz's "Human Welfare: What It Is Not," this volume, Chapter 12.

3. Talk of satisfying desires is ambiguous. It can refer to the *feelings* of satisfaction one experiences as a result of getting what is desired, or it can mean simply that the feature or state of affairs desired comes to be, no matter how the person feels about it. The latter is what I have in mind.

4. Philip Quinn was the first of many to call this problem to my attention.

5. Cf. C. D. Broad, "Egoism as a Theory of Human Motives," *Ethics and the History of Philosophy* (New York: Humanities Press, 1952), 219-220.

6. This is misleading, since we will want the agent to take the causal consequences of his having the desire, which do involve him as an essential constituent, into account. The desire itself is excluded from playing a role, but his desires for its causal consequences will enter in if they meet the condition.

7. Cf. Schwartz, pp. 195-196.

8. Cf. Brandt, "Two Concepts of Utility," this volume, pp. 179-181.

9. Cf. J. C. Thornton, "Can the Moral Point of View Be Justified," *Australasian Journal of Philosophy* 62 (1964).

12 Human Welfare: What It Is Not

Thomas Schwartz

For all the criticisms leveled at utilitarianism, one conspicuous and questionable part of the utilitarian legacy remains largely unchallenged and widely embraced. It is the utilitarian conception of human welfare. I call this conception *subjectivist*. It treats a person's own preferences, tastes, or desires as the sole measure of his welfare—his level of well-being. According to the classical utilitarians, something is good for a person to the extent that it makes him pleased, happy, or satisfied. To what extent someone is pleased, happy, or satisfied depends on his preferences, tastes, or desires, broadly construed. And recent theorists in the utilitarian tradition (including most economists who talk about social welfare) have tended to characterize human welfare expressly in terms of preference or desire.

The subjectivist conception is preposterous. Human welfare, ordinarily so-called, is nothing like what the subjectivist says it is. Neither can the subjectivist surrogate bear the normative burden of the genuine article.

1. DEFECTIVE PREFERENCES

One reason for either rejecting the subjectivist conception or taking special care with its formulation is that a person's preferences can be defective in ways that discredit them as a measure of his welfare.

Here are four varieties of defective preference:

(i) *Ill-informed preferences* are based on incomplete or false information. Owing to ill-informed preferences, someone can prefer what is bad for him. Example: Standing next to a tall building, unaware that a safe dropped from

---

In a number of places I have borrowed from my paper "Von Wright's Theory of Human Welfare: A Critique," written in 1973-74 for P. A. Schilpp, ed., *The Philosophy of Georg Henrik von Wright*, which has been forthcoming for some time but has yet to see the light of day.

an upper window is about to land on him, Ignatz prefers that I not push him aside. To do what is good for him—to prevent harm to him—I must act contrary to one of Ignatz's preferences.

(ii) *Irrational preferences* conflict with canons of rational decision-making—with reasonable rules for pursuing one's own objectives, whatever those objectives happen to be. Example: Seeking above all to minimize pain, and aware that going to the dentist right away would cost her less pain in the long run than not going, Bertha nevertheless prefers not to go, owing to weakness of character.

(The reason I have characterized the defect at issue as irrationality rather than character weakness is that I want to allow the possibility of irrational preferences not associated with weakness of character—preferences resulting from poor estimation of probabilities, from incorrect computations, from erroneous canons of decision-making under uncertainty, or the like. One could argue, however, that irrational preferences of these kinds also are ill-informed. I used the character-weakness example to show that irrational preferences do not just constitute a subcategory of ill-informed preferences.)

(iii) *Poorly cultivated preferences* are the result of not having cultivated certain powers of appreciation. You will not much like to ride or play squash if you have not learned how—if you have not developed the necessary skills. Similarly, you will not much like fine wines, great music, or the philosophic classics if you have not learned how to enjoy them—if you have not cultivated the necessary powers of appreciation. To lack such cultivation is not exactly to have wrong or skewed tastes. It is to lack an *ability*—the ability to perceive those features of fine wines, great music, and the philosophic classics whose perception gives people enjoyment.

It is a common belief that we promote the welfare of children and adolescents when we provide them with a good education, including cultivation of their powers of appreciation. And we tend to feel that a person is less well off than he could have been if he has grown up without the benefit of such education, hence without having cultivated his powers of appreciation, even if *he* feels no lack.

(iv) *Malconditioned preferences* have been warped or distorted in unhealthy ways; they are the products of illicit or unfortunate conditioning. Commercial advertising can condition one to relish unwholesome foods. Religious training can condition one to loath sexual pleasure. Political propaganda can condition one to prefer national glory to one's own continued existence. Peer pressure can condition one to want to try dangerous drugs.

A major theme of such social theorists as Plato, Marx, and Skinner is that bad social systems condition people's preferences in ways that favor those systems but conflict with people's "true needs," whereas an ideal society would condition preferences differently. According to this view, the reformer or revolutionary bent on promoting people's *welfare* often must act in ways contrary to people's *preferences*, forcing his beneficence upon unwilling beneficiaries.

There are four things a subjectivist might say to avoid basing welfare judgments on preferences unsuited to the purpose because defective:

Thing 1. Preferences never are defective in any way that discredits them as a measure of their subjects' welfare. Ostensible defects either are not real defects or are not discrediting.

Some will find this position attractive when applied to poorly cultivated preferences. But it is absurd when applied to ill-informed and irrational preferences. And in an age of sophisticated mind-altering techniques, it is hard to swallow when applied to malconditioned preferences.

Thing 2. Instead of defining human welfare in terms of *actual* preferences, we can define it in terms of *hypothetical rectified* preferences—those preferences the subject would have but for certain specified defects.

This approach deviates from pure subjectivism. It bases welfare judgments, to some extent, on factors other than subjects' preferences. How much it deviates depends on what defects are specified. *Any* theory of human welfare can be cast in the seemingly subjectivist mold:

> X is good for a person to the extent that X satisfies those preferences the person would have but for such-and-such defects,

so long as failure to conform to the given theory is a specified defect. Besides, some of the more salient defects, notably lack of cultivation and malconditioning, might be impossible to define without using some such locution as "welfare" or "good for."

Thing 3. Whenever someone has a preference unsuited to welfare judgments by dint of some defect, that preference must conflict with another of his preferences, one that is both stronger and nondefective. So the subject's preferences *as a whole* would be best satisfied if his *defective* preferences were *not* satisfied. In short, defective preferences do not interfere with welfare judgments when welfare is equated with *net* preference-satisfaction (pleasure, happiness).

Unaware of the falling safe, Ignatz prefers not to be pushed aside. But he also (we may suppose) has a stronger preference not to be mashed on the pavement: He prefers being pushed and not mashed to being mashed and not pushed. So although Ignatz prefers not to be pushed, his preferences as a whole would be better satisfied if he were pushed.

Or consider Bertha, weak in character, who prefers not to go to the dentist. She prefers having gone, pain and all, to not having gone. Although the act of going is a necessary means to the end of having gone, Bertha prefers not going to going. Because she cannot have the end without the means, her preferences conflict. Unlike Ignatz, she is aware—painfully aware—of the conflict.

She would doubtless agree that her preference for having gone takes priority over her preference for not going. After all, her preference for having gone already takes account of the cost of having gone and therewith the unpleasantness of going. This does not mean she will go. And it does not mean she should be forced to go. It just means her preferences, taken as a whole, would be better satisfied if she went to the dentist, and so, if welfare is *net* preferences-satisfaction, she would be better off if she went.

Applied to ill-informed and irrational preferences, Thing 3 is plausible. What about poorly cultivated and malconditioned preferences? Defective preferences of these types do not seem to conflict in all cases with other, nondefective preferences.

One might argue, though, that poorly cultivated and malconditioned preferences always conflict with their subjects' "true" or "real" or "underlying" preferences, these being subconscious or otherwise nonapparent. But this is of a piece with Thing 2. It amounts to treating nonpreferential factors — misleadingly described as preferences of a mysterious kind — as the basis of welfare judgments.

Thing 4. Even when defective preferences do not conflict with other preferences, their subject obtains less satisfaction than he would if his preferences were not defective. It follows that a person with defective preferences would obtain more preference-satisfaction if his defective preferences were somehow rectified at low enough cost and his rectified preferences were then satisfied. Often defective preferences are indeed rectified at little cost. Sometimes verbal persuasion works. And sometimes satisfying a person's hypothetical rectified preferences instead of his actual but defective preferences is enough to rectify his preferences: Experience of good things can breed a preference for good things. So the subjectivist equation of welfare with preference-satisfaction adequately accounts for the fact that people who have defective preferences would be better off (other things being equal) if they had nondefective preferences. It also adequately accounts for the fact that sometimes what is good for a person violates his preferences.

This is, I think, the subjectivist's best ploy. But it rests on two questionable, quasi-empirical contentions. One is that nondefective preferences are more felicifically efficient (other things being equal) than defective ones: their satisfaction is more satisfying. Not only is this not obviously true; it is not obvious how to tell if it is true. For it is one thing to compare actions or their consequences according to a fixed set of preferences, quite another to compare sets of preferences: how does one tell, in general, whether one set of preferences has the capacity to be satisfied to a greater degree than another? Can one compare levels of satisfaction without using some fixed set of preferences as measure?

The other quasi-empirical contention is that defective preferences often can be rectified at low enough cost — low enough, that is, to be offset by the gain in satisfaction resulting from increased felicific efficiency. It is far from clear that this contention is true and far from clear how to assess the cost of rectifying preferences. Can one do this without using some fixed set of preferences as measure?

2. SELF-REGARDING AND OTHER PREFERENCES

Say both my daughter and I need medical treatment badly. I can afford the treatment for either one of us but not for both. My preferences are in no way defective. Fully aware of all the relevant information, I decide that my daughter will get the treatment, not I. All things considered, I prefer my daughter's getting the treatment she needs to her not getting it, and so prefer my not getting the treatment I need to my getting it. (I prefer this, of course, not as an end in itself, but as a means to my daughter's health.) I should be happier, more pleased, better satisfied if my daughter got the treatment and I did not than if I did and she did not.

The subjectivist conception has the preposterous consequence that *my daughter's* getting the treatment *she* needs would be better for *me* than *my* getting the treatment *I* need.

The truth: What would better satisfy my preferences (please me more, make me happier) is worse for me, not better. The reason: My preferences are *not self-regarding*: I prefer my daughter's welfare to my own.

Roughly speaking, self-regarding preferences are ones not based on any ultimate objective of promoting the welfare, the goals, or the happiness of anyone but their subject. Only such preferences (and perhaps not even they) constitute strong evidence of what is good for their subject.

My criticism of the subjectivist conception is that it amounts to a form of *psychological egoism* — the doctrine that everyone, at bottom, wants, seeks, or prefers only his own good. If whatever I prefer is good for me, then I prefer only what is good for me. If to be good for me is to satisfy my preferences, to please me, to make me happy, or some such thing, then only what is good for me can satisfy my preferences, please me, make me happy, or whatever. Depending on how it is formulated and qualified, any subjectivist analysis of human welfare will have the following consequence or some variant thereof, suitably qualified:

> Each person is satisfied (pleased, made happy) only by what is good for him.

You might object that this is not quite psychological egoism because to be satisfied or pleased only by what is good for oneself is not the same as seeking or desiring only one's own good: One can prefer what (and only what) is good for oneself because that happens to serve some further, selfless objective. But this could hardly happen *in all cases* if it were true — true by definition, yet — that *everyone always* is satisfied *only* by what is good for himself.

Besides, the consequence just cited is objectionable in just the way psychological egoism is objectionable. It denies the fact of selfless behavior—of self-sacrifice. It denies that a fully informed person can ever sacrifice his own welfare for someone else's—or for a higher goal. It implies that the soldier who throws himself on a live grenade to save his fellows really is doing *himself* some good.

Perhaps the ostensible self-sacrificer always seeks (or at least expects) some sort of *personal satisfaction* (pleasure, gratification). But to reason from this to the conclusion that even the ostensible self-sacrificer always seeks *his own good* is to beg the question whether (as the subjectivist contends and I deny) to satisfy someone is perforce to do him good. In other words, the argument:

> Ostensible self-sacrificer always seeks personal satisfaction
> ∴ Ostensible self-sacrificer always seeks his own welfare

is not valid as it stands, and to make it valid we must add a premise equating personal satisfaction with one's own welfare—the very equation I am challenging.

An analysis of human welfare in terms of strictly *self-interested* preferences would avoid the commitment to psychological egoism. But it would hardly qualify as subjectivist. And it would be circular or nearly so.

An analysis in terms of *nonethical* preferences, besides being nonsubjectivist, would be false: not all selfless preferences are ethical in any sense. Some are downright unethical. Imagine a Mafia godfather happily incurring personal sacrifices that his son might prosper in villainy.

Defining human welfare in terms of preferences that *ignore all people but their subject* (preferences for things specifiable without reference to other people) also would be wrong: sometimes it is good (bad) for a person to marry, to dissolve a business partnership, to visit a doctor, or the like, although such activities cannot satisfy those of the person's preferences that ignore other people.

3. WELFARE AS MINIMAL

Say I want a drink. I prefer having it to not having it. My preference is *not* in any way *defective*. It *is self-regarding*: I want the drink solely for my own sensory enjoyment.

Still, we cannot conclude that the drink would be *good* for me. In the circumstances, if you said the drink would be good for me, you would likely be taken to mean that it would calm my nerves, or that it has some nutritional or medicinal value,—or some such thing. Although I have a nondefective, self-regarding preference for the drink, it is unlikely that the drink would favorably affect my *welfare*. It is merely something I should enjoy.

Sometimes, indeed, a person has a nondefective, self-regarding preference whose satisfaction would be *bad* for him. Someone who prefers to eat too much, knowing that it is too much, could have a character defect, hence an irrational preference. But not necessarily: The person who knowingly sacrifices his welfare for the sake of enjoyment could have made the rational decision to risk shortening his life that he might enjoy it more.

Even if a person's preferences be completely nondefective and self-regarding, his welfare cannot be equated with his level of satisfaction. Welfare does not encompass all aspects of a good or satisfying life, but only certain minimum requisites of good living.

The reason, I suggest, is that to promote someone's welfare is not to provide him directly with satisfaction of any sort; it is to provide him with *certain enduring means of achieving* satisfaction of many sorts—with health, wealth, intelligence, shelter, and the like. It is good for a person to have such things as a cultivated palate, a musical ear, and the strength and motor skills to do well at sports; these things (along with many others) constitute his welfare. Normally, though, delicious tastes, beautiful sounds, and the joy of athletic competition are not properly called good for their subject; they do not constitute his welfare, and they need not contribute causally to his welfare.

4. VARIETIES OF "GOOD FOR"

We call things good for beasts, plants, artifacts, and categories of such, not just for people. Sometimes we call a thing good for a person or category of persons without meaning that the thing would favorably affect anyone's *welfare*. These uses of "good for" resist any subjectivist construction. Yet they do not seem radically different from the "good for" of human-welfare judgments.

When we call something good for a beast or plant, we apparently mean it would favorably affect (enhance, restore, protect) the creature's health. This includes health in the broad, positive sense of strength, hardiness, growth, and long life, not just the narrow, privative sense of freedom from injury, abnormal weakness, and disease.

"Good for" is used *functionally* when we say that lead-free gasoline is good for car engines, that jumping rope is good for prize fighters, that a new type of oil would be good for your car engine, or that increased practice with a sparring partner would be good for Muhammad Ali.

The functional "good for" comes in two varieties: *generic* and *singular*. The generic "good for" always precedes a functional (as opposed to a morphological) general term ("car engines," "prize fighters"). The singular "good for" always precedes a singular term ("your car engine," "Muhammad Ali").

In the generic functional sense, to say of something that it is good for so-and-sos is to say that it helps so-and-sos to function—or to function well—as so-and-sos. "Oil is good for engines" means (roughly) "Oil helps engines to function well as engines." "Jumping rope is good for prize fighters" means (roughly) "Jumping rope helps prize fighters to function well as prize fighters."

Understood this way, something is good for a *kind* of thing, functionally specified, not an *individual* thing.

In the singular functional sense, to say of a thing X that it is good for a thing Y (an individual thing, not a kind of thing) is to say that X helps Y to perform—or to perform well—a certain function. What function? Just some contextually specified function, perhaps; or maybe the function for which Y has been designed or intended or used. If I say, "This new oil would be good for your car engine," I mean the oil would help the engine to work better, to do better the job for which it was designed. Or if, in normal circumstances, someone said, "Increased practice with a sparring partner would be good for Muhammad Ali," I should take him to mean that the recommended activity would help Ali fight better. I should not take him to mean that this activity would favorably affect Ali's welfare.

In a way, to be healthy is to function well. To restore, protect, or enhance the health of an organism is to enable it to get what it needs to function normally and even to flourish, to eliminate function-impairing conditions, and to combat and survive such conditions. So the "good for" of beast and plant health is a special case of the functional "good for." (This requires, of course, that labels like "hemlock" and "armadillo" be understood functionally, not just morphologically. And that gives rise to philosophic problems I shall not now discuss.)

Suggestion: The "good for" of human welfare, too, is a special case of the functional "good for": Something is good for human beings to the extent that it helps them to function (or to function well) as human beings, and something favorably affects the welfare of a particular human being to the extent that it helps him to function (or to function well) as a human being. (This requires that "human being" be construed functionally—that there be a function or set of functions constitutive of the human role or mechanism.) On this view, the concept of human welfare is an extension or generalization of the concept of human health.

Consider the objectives parents pursue when they seek to protect and enhance their offsprings' welfare. Each of these objectives involves some common human function or functions. Each can be regarded as an aspect of health in a very much extended sense. The most conspicuous such objective is health itself, positive and privative, somatic and psychological.

The good parent also ensures that his child is properly educated. I mean this to include, not just formal schooling, but all those things we call training and upbringing and regard as essential to a child's welfare. The principal overall aim of such education is to promote strengths and excellences of the intellect, the character, the neuromotor functions, and the higher perceptual faculties— the intellectual, moral, athletic, and aesthetic virtues.

Might not this objective be described as the *health* of the intellect, character, neuromotor functions, and perceptual faculties? To pursue this objective, after all, is to help ensure that certain "parts" of a person function well, "parts" that admit of defect and weakness as well as normality and strength.

True, this sort of health does not attach to those faculties or parts of the body or the psyche to which we customarily ascribe illness and health. But that may just be a historical accident: As the medical arts grew, they extended their stewardship from bodily organs to *certain* parts of the mind, leaving other parts to other arts. Because functional deficiencies in these parts have come to be treated by professions other than medicine, the corresponding strengths and excellences tend not to be thought of under the rubric of health.

Much else that parents do in promoting their children's welfare can be regarded as providing and securing protections from conditions that could impair the somatic and psychological strengths and excellences (the aspects of "health") just surveyed. These protections include shelter, clothing, food, financial solvency, and the like.

The functions whose strengths and excellences constitute human welfare are those functions that all normal persons possess and value, not those functions that are peculiar to certain roles or objectives. Thus, one who says, "More practice with a sparring partner would be good for Muhammad Ali" probably is not making a welfare judgment. The recommended activity probably is supposed to be good for Ali *as a prize fighter*, not necessarily *as a man*. Of course, if successful prize fighting were the only way Ali could support himself or avoid despondency, then most activities that were good for him as a prize fighter also would be good for him as a man, although probably less directly and to a lesser degree.

5. HUMAN WELFARE, ITS CLOSE COUSINS, AND ITS DISTANT RELATIONS

The concept of human welfare is one of a variety of related concepts I call *value-for* concepts. Each is the concept of a kind of value something can have *for* a subject. Here are seven such concepts:

Goal-relative value for a subject is expressed by the following predicates:

    _____ is useful for . . .
    _____ is valuable for . . .
    _____ benefits . . .
    _____ favors (is favorable to) . . .
    _____ is advantageous for (is to the advantage of) . . .
    _____ is in the interest of . . .

These stand for the relation of a thing to a subject when the thing is efficacious in realizing a *contextually specified goal* of the subject's—or, at least, a contextually specified goal that the subject might reasonably be expected to have.

That goal can be anything. It need have nothing to do with the subject's *welfare*. If it is clear from context that a person is pursuing a certain athletic, commercial, or military goal, and if a change in the weather helps realize that goal, it would be natural to say that the weather change *benefited* the person, was *advantageous* to him, was *in his interest* — although the goal were not his welfare. Sometimes, of course, the contextually specified goal *is* the subject's welfare or some aspect thereof. But not always. Example: Debating Jimmy Carter during the 1976 presidential-election campaign, President Ford, in a slip of the tongue, denied that Russia dominated Eastern Europe. That slip (it is widely held) *benefited* Carter; Ford's assertion followed by Carter's disagreement with it was *to Carter's advantage*.

Welfare value is expressed by these predicates:

    ____ is good for . . .
    ____ is beneficial for . . .

They stand for the relation of a thing to a being whose *welfare* (well-being) the thing favorably affects (promotes, restores, protects).

In a way, the predicates listed under "goal-relative value for a subject" also are commonly used to express welfare value. But only in the sense that they are commonly used in cases in which the subject's contextually specified goal happens to be (an aspect of) his own welfare.

Functional value is expressed by the functional use of "good for," explained earlier. I have argued, in effect, that welfare value is a special case of functional value. Such was Aristotle's general approach.

Human-welfare value is just welfare value applied to humans. I list it separately only because there is a tradition, stemming at least from Bentham, of analyzing human welfare as though it bore no resemblance to the welfare of beasts and plants.

Subjective value is expressed by such predicates as the following:

    ____ makes . . . pleased
    ____ makes . . . happy
    ____ makes . . . content
    ____ satisfies . . . 's preferences
    ____ helps bring about . . . 's goals
    ____ gratifies . . .

Each stands for a relation of a thing to a subject when the thing contributes to bringing about consequences that *he*, in some sense, *values*.

I have already pointed out the striking differences between human-welfare value and subjective value — differences totally ignored by the subjectivist.

Self-interest value is akin to both subjective value and welfare value. It is typically expressed by the predicate:

    ____ is in . . . 's own self-interest

This stands for the relation of a thing to a subject when the thing helps realize some *self-regarding goal or preference* of the subject's.

That goal or preference can, but need not, coincide with the subject's welfare. Suppose I praise Peter's generosity in offering to help Paula carry some books up to her apartment. Someone inclined to a more cynical analysis of Peter's action might say, "Peter was really just acting in his own self-interest, hoping Paula would succumb to his amorous advances when they reached her apartment." If the cynic is right, Peter has pursued a self-regarding goal, but the achievement of that goal probably would not favorably affect Peter's *welfare*. More likely it would merely *please* him. Peter's act of apparent generosity may have been self-serving, but it would be misleading to call the act *good* for Peter. It could even have been bad for him, although he were well aware of its consequences—if, for example, it kept him from keeping a badly needed dental appointment.

Life value is closely related to welfare value as well as subjective value. It is expressed by the following predicates:

> _____ helps . . . to thrive
> _____ helps . . . to flourish
> _____ helps . . . to enjoy a good life

Roughly speaking, these predicates stand for the relation of a thing to a subject when the thing helps the subject to lead a life in which he enjoys a high level of well-being (welfare), develops his peculiar potentials, has ample opportunity to realize those potentials, and enjoys their realization.

The utilitarians have completely failed to appreciate the differences among the various value-for concepts.

6. WHY WELFARE?

Having defined *utility* as happiness, pleasure, preference-satisfaction, or some such thing, a utilitarian might argue thus: "Maybe welfare, ordinarily so-called, is not the same thing as utility. But what is so great about welfare? I contend that moral judgments and public-policy decisions ought to be based on aggregate utility rather than aggregate welfare."

I disagree. To base moral judgments or public-policy decisions on utility rather than welfare is to attach undue weight to the preferences of those who are mercurial, lustful, greedy, bigoted, earnest, meddlesome, and the like, bringing about unjust allocations of social benefits. Suppose Crusoe and Friday have contributed equally to the day's catch of fish and have equal appetites and similar metabolisms. But suppose Crusoe is much *greedier*: Unlike Friday, he gets a big kick out of the mere perception that he has a larger share of fish (or whatever). The most reasonable allocation of fish would surely be an equal division of the day's catch, which also would maximize aggregate welfare. But an allocation that maximized aggregate utility (discounted, if you like, by some index of dispersion) would give the lion's share to Crusoe, unfairly rewarding his greed.

That Crusoe's utility depended on a perceived comparison of his share of fish with Friday's was inessential. Just suppose Crusoe is not greedy but gluttonous: he always wants to eat more at a sitting than can be justified on grounds of nutrition, gustatory appreciation, or postprandial comfort, and he always becomes very unhappy if he does not get all he wants. Once again, an allocation of fish based on welfare would give Crusoe and Friday equal shares, whereas an allocation based on utility would unfairly give Crusoe more than Friday. Or suppose Crusoe and Friday are equally strong and skilled fisherman but Crusoe is much lazier. Then an allocation of fishing chores based on welfare would (we may suppose) divide the burden about equally, whereas an allocation based on utility would unfairly assign more work to Friday (assuming he is not resentful).

If there is some value that individual actions and public choices ought to maximize (a fashionable but questionable contention), it is more akin to aggregate welfare than to aggregate utility (happiness, pleasure, preference-satisfaction).

Objection: It is *undemocratic* not to base public-policy decisions on aggregate preference-satisfaction.

Reply: This assumes that the purpose of democratic decision-making procedures is to satisfy people's preferences, on the whole, to the greatest extent possible. I disagree. Democratic procedures have other, worthier purposes. One is to distribute power widely, preventing concentrations of power and so minimizing the abuse of power. Another purpose is to broaden the pool of ideas by which choices are informed. Still another is to enhance people's sense of participation in, and therewith their allegiance to, the institutions that govern them. Perhaps the most important purpose is to institutionalize such power-shifting, or governmental change, as would otherwise occur in a more violent, less predictable, and therefore most costly manner.

Section IV: Utilitarianism and the Moral Community

In his essay in Section II, Gauthier accepted the thesis that prisoners' dilemma situations reveal a place for a rational ethics embodying a positive, impartial concern for the interests of interacting parties. He argued, however, that rationality coupled with such concern excludes act utilitarianism. The latter, he argued, incorporating a model or rationality suitable to self-interest but not to morality, cannot lead us out of prisoners' dilemma problems in a morally acceptable way.

The adequacy of act utilitarianism is brought into question in another way by prisoners' dilemma situations, arising now in connection with the prospects for voluntary cooperation in the provision of public goods. Rolf Sartorius argues that from the perspective of act utilitarianism, as well as from that of self-interest, an agent will in many typical situations lack a reason to give his uncompelled cooperation in producing goods that by their nature would be enjoyed by all and that would constitute an aggregate net benefit despite the costs of cooperation. These are situations in which one's cooperating or not has little likelihood of determining whether or not the public good in question will be secured. In such situations some form of rule utilitarianism would provide the moral basis for cooperation (as presumably would contractarian principles). *Ceteris paribus*, this would tend to confirm these competing views as against act utilitarianism, but Sartorius claims to find these inadequate on other grounds.

Lawrence Becker argues against Sartorius that as rational, individual maximizers we have good reason to cultivate in ourselves and in others feelings of solidarity and so forth that will lead us to set aside maximizing calculations and to act generally in cooperative ways. This principle will defeat prisoners' dilemmas in those instances where the presence of such attitudes in interacting parties ensures that cooperation has no costs. Provision of public goods will result in such instances as a by-product of the defeat of the dilemma. It would not seem to follow, however, that those who eschew in this way the individual maximizing perspective are led thereby to adopt a utilitarian one. To the extent that attitudes of good will, cooperativeness, and solidarity translate into principle, their view might better be described as contractualist.

If act utilitarianism will not generally provide adequate justification for voluntary cooperation in the provision of public goods, it may, on the other hand, require more of persons in the way of aid to others than will seem acceptable. Dan Brock and Thomas Carson examine this issue in different connections and suggest different assessments of the adequacy of act utilitarianism.

13 Benevolence, Collective Action, and the Provision of Public Goods

Rolf Sartorius

Numerous instances may be cited in which voluntary cooperation among a number of individuals would be sufficient, and might be necessary, to achieve shared social goals. Some familiar and important examples: prevention of inflation, preservation of scarce natural resources, control of population growth and pollution, widespread political participation in a democratic society.

In spite of the important differences among them, these examples share the following significant features: (1) Properly coordinated actions on the part of some but not all of the members of a group are sufficient to provide each member of the group with a social good that each desires. (2) If the good in question is actually produced, its availability to some ensures its availability to all, even those who did not contribute toward providing it (jointness of supply). (3) It is either practically impossible or not worth the costs to exclude free riders (nonexcludability); and in some cases those who would prefer not to go for the ride at all cannot even exclude themselves. The last two features are usually taken to define the class of *public goods*, as opposed to private goods that individuals may purchase and enjoy to the exclusion of others. Contrary to what is often implied by writers on the subject, the possibility of voluntary collective action leading to the provision of a public good does not necessarily create a free rider problem; as in the case of conventions that represent solutions to pure coordination problems, each individual might prefer to cooperate contingently upon others doing so.[1] The problematic aspect shared by our examples arises only when we add: (4) The required form of social cooperation is burdensome; it represents the assumption of real costs by the individuals in question, and (5) the potential value of the collective benefit to each individual is greater than his fair share of the total costs of the cooperation required to provide it.

This paper is a product of research supported by a Population Policy Research Grant from the Ford and Rockefeller Foundations.

A public good, by definition, is some state of affairs such that if it may be enjoyed by some of the members of the group over which it is defined, it may be enjoyed by the other members of that group free of cost, even if they have not shared in assuming the costs of providing it. Assuming that cooperation toward the production of a public good represents the assumption of genuine burdens or costs, how would the rationally self-interested individual view the choice between cooperation and noncooperation?

For any given individual, if a collective benefit that is also a public good is available within a group to which one belongs, it is available to that person free of charge. Once available, no further benefit, to oneself or anyone else, could come from one's sharing in the costs of providing it, at least in those kinds of cases (with which we are concerned) in which the number of individuals whose cooperation is called for is very large, and the contribution that each person is in a position to make, relative to that required from the group collectively, very small. Where a public good is available to the individual, then, rational self-interest dictates that he be a "free rider" and avail himself of it without sharing in the costs of providing it. On the other hand, if the public good is not available, owing to the failure of others to cooperate toward providing it, and one man alone is in no position to provide it all by himself,[2] then assuming the burden of cooperation would simply be a wasted effort and surely not called for by self-interest. So either way, regardless of how others are acting, noncooperation is that which is required of the individual by rational self-interest. Such reasoning on the part of each individual member of a group in a position to provide itself with a public good through collective action leads of course to the goods' not being provided (at least through their voluntary cooperation), and all members of the group are thus worse off than they might have been had they acted otherwise. The individual members of a group that fails to provide itself with a collective benefit in this way are in what has come to be called an n-person prisoners' dilemma.[3]

The choice situation for each individual may be represented in terms of the possible outcomes of the alternative decisions, to cooperate or not to cooperate, where it is assumed that others' cooperating is sufficient to ensure the production of the public good in question and their noncooperation its nonproduction:

	Others	
	Cooperate	*Don't Cooperate*
Individual — Cooperate	Benefits of G Costs of cooperation	No benefits Cost of cooperation
Individual — Don't Cooperate	Benefits of G No costs	No benefits No costs

Given that the benefits of the public good (G) are of a positive value for the individual, and that the costs of cooperation are of negative value, the rationally self-interested maximizer of expected value must have the following preferences over the possible outcomes (expressed in descending rank order):

	Others	
	Cooperate	*Don't Cooperate*
Cooperate	2	4
Individual		
Don't Cooperate	1	3

In the parlance of the decision theorist, the point is that, for each individual, noncooperation strictly dominates cooperation; regardless of how others are behaving, noncooperation is that which maximizes expected value. The situation in which all choose not to cooperate (the lower right-hand cell in the matrix) is a *strongly stable equilibrium point*; it is the best strategy choice for each individual against whatever choices are made by others. But since there is a situation (the upper left-hand cell in the matrix) that each would prefer to it and that could have been brought about by appropriately coordinated individual choices, the outcome is *not Pareto-optimal*. This matrix, as defined by the order of preferences represented within it, has been shown to be the only two-by-two matrix having this unfortunate combination of properties, that is, a strongly stable equilibrium point that is not Pareto-optimal.[4] All can realize that each will be worse off than he might otherwise be, but this will not provide any individual with a reason to change his choice from noncooperation to cooperation. Like Hobbesian individuals unable to rationally contract themselves out of a state of nature and into civil society, they must forgo the benefits of those public goods the creation of which depends on their mutual cooperation.

Having mentioned the notion of a contract, we should take pause here and consider what difference, if any, would be made if the individuals in question were in a position to enter into binding agreements, either because of the existence of some reliable mechanism for the enforcement of promises or because of their recognition of a moral obligation to keep promises. Might not each agree to cooperate contingently on others doing likewise? Not if each reasons that either enough others so agree and the public good thus becomes available to him free of charge or that enough others do not and thus there is no point to agreeing in the first place. General agreement to cooperate toward the provision of a public good, in short, is itself a public good, and the dilemma of collective action can arise with respect to it.

Does not the possibility of this dilemma's arising depend on people acting selfishly? Would not moral individuals—in particular those motivated by a benevolent concern to promote the general welfare even at the cost of personal sacrifice—be inclined to act cooperatively in such situations? Garrett Hardin, whose oft-reprinted "The Tragedy of the Commons" implicitly treats population and pollution control from a public goods perspective, quite clearly assumes an affirmative answer to this question.[5] But although he believes that those responsive to the demands of "conscience" (as he calls it) would voluntarily cooperate toward the provision of public goods, he contends that it would be unwise to call on them to do so. Rather than relying on voluntary cooperation in such cases, Hardin argues that "mutual coercion, mutually agreed upon"[6] is the appropriate approach from the standpoint of public policy. Although the financing of public goods through compulsory taxation is all too familiar, it should be noted that Hardin's position might call for very strong forms of governmental interference with individual freedom of choice where we are concerned with such things as limitation of population growth—e.g., compulsory abortion or sterilization, or criminalization of overfecundity. Why not rather depend on appeals to "conscience"? Hardin's response is double barreled. First, he contends that the long-range consequences of such a policy would be self-defeating, because those who would be responsive to such appeals would eventually be outbred by those who are not—the wicked would inherit the earth, and in excessively large numbers to boot. Second, calling on people voluntarily to limit family size, refrain from polluting activities, and so on would place them in an undesirable psychological "double bind." They would either fail to cooperate and feel guilty for doing so, or cooperate and feel that they were being played for suckers by those who did not.

Neither of Hardin's arguments is very convincing. The first assumes that being inclined to act cooperatively or benevolently is a heritable characteristic — either genetically or culturally. I know of no evidence for this dubious proposition. The second argument has the absurd consequence that one should never call for voluntary compliance with the demands of conscience or morality when this may require self-sacrifice, i.e., in virtually all interesting cases. If Hardin is correct in assuming that a moral basis exists for voluntary cooperation toward the provision of public goods, then I do not believe that we have been given any good reason not to cooperate voluntarily. The resort to "mutual coercion mutually agreed upon"—i.e., governmental regulation—should be viewed only as a *last* resort.

The question, then, is whether or not there is any moral basis for voluntary cooperation toward the provision of public goods. To answer it, it would be necessary to canvass a number of putative moral principles, exploring their defensibility and investigating their implications in cases where public goods provision is at issue. I cannot undertake that task here, although I should note that a preliminary investigation along these lines that I have undertaken elsewhere supports the somewhat disturbing (at least to one with libertarian leanings) conclusion that there are no defensible general moral principles on the basis of which voluntary cooperation toward the provision of public goods might be required.[7] In this paper, I shall confine my remarks to an analysis of what the act-utilitarian principle implies in such cases. (Rule utilitarianism provides a ready solution, I believe, but I am not aware of any acceptable version of that theory.)

In his well-known *The Logic of Collective Action*, Mancur Olson writes:

Even if the member of a large group were to neglect his own interests entirely, he would still not rationally contribute toward the provision of any collective or public good, since his own contribution would not be perceptible.[8]

Brian Barry has called attention to a difficulty with this position: "If each contribution is literally 'imperceptible' how can all the contributions together add up to anything?"[9] Barry's claim, I take it, is that benevolent people, moved by a sense of community, would calculate the benefits of a public good in terms of the entire group to which it would be available. Although the difference that any individual's contribution would make might be very small with respect to the level at which the good was provided, it must nonetheless make a difference; and since the number of people to whom it would make such a difference would be very large, cooperation would be called for on the basis of a calculation of expected utility.

The disagreement between Olson and Barry may, I believe, be at least partially resolved along the following lines: Cooperation toward the provision of a public good may be required of benevolent persons when but only when no significant *threshold effects* are involved, threshold effects being those consequences of individual action that result or fail to result depending on whether or not a sufficient number of others are acting in the appropriate way. Consider, for example, two public goods aspects of the problems surrounding fuel consumption: price inflation and the possibility of the imposition of gasoline rationing. If we assumed that our monetary unit were infinitely divisible, price theory would tell us that, with supply held constant, price *will* vary continuously with demand. An individual's decision to refrain from consuming those extra gallons of fuel oil per month required to heat his home to a very comfortable 70° F rather than a merely tolerable 65° F would thus (in theory) make a difference; a small one, to be sure, but one that would extend to millions of people. So, perhaps, as benevolent persons, we are morally required to turn our thermostats down. Let us also suppose that at some point high levels of consumption would produce such scarcity that the government would impose gasoline rationing. Is *this* also a reason why we should turn our thermostats down? Surely not. Whatever the *threshold* point that would have to be crossed before rationing would be imposed, the likelihood of any individual's level of consumption determining whether or not it is crossed is virtually nil. If this were the only aspect of the problem, each consumer would quite rightly reason that either enough others were "cooperating" so as to avoid rationing or that they were not; either way, the rational and "noncooperative" decision must be to wait and see and remain very comfortable at 70° F in the meantime. Where strong threshold effects are involved, even those motivated by considerations of benevolence may have no reason to cooperate toward the provision of public goods.

Where significant threshold effects are involved, two different kinds of case are worth distinguishing: (1) Those where some one individual will be responsible for the threshold being crossed, but where, because of the large numbers involved, the probability of any given person being so responsible is virtually nil. (2) Those where it is virtually certain that the conjoint effect of the actions of a number of individuals will either fall well below a given threshold or well beyond it. In such cases, the probability of a given individual's act being responsible for the threshold being crossed is zero. For example, the probability of my casting a swing vote in a national election is, for all intents and purposes of moral significance, zero, for the simple reason that it is a virtual certainty that no such election will be won by a single vote.[10]

The situation, though, is still more complex that either Barry or Olson seems to realize. Barry is clearly wrong in maintaining that a number of contributions each of which makes an imperceptible difference cannot add up to a perceptible one; as anyone familiar with the psychology of perception realizes, differences in perceptual magnitudes that are not noticeable may add up to ones that are (for example, adding sugar to a cup of coffee one grain at a time). Olson is clearly mistaken in assuming that the effects of individual cooperative acts will be imperceptible whenever large numbers are involved. If the concept of utility incorporated into the act-utilitarian principle is to be understood in terms of experienced satisfactions (or any similar notion), it would seem that cooperation toward the provision of public goods could be required of the benevolent man only where it would make a perceptible difference. With respect to many important social issues where the provision of public goods is at issue, I suspect that Olson *is* correct in maintaining that the individual is not in a position to make a perceptible difference in the welfare of others even if threshold effects are not involved.

In sum, it would appear that the range of cases in which cooperation toward the provision of public goods would be required of one acting on the basis of the act-utilitarian principle is limited to those in which (a) no significant threshold effects are involved, and in which (b) the individual is in a position to act in a manner that will have a perceptible effect on the welfare of others.

Of course, as suggested earlier, some particular individual might be in a position to produce a given public good all by himself. The self-interested individual will do so where the benefits to him outweigh the total costs of production (including opportunity costs). Such cases do arise; we are well aware that not all actions that in fact work to the public benefit are motivated by a sense of public spirit on the part of those who undertake them. The benevolent individual will bear the entire cost of providing a public good when the benefits to the entire group to which it will be available outweigh that individual's private costs. Such cases also arise, and represent genuine philanthropy. Of course we are often in no position to *know* whether an individual providing a public good has been motivated by considerations of self-interest or benevolence; such institutional mechanisms as tax deductions for charitable contributions muddy the waters (and, in a sense, may be understood as deliberately designed to do so). Whatever their motives, though, individuals are not in a position to produce by themselves the kinds of public goods with which we are primarily concerned; no individual (or family), not even a large number of individuals (or families), can end a fuel shortage, prevent inflation, or limit population growth on a national level. In such cases, the production of public goods clearly depends on the coordinated action of *very* large numbers of people — typically many millions. It is for this reason that each individual can only view a personal potential contribution toward the production of a public good as so minute as to be insignificant, treating the availability of a public good as a benefit of which one can avail oneself free of charge and its absence as something which one person alone can do nothing about.

It must also be noted that behind the construction of the matrix representing the dilemma of collective action lies the assumption that the cooperation of a sufficient number of others to produce the public good in question exists or does not exist *independently* of the decision of the individual to cooperate or not to cooperate. Although this is typically the case, especially with regard to the kinds of cases with which we are primarily concerned, it surely need not be.[11] For a particular individual may be in a position to set an example that others, for whatever reasons, will be inclined to follow. In theory, a given individual might be able to attach specific values to the probabilities that one's cooperation or noncooperation will set an example that will be followed by a sufficient number of others so as to lead to the production of a particular public good. Taking into account the costs of cooperation, the value of the public good, and the probabilities of others following the examples of cooperation or noncooperation, cooperation might be called for as that action which would maximize expected utility. On the assumptions that the value of the public good would outweigh the cost to the individual of contributing toward its production, and that others would in fact follow whatever one set by way of an example, cooperation would be required of either the self-interested or the benevolent individual, for the choice would be tantamount to one between the upper left-hand cell of the matrix and the cell in the lower right, and it is the former that ranks higher in the individual's order of preferences.[12] Examples in which the cooperation or noncooperation of some is likely to influence the behavior of others do abound, but they do not typify our examples. For it is typically in small groups that some person is in a position to set an example of the sort in question, and the setting of such an example will be of value only when the group itself is in a position to provide itself — without the cooperation of other groups — with some positive benefits. When public goods range over very large groups, as is the case with the benefits of limited population growth, resource conservation, and so on, no individual or small subgroup is in a position to influence enough of those others whose cooperation is also required to ensure the production of a public good.

Many current social issues, especially in the environmental area, quite clearly involve the provision of public goods. Although calls for voluntary cooperation in such contexts are frequent and politically understandable, the analysis sketched above suggests that the act utilitarian must conclude that they lack foundation in moral principle. However reluctantly, the act utilitarian thus should also conclude, with Hardin and others, that governmental regulation is required to bring about the changes in incentive structure that will lead both self-interested and benevolent individuals to act cooperatively. At least within democratic societies, those who understand the need for such measures can indeed view them as forms of "mutual coercion, mutually agreed upon."[13]

Notes

1. See David Lewis, *Convention* (Cambridge, Mass.: Harvard University Press, 1969).
2. Either because this would be impossible or because the cost of doing so would outweigh the benefits. Even where an individual could provide some public good by acting unilaterally, he might fail to do so because he believes that someone else will.
3. See Russell Hardin, "Collective Action as an Agreeable n-Person Prisoners' Dilemma," *Behavioral Science* 16 (1971).
4. *Ibid*.
5. Garrett Hardin, "The Tragedy of the Commons," *Science* 162 (1974).
6. *Ibid.*, p. 1247.
7. Rolf Sartorius, "The Limits of Libertarianism," in Robert Cunningham (ed.), *Law and Liberty: Essays in Honor of F. A. Hayek* (College Station and London: Texas A & M University Press, 1979).
8. Mancur Olson, *The Logic of Collective Action* (Cambridge, Mass.: Harvard University Press, 1971), p. 64.
9. Brian Barry, *Sociologists, Economists, and Democracy* (London: Collier-Macmillan Ltd., 1970), p. 32.
10. See Paul Meehl, "The Selfish Voter Paradox and the Thrown-Away Vote Argument," *American Political Science Review* 71 (1977).
11. This point is elaborated upon in James Buchanan, "Ethical Rules, Expected Values, and Large Numbers," *Ethics* 76 (1965).
12. Assuming that the individual does not believe that someone else will set the example. Cf. note 2.
13. Two papers of which I was unaware at the time I wrote this speak to the sort of coordination problems in question. One, by Wayne Sumner ("Cooperation, Fairness, and Utility," *Journal of Value Inquiry* 5 (1971), calls for the selection of fair procedures to determine who shall cooperate and who shall free ride, and argues that cooperation may be called for in the absense of such procedures as that which would maximize expected utility where it is uncertain how others will act. The other, by Jan Narveson, ("Utilitarianism, Group Action, and Coordination," *Nous* 10 (1976), also stresses the importance of procedures and calls attention to the alternative of acting so as to encourage others to cooperate in such situations. Between them, they provide good reasons to believe that the act utilitarian will have grounds for acting cooperatively toward the provision of public goods in many situations. My paper may be viewed as an attempt to establish that there will still be cases not caught by the wide net that their arguments cast.

14 The Free-Rider Problem

Lawrence C. Becker

I

People are often uneasy about the utilitarian requirement: *Act so as to maximize aggregate welfare.* The emphasis on the welfare of all is, of course, one of the things that distinguishes utilitarianism from egoism. But one may be unsatisfied with egoism,[1] be satisfied that a concern for aggregate welfare is the proper direction to take, and yet be wary of the level of self-sacrifice implicit in the utilitarian requirement.[2] That is why Invisible Hand theses are a constant source of fascination. If, for a large range of important cases, the way to maximize aggregate welfare is for each person to behave like a rational egoist, we can have the best of both worlds. We can be utilitarians by acting out rational, self-maximizing strategies.

The disappointments to such hope are well known. The prisoner's dilemma[3] provides one of them. And in public policy cases, sometimes an analogous situation occurs: the free-rider problem.

The problem arises when people want to produce some public good. (A public good is defined as one that, if it is available at all, is *necessarily* available equally to everyone. A paradigm example is clean air. Such a good cannot be "partitioned"—so as, for example, to exclude recalcitrant polluters from the enjoyment of it.) Now if people want some public good; if it can be produced only by the joint activity of a group of people; if people also want that joint activity to be voluntary (rather than coerced) cooperation;[4] and if voluntary cooperation would impose costs on each cooperator; then the following dilemma arises for each rational self-maximizer:[5] Either enough other people will cooperate to produce the desired public good (no matter what I do), or they will not. If they do, and if cooperating would cost me something, then it would be irrational for me to incur the costs of cooperation, for I can reap the benefits no matter whether I cooperate or not. On the other hand, if *not*

I am much indebted to Sarah Crenshaw, Art Poskocil, and Rolf Sartorius for discussion of an earlier draft.

enough others cooperate to produce the desired public good, then the probability of my cooperation's being the increment that makes the difference between success and failure is so small that *again* it is not rational for me to incur the costs of cooperation. So we seem to be in a situation in which each rational self-maximizer must choose to be uncooperative, and in which the Invisible Hand will not produce the desired public good.

I want to argue, however, that the free-rider problem is soluble on its own terms.[6] In a nutshell, my argument is that rational self-maximizers, facing the free-rider problem, would not necessarily have to accept defeat (either by accepting "mutual coercion, mutually agreed upon" or by abandoning the effort to produce the desired public good). Rather, in many imaginable circumstances, they would each embark on a project in moral education designed to defeat the dilemma—a project that required exactly that cooperative behavior from them that they would otherwise refuse to give.

II

The argument begins with a simple observation. Rational calculation is what gets people into this dilemma. Further rational calculation (leading to a conclusion about what one ought to do about the dilemma) must necessarily include an attempt to escape from the dilemma, and the rational self-maximizer must necessarily *prefer* an escape to a defeat—as long as the costs of escape do not exceed those of defeat. (This is so by definition: If rational self-maximizers do not want—equally—*both* the public good at stake *and* the liberty to produce it voluntarily, there is no dilemma.)[7]

The next step, then, is to look for an escape. Rolf Sartorius has considered one—the moral exemplar argument—and rejected it as inapplicable to most cases.[8] I want to consider an escape that, while it may be inapplicable to some cases, *is* applicable to a large range of important ones.

To begin, consider two common occurrences. One is that people often cooperate for the sake of realizing the values inherent in the cooperation itself—quite independently of whether their efforts are likely to produce the public good at which they are ostensibly aimed. People give blood, in part, to get the feelings of solidarity, conviviality, and fraternity that the activity itself provides—and might well continue to do so even if convinced that the expected utility to them of having their blood in the bank could not conceivably offset the costs to them of donating it. They do this because their donation costs are offset by the values inherent in the *process* of donating.

The other frequent occurrence to consider is this: People know the utility (for themselves and others) of spontaneity, of habit, and of learned reflexes. That is, they know that in some areas of human conduct, rational self-interest is best served by acts that are not themselves taken as result of rational calculation. Tennis players can think so much on the court that they play badly; drivers can think so much on the road that they drive dangerously; lovers can be so analytical that they destroy the pleasure they seek. These are familiar problems, but they are not usually thought to raise any theoretical difficulty. Rational self-interest dictates that one define with great care the situations in which it would maximize utility to act reflexively, or on impulse, or out of habit, and then *train oneself to do it* (assuming the expected payoffs outweigh the training costs). That is why a rational self-maximizer who wanted to beat Jimmy Conners at Forest Hills would *practice*—even though the practice were painful. That is why pilots and drivers have *routines*—even though the routines are irksome. That is why, at some point, lovers have to try to stop remembering what the marriage manuals say.

My proposal for an escape from the prisoner's dilemma, then, requires one of two things: either the cultivation (in others) of a set of attitudes that offsets the costs of cooperative action for them (this is what socialists see as one of the functions of feelings of solidarity, conviviality, and fraternity); or it requires the deliberate decision to train others to refrain from thoroughgoing calculative deliberation in these situations (much as realizing the values of loving another person occasionally requires training oneself in the deliberate suspension of calculation). Once that is done, or rather, once agents are embarked on the project of doing it, egoistic calculations may require that the agents themselves behave cooperatively. The argument for this proposal therefore has two basic parts: one designed to show that a rational self-maximizer would try to persuade others to cooperate; and one designed to show that these same self-maximizers would, as a part of their attempt to persuade others, cooperate themselves.

Here is the argument, step by step. First, to rehearse the dilemma, recall that it is *given* that:

(1) Everyone wants public good X.
(2) Everyone prefers voluntary cooperation (as a means to it) over mutual coersion, mutually agreed upon.
(3) Cooperation is costly. And
(4) Anyone who is a rational self-maximizer will refuse to cooperate to produce X directly.

But now, given these points, it follows that:

(5) If enough others could be *persuaded* to cooperate (voluntarily) to produce X, the problem would be solved.
(6) There are at least two ways to persuade (enough) other rational self-maximizers to cooperate voluntarily.
   (a) One way is to (*actually*) offset their cooperation costs by providing substitutes of equivalent value. (Substitutes of equivalent value might include feelings of solidarity, conviviality, and fraternity derived from cooperation, regardless of its success or failure in producing the aimed at public good.)
   (b) The other way to persuade people is to convince them to forgo thoroughgoing rational calculation in these prisoners' dilemma cases (for example, on analogy with the rationality of spontaneity,

habit, and reflex in other areas of life). The point here is to get others to believe that a satisfying life is one in which—in these dilemmas as well as in love, or tennis, or driving a car—one doesn't consider the consequences. (This is a common enough practice. We even have a long history of fossil evidence in the form of slogans: "Give me liberty or give me death." "Damn the torpedoes, full speed ahead." "Death before dishonor." "Don't just stand there, *do* something.")

(7) Now it is assumed, here, that rational agents will not engage in either of these two sorts of attempts to persuade others unless their attempts are "cost-effective"—that is, unless the benefits they themselves will reap from the attempt are larger than what it will cost them to make the attempt.

(8) It is also assumed that the expected utility of their attempts to produce the desired public good is *not* enough, by itself, to offset their attempt costs. (That is, we are here ruling out the cases in which one can persuade others to cooperate just by setting an example.)

(9) It follows, then, that to offset the costs of one's attempts to persuade others, one will have to engage in activities that *serve a double purpose:* that is, activities that are not only designed to persuade but that are cost-beneficial to oneself *whether* they succeed (in persuading others) or not.

(10) It seems plausible to suppose that the likeliest candidate for this double-purpose activity is cooperation itself. That is, it seems reasonable to suppose that to offset others' cooperation costs with conviviality, etc.—*at a cost to oneself that is rational*—one would have to plunge into cooperative acts with the dual intent of persuading others to do likewise and at the same time covering one's losses by reaping the rewards of conviviality, fraternity, and eventually, perhaps, solidarity that often accrue to the generous, friendly, and openhearted. Similarly, it seems reasonable to suppose that persuading others to forgo rational calculation in these cases—again at a cost to oneself that is rational—will require actually *becoming* a person who does not count the cost of cooperation in these cases, so as to be a persuasive example without cost to oneself.

(11) In either case, beginning with a purely self-interested calculation, one is *likely* to find that the expected utility of cooperation is *higher* than that of noncooperation. This is so because, first, one's cooperation costs are offset by other values (fraternity, conviviality, a Stoic/Buddhist indifference to the outcome); and second, there is, after all, some probability that one—together with other rational self-maximizers—will *succeed* in producing the otherwise unobtainable double benefit of the desired public good achieved through voluntary cooperation.

(12) Indeed, if it is rational for a self-maximizer to cooperate, then the probability that the public good will be produced is just the probability that enough people will act rationally for it to be produced.

In short, what I have argued for is *not* the rationality of cooperating in order to produce the desired public good. I have argued for the rationality of cooperating to defeat the dilemma—one by-product of which will be the production of the desired public good.

An interesting consequence of this for public policy deliberations is this: The necessity for governmental coercion in the production of public goods does *not* come from the "fact" that it would be rational for people to be free riders. Rather, in some cases it comes from the fact that we do not want people to be at liberty to cooperate or not, as they wish. (Think of the public good produced by criminal law enforcement.) Or in other cases, the necessity for coercion arises because we cannot expect enough people to be rational to guarantee the production of the public good. The *existence* of rational self-maximizers is not the problem: The problem is the *absence* of them.

III

I want to conclude by considering some objections that might be leveled at my argument.

Objection: Doesn't the free-rider problem just arise again at the second level, here? That is, won't rational self-maximizers reason as follows? Either enough people will choose to cooperate for the purpose of defeating the dilemma, or they won't. ("Enough people" here means enough to produce the public good.) If they do, then I should be a free rider. If they don't, then the probability of my behavior's helping to produce the public good is so low that again I should not cooperate. And so we are back in the dilemma.

Reply: The prisoner's dilemma in public goods cases depends upon the assumption that cooperative behavior imposes *costs* on the agent—costs that can be offset only by the production of the public good. The escape I have argued for imposes no net costs on cooperative behavior. The costs of cooperation are either offset by other values or are necessary to the development of traits of character that are justifiable whether or not the specific public good at issue gets produced. Added to that, there is a finite probability that one's cooperative act will contribute to producing the desired good. Hence, there is no free-rider problem, because the benefits necessary to make cooperation rational do not depend on the behavior of others (as they do in the prisoner's dilemma).

Objection: But surely the benefits of conviviality and so forth *do* depend on others—if not on their being cooperative themselves, at least on their "appreciation" of such efforts. Otherwise there could be no conviviality.

Reply: True enough. But even in that case it would still be rational to try to persuade others not to count the costs of cooperation—to persuade them to become the sort of person who does not do that. And to the extent that *that* required one to become such a person (and act cooperatively oneself) cooperation would still be rational.

Objection: But when one has become the sort of person who does not count the cost in these situations, hasn't one ceased to be a rational self-maximizer? And doesn't a proposal for abandoning rational calculation violate the ground rules for defeating the dilemma on its own terms?

Reply: Not in this case. If it is rational to become X, then one can remain rational only by choosing to do so—even if the result of the process of doing so is the abandonment of rationality itself.

Objection: If the escape recommended here is really rational for self-maximizers, why does it seem (in the abstract) so implausible to expect that certain public policy theorists will accept it—namely, precisely those theorists who advocate thoroughgoing rational self-maximizing calculations on the part of everyone.

Reply: I think some of the resistance to proposals like mine arises because commitment to rational self-maximization as a means to making policy decisions is closely connected to a commitment to an individualist political theory. After all, people will often wallow in a misery of depression because—although they know how to get themselves out of it—they are repelled by what they would have to do to get themselves out. Similarly, individualists are sometimes repelled by the obvious cooperative solutions to their dilemmas. They prefer to wallow in the miseries of individualism. What my argument shows, I think, is that in some important prisoner's dilemma cases, the refusal to cooperate is not the act of a rational self-maximizer. It may well be, of course, the act of a stubborn individualist.

A final objection: Isn't the escape proposed here just a disguised form of rule-utilitarian escapes from these dilemmas?

Reply: No. I am not recommending the adherence to a rule, regardless of the cost in a specific case. I am recommending (repeated) self-interested decisions to cooperate for its own sake, or self-interested decisions to train oneself to become a certain sort of person.

In short, and to repeat, I think this proposal defeats the dilemma on its own terms—not by arguing for the rationality of cooperating in order to produce the desired public good, but by arguing for the rationality of cooperating in order to defeat the dilemma. And the probability that the desired public good will be produced as a by-product is just the probability that enough people will act rationally for it to be produced.

Notes

1. Because, for example, it provides no principle for the moral assessment of the enormous class of acts that have no bearing on one's own welfare.

2. Peter Singer has argued, for example, that utilitarianism collapses the distinction between duty and charity. See his "Famine, Affluence and Morality," *Philosophy & Public Affairs* 1 (1972):229-243.

THE FREE-RIDER PROBLEM   223

3. "Prisoner's dilemma" is understood here in its usual sense—as the name given to a class of non-zero sum, noncooperative games in which each player is faced with two undesirable options—typically represented in a two by two matrix.

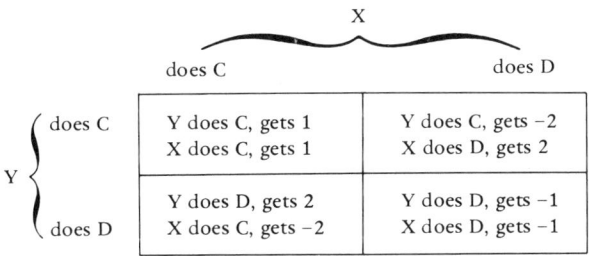

	does C	does D
does C	Y does C, gets 1 X does C, gets 1	Y does C, gets −2 X does D, gets 2
does D	Y does D, gets 2 X does C, gets −2	Y does D, gets −1 X does D, gets −1

These payoffs—and the provision that the players may not make collusive agreements—make each player's options problematic. Each player will want to try for the biggest payoff, which can only be achieved by doing D. But if the other player does the same thing, both players will "lose." (The "D D" cell of the matrix.) On the other hand, a player who does C (hoping for the modest payoff of the "C C" cell) risks disaster. Hence the dilemma. Payoffs may vary widely as long as they maintain the ordinal inequalities in the above matrix (i.e., the best payoff for a player comes when he/she does D and the other does C; the next best when both do C, the next best when both do D; and the worst when he/she does C and the other does D). Some people recommend a further condition—namely that the sum of the payoffs for options in which one player does C and the other D be larger than the sum of the payoffs when both do C. See Anatol Rapoport and Albert M. Chammah, *Prisoner's Dilemma* (Ann Arbor: University of Michigan Press, 1965), p. 34.

4. Some public goods (for example, safety from violent crime) are not in this category. That is, people want them, but they don't want everyone to be free to choose whether or not to contribute to them.

5. There is one other condition that must be met: No member of the group must be able to profit so much from the public good that he or she would be willing to pay the whole cost of its production. In a recent paper, Allen Buchanan has shown that the same free-rider dilemma arises for (rational) *social* utility maximizers. See his "Revolutionary Motivation and Rationality," *Philosophy & Public Affairs* 9 (Fall, 1979):59-82 at 65.

6. Mancur Olson argues that voluntary cooperation to produce public goods (on the basis of uncoordinated and rationally self-interested action by each individual) is sometimes possible—namely when one or more members of the group can expect a benefit in excess of the total cost of providing the good. But this occurs, he says, only in rather small groups. See Mancur Olson, Jr., *The Logic of Collective Action* (Cambridge: Harvard University Press, 1965), pp. 33-34. For large groups—defined as groups "distinguished by the fact that, if one member does or does not help provide the collective good, no other member will be significantly affected and therefore [have] any reason to react"—Olson argues that

> Only a *separate and "selective" incentive* will stimulate a rational individual . . . to act in a group oriented way. In such circumstances group action can be obtained only through an incentive that operates, not indiscriminately, like the collective good, upon the group as a whole, but rather *selectively* toward the individuals in the group. . . . These "selective incentives" can be either negative or positive, in that they can either coerce by punishing those who fail to bear an allocated share of the costs of

the group action, or they can be positive inducements offered to those who act in the group interest.

See Olson, *ibid.*, pp. 50-51. In Olson's terms, my proposal for an escape from the dilemma invokes a "positive inducement." Further, one part of the proposal is an example of what he calls a "social" incentive. And he thinks that, in general, social incentives are effective only in small and intermediate groups (*Ibid.*, pp. 61-62). I disagree. Large groups can certainly be "mobilized" toward a public good by the provision of positive incentives; and these incentives can be social in nature. An example is the blood donation system in England. My proposal, however, is not an argument for the manipulation of incentives by an organization (such as a government). It is rather for the rationality of each agent's acting to provide those incentives for himself and others. (For completeness, one should note that "intermediate" groups, in Olson's argument, are judged able to provide public goods only when the actions of their members are coordinated and organized. An "intermediate group" is one in which "no single member gets a share of the benefit sufficient to give him an incentive to provide the good himself, but which does not have so many members that no one member will notice whether any other member is or is not helping to provide the collective good," p. 50.) For other attempts to beat the dilemma on its own terms, see Jan Narveson, "Utilitarianism, Group Action, and Coordination," *Nous* 10 (1976):173-194, and Wayne Summer, "Cooperation, Fairness, and Utility," *Journal of Value Inquiry* 5 (1971):105-119.

7. A word about "giving up." The option often recommended for getting out of the dilemma—"mutual coercion, mutually agreed upon"—is not an escape from the dilemma. It is a defeat. It is a defeat because the dilemma begins with these assumptions (among others): first, that everyone prefers mutual liberty over mutual coercion; second, that everyone prefers the production of some specified public good over its nonproduction; and third, that liberty and the public good are desired *equally*. (If this last condition were not met, of course, the way out of the "dilemma" would be clear: Sacrifice the lesser good for the greater.) Given mutual liberty, the specified public good is obtainable only through voluntary cooperation. But given mutual liberty, rational self-maximizers will not cooperate. To give up liberty in this situation—to get the public good—is one sort of defeat. To give up the desired public good—in order to preserve liberty—is another.

8. Sartorius mentions that occasionally one can lead others into cooperating just by setting an example. For large-scale socieities as a whole, however, the instances of this are rare. See Rolf Sartorius, "Benevolence, Collective Action, and the Provision of Public Goods," this volume, pp. 214-215.

15 Utilitarianism and Aiding Others

Dan W. Brock

Utilitarianism is the moral view that right action is that action among alternatives open to an agent that will produce at least as much utility as any other alternative. For this quite general and abstract principle to become a precise moral theory, a number of rather complex issues must be resolved, among them the account of utility to be adopted, the way in which utility is to be interpersonally measured, the criteria for delineation of alternatives and consequences, the way in which rules may enter into calculations, and so forth. For the purposes of this paper I shall assume utilitarians can give a satisfactory treatment of them.[1] The issue I want to address here is whether utilitarianism supports a satisfactory theory of mutual aid or aiding others, and if it does not, whether the issue of aiding others helps illuminate one place where utilitarianism is defective. I shall construe the problem of aiding others as raising a subset of the class of distributive issues. My question can be taken as: What does one person (group, nation) morally owe in aid to others? Whatever we decide is owed can be understood as a morally required redistribution, I shall try to avoid the overall problem of distributive justice, that is, how benefits and burdens, for example, income, ought to be distributed. And I shall exclude in turn questions of compensatory justice, that is, what ought to be done to rectify past departures from just distributions. Issues of aiding others are most clearly and pressingly raised when special circumstances create situations in which significant harm to someone will be prevented (or substantial benefits secured) only if some form of aid is received from another person, aid that would in the absence of the special circumstances not be required.

A *theory* of aiding others will provide general principles that specify when such aid is morally required. As a preliminary account, utilitarianism treats this like any other issue and so seems to require that such aid be given whenever doing so will produce a net gain in utility as compared with not giving the aid (and other alternatives). It is simply a matter of weighing up where the gain in utility lies. As has often been noted, utilitarianism seems to place extremely stringent moral requirements on us in cases of aiding others, and in particular it seems to make aid required or obligatory in instances where it is commonly considered supererogatory, i.e., good to do but nor morally required.[2] I shall discuss some of these cases shortly, but before doing so I want to indicate some of the principal issues that a satisfactory theory of aid ought to address. For a utilitarian, these questions may generally be understood as asking for justification of possible limitations on the aid that his theory would seem to make morally required.[3]

(1) Are there any limits as to *whom* one may owe aid? For example, may a stranger starving half-way around the world in Bangladesh be a proper object of my obligatory aid? An important subsidiary question here is whether, and if so to what extent and why, I am morally justified in giving preference in my aiding activities to those I especially care about, or those with whom I have some special or personal relation, such as my friends, family, or countrymen?

(2) In cases where more persons can give the aid than are needed to do so, how is the question resolved of who owes the aid, or who has the strongest obligation to provide aid? And is the strength of my obligation to provide aid affected if others could as (more) easily (or at less cost) provide it?

(3) Is an obligation to provide aid to specific persons affected by whether those persons have provided (would provide) aid when they were in a comparable position to do so? Do we want a theory of *mutual* aid, where the requirement is a reciprocal or conditional one?

(4) Are there any limitations on the *kinds* and *amounts* of aid that one can be morally required to provide to others? There are at least three central subsidiary issues here.
   (a) Are there any moral limits on the extent or kinds of *efforts* that may be morally required of us in providing aid to others?
   (b) Are there any limits on the extent to which we may be required to use our justly acquired *resources* to provide aid for others?
   (c) Are there any moral limits on the extent to which we may be morally required to give the use of, or parts of, our *bodies* to provide aid for others?

Before taking up some of these issues, a preliminary point should be made. Most clearly in cases involving transfer of essential bodily organs, many persons are inclined to object to any position according to which they could properly be obliged to provide aid. Even after reflection, when we have what Rawls has characterized as considered judgments,[4] such objections generally persist. I shall assume here (though for other purposes and contexts it would require argument) that if the implications of utilitarianism on mutual aid conflict with our considered moral judgments, this counts against (though not necessarily decisively) the adequacy of the utilitarian account of aiding others, and in turn against the adequacy of utilitarianism as a general moral theory. However, more must be said to remove the possibility that our objections to considering our organs as proper objects of aid to others in need are merely reflections of ad hoc prejudices and rationalizations based, for example, on our own lack of need for the organs of others, or on some form of nonrational taboo concerning physical intrusions to our bodies. What we must try to do is to identify the more general moral notions or principles that underlie the objection to the utilitarian treatment of aiding others in such cases, and in turn to demonstrate the place such notions or principles have in an alternative, comprehensive moral theory. Only when we have done this will it have been shown that the objections to the utilitarian account of aid are expressions of an alternative, coherent moral conception or theory, whose appeal is not exhausted by its more acceptable account of the particular issue of aid owed to others. Little of that can be done in this paper, but, as space permits, I shall attempt at least to suggest some of the outlines of the more acceptable moral conception.

Now let us look a bit more closely at how a utilitarian will treat some of the issues noted above in a theory of aiding others. First, to whom can aid be owed? Utilitarianism rightly does not exclude anyone as a possible object of our obligatory aid. Aid could be owed to strangers, persons on the other side of the world, citizens of other countries, and so on. However, other things equal, we will be in a better position to aid those we know, whose needs we are aware of and understand; moreover, we can use our resources and efforts more efficiently for those who are in relatively close proximity. These considerations are more forceful still concerning persons attending, other things equal, to satisfaction of their own interests, while others attend to their own interests.[5] Second, a utilitarian can accept the utility of having some settled arrangements, such as the family, for assigning special obligations and responsibilities for those who would otherwise be in need of aid, for example, children and the elderly. An institution that assigns definite responsibility for giving this aid will almost certainly have higher long-run utility than the alternative of each person continually calculating anew with no prior restrictions where his efforts and resources will be most useful. Thus, other things equal, some preference in the use of one's resources for members of one's family is justified on utilitarian grounds. Finally, and perhaps less obviously, the utilitarian can accept the implications here of certain features of personal relationships like friendship and love. These are relationships that answer deep human needs—needs to be befriended and loved, and to give friendship and love in return. Such relations provide important satisfactions and happiness, or in utilitarian terms substantial utility. These relations are not merely a matter of friendly or loving feelings toward another, but rather involve structured expectations, commitments, and responsibilities.[6] In particular, they involve commitments to do things for and with friends that one is not committed to doing for or with just anyone; we can "count on" our friends in various ways that we cannot count on just anyone. And these relationships are such that their value lies in part in their being freely chosen and entered into; it is an important feature of friendship that we are entitled to choose to whom we will make the commitments that friendship involves. Utilitarians can then accept a preference for aiding and caring for one's friends and loved ones, friends and loved ones who will generally be chosen independently of their need for what our friendship or love may provide, because of the high utility of such relationships. Given that it is important to these relationships that they be freely entered into, it follows that some persons will be "unfairly" rich or poor in such relationships and the satisfactions and care they provide.[7] Thus, on the issues of to whom aid may be owed, and on whether and when we are justified in preferring some to others, utilitarianism may be able to provide at least the broad outlines of a satisfactory account. Moreover, up to a point at least, it seems to capture correctly the basis many persons would on reflection offer for these preferences of whom they give aid to. One place it may fail is in its account of the moral justification of the relationships of friendship and love with the special commitments and responsibilities they entail—the utilitarian finds their justification in their high utility, whereas nonutilitarians often appeal to a right or entitlement to enter into such relations independent of their high utility, a right usually embedded within some broader right to self-determination, autonomy, or liberty.

In the rest of this paper, I shall consider whether any limits may be placed on the extent to which our efforts, resources, and bodies may be owed in aid. On this, the utilitarian account seems less acceptable. To see this, consider the following three cases.

Case 1. A great many Americans (as well as members of other developed countries) have or could acquire technical, educational, agricultural, medical, and other skills that if put to work in underdeveloped countries (or parts of our own country) would produce benefits (utility) far in excess of what they will produce in the jobs skilled Americans commonly hold in this country. There are unmet human needs of sufficient importance in parts of the world to make it entirely plausible on utilitarian grounds that many Americans are morally required to devote their lives to meeting those needs; something like a life-long Peace Corps commitment seems morally obligatory.

Case 2. Much of the income of the average middle-class American (and Americans and members of other developed countries as well or better off) is spent on goods and services relatively inefficient in the production of utility in comparison with donating that money to, for example, organizations such as Oxfam and CARE devoted to aiding victims of famine and poverty. Utilitarianism seems to require us to reduce drastically our living standards by donating our income toward such ends, up to the point that it is reasonable to believe doing so produces a net loss of utility; at the least that would require our giving up many or most of the goods, services, and activities of modern American life.

Case 3. Imagine a now only mildly unrealistic situation in which Jones has some special properties that make it the case that only his organs will transplant successfully in Doe and Roe. Doe and Roe will lose their lives unless each receives one of Jones's organs, say a heart and Jones's last kidney, whereas Jones will lose his life if the transplants are made. There are no special personal relations between the three (Jones has been picked out with information on a computer data bank), and other utility affecting factors concerning each are substantially the same. Assuming there is a substantial disutility to a person in losing his life against his will (and if there is not, *that* is a serious problem for utilitarianism), then utilitarianism seems morally to require Jones to give his organs for transplant to Doe and Roe, even though in so doing he will lose his own life, and to justify others in forcibly carrying out the transplants.

In each of these cases, providing the aid needed can be done only at substantial sacrifice to the provider. We may on reflection view one who does provide the aid in such cases as worthy of our admiration and respect—he evidences an uncommon concern for the needs of others. But certainly many persons (I suspect, most) will not hold on reflection that giving aid in these cases is morally required or obligatory, and the failure to do so morally wrong. Either a utilitarian must try to show that in cases like 1, 2, and 3 above utility would not in fact be maximized by giving the aid, or he must accept that giving the aid is in fact morally required.

Consider the former alternative. What arguments can utilitarians employ to place limits on the kinds and amounts of aid owed to others? First, they can note the important general point that the value to us of many activities lies in our (at least within broad limits) unaided performance of them; we generally do not wish others to come to our aid when we are making love or playing a bridge hand. However, this leaves most important forms of aid, for example food, shelter, medical care, and the like untouched. A second general consideration in this area to which a utilitarian might appeal is the security and consequent high utility of being able to form settled expectations about, and exercise control within some limits over, our own efforts, resources, and bodies. The point is most obvious in the case of our bodies—the insecurity of knowing that we could be required, forcibly, to give up our organs to others who "need them more than we do" would be substantial. A public program of involuntary organ transfer might be expected to produce considerable anxiety, even terror, in the general population. And so it might seem that the general insecurity all in a society would likely experience from such a program would be sufficient to outweigh any gain in utility it might produce. After all, only a few would ever need such organ transfers and so be recipients of their benefits, whereas all would be subject to the insecurity and fear of having to give an eye, a kidney, a heart, to another. For utilitarians, however, any substantial insecurity or fear from such a system of organ transfers would appear to be irrational. A system of forcible organ transfers would provide the considerable security, and consequent high utility, to all of knowing that should they need an organ from another, that another would be required to give it and they would be assured of getting it. Although few would ever need the organs of others, just as few (or even fewer) would be required to give them. And the high utility to the person needing a kidney transplant of in fact getting it is obvious. Now of course should such insecurity and fear persist, despite its "irrationality," the utilitarian must take account of it, but he is then able to avoid endorsing the organ transfer system only by appeal to the insecurity and fear that his own theory condemns as irrational. And this consideration, in any case, counts principally against others' being justified in forcing one to give up one's organ, not against it being morally required for one to do so; any consequentialist moral theory will include a distinction between A being morally required to do x, and others being morally justified in coercing A to do x or punishing A for failing to do x.

A third seemingly relevant consideration is not available to a utilitarian. Consider the case of famine. It might be claimed that many persons ought each to contribute a very small amount that would together be sufficient to relieve the famine, but that given that almost all others are not giving what they ought, one is not required to give the now quite large amount of aid that is needed; this large sacrifice is not required, as it is only needed as a result of the failure of others to act as they ought. Although the latter would be true, it does not show that a utilitarian is relieved of the requirement to provide all the aid needed, where he can do so and others are not doing so. The failure of others to act is simply one of the background circumstances in which he acts, and in which the utility of different alternatives is to be calculated; it is like the famine itself, in making the need he could alleviate greater than it would otherwise be. Thus, the failure of others to help will often increase what one ought on utilitarian grounds to do in aiding situations; their failure will not limit what a particular individual must as a result provide. This situation does, on the other hand, suggest utilitarian grounds for setting up a system of aid provision to which everyone would be required to contribute.

The most important consideration a utilitarian can successfully use is probably the necessity for incentives. Unless some limits are set to the extent to which persons' resources can be taken from them to meet the needs of others, as in Case 2, they will not be willing to expend the efforts necessary to produce those resources, or at least their efforts and so production will be substantially reduced. Overall utility would be greater if such self-interested motivation were replaced by fully altruistic motivation, for then we could redistribute resources to the needy without any loss over time in the stock of resources produced and so available for redistribution. However, given the necessity to provide assurance that the results of our efforts will in some degree be left available to us, to secure incentives to produce, there will be limits to the redistribution of our resources. The proper limit will depend on complex empirical information, in the absence of which it is difficult to be specific about *how much* this consideration will help with situations like Case 2. The necessity for incentives will have *some* applicability in Case 1 type situations as well, though it seems not applicable to Case 3 situations.

I believe we can tentatively conclude from this brief examination of some utilitarian considerations relevant to Case 1, 2, and 3 that serious conflict remains between many persons' considered moral judgments in such cases and utilitarian requirements. In support of revising these considered judgments in favor of the stronger utilitarian requirements, a utilitarian can point out that in each of the three cases giving the aid *does* produce more happiness than failing to do so, and he can in turn offer whatever arguments are possible in direct support of the general utilitarian principle. This again suggests that some explication is needed, beyond mere appeal to our nonutilitarian judgments in the three cases at hand, of the moral concepts or principles inadequately accounted for by the utilitarian view and of why persons would want to hold those principles.

Before proceeding, I want to make explicit that on the nonutilitarian view I favor, some principle of the following sort is acceptable: When one can relieve the suffering, or prevent a substantial harm or injury to or loss of life of another, at little cost or risk to oneself, one has a moral duty to do so.[8] (See the discussion below of the Brazen Rule for an important qualification on this principle.) But the issue here is why a duty to aid others has limits of this sort. Case 1, and to a lesser extent Case 2, are both instances of situations in which the needs of others with whom I stand in no special moral or personal relation would morally require the substantial redirection of my plan of life, of the direction my life will take, from the direction I would otherwise choose for my life.[9] This is more clearly true in Case 1 than 2 and suggests a distinction between a person's plan of life and his style of life; I am most concerned here with the former sort of case. Now if what is intrinsically valuable is simply utility, for example human happiness, or the satisfaction of human needs, then Cases 1 and 2 are merely instances where the net balance of human happiness or need satisfaction conflicts with my carrying out my own ends and purposes. Part of what utilitarianism misses here is that we have an important interest in choosing or determining our own ends or purposes according to our own conception of the good, an interest which is independent of whether our doing so will best promote our own, or everyone's happiness or need satisfaction. That is, our good is to be importantly identified with our continuing status as rational and purposive agents or choosers, able to and free to form and modify our plan of life and conception of the good, and not simply with the particular ends or purposes that give content to that plan of life.[10] This issue in a more general form traditionally has often been conceived as the inadequate place utilitarianism seems to give to human liberty, and to personal autonomy of self-determination in directing our lives, and in turn to the excessive place it gives to interventions in people's choices and lives on both paternalistic and general utilitarian grounds. Moral rights—at least so-called claim rights, with their conceptual feature of providing the right-holder with the entitlement to act as he chooses within the area protected by the right, to exercise, waive, and so on, the right as he sees fit—are especially suited to give recognition to this view that our good rests in being free to determine our plan of life and does not rest simply in the content of that plan and the ends and purposes it includes.

The element of autonomy that is relevant here is the feature of persons as able to form purposes, to weigh alternatives according to how they fulfill those purposes, to choose the alternative that best fulfills out purposes, and to act on the result of this deliberative process. What is to be emphasized is that we ascribe independent value to our behavior being determined by our own conscious choice process, value independent of either our own welfare, or society's generally, being best promoted by such choice. Each person's own life is uniquely important to him, in a way that the lives of others, even others to whom he is closely related and about whom he cares a great deal, are not. Our own freely chosen ends and purposes in turn have a special importance to us that the ends and purposes of others do not have. On the utilitarian view, anyone's end or purpose has in principle just as much claim on me and on my action as does my own, and this is why our own ends and purposes on the utilitarian view are too easily overwhelmed by the needs and purposes of others, most especially in "aid to others" sorts of cases.

We can briefly note here that on any moral view that incorporates some right to determine the major directions of our own life on the basis of our own desires and values, it is plausible to argue that we have a responsibility for the foreseeable and reasonably preventable consequences of the decisions we make in determining our life plan. "Responsibility for" not just in the causal sense, but in the sense that each must bear the consequences of his choices, and will have (at least within broad limits) no claim on others to relieve him of those consequences. This is necessary to distinguish cases in which a person through no fault of his own is in need of aid from others — as for example when he needs food to avert starvation in a famine resulting from unforeseeable and unpreventable circumstances such as a long drought — from cases in which he is responsible for his plight — as for example when he lacks food supplies that he possessed and that would have sufficed, because he gambled and lost them or simply let them spoil. In the latter case, a right to aid that could obtain in the former case has been forfeited; the claim he would have had to aid has been forfeited by his responsibility for his situation. Others, out of sympathy for him and his plight, might provide him with the food he needs, but he would not have any moral claim or entitlement to their doing so. The responsibility for determining our life plan then cuts two ways — it provides us with an area of free choice, and it leaves us to bear the foreseeable and reasonably preventable consequences of that choice. There are at least two ways of explaining this feature of forfeitability of an entitlement to aid. First, if our capacities as rational choosers are to support rights within limits to the unimpeded exercise of those capacities, then we "hold" this right to control or determine how we shall act (even in cases when the interference of others with our choice would maximize utility) only on condition of giving up any entitlement to have others intervene to alleviate the bad consequences of our choice (even when utility would be maximized by their doing so). Second, a moral theory that makes some rights basic moral principles takes seriously (and as primary) the moral claims particular individuals have on particular other individuals; it does not view individuals merely as objects for others' benevolence, as more or less promising places where utility or disutility can be promoted or prevented. If we use, as Rawls does, some contract or agreement between distinct individuals as a device for settling which claims are to be acknowledged valid claims, then I believe it is plausible to suppose that parties to that agreement would wish to distinguish between the two sorts of cases considered above in the claims they generate.

The foregoing suggests an even clearer, though likely infrequent, case in which a claim to aid can be forfeited, despite its being true that giving the aid would maximize utility. Suppose Jones needs aid to finance an unexpected and very expensive operation, and in accordance with some acceptable principle of aiding others, the money for the operation has been provided him; but then Jones, instead of getting the operation, gambles and loses the money. Jones at this point will still have the same need as before, and whatever gain in utility would be produced by his having the operation could still be produced by giving him the money for it again. As in the earlier case, some might still, out of sympathy for Jones's continuing medical need, provide him again with the necessary funds (though, no doubt, taking greater care to ensure they are properly spent). But I believe it is clearer still in this case that Jones would have no moral claim on others to receive the necessary funds a second time; it is false that even basic needs in all cases generate claims. The claim he did have was satisfied in the first instance when the necessary funds were provided, and having squandered the funds, nothing further is owed him.

The utilitarian's treatment of both this and the earlier case will likely be similar. In each, he can argue that long-term utility will be maximized by a settled and known policy of not recognizing claims to aid when a person's need for it is a foreseeable and reasonably preventable consequence of his action, of which this latter case is simply one particular instance. Persons will be more inclined to take available and reasonable precautions not to get themselves into situations where substantial aid from others is necessary, if they know that should they not take adequate care, aid will not be forthcoming. This policy will help minimize the number of cases in which such aid will be needed, and though a few may suffer from the policy who do not exercise sufficient care, overall utility will be maximized by the policy over the long term. I do not want to deny either that such reasoning is generally sound or that it is a part of our views about such cases. But it is only a part and leaves out something important. It is important that in each of these cases the needy person has no moral *claim*, in the first case because claims to aid do not extend to cases where the need is "one's own fault," and in the second because what claim there was has been met, and the continuance of the need is not sufficient to establish a continuing claim. On the utilitarian account, were it possible to show that providing the aid in either of the two cases would have no future effects on anyone's disposition to take sufficient care to prevent such cases from arising, perhaps because the provision of aid could be kept secret, then giving the aid would be required and the potential recipient could make a valid claim to it. But showing that the best future consequences can be produced by providing the aid in the case at hand fails to establish that the recipient can claim it *as his due*.

Another important limitation on people's moral claims to aid consists of cases where claims are defeated or forfeited, claims that a principle of mutual aid would otherwise sustain. Michael Slote has formulated what he calls the Brazen Rule to capture this sort of case:

> It is not wrong to omit doing for others what others would have omitted doing for you, if your positions had been appropriately reversed.[11]

Slote's principle is intended to apply only to omissions, in particular the question of retaining or giving away wealth, and does not apply to what he calls commissive immoralities; so, for example, it does not entail that I may rightly kill another who would kill me if he had the chance. Slote argues for the Brazen Rule on the basis of its intuitive appeal, its fit with our considered judgments, and over at least some range of cases its appeal is strong. Perhaps everyday, relatively trivial cases of social or neighborly aid or cooperation show this best. Should I ask a neighbor to help me carry a heavy piece of furniture, and he simply refuse to do so, I would feel he has no right to expect me to help him carry a piece of his furniture later; he then has no claim on my aid. This is a case where the aid is perhaps not required in the first place, but is rather supererogatory, and so I would incur an obligation to help him, for example, only if I had earlier accepted (and requested?) his help. Cases of aid required by the principle of aid supported above are less clearly defeated by the Brazen Rule, but there is still some basis for holding that the aid is even here not required. Again, the clearest cases are ones in which the aid seeker has in fact refused in the past to give the same aid to you. Suppose that in a medical emergency your only nearby neighbor refuses to drive you to the hospital because doing so would interrupt his favorite television program, and you suffer serious and permanent injury as a result. And now that same neighbor, himself in the same sort of emergency, comes to you for transportation. Are you morally required to help him?

Even more clearly here than in the earlier case where the money given for a needed operation was squandered, since the burden to the aid giver is small, we might out of sympathy for his plight provide him with the needed transportation. But this is not to say that he has any moral claim to the aid, nor that we are morally obligated or required to provide it. A person might have adopted a moral ideal for himself according to which one does not refuse such aid to another person; he might believe that no decent person would refuse the aid, even to an indecent person who had refused it to him, and so his moral conception of himself would require giving the aid. In a moral conception that included such an ideal, the Brazen Rule would have to be substantially modified, if not simply rejected. But there is an alternative and plausible moral conception that I believe accounts for the appeal of the Brazen Rule and underlies its defense. This is the contract or agreement account of morality, which has been most fully developed by Rawls for principles of justice, and according to which acceptable moral principles are those principles persons would all agree to in a suitably defined initial position. Such a view is sometimes characterized as morality as reciprocity or fairness, where moral constraints on action, in particular on self-interested action, are viewed as reciprocal or mutually acknowledged and abided-by constraints; each agrees to limit or constrain behavior in the specified way on the condition that others do so as well. Now I cannot, of course, spell out here the suitable agreement conditions or initial position of such a theory, nor make the argument from such a choice framework to a conditional principle of mutual aid, including something like the Brazen Rule. But I believe that the Brazen Rule may be seen as an expression of this view of morality as mutually acknowledged constraints, with its corollary that the constraints do not apply when a person is dealing with those who refuse themselves to acknowledge them. They have by their refusal forfeited their right to have others abide by the constraints in their behavior toward them, and have forfeited their right to criticize behavior of others that violates the principle they have themselves rejected. Care must be taken, however, in any attempt to derive a Brazen Rule from an agreement or contract view of morality, since the agreement view leaves it an open question which, if any, moral principles agreed to would themselves be of the conditional sort exemplified by the Brazen Rule. At least some moral prohibitions could be expected not to be fully conditional in the manner of the Brazen Rule, though it is worth noting that the exception of self-defense to as important a prohibition as that against killing persons may be interpreted as a conditional feature, though of a more limited sort than that in the Brazen Rule. All that I can do here is to suggest that situations of aid to others of the sort under consideration here seem to me especially plausible places for such conditional duties on the agreement or contract view. As Slote has noted, serious difficulties arise in both the interpretation and application of a Brazen Rule, for example, in the meaning of positions being appropriately reversed; I shall not pursue these here. Rather, what I have wanted to suggest is that we can do more than illustrate the intuitive plausibility of a Brazen Rule, as Slote does. We can show as well the sort of general moral theory in which such a rule will, or will not, have a place; and since such general moral theories may be supported or argued for independent of their fit with our particular moral intuitions or considered judgments, what sort of theory the Brazen Rule will fit will be partially determinative of its acceptability.

Finally, consider Case 3 above, where the needed aid takes the form of organ redistribution, and is possible only at the high cost of the loss of life of the aid giver.[12] In many respects, this case raises the most complex issues of the three and is least amenable to brief treatment. It is not possible here even to begin a full defense of the nonutilitarian position, but at least the nature of that position and what the issues are can be suggested. At least two important moral rights seem relevant here, the first being the right not to be killed. Jones would then be acting within his rights in refusing to grant permission to others to take the needed organs from him, and others would violate his right not to be killed were they to attempt forcibly to kill him to do so. The second relevant right is a property right. Surely, if we own anything, we own our bodies and the important parts thereof. If so, this property right would seem to protect our free choice of how to use and dispose of our body so as to cover the case at hand; it gives Jones a moral claim on Jones's organs that Doe and Roe do not have. It is not a case of Jones having forfeited either right, as he would have were he intentionally and wrongly attempting to kill Doe or Roe, nor does it seem a kind of use of his body to which his right does not extend, as in a case where he is about deliberately to bring his fist into forceful contact with Doe's jaw. Nor is it a case of his having waived his right, as for example if he had freely and voluntarily promised his organs to Doe and Roe should circumstances of the sort imagined in fact occur. Nor, finally, is it a case simply of choosing whom to save when we cannot save all who need saving, for example, if we could use scarce medicine to save Jones but not Doe and Roe, or Doe and Roe but not Jones, whereas if we give the medicine to none of them all will die. In cases of this latter sort where no one person has any greater claim on the scarce medicine than the others, we would be justified in attempting to save the most lives possible.[13] However, just because the organs are Jones's, he has a claim the others do not have. That Jones has a claim on his organs that Doe and Roe do not have is part of what is wrong with it being obligatory for Jones to give up his organs, and for others forcibly to take them, though I believe there is more as well.

Just how to formulate what else is relevant here is by no means clear. What is needed, I believe, is some distinction between what we deliberately or intentionally do to others, as opposed to what we merely allow to happen.[14] In Case 3 we must intentionally kill Jones, as well as take from him what is his, to save Doe and Roe, and not merely allow him to die; whereas if we do nothing, it is the diseases that will kill Doe and Roe, not Jones who refuses to give up his organs and his life for them. There is no agreement among nonconsequentialists even about what is the correct distinction to be applied to cases of this sort, much less on how the distinction is to be coherently and precisely drawn, and why in turn it is morally relevant. The appropriate distinction here is not, as is sometimes thought, that between acts and omissions, since, as is made clear in the literature on this topic, one can deliberately bring about another's death, by omitting to act, in a way just as blameworthy as if one had killed him. Nor in turn, I believe, is the necessary distinction that between killing and letting die or failing to save; once again, there seem to be pairs of cases in which the only relevant difference is that one is an instance of killing and the other of letting die, but where there is no moral difference in the wrongness.[15] Other philosophers have thought the distinction lies in the difference between positive (here, to save) and negative (here, not to kill) duties, and the putative greater strength of the latter, but this too seems difficult to defend over all possible cases.[16]

Using the distinction between what we deliverately do to others, or intend to bring about as opposed to what we merely allow to happen or fail to prevent, we can appeal to the common belief that we each have a greater responsibility for the former than the latter. Despite their obvious importance, I shall not attempt here either to formulate this distinction more precisely or to extend the defense of its moral relevance; in my view, this latter would require developing the full moral conception in which this distinction plays a part.

A utilitarian might make a number of responses, of which I shall consider three. David Gauthier has suggested in discussion the following scheme to avoid the utilitarian commitment to forcible organ transfers. Establish an insurance system under which one can obtain an organ for transplant, should it become needed. The "cost" of this insurance is participation in the pool from among whom "donors" will be chosen, presumably by a lottery method (or utilitarian calculus?) when there is more than one possible donor in the insurance system. In any such insurance system, the principal benefit to be gained is an organ, should it become needed, and the burden is the risk of losing an organ to another. Given different values placed on length of life, bodily integrity, and so on, by different persons, how do we know whether such an insurance scheme would maximize utility? If utility is in some way linked to preferences, then perhaps we can assume that those who freely choose to enter the insurance scheme calculate the potential benefits of the scheme to be greater than its burdens, while those who freely forgo participation calculate that participation would create for them a net disutility. Those who found the potential gain of getting a needed organ greater than the potential loss of losing one to another would be in the insurance system and would get an organ when necessary. Those who found the potential loss of an organ worse than the potential gain of one would not be in the system and would not have claim on another's organ. Utility would seem to be maximized over the two groups, as members of each obtain their higher valued alternative.

There would clearly be a number of serious practical difficulties in instituting and operating such an insurance system. But even assuming that such a system was in operation, it seems not to meet this objection to utilitarianism. One difficulty is that it is probably not possible plausibly to equate utility with the actual, voluntary choices of persons to join or not to join the system in the manner necessary to sustain the claim that the system would maximize utility; too many features of such decisions would likely make them not fully rational. Second, it need not be the case that having such an insurance system would produce greater utility than not having one. All the system allows us to assume is that for each member, the utility to him of getting a needed organ is greater than the disutility in having to provide one. But this is consistent with the operation of the insurance system producing overall a net disutility. To see this, suppose we can make interpersonal cardinal utility assignments and that there are, for simplicity, only two participants, Jane and John, with the following utility assignments, already discounted for the probability of needing or having to give an organ.

	Utility of Getting an Organ When Needed	Disutility of Giving an Organ to Another
Jane	40	-30
John	100	-80

Suppose Jane needs the organ and it must come from John. Although both are voluntary participants in the system, the organ transfer will produce a net utility of -40. On utilitarian grounds, it ought not to be made.

But this suggests the more serious difficulty that utilitarianism *would* require transfers from members of the insurance system to nonmembers, from nonmembers to members, as well as from nonmembers to other nonmembers. Consider the cases where Sam and Sarah are participants in the insurance system, and Peter and Paula are nonparticipants, with the following utility assignments.

	Utility of Getting an Organ When Needed	Disutility of Giving an Organ to Another
Sam	40	-30
Sarah	100	-80
Peter	80	-100
Paula	30	-40

If nonparticipant Peter needs an organ that can be given only by participant Sam, utility is increased by making the transplant. On the other hand, if participant Sarah needs an organ that only nonparticipant Paula can provide, then utilitarianism again requires making the transplant. And if nonparticipant Peter needs an organ that only nonparticipant Paula can provide, utilitarianism again requires the transplant. So the insurance system would not preclude utilitarians from having to endorse involuntary organ transplants. And finally, even if some voluntary insurance scheme did preclude the possibility of utilitarianism's requiring involuntary organ transfers, in the absence of the existence of such a scheme, the transfers would still be required. But even that is in sharp conflict with most persons' considered moral judgments about such cases.

The second utilitarian response questions why we should accept rights not to be killed and to property that would protect Jones in Case 3. Rather, if we view the situation impartially, we can see that Jones is required to sacrifice his life for Doe and Roe, and others would be justified in forcibly intervening to bring this about. And, surely, taking the moral point of view, considering the case from a moral point of view, entails considering it impartially. So, suppose we ensure impartiality by assuming that you are under a veil of ignorance such that you do not know who you are in the situation—Jones, Doe, or Roe—and must agree to a principle covering the case knowing you could turn out to be any of the three. Wouldn't you agree that Jones should give his life to save Doe and Roe, since you would thereby, under your veil of ignorance, maximize your probability of continuing to live? It is only if you know that you are Jones, and are thereby able to bias your moral judgment to your own known position, that you would defend Jones's right not to give his organs to Doe and Roe. And perhaps similar reasoning could prevail against the well-off Americans in Cases 1 and 2.

The third utilitarian response to Case 3 adapts an argument used by Rawls for different purposes. (Whether in fact this argument is compatible with utilitarianism is problematic, but it is an important one that merits consideration, and so largely for convenience sake I attribute it to a utilitarian.) It is only one's luck in the natural lottery that one has a complete set of sound organs whereas unlucky Doe and Roe do not. One does not from a moral point of view deserve that advantage any more than Doe and Roe deserve their disadvantage. Thus, from a moral point of view, we should view bodily parts, like talents and abilities, as in a common pool belonging equally and in common to all, and only accidentally attached to or located in individual persons. That the sound organs happen by chance now to be located in Jones provides no moral basis for a claim by Jones that they ought to remain there. And so, we must consider the case from an impartial moral standpoint where no moral weight is given the present location of organs. But if we do this, we seem led to accept the line of reasoning of the second utilitarian response above.

These last two responses to Case 3 raise a number of very difficult issues with which it will not be possible to deal adequately here. One point to note is what happens to the notion of a "person" on the third response, namely, it seems to be in danger of disappearing. The proper philosophical account of the relation of a person to his body is an extremely difficult and controversial issue, but the relation is surely a close and intimate one. It is not only that persons as a matter of fact require bodies in working order for continued survival, but also that our sense of ourselves, and our self-image, is commonly tied in close and deep ways to our physical self-image. Moreover, as has already been suggested, a central feature of the concept of person in its role in moral philosophy is the property of purposive being, possessor of interests, and able to deliberate on and act so as to further those interests. But to view persons and their bodies as the second utilitarian response would do is not to view and in turn treat them as persons in this sense, but is rather to make them into a scarce resource, to be used in whatever way will maximize overall utility; a person's body, and its organs, become like a piece of meat to be cut up and fed in the most efficient manner possible to starving others. Rights, including rights to privacy and specific liberties, as well as the right not to be killed, acknowledge an inviolability of each person, and limits on how we may deliberately use a person to further the ends of others. In so doing, they allow a stronger and more plausible account of the notion of respect for persons than does utilitarianism.

Both the second and third utilitarian lines of response fail adequately to take account of the particularity and separateness of individual persons, and as a result they are insensitive to the issue of whether a specific individual deserves to be disadvantaged or harmed so as to benefit others, and to the issue of proper compensation of persons so disadvantaged or harmed.

Within a single person's life, an at least initially plausible principle of rational choice would justify choosing so as to maximize satisfactions over time, and sacrificing satisfactions at one time for greater compensating satisfactions at another time. If there is not a serious problem about whether gains to my future self could justifiably compensate me for losses to my present self, it is because the gains and losses are both to one, single and unified self—me[17] It is because I have a concept of myself as a self that persists through time that it is plausible to defend such a principle of rational, individual choice with the intrapersonal trade-offs and compensations over time that it allows. The utilitarian treatment of Case 3, however, requires the justification of trade-offs and compensaton between distinct and separate individual selves. But the benefits to Doe and Roe seem in no way to compensate Jones for the loss to him necessary to bring about those benefits. And this problem of interpersonal compensation is, of course, especially acute when the loss is of one's life, because that is a loss that in only very limited respects one can be compensated for at all; if my life is sacrificed now, there is no way I can be compensated by future benefits to make up for my loss because there will be no future "me" to benefit. Just because the possibilities of compensation are extremely limited in such cases, it is especially important to show that the sacrifice is just or fair to *Jones*, that *he* deserves to be sacrificed for Doe and Roe. Merely showing that there would be a gain in lives preserved is not sufficient to establish that. Jones, like the rest of us, has but one life to live, and the life he has is uniquely important to him; it is in part this fact that the strength of the right not to be killed reflects.

Much work remains to be done in developing a theory of aid owed to others. In this paper, I have attempted only to indicate, first, what some of the issues are in the development of such a theory; second, the main considerations in the utilitarian treatment of those issues; and, finally, some broad outlines of a more adequate nonutilitarian theory of aid.

Notes

1. I have reviewed these issues in my, "Recent Work in Utilitarianism," *American Philosophical Quarterly* 10 *(1973):241-76.*

2. For example, cf. Fred Feldman, *Introductory Ethics* (Englewood Cliffs' Prentice-Hall, 1978), Ch. 4.

3. There is one issue that clearly cannot be so understood, viz. whether there is morally required aid that on the utilitarian view it is not required (and so wrong?) to give. If so, then in these areas, utilitarian requirements are not stringent enough. I do not consider this question in the present paper.

4. See John Rawls, *A Theory of Justice* (Cambridge: Harvard University Press, 1971), especially Ch. 1.

5. Since the preference for oneself is one that each person is, other things equal, entitled to exercise, it need not be in conflict with the conditions of impartiality or universalizability commonly placed on moral judgments. The issue between utilitarians and their critics is whether the justification for the preference lies in the overall high utility of persons acting on it, or elsewhere. Some, though I believe not all, nonutilitarian justifications of this preference may turn out to be incompatible with a plausible condition of impartiality or universalizability.

6. An example of such an account of the relationships of friendship and love, with an attempt to display its implications for morality, can be found in Charles Fried, *An Anatomy of Values* (Cambridge: Harvard University Press, 1970), Ch. 5.

7. Thomas Carson has suggested that utilitarianism may imply that we are required to

befriend friendless, or relatively friendless, people whom we don't really like very much. It is not clear to me that this is correct, but if it is, then utilitarianism seems incompatible with the social institution of friendship as it is commonly understood, and so much the worse for utilitarianism, not friendship.

8. See, for example, Rawls's defense, *A Theory of Justice,* of some such limited duty of mutual aid.

9. On this point, cf. Michael Slote, "The Morality of Wealth," in *World Hunger and Moral Obligation,* ed. William Aiken and Hugh LaFollette (Englewood Cliffs: Prentice-Hall, 1977).

10. Thomas Scanlon, in his "Rawls' Theory of Justice," reprinted in *Reading Rawls,* ed. Norman Daniels (New York: Basic Books, 1977), attributes such a view to Rawls.

11. Slote, *op. cit.*

12. After this paper was largely completed, I came across three papers that discuss this sort of case. In "The Survival Lottery," *Philosophy* 50 (1975):81-87, John Harris argues that a mandatory organ redistribution system would be both efficient and fair; Harris's position is criticized by Richard Trammell and Thomas Wren, "Fairness, Utility and Survival," *Philosophy* 52 (1977):331-37. Judith Jarvis Thomson argues that in some cases an agent may not kill instead of letting die in "Killing, Letting Die, and the Trolley Problem," *The Monist* 59 (1976):204-17.

13. I discuss the issue of saving the most lives possible in medical contexts, and when it is not permissible to do so, in more detail in my "Moral Rights and Permissible Killing," in *Ethical Issues Relating to Life and Death,* ed. J. Ladd (New York: Oxford University Press, 1979).

14. See, for example, Thomas Nagel, "War and Massacre," *Philosophy and Public Affairs* 1 (1972):123-24, and Charles Fried, *Right and Wrong* (Cambridge: Harvard University Press, 1978)

15. Cf. Thomson, "Killing, Letting Die and the Trolley Problem."

16. See, for example, Philippa Foot, "Abortion and the Doctrine of Double Effect," *Oxford Review* 5 (1967).

17. In the extremely interesting paper, "Later Selves and Moral Principles," in *Philosophy and Personal Relations,* ed. A. Montefiore (Montreal: McGill-Queens University Press, (1973), Derek Parfit defends an alternative view of personal identity, and argues in turn that it lends support to utilitarianism over the sort of moral view I propose in the text.

16 Utilitarianism and World Poverty

Thomas L. Carson

I

Act utilitarianism is a moral theory that states that one ought always to act so as to bring about the best possible balance of good consequences relative to bad ones. Most utilitarians hold that the only things that are instrinsically good or bad are the well-being and ill-being of human beings and other sentient creatures. According to this view, an agent's own interests are not entitled to any special weight in determining what he ought to do. One ought to promote the general welfare even if it is contrary to one's own self-interest. In principle, there is no limit to the sacrifices that may be required of one by act utilitarianism. If sacrificing one's life or giving away all of one's money would have better consequences than any alternative courses of action, then that is what one ought to do. Utilitarianism is an extremely demanding moral theory. Many philosophers take this to be an objectionable feature of utilitarianism.[1]

Many hundreds of millions of people throughout the world lack the basic material requirements for a satisfactory life. On the other hand, the vast majority of people in industrialized nations possess far more material goods than are *necessary* for a satisfactory life. *Prima facie,* the present distribution of wealth and resources cannot be considered optimal from the utilitarian point of view. Utilitarian principles require those who live in the industrial world to make considerable sacrifices for the sake of those who live in less fortunate economic circumstances. The per capita income or economic product of North America (the United States and Canada) is 4.5 times as great as that of the world as a whole, 18.2 times that of Africa, 25.3 times that of Asia (excluding the Middle East and Japan), and 50.7 times that of India.[2] To even begin to approach equality of wealth and income would involve huge sacrifices on the part of wealthier nations. Yet, given act utilitarianism, there is a *prima facie* case for strict equality. If (contrary to fact) a redistribution of wealth and resources would have no effect on economic production or population growth, then

---

I am indebted to Palmer Talbutt, Bob Fullinwider, Harlan Miller, and Bill Williams for helpful criticisms of earlier versions of this paper.

the phenomenon of "decreasing marginal utility" would seem to commit the utilitarian to something approaching strict equality.

Some argue that we have no obligation to provide assistance to impoverished societies because such aid would cause dramatic population increases and lead to even greater problems of poverty and famine in the future.[3] Such aid, it is argued, would only *postpone* suffering and starvation and, at the same time, ensure that they will occur on a greater scale. At best this argument shows only that it wouldn't do any good to help feed other nations without at the same time helping curb population growth.[4] The argument under consideration rests on very dubious empirical assumptions. Of course, the principle to which it appeals is entirely correct: If there is nothing we can do to help someone, then we don't have a duty to try.

Offhand, I can think of two considerations (there are no doubt others) that militate against the claim that utilitarian principles require a strictly equal distribution of the world's wealth and resources. First, much of the world's wealth is in the form of immovable buildings or land that cannot be transferred for foreign aid. Of course, the industrial nations could change their immigration policies and allow the poor to move themselves to where the wealth is. Second, large transfers of wealth from the industrial nations might diminish the productivity of their labor force. (The importation of workers from impoverished nations would be a partial remedy for this.) So, an optimal utilitarian strategy for the redistribution of wealth from rich nations to poor ones would probably not have to approach strict equality. There are thus good utilitarian reasons why the governments of wealthy nations should not attempt to bring about an equal distribution of wealth by means of involuntary transfers. But this is only because most people are not good utilitarians and cannot be compelled to act like ones. A good utilitarian would work hard and be productive even if much of his income were given to those less well-off than himself. It would seem that the utilitarian must still say that wealthy individuals ought to try of their own free will to effect a redistribution of wealth bordering on strict equality.

The consequences of utilitarianism for the question of our obligation to assist others would be thought by most people to be highly counterintuitive. Few people in the industrial world believe that they have a duty to donate their resources to organizations like CARE to the point when doing so would involve a net loss of utility, i.e., to the point when any further giving would do more harm than good.[5] Such acts are thought to be supererogatory. However, the appeal to considered judgments and moral intuitions is rather feeble in the present context. For there is strong reason to think that such judgments are seriously prejudiced by a concern for our own self-interest. Almost none of us who live in wealthy nations come anywhere near to discharging all of the duties to provide assistance to others that we would have if utilitarianism were true. We have a personal interest in denying that we have such obligations. Not only do we have an interest in avoiding the sacrifices that may be required for the sake of other people, but we also have an interest in defending our self-esteem against the view that we fall seriously short of doing what we ought to do in such matters.

The ordinary view about our obligation to assist others rests, I think, on the view that there is a morally significant difference between harming someone and failing to prevent him from being harmed. Although most people would see nothing wrong with spending $100 on luxury items for oneself (and thereby failing to use the money to save someone from starvation), almost no one would think it permissible to murder someone to obtain $100 to spend on luxury items. The view is that, all other things being equal, we are under a much stronger obligation to refrain from harming a person than to prevent harm from befalling from other sources. The merits of this position have been a topic of much recent debate. I am unconvinced by the examples given in support of the relevance of the distinction. Those who take this distinction to be morally relevant would no doubt reject my intuitions about those cases that I take to show that the distinction is not relevant. I don't see much point in appealing to intuitions about particular cases, for that is precisely what is in dispute. James Rachels has tried to show that in many of the cases thought to support the relevance of the distinction, there are other morally relevant differences between the two acts in question. Therefore, the fact that harming someone may indeed be worse than failing to prevent him from being harmed, in such cases, does not count against the view that "the bare fact that one act is an act of killing, while another act is an act of 'merely' letting die, is not a morally good reason in support of the judgment that the former is worse than the latter."[6] Another line of argument would be to appeal to more general principles that are justified on grounds other than their implications for the kinds of classes being considered. This paper constitutes the *beginning* of such an argument. In the following sections of the paper I will argue that the golden rule, Kant's categorical imperative, and the framework of Rawls's *A Theory of Justice* all have implications similar to those of utilitarianism for the question of our obligation to assist others.

There are, no doubt, other normative theories that have implications contrary to those of utilitarianism. Contractarianism is one of these. By "contractarianism" I mean the view that all moral rights and duties are derived from actual or possible agreements between people who possess full knowledge of their own circumstances of life. (By contrast, Rawls's theory is based on the idea of a hypothetical contract between people who are ignorant of their own personal circumstances.) Gilbert Harman argues, rightly, I think, that contractarianism supports the moral relevance of the distinction between harming and failing to help.

> For we also think that he has a stronger duty to try not to harm any of his patients (or anyone else) even if by so doing he could help five others.
>
> This aspect of our moral views can seem very puzzling especially if one supposes that moral feelings derive from sympathy and concern for others. But the hypothesis that morality derives from an agreement among people of varying powers and resources provides a plausible explanation. The rich, the poor, the strong, and the weak would all benefit if all were to try to avoid harming one another. So everyone could agree to that arrangement.

But the rich and the strong would not benefit from an arrangement whereby everyone would try to do as much as possible to help those in need. But poor and weak would get all of the benefit of this latter arrangement. Since the rich and the strong could foresee that they would be required to do most of the helping and that they would receive little in return, they would be reluctant to agree to a strong principle of mutual aid. A compromise would be likely and a weaker principle would probably be accepted. In other words, although everyone could agree to a strong principle concerning the avoidance of harm, it would not be true that everyone would favor an equally strong principle of mutual aid. It is likely that only a weaker principle of the latter sort would gain general acceptance.[7]

II

The intuitive judgments of those of us who live in wealthy societies concerning our obligation to assist other people are suspect because we are, to varying degrees, incapable of viewing the issue impartially and disregarding our own personal interests. People who are in need of aid are no more capable of being impartial than those who are in a position to provide it. How can one attain an impartial perspective on these questions? Or, better, what *would constitute* an impartial perspective?

In *A Theory of Justice* Rawls uses the notion of a "veil of ignorance" to ensure that people do not contrive principles of justice to suit their own personal interests. The basic idea is that an individual cannot tailor principles to his own advantage without having some knowledge of his own circumstances in life. A self-interested person who was ignorant of his own personal circumstances (his age, sex, race, abilities, etc.) could be relied on to choose moral principles in an impartial manner. I suggest that we ought to consider the question of our obligation to assist others from the standpoint of someone who does not know whether he is in need of aid or in a position to offer it. Or more precisely:

(A) A ought to assist B by doing x at t if and only if: a rational person who was motivated solely by considerations of self-interest and who was in a veil of ignorance concerning the circumstances of his own life (but knew that he had an equal chance of being A or B or anyone else affected by A's decision at 5) would prefer that A do x rather than any other course of action open to him at the same time.

(A) A can be expanded to give us a more general account of right action:

(G) It is right for S to do x at t if and only if: if S were (a) in a veil of ignorance concerning the circumstances of his own life — among other things this means that he cannot know that he is S — but knew that he had an equal chance of being any of the people who will be affected by S's choice of what to do at t, (b) self-interested, and (c) fully informed about all of the facts that are not denied him in virtue of (a), then he would not prefer that S perform any other act at t.

(G) says that right and wrong are to be determined by the preferences the agent would have if he were rational, self-interested, fully informed about all of the relevant facts of a general sort, and ignorant of his own circumstances in life. So circumstanced, the agent would desire, all other things being equal, to promote the welfare of any given person, because, for any given person, there is some chance that S will turn out to be that person. Thus, everything else being equal, for any act that will contribute to x's welfare (utility), S will desire that that action be performed. But what does this desire amount to? Does S desire to (a) bring about events to which x would assign high utility, or (b) bring about events that would increase the utility that he (S) would assign to his being x? (a) and (b) clearly are different. For example, x may attach such great value to pleasure that being a "contented pig" or living in a pleasure machine would have a very high utility for him. On the other hand, S may assign very little value to pleasure. In that case, it is likely that he would assign a very low utility to the state of affairs his being x and being in a pleasure machine. Certain courses of action might result in x's becoming a contented pig. S's preferences concerning these actions will differ depending on whether we take him to be trying to bring about states of affairs to which x assigns a high utility, or trying to do things that make the prospect of his (S's) becoming x as attractive to him as possible.[8] (Ga) and (Gb) do not have significantly different consequences for the kinds of cases under consideration, and, therefore, I will not attempt to argue for one over the other.

The implications of (A) and (G) for the question of our duty to assist others are little different from those of act-utilitarianism. The marginal utility of a given amount of wealth is much greater for a given member of a poor society than a given member of a rich one. Therefore, any self-interested person who believed that he had an equal chance of being anyone would desire that rich societies make large transfers of wealth to poorer ones. Any act that maximizes the utility of humanity at large also maximizes *the expected individual utility* of the person behind the veil of ignorance in (Ga). Therefore, *if* rationally pursuing one's own self-interest is the same as maximizing one's expected utility, then (Ga) is extentionally equivalent to act utilitarianism. So, whatever reasons can be given in support of (A) or (G) also provide support for the utilitarian position concerning the stringency of our obligation to aid others.

The golden rule and Kant's categorical imperative are most plausible if we formulate them so as to include something analogous to Rawls's veil of ignorance and when formulated in this way these principles are very nearly equivalent to (G). So whatever general sorts of reasons there may be for accepting the golden rule or the categorical imperative can also be given in support of the utilitarian's claim that our obligations to assist others are of a very stringent sort.

Christ states the Golden Rule as follows: "And as you would wish that men would do unto you, do so to them".[9] As stated, the Golden Rule is ambiguous. Am I to do to others what I wish that they would do to me given my present circumstances and desires? Or, should I do to them what I would want them to do to me if I were in their position with their desires and aversions, etc.? Given the former interpretation the Golden Rule has extremely counterintuitive consequences, among them being that it would be permissible for a person who wants to die to murder anyone whom he pleases. To be plausible, the Golden Rule must be taken to mean that we should treat others as we would wish to be treated if we were in their position, with their likes and dislikes, etc.[10] This is equivalent to saying that we should treat others as they would like to be treated. Consider the following:

(1) It is right for A to do x to B if and only if: B would not object to A's doing x.
(2) It is right for A to do x to B if and only if: B would not prefer that A perform some other act.

(1) and (2) have the extremely counterintuitive consequence that one can never be justified in treating another person in a way which that other person doesn't like. (1) implies that it could never be right for a judge to send a person to jail against his will. (2) implies that it is wrong for Rockefeller not to give me all of his money. (1) and (2) are incoherent in cases in which what one person wants one to do is incompatible with what someone else wants one to do. For example, suppose that I want Rockefeller to give *me* all his money and you want him to give *you* all his money. (2) implies that Rockefeller ought to give all of his money to me and also that he ought to give you all of his money. But, of course, he cannot do both, and assuming that "ought" implies "can," he cannot be obligated to do both. To avoid incoherence in cases in which what one does will affect more than one person, the Golden Rule must be formulated so as to involve a consideration of the wishes of all the other affected parties. Or, more precisely:

(GR) An act is right if and only if it is the act (or one of the acts) that the agent would most want to perform if he were to try to perform the act most acceptable to the other affected parties, giving equal weight to each of their wishes.

I take it that this is equivalent to saying that an act is right if and only if it is the act or one of the acts that the agent would most want to perform if he were rational, self-interested, fully informed about all the facts, and acting on the assumption that he has an equal chance of being any of the other affected parties. This is very nearly equivalent to (G). Both principles imply that the rightness or wrongness of an action is to be determined by the preferences the agent would have in a certain hypothetical situation. The only difference is that in the hypothetical situation envisaged in (G), one operates on the assumption that one has an equal chance of being any of the affected parties (including the agent), as opposed to any of the *other* affected parties.

Kant's categorical imperative can be stated as follows:

(CI) An Act is right if and only if the agent would be willing to have others act on the same principles—or willing to have others do the same thing in similar circumstances.[11]

One trouble with this formulation of the categorical imperative is that a person can be willing to have others act on patently immoral principles if he knows that his own circumstances are such that he cannot be harmed by people who follow those principles. Consider the following scenario: A leader of the local Ku Klux Klan is in the process of lynching a black man who has been found guilty of "upptiness." When confronted by his victim with charges of moral turpitude, the philosophically astutue Grand Wizard offers the following reply: "How can you accuse me of any wrong-doing? After all, I'm acting in accordance with the categorical imperative. I am acting on the principle 'lynch all uppity blacks.' Not only am I *willing* to see others act on this principle, but I actually encourage them to, as my Klan recruitment activity suggests. I am also happy to have other Grand Wizards take similar action in such cases." Can (CI) be revised to as to avoid this objection? One approach would be to stress the importance of how one describes people's actions. "Lynching uppity blacks" is the sort of act that the Grand Wizard would be willing to have become common practice. The problem with this is that there seems to be no reason for preferring the latter description to the former (both are perfectly correct descriptions of the Grand Wizard's action) and no general way of ruling out descriptions of acts that lead to counterintuitive consequences.

It seems to me that what is wrong with the Klansman's reply to his victim is that his knowledge of his own circumstances in life makes it certain that he could never be harmed by people acting on the principles which he endorses. He is willing to have others act on the principle "lynch all uppity blacks" only because he knows that he is not black himself. We need to find a version of the categorical imperative that incorporates some kind of veil of ignorance. For example:

(C) An act is right if and only if it is consistent with the set of rules that one would most like everyone to follow if one were ignorant of the particular circumstances of one's life.

A prudent person in such a veil of ignorance would want others to follow strongly egalitarian principles of mutual aid, for his expected utility would be maximized in that case. So, (C) requires those who would be strongly moved by considerations of self-interest in such circumstances (this surely includes most people) to follow strongly egalitarian principles of mutual aid. For those who would try to maximize their own expected utility in such a situation, following (C) is extentionally equivalent to following some kind of rule utilitarian—following principles the general observance of which would maximize the general welfare. The only persons who are not required by (C) to follow strong principles of mutual aid are those who would not want such principles to be adhered to, even in situations in which they would likely to be harmed as a result.

III

John Rawls's celebrated work *A Theory of Justice* attempts to justify a distinctive theory of social justice by showing that it would be preferred to other conceptions of justice by people in what Rawls calls the "original position." The original position is a hypothetical situation in which rational self-interested people who are in a veil of ignorance with respect to their own particular situation in life choose principles of justice for a society of which they will all be members. According to Rawls, a society or social institution is just if and only if it satisfies the following two conditions:

(a) It gives its members the most extensive system of liberties possible — compatible with everyone's having equal liberty.
(b) All inequalities in the distribution of other primary goods, wealth, power, self-respect, and so on are to the advantage of the least advantaged members.[12]

Rawls does not attempt to offer a full-blown theory of justice concerning the relations between different nations. However, he suggests that the original position would be an appropriate framework for constructing such a theory.[13] There is no reason for thinking that the original position has any special merits as a device for justifying conceptions of justice for particular societies that it lacks as a device for justifying principles of justice for the relations between nations (or to use Rawls's own terminology "the law of nations"). So, whatever justification we can provide for a conception of justice for an individual society by showing that it would be chosen in the original position, we can also provide for a conception of justice for relations between nations by showing that it would be chosen in the original position.

I believe that the Rawlsian framework of the original position is essentially correct and that it is an adequate device for justifying moral principles. I will not attempt to argue for this here. Rather, I will attempt to show that given the adequacy of this framework, it follows that it is unuust that the industrial nations of the world do not require great sacrifices of their members to benefit people in impoverished countries. For the principles of justice for relations between nations that would be chosen in the original position would require such sacrifices.

The parties to the original position for the law of nations are representatives of individual states who are concerned to advance the interests of their own particular nation but who "know nothing about the particular circumstances of their own society, its power in comparison with other nations, nor do they know their place in their own society."[14] Rawls gives a rough picture of the principles that would come out of the original position for the law of nations.

> The basic principle of the law of nations is a principle of equality. Independent peoples organized as states have certain fundamental equal rights. This principle is analogous to the equal rights of citizens in a con-

stitutional regime. One consequence of this equality of nations is the principle of self-determination, the right of a people to settle its own affairs without the intervention of foreign powers.[15]

This concern for the equality of nations seems to be inconsistent with Rawls's claim that securing individual liberty would be the (or a) primary concern of those in the original position.[16] For it is notorious that a society may disregard the rights and liberties of its own members. Concern for one's own individual rights and liberties would give one no special reason to be concerned about guaranteeing the "self-determination" of entire nations. In fact, this concern might incline one to choose principles that would allow for violations of the national sovereignty of individual nations when doing so would be necessary to protect the rights and/or liberties of their citizens. One must also keep open the possibility that the representatives in the original position would prefer some sort of world government and reject national sovereignty altogether.

Rawls does not say whether the law of nations would include any principles governing the distribution of wealth or income. However, in the situation Rawls describes, the representatives would choose strongly egalitarian principles providing for the redistribution of wealth from rich nations to poor ones. For they would be concerned to promote the interests of the members of their nation and know that (a) there is some probability that the nation they represent is poor and (b) that the marginal utility of a given amount of wealth is much greater for a poor person than a rich person. Even if one accepts Rawls's general approach to the question of justice, his description of the original position is questionable. Why shouldn't individuals (as opposed to representatives of nations) be the parties to the original position for the law of nations? If we suppose that individuals are the parties to the original position and if, as Rawls supposes, they would adopt a "maximin" strategy of ensuring the best possible worst outcome instead of trying to maximize their own expected utility, then the law of nations chosen would include something like the following:

(WDP) All social and economic inequalities must be to the advantage of the least well-off group in the world.

Whatever reasons can be given for thinking that Rawls's "difference principle" would be chosen as a principle of justice for individual societies are equally good reasons for thinking that the principles chosen in the original position as it is construed here would include something like (WDP). I believe that on any plausible interpretation, the original position for the law of nations will yield strongly egalitarian principles for the redistribution of wealth. For on any such interpretation, the parties to the original position will know that there is some probability that they are members or representatives of a poor society and that the marginal utility of a given amount of wealth is much greater for a poor person than a rich one.

Conclusion

Act utilitarianism is an extremely stringent and demanding moral theory. In particular, it requires that "we" make great sacrifices to assist impoverished people.

This is a counterintuitive consequence to the vast majority of people who live in wealthy nations. According to their common-sense beliefs about morality, providing such aid is "above and beyond the call of duty." However, as we have seen, we cannot place great trust in our common-sense beliefs about such issues. These questions must be considered in the light of moral principles and moral theories. Several historically important normative theories have implications similar to those of utilitarianism for the question of our duty to assist others.

Two related questions that I have not considered here are the following:

(1) Can a society be justified in *forcing* its members to provide assistance to others via taxation, etc.?
(2) Can a nation or group of nations be justified in forcing other nations to assist it (them)?

In this context it is necessary to stress the importance of the distinction between:

(i) The obligation of an individual (or society) to do something—in this case, to provide assistance to the members of impoverished societies.
(ii) The rightness or permissibility of forcing an individual or group to do what it ought to do.

That an individual or group has an obligation to do something does not necessarily imply that it would be right to *compel* him (or it) to do it. This can be put somewhat paradoxically, saying that an individual or a group may have a (moral) right to do something that is morally wrong. For example, it would be morally wrong for me to watch the fights on television rather than visit a dying aunt whom I've promised to see. However, I have a right to do this—it would be wrong for anyone to force me to visit her.

Both utilitarianism and Rawls's theory have the consequence that rich nations and citizens of such nations may be rightfully compelled to assist others. Doing so would maximize utility in many situations. The "law of the nations" that would come out of a Rawlsian original position would include principles that provide for measures for compelling nations to comply with the other principles—including those providing for a redistribution of wealth.

Notes

1. Cf., John Rawls, A Theory of Justice (Cambridge: Harvard University Press, 1971), p. 117; John Arthur, "Rights and the Duty to Bring Aid," in *Morality and World Hunger*, William Aiken and Hugh La Follette, eds., (Englewood Cliffs, N. J.: Prentice Hall: 1977), pp. 37-49; Richard Trammell, "Saving Life and Taking Life," *Journal of Philosophy* 72 (1975):131-137; Glenn Ebish, "Nationality and Moral Obligations," *Journal of Social Philosophy* (1978):5-10.

2. I have computed these figures from data on pp. 10 and 16 of the 1977 *World Bank Atlas*. To my knowledge, there are no reliable figures concerning national wealth.

3. Garrett Hardin, "Lifeboat Ethics: The Case Against Helping the Poor," in *Morality and World Hunger*, pp. 12-21.

4. Cf., Peter Singer, "Famine, Affluence and Morality," in *Morality and World Hunger*, pp. 32-35.

5. C. D. Broad argues that the position that he calls "self-referential altruism" best de-

scribes the morality of common sense. "Self-referential altruism" can be summed up as follows: (1) we have negative duties (i.e., duties to refrain from harming others) to the entire human race, but (2) the only people toward whom we have any positive duties (e.g., the duty to provide assistance) are people who are members of special groups of which we are a part, e.g., *our* family, *our* country, etc. "Self and Others," in Broad's *Critical Essays in Moral Philosophy,* D. Cheney, ed. (allen and Unwin: 1971), pp. 279-80.

6. James Rachels, "Killing and Starving to Death," *Philosophy* 54 (1979):163-164.

7. Gilbert Harman, "Moral Relativism Defended,"*Philosophical Review* 84 (1975):12-13.

8. This example and the distinction that it illustrates are drawn from David Gauthier's "The Refutation of Utilitarianism," this volume, p. 157.

9. Luke 6:31; also see Matthew 7:12.

10. Cf., Marcus G. Singer, "The Golden Rule," in *The Encyclopedia of Philosophy,* Paul Edwards, ed., (New York: Macmillan, 1967), vol. III, p. 366.

11. Kant presents three different formulations of categorical imperative in *The Groundwork of the Metaphysics of Morals.* (1) *"Act as if the maxim of your action were to become through your will a universal law of nature"* (p. 89); "I ought never to act except in such a way *that I can also will that my maxim should become a universal law"* (p. 70; also see p. 88); (2) *"Act in such a way that you always treat humanity, whether in your own person or in the person of any other, never simply as a means, but always at the same time as an end"* (p. 96); (3) "A rational being must always regard himself as making laws in a kingdom of ends . . . " (p. 101) My (CI) is most nearly equivalent to Kant's (1). On pp. 88 and 104 Kant makes statements that suggest that he takes (2) and (3) to be equivalent to (1), "there is therefore only a single categorical imperative and it is this: *'Act only on that maxim through which you can at the same time will that it should become a universal law"* and "we . . . take as our basis the universal formula of the categorical imperative: 'Act on the maxim which can at the same time be made a universal law.'" *Groundwork of the Metaphysics of Morals,* trans., H. J. Paton (New York: Harper and Row, 1964).

12. This is a very oversimplified statement of Rawls' theory. See *A Theory of Justice,* 60, 205, 244, 250, and 302.

13. *Ibid.,* pp. 8 and 377-382.

14. *Ibid.,* p. 378.

15. *Ibid.,* p. 378.

16. *Ibid.,* pp. 541-548.

Bibliography

Bibliography

In addition to works cited by the authors, the following general bibliography contains what the editors hope is a nearly exhaustive list of books and articles pertaining to utilitarianism written during the last fifty years or so, i.e., roughly 1930-1980. It contains, of course, a good deal more: for example, listings of relevant classical works of the eighteenth and nineteenth centuries, and many works on utilitarianism produced during the first thirty years of this century. In addition, many works in such related fields as game theory, decision theory, value theory, economic theory of utility and welfare economics are included, as well as a goodly number of essays on social, economic, and retributive justice, and punishment, representing both utilitarian and anti-utilitarian points of view. It was not our aim to provide anything like exhaustive coverage of these last areas, but to include works that have figured in the literature on utilitarianism, especially during the half-century on which we have focused our attention.

In compiling the bibliography we have drawn on numerous sources, the chief of which we might usefully mention.

The Philosopher's Index file on the DIALOG retrieval system; Brock, Dan. "Recent Work in Utilitarianism," *American Philosophical Quarterly* 10 (1973): 270-276; Rescher, Nicholas. *Distributive Justice*. Indianapolis: The Bobbs-Merrill Company, Inc., 1965, 125-155; Schneewind, Jerome B. *Sidgwick's Ethics and Victorian Moral Philosophy*. Oxford: At the Clarendon Press, 1977, 423-456.

Some utilitarian classics, e.g., works of Hume, Bentham, and Mill that exist in numerous editions, are listed with only the original date of publication. It may be helpful here to mention the following:

Mill's *Collected Works* now under the general editorship of J. M. Robson and published by the University of Toronto Press and Routledge and Kegan Paul—especially volume 10, *Essays on Ethics, Religion, and Society*, 1969, for *Utilitarianism*; volume 18, *Essays on Politics and Society*, 1977, for *On Liberty*; and volume 19, *Essays on Politics and Society*, 1977, for *Considerations on Representative Government*.

Bentham's *Collected Works* under the general editorship of J. H. Burns—especially *An Introduction to the Principles of Morals and Legislation*. Edited by J. H. Burns and H. L. A. Hart. London: The Athlone Press, 1970.

Hume's *A Treatise of Human Nature*. Edited by L. A. Selby-Bigge. 2nd edition, rev. Edited by P. H. Nidditch. Oxford: Oxford University Press, 1978; and Hume's

BIBLIOGRAPHY

Enquiries Concerning Human Understanding and Concerning the Principles of Morals. Edited by L. A. Selby-Bigge. 3rd edition, rev. Edited by P. H. Nidditch. Oxford: Clarendon Press, 1975.

Readers interested in the history of utilitarianism may wish to consult Schneewind (supra.) and Rescher (supra.), especially pages 127-133.

Abraham, J. "J. S. Mill and Utilitarianism." *The Listener* 69 (1963):1031-1032.
Ackermann, Robert J. "The Consequences." In *Logic and Art: Essays in Honor of Nelson Goodman,* edited by Richard Rudner and Israel Scheffler, pp. 43-57. Indianapolis: Bobbs-Merrill, 1972.
Ackoff, Russell L. "On a Science of Ethics." *Philosophy and Phenomenological Research* 9 (1949): 663-672.
──── . "The Development of Operations Research as a Science." *Operations Research* 4 (1956): 265-295.
──── , ed. *Progress in Operations Research.* New York: Wiley, 1961.
Acton, H. B. "Animal Pleasures." *Massachusetts Review* 2 (1961): 541-548.
──── . "Negative Utilitarianism," Part I. *Aristotelian Society Supplementary Volume* 3 (1963): 83-94.
──── . "Introduction." In *The Philosophy of Punishment.* London: Macmillan, 1969.
Adams, E. Maynard. "Classical Moral Philosophy and Metaethics." *Ethics* 74 (1964): 97-110.
──── . "The Philosophical Grounds of the Present Crisis of Authority." *Southern Journal of Philosophy* 8 (1970):129-142.
Adams, Robert M. "Motive Utilitarianism." *Journal of Philosophy* 73 (1976): 467-481.
Aiken, Henry D. "Definitions, Factual Premises, and Ethical Conclusions." *Philosophical Review* 61 (1952):331-348.
──── . *Reason and Conduct.* New York: Alfred A. Knopf, 1962 (see especially Chapter 14).
Albee, Ernest. "An Examination of Professor Sidgwick's Proof of Utilitarianism." *Philosophical Review* 10 (1901):251-260.
──── . *A History of English Utilitarianism.* New York: Collier, 1962.
Allen, Derek P. H. "The Utilitarianism of Marx and Engels." *American Philosophical Quarterly* 10 (1973):189-199.
──── . "Is Marxism a Philosophy?" *Journal of Philosophy* 71 (1974):601-612.
──── . "Reply to Brenkert's 'Marx and Utilitarianism'." *Canadian Journal of Philosophy* 6 (1976):517-534.
Allen, Glen O. "Beyond the Voter's Paradox." *Ethics* 88 (1977): 50-61.
Allen, H. J. "A Logical Condition for the Redescription of Actions in Terms of Their Consequences." *Journal of Value Inquiry* 1 (1967):132-134.
Alston, W. P. "Pleasure." In *The Encyclopedia of Philosophy,* edited by Paul Edwards, pp. 341-347. New York: Macmillan, 1967.
Anderson, John. *Studies in Empirical Philosophy.* Sydney: Angus and Robertson, 1962 (see Chapter 20).
Anglin, Bill. "The Repugnant Conclusion." *Canadian Journal of Philosophy* 7 (1977):745-754.
Annas, Julia. "Mill and the Subjection of Woman." *Philosophy* 52 (1977):179-194.
Anschutz, R. P. *The Philosophy of J. S. Mill.* Oxford: Clarendon Press, 1953.
Anscombe, G. E. M. "Modern Moral Philosophy." *Philosophy* 33 (1958):1-19.
──── . "On the Grammar of 'Enjoy'." *The Journal of Philosophy* 64 (1967):607-614.
Aqvist, Lennart. "Improved Formulations of Act-Utilitarianism." *Nous* 3 (1969):299-323.
Ardal, Pall S. "Promises and Reliance." *Dialogue* (Canada) 15 (1976): 54-61.
Armstrong, K. G. "The Retributivist Hits Back." *Mind* 70 (1961):471-490.

Armstrong, W. E. "Uncertainty and the Utility Function." *Economic Journal* 58 (1948): 1-10.
_____. "Utility and the Theory of Welfare." *Oxford Economic Papers, New Series* 3 (1951): 259-271.
Arneson, Richard J. "Benthamite Utilitarianism and 'Hard Times'." *Philosophy and Literature* 2 (1978):60-75.
Arrow, Kenneth J. "A Difficulty in the Concept of Social Welfare." *Journal of Political Economy* 58 (1950):328-346.
_____. "Alternative Approaches to the Theory of Choice in Risk-Taking Situations." *Econometrica* 19 (1951):494-537.
_____. *Social Choice and Individual Values*. 2nd edition. New Haven and London: Yale University Press, 1963. (Originally published by John Wiley & Sons, Inc. [New York], 1950.)
_____. "Values and Collective Decision-Making." In *Philosophy, Politics and Society: Third Series*, edited by P. Laslett and W. G. Runciman, pp. 215-232. Oxford: Basil Blackwell, 1967.
_____. "A Utilitarian Approach to the Concept of Equality in Public Expenditures." *Quarterly Journal of Economics* 85 (1971):409-415.
_____. "Gifts and Exchanges." *Philosophy & Public Affairs* 1 (1972):343-362.
_____. "Some Ordinalist-Utilitarian Notes on Rawls' Theory of Justice." *Journal of Philosophy* 70 (1973):245-263.
Arthur, John. "Rights and the Duty to Bring Aid." In *Morality and World Hunger*, edited by William Aiken and Hugh LaFollette, pp. 37-49. Englewood Cliffs, N. J.:Prentice-Hall, 1977.
Ashmore, Robert B., Jr. "Deriving the Desirable From the Desired." *Proceedings of the American Catholic Philosophical Association* 44 (1970):152-160.
_____. "Ewingon 'Higher' Egoism." *The New Scholasticism* 51 (1977): 513-523.
Atkinson, Ronald F. "J. S. Mill's 'Proof' of the Principle of Utility." *Philosophy* 32 (1957): 158-167.
_____. *Sexual Morality*. London: Hutchinson, 1965.
Atwell, J. E. "Oldenquist on Rules and Consequences." *Mind* 78 (1969):576-579.
August, Eugene R. *John Stuart Mill: A Mind at Large*. New York: Charles Scribner's Sons, 1975.
Austin, Jean. "Pleasure and Happiness." *Philosophy* 43 (1968):51-62.
Austin, John. *The Province of Jurisprudence Determined*. 1832.
_____. *Lectures on Jurisprudence*. Edited by Sarah Austin. 3 vols. 1861-1863.
Ayer, A. J. "Freedom and Happiness." *New Statesman, Supplement* 18 68 (1964): 390-392.
Bach, Kent. "When to Ask, 'What if Everyone Did That'." *Philosophy and Phenomenological Research* 37 (1977):464-481.
Baier, Kurt. "Is Punishment Retributive?" *Analysis* 16 (1955):25-32.
_____. *The Moral Point of View*. Ithaca: Cornell University Press, 1958.
_____. "Pains." *Australasian Journal of Philosophy* 40 (1962):1-23.
_____. "Acting and Producing." *The Journal of Philosophy* 62 (1965):245-248.
_____. "Moral Obligation." *American Philosophical Quarterly* 3 (1966):210-226.
_____. "Welfare and Preference." In *Human Values and Economic Policy*, edited by Sidney Hook. New York: New York University Press, 1967.
Baker, John M. "Utilitarianism and Secondary Principles." *Philosophical Quarterly* 21 (1971):69-71.
Bales, R. Eugene. "Act-Utilitarianism: Account of Right-Making Characteristics or Decision-Making Procedure?" *American Philosophical Quarterly* 8 (1971):257-265.
_____. "Utilitarianism, Overall Obligatoriness and Deontic Logic." *Analysis* 32 (1972): 203-205.
_____. "Czego Nalezy Oczekiwac od Utylitaryzmu Czynow?" *Etyka* 11 (1973):87-109.
Bar-Hillel, Maya, and Margalit, Avishai. "Newcomb's Paradox Revisited." *British Journal for the Philosophy of Science* 23 (1972):295-304.

Barker, Henry. "A Recent Criticism of Sidgwick's *Methods of Ethics*." *Philosophical Review* 11 (1902):607-614.
Barnes, Gerald W. "Utilitarianisms." *Ethics* 82 (1971):56-64.
Barnhart, J. E. "Egoism and Altruism." *The Southwestern Journal of Philosophy* 7 (1976): 101-110.
Barone, Enrico. "The Ministry of Production in the Collectivist State." Rome, 1908. *Collectivist Economic Planning*, edited by F. A. Hayek, pp. 245-290. London: Routledge, 1935.
Barrow, Robin. *Plato, Utilitarianism and Education*. London: Routledge and Kegan Paul, 1975.
Barry, Brian M. "Justice and the Common Good." *Analysis* 21 (1961):86-90.
_____. "Preferences and the Common Good." *Ethics* 72 (1962):141-142.
_____. "The Public Interest." *Aristotelian Society Supplementary Volume* 38 (1964): 1-18.
_____. *Political Argument*. New York: Humanities press, 1965.
_____. "On Social Justice." *Oxford Review* (Trinity Term, 1967):33-43.
_____. *Sociologists, Economists and Democracy*. London: Collier-Macmillan, Ltd., 1970.
_____. *The Liberal Theory of Justice*. Oxford: Oxford University Press, 1973.
_____. "Rawls on Average and Total Utility: A Comment." *Philosophical Studies* 31 (1977):317-325.
_____. "Don't Shoot the Trumpeter, He's Doing His Best: Reflections on a Problem of Fair Division." *Theory and Decision* 11 (1979):153-180.
Bates, James. "A Model for the Science of Decision." *Philosophy of Science* 21 (1954): 326-339.
Baumgardt, David. "Bentham's 'Censorial' Method." *Journal of the History of Ideas* 6 (1945):456-467.
_____. *Bentham and The Ethics of Today: With Bentham Manuscripts Hitherto Unpublished*. Princeton, N. J.: Princeton University Press, 1952.
Baumol, William J. "The Neumann-Morgenstern Utility Index: An Ordinalist View." *Journal of Political Economy* 59 (1951):61-66.
_____. *Welfare Economics and the Theory of the State*. 2nd edition. Cambridge, Mass.: Harvard University Press, 1965.
Bayles, Michael. "Singer's Moral Principles and Rules." *Philosophical Studies* 16 (1965): 61-64.
_____, ed. *Contemporary Utilitarianism*. Garden City, N. Y.: Anchor Books, 1968.
_____. "A Rule Utilitarian Moral Code." *Journal of Value Inquiry* 3 (1969):258-269.
_____. "Mill's 'Utilitarianism' and Aristotle's 'Rhetoric'." *The Modern Schoolman* 51 (1974): 159-170.
_____, ed. *Ethics and Population*. Cambridge, Mass.: Schenkman, 1976.
Baylis, Charles A. "Intrinsic Goodness." *Philosophy and Phenomonological Research* 13 (1952):15-27.
_____. "Comments" on Symposium on Utilitarianism and Moral Obligation. *Philosophical Review* 61 (1962):327-330.
Beardsley, Elizabeth L. "A Plea for Deserts." *American Philosophical Quarterly* 6 (1969): 33-42.
Beardsmore, R. W. "Consequences and Moral Worth." *Analysis* 29 (1968-69):177-186.
Becker, G. M. and McClintock, C. G. "Value: Behavioral Decision Theory." *Annual Review of Psychology* 18 (1967):239-286.
Becker, Gordon. "Difficulties with Bare Preferences." *Theory and Decision* 5 (1974):329-331.
Becker, Lawrence C. *Property Rights: Philosophic Foundations*. London: Routledge and Kegan Paul, 1977.

Bedau, Hugo A. "Justice and Classical Utilitarianism." In *Nomos VI Justice*, edited by C. Friedrich, pp. 284-305. New York: Atherton Press, 1963.
_____, ed. *Justice and Equality*. Englewood Cliffs, N. J.:Prentice-Hall, 1971.
Beitz, Charles R. "Justice and International Relations." *Philosophy & Public Affairs* 4 (1975):360-389.
Bell, Linda A. "Utilitarianism and the 'Reductio Ad Absurdum'." *Metaphilosophy* 9 (1978): 233-241.
Benditt, Theodore M. "The Public Interest." *Philosophy & Public Affairs* 2 (1973):291-311.
_____. "Happiness." *Philosophical Studies* 25 (1974):1-20.
_____. "The Concept of Interest in Political Theory." *Political Theory* 3 (1975):245-258.
Benn, S. I. "An Approach to the Problem of Punishment." *Philosophy* 33 (1958):325-341.
_____, and Mortimore, G. W. "Technical Models of Rational Choice." In *Rationality and the Social Sciences*, edited by S. I. Benn and G. W. Mortimore, pp. 157-195. London: Routledge and Kegan Paul, 1976.
_____, and Peters, R. S. *Social Principles and the Democratic State*. London: Allen & Unwin, 1959.
Bennett, John. "Whatever the Consequences." *Analysis* 26 (1965-66):83-102.
Bentham, Jeremy. *Introduction to the Principles of Morals and Legislation*. 1789.
_____. *Table of the Springs of Action*. 1815.
_____. *Deontology*, 2 vols. 1834.
Berger, Fred R. "Gratitude." *Ethics* 85 (1975):298-309.
_____. "Mill's Concept of Happiness." *Interpretation* 7 (1978):95-117.
_____. "John Stuart Mill on Justice and Fairness." *Canadian Journal of Philosophy, Supplementary Volume* 5 (1979):115-136.
Bergson, A. "A Reformulation of Certain Aspects of Welfare Economics." *Quarterly Journal of Economics* 52 (1938); reprinted in Bergson, A., *Essays in Normative Economics*. Cambridge: Harvard University Press, 1966.
_____. "On the Concept of Social Welfare." *Quarterly Journal of Economics* 68 (1954): 233-252.
Bergstrom, Lars. *The Alternatives and Consequences of Actions*. Stockholm: Almqvist and Wicksell, 1966.
_____. "Alternatives and Utilitarianism." *Theoria* 34 (1968): 163-170.
_____. "Utilitarianism and Deontic Logic." *Analysis* 29 (1968):43-44.
_____. "Utilitarianism and Alternative Actions." *Nous* 5 (1971):237-252.
_____. "Reply to Bronaugh." *Theoria* 38 (1972):148-149.
_____. "On the Coherence of Act-Utilitarianism." *Analysis* 33 (1973):98-102.
_____. "On the Formulation and Application of Utilitarianism." *Nous* 10 (1976): 121-144.
_____. "Utilitarianism and Future Mistakes." *Theoria* 43 (1977):84-102.
Berkeley, George. *Passive Obedience, or the Christian Doctrine of not Resisting the Supreme Power, Proved and Vindicated Upon the Principles of the Law of Nature*. London, 1712.
Bernays, Paul. "Das Moralprinzip bei Sidgwick und bei Kant." *Abhandlung der Fries' schen Schule*, NF iii. Band, 3. Heft (1910):501-582.
Bernstein, Richard F. "Legal Utilitarianism." *Ethics* 89 (1979):127-146.
Beveridge, William. *Full Employment in a Free Society*. London: Allen & Unwin, 1944. New York: W. W. Norton, 1945.
Bierman, A. K. "Spying, Liberalism, and Privacy." *Journal of Social Philosophy* 5 (1974): 11-14.
Birmingham, Robert L. "The Prisoner's Dilemma and Mutual Trust: Comment." *Ethics* 79 (1969):156-158.
Birnbacher, Dieter. "Rawls' 'Theorie Der Gerechtigkeit' und Das Problem Der Gerechtigkeit Zwischen Den Generationen." *Zeitschrift fur Philosophischen Forschung* 31 (1977): 385-401.
Bishop, Donald. "What is the Good?" *Indian Philosophy and Culture* 17 (1972): 142-148.

Black, Duncan. *The Theory of Committees and Elections.* Cambridge: Cambridge University Press, 1963.
Black, Max. "Notes on the Meaning of 'Rule'." *Theoria* 24 (1958):121-122.
Blackstone, William T. *Francis Hutcheson and Contemporary Ethical Theory.* Athens: University of Georgia Press, 1965.
_____. "The American Psychological Association Code of Ethics for Research Involving Human Participants: An Appraisal." *Southern Journal of Philosophy* 13 (1975):407-418.
_____. "Compensatory Justice and Affirmative Action." *Proceedings of the American Catholic Philosophical Association* 49 (1975):218-227.
Blanshard, Brand. *The Impasse in Ethics, and a Way Out.* Berkeley: University of California Press, 1955.
_____. "Sidgwick the Man." *Monist* 58 (1974):349-370.
Blegvad, Mogens. "Equality, Utility, and Moral Rules." *Danish Yearbook of Philosophy* 1 (1964):23-36.
Block, Walter. "Coase and Demsetz on Private Property Rights." *Journal of Libertarian Studies* 1 (1977):111-115.
Blum, Roland Paul. "The True Function of the Generalization Argument." *Inquiry* 13 (1970):274-288.
Blum, W. J. and Kalven, H. *The Uneasy Case for Progressive Taxation.* Chicago: University of Chicago Press, 1953.
Bogen, Daniel and Farrell, D. M. "Freedom and Happiness in Mill's Defense of Liberty." *Philosophical Quarterly* 28 (1978):325-338.
Bohnert, Herbert G. "The Logical Structure of the Utility Concept." In *Decision Processes,* edited by Robert M. Thrall, et al. New York: Wiley, 1954.
Botwinick, Aryeh. "A Case for Hume's NonUtilitarianism." *Journal of the History of Philosophy* 15 (1977):423-435.
Boulding, Kenneth E. "Some Contributions of Economics to the General Theory of Value." *Philosophy of Science* 23 (1956):1-14.
_____. *Principles of Economic Policy.* Englewood Cliffs, N. J.: Prentice-Hall, 1958.
Bourke, Vernon J. "Recent Trends in Ethics." *The New Scholasticism* 44 (1970):396-425.
Bower, Howard B. *Toward Social Economy.* New York: Rinehart, 1948.
Bowie, Norman E. *Towards A New Theory of Distributive Justice.* Amherst: University of Massachusetts Press, 1971.
Bowle, John. *Hobbes and His Critics: A Study in Seventeenth Century Constitutionalism.* New York: Oxford University Press, 1952.
Bradley, F. H. "Mr. Sidgwick on Ethical Studies." *Mind,* O. S., 2 (1887):122-125.
Bradley, M. C. "Professor Smart's 'Extreme and Restricted Utilitarianism'." *Philosophical Quarterly* 7 (1957):264-266.
Braithwaite, Richard Bevan. "Moral Principles and Inductive Policies." *British Academy Proceedings* 36 (1950):51-68.
_____. *Theory of Games as a Tool for the Moral Philosopher.* Cambridge: Cambridge University Press, 1963.
Brandt, Richard B. *Ethical Theory: The Problems of Normative and Critical Ethics.* Englewood Cliffs, N. J.: Prentice-Hall, 1959.
_____. *Social Justice.* Englewood Cliffs, N. J.: Prentice-Hall, 1962.
_____. "Toward a Credible Form of Utilitarianism." In *Morality and The Language of Conduct,* edited by H.-N. Castaneda and George Nakhnikian, pp. 107-143. Detroit: Wayne State University Press, 1963.
_____. "Utility and the Obligation to Obey the Law." In *Law and Philosophy,* edited by Sidney Hook, pp. 43-55. New York: New York University Press, 1964.
_____. "Review of *Freedom and Reason* by R. M. Hare." *The Journal of Philosophy* 61 (1964):139-150.
_____. "The Concept of Welfare." In *The Structure of Economic Science: Essays on*

Methodology, edited by Sherman R. Krupp, pp. 257-276. Englewood Cliffs, N. J.: Prentice-Hall, 1966.
———. "Happiness." In *The Encyclopedia of Philosophy*, edited by Paul Edwards, Volume 3, pp. 413-414. New York: Macmillan, 1967.
———. "Personal Values and the Justification of Institutions." In *Human Values and Economic Policy*, edited by Sidney Hook. New York: New York University Press, 1967.
———. "Some merits of One Form of Rule Utilitarianism." In *University of Colorado Studies Series in Philosophy*, No. 3. Denver: University of Colorado Press, 1967.
———. "Review of *Morality and Utility* by Jan Narveson." *The Journal of Philosophy* 65 (1968):544-550.
———. "A Utilitarian Theory of Excuses." *Philosophical Review* 78 (1969):337-361.
———. "Rational Desires." *Proceedings of the American Philosophical Association* 43 (1969-70):43-64.
———. "Traits of Character: A Conceptual Analysis." *American Philosophical Quarterly* 7 (1970):23-37.
———. "The Interpersonal Comparison of Utility." Paper presented at the meetings of the American Philosophical Association, Western Division, Spring, 1971. Mimeographed.
———. "Utilitarianism and the Rules of War." *Philosophy & Public Affairs* 1 (1972):145-165.
———. "Rationality, Egoism and Morality." *Journal of Philosophy* 69 (1972):681-697.
———. "The Psychology of Benevolence and Its Implications for Philosophy." *Journal of Philosophy* 73 (1976):429-453.
———. *A Theory of the Good and the Right*. Oxford: Clarendon Press, 1979.
Braybrooke, David. "Farewell to the New Welfare Economics." *Review of Economic Studies* 22 (1954-1955):180-193.
———. "Collective and Distributive Generalization in Ethics." *Analysis* 23 (1962-63):45-48.
———. "The Choice Between Utilitarianisms." *American Philosophical Quarterly* 4 (1967): 28-38.
———. "Let Needs Diminish that Preferences May Prosper." In *American Philosophical Quarterly*, Monograph 1, *Studies in Moral Philosophy*, edited by Nicholas Rescher, pp. 86-107. Oxford: Basil Blackwell, 1968.
———. *Three Tests for Democracy: Personal Rights, Human Welfare, Collective Preference*. New York: Random House, 1968.
———. "Utilitarianism With A Difference: Rawls' Position in Ethics." *Canadian Journal of Philosophy* 3 (1973):303-331.
———. "The Insoluble Problem of the Social Contract." *Dialogue* (Canada) 15 (1976):3-37.
———, and Lindblom, Charles E. *A Strategy of Decision: Policy Evaluation as a Social Process*. New York: Free Press, 1963.
Brenkert, George G. "Marx and Utilitarianism." *Canadian Journal of Philosophy* 5 (1975): 421-434.
———. "On Welfare and Rescher." *Personalist* 57 (1976):299-307.
Britton, Karl. "What Does a Moral Judgment Commit Me To?" *Proceedings of the Aristotelian Society* 54 (1954):97-114.
———. "Utilitarianism: The Appeal to a First Principle." *Proceedings of the Aristotelian Society* 60 (1960):141-154.
———. *John Stuart Mill*. 2nd edition. New York: Dover Publications, 1969.
Broad, Charlie Dunbar. "Henry Sidgwick." *Hibbert Journal* 37 (1938):25-43.
———. "Egoism As A Theory of Human Motives." *Hibbert Journal* 48 (1949):105-114.
———. *Ethics and the History of Philosophy*. London: Routledge and Kegan Paul, 1952.
———. "Berkeley's Theory of Morals." *Revue Internationale De Philosophie* 7 (1953):72-86.
———. *Five Types of Ethical Theory*. Paterson, N. J.: Littlefield Adams, 1959.
———. "Self and Others." In *Broad's Critical Essays in Moral Philosophy*, edited by D. Cheney, pp. 262-282. London: Allen & Unwin, 1971.
Brock, Dan W. "Contractualism, Utilitarianism and Social Inequalities." *Social Theory and Practice* 1 (1971):33-44.

_____. "Recent Work in Utilitarianism." *American Philosophical Quarterly* 10 (1973):241-276.

_____. "Moral Rights and Permissible Killing." In *Ethical Issues Relating to Life and Death*, edited by J. Ladd. New York: Oxford University Press, 1979.

Brody, Baruch A. "The Equivalence of Act and Rule Utilitarianism." *Philosophical Studies* 18 (1967):81-87.

Brogan, A. P. "John Locke and Utilitarianism." *Ethics* 69 (1959):79-93.

Broiles, R. David. "Is Rule Utilitarianism Too Restricted?" *Southern Journal of Philosophy* 2 (1964):180-187.

Bronaugh, Richard N. "The Next Best Thing." *Logique Et Analyse* 16 (1973):581-589.

_____. "The Quality of Pleasures." *Philosophy* 49 (1974):320-322.

_____. "The Utility of Quality: An Understanding of Mill." *Canadian Journal of Philosophy* 4 (1974):317-325.

_____. "Utilitarian Alternatives." *Ethics* 85 (1975):175-178.

Bross, Irwin. *Design for Decision*. New York: Macmillan, 1953.

Brown, D. G. "Mill on Liberty and Morality." *Philosophical Review* 81 (1972):133-158.

_____. "What is Mill's Principle of Utility?" *Canadian Journal of Philosophy* 3 (1973):1-12.

_____. "John Rawls: John Mill." *Dialogue* (Canada) 12 (1973):477-479.

_____. "Mill's Act Utilitarianism." *Philosophical Quarterly* 24 (1974):67-68.

Brown, P. M. "Distribution and Values." *Journal of Philosophy* 66 (1969):197-212.

Brown, Stuart M., Jr. "Duty and the Production of Good." *Philosophical Review* 61 (1952):299-311.

Browne, S. S. S. "Independent Questions in Ethical Theories." *Philosophical Review* 61 (1952):188-197.

Brownsey, Paul. "Hume and the Social Contract." *Philosophical Quarterly* 28 (1978):132-148.

Buchanan, Allen, "Distributive Justice and Legitimate Expectations." *Philosophical Studies* 28 (1975):419-425.

_____. "Revolutionary Motivation and Rationality." *Philosophy & Public Affairs* 9 (1979):59-82.

Buchanan, James M. "Ethical Rules, Expected Values, and Large Numbers." *Ethics* 76 (1965):1-13.

_____. *The Demand and Supply of Public Goods*. Chicago: Rand McNally & Company, 1968.

_____. *The Limits of Liberty: Between Anarchy and Leviathan*. Chicago: University of Chicago Press, 1975.

_____, and Tullock, Gordon. *The Calculus of Consent*. Ann Arbor: University of Michigan Press, 1962.

_____, and _____. "Economic Analogues to the Generalization Argument." *Ethics* 74 (1963-64):300-301.

Bunzl, Martin. "The Moral Development of Moral Philosophers." *Journal of Moral Education* 7 (1977):3-8.

Burkholder, L. "Rule-utilitarianism and 'Two Concepts of Rules'." *Personalist* 56 (1975):195-198.

Burne, P. "Bentham and the Utilitarian Principle." *Mind* 58 (1949):367-368.

Burns, J. H. "Utilitarianism and Democracy." *Philosophical Quarterly* 9 (1959):168-171.

Burrill, Donald. "The Rule-Egoism Principle." *Personalist* 57 (1976):408-410.

Burris, Harold W., Jr. "Utilitarianism: Benthamism in Disguise." *Dialogue* (Phi Sigma Tau) 19 (1977):58-62.

Callebaut, Werner. "Practical Rationality From an Evolutionary Perspective." *Philosophica* 22 (1978):119-166.

Camacho, Antonio. "On Cardinal Utility." *Theory and Decision* 10 (1979):131-145.

Campbell, Richmond. "A Short Refutation of Ethical Egoism." *Canadian Journal of Philosophy* 2 (1972):249-254.

_____. "The Pursuit of Happiness." *Personalist* 54 (1973):325-337.
_____. "Replies to MacDonald and Dwyer on Pursuing Happiness." *Personalist* 58 (1977): 182-186.
Campbell, T. D. *Adam Smith's Science of Morals.* London: Allen & Unwin, 1971.
_____. "Rights Without Justice." *Mind* 83 (1974):445-448.
_____. "Equality of Opportunity." *Proceedings of the Aristotelian Society* 75 (1974-75): 51-68.
Caplan, Arthur L., ed. *The Sociobiology Debate.* New York: Harper and Row, 1978.
Care, Norman S. "Contractualism and Moral Criticism." *Review of Metaphysics* 23 (1969): 85-101.
Cargile, James. "Utilitarianism and the Desert Island Problem." *Analysis* 25 (1964):23-24.
_____. "On Consequentialism." *Analysis* 29 (1969):78-88.
Carlson, George R. "Plans, Expectations and Act-Utilitarian Distrust." *Philosophical Studies* 36 (1979):295-300.
Carmichael, Peter A. "Mill and 'Desirable'." *Philosophy and Phenomenological Research* 34 (1974):435-436.
Carney, David. "Marginal Utility, Interpersonal Comparisons and the Theory of Taxation." *American Journal of Economics* 22 (1963):173-184.
Carney, Frederick. "On McCormick and Teleological Morality." *Journal of Religious Ethics* 6 (1978):81-107.
Carpriata, Manlio. "Alcune Lettere Inedite di Croce a Camillo Spinedi." *Rivista Di Studi Crociani* 15 (1977):149-160.
Carr, Spencer. "The Integrity of a Utilitarian." *Ethics* 86 (1976):241-246.
Carritt, Edgar Frederick. *The Theory of Morals: An Introduction to Ethical Philosophy.* New York: Oxford University Press, 1928. (See Chapter 12.)
_____. "Thinking Makes it So." *Proceedings of the Aristotelian Society* 30 (1929-30):277-284.
_____. *Ethical and Political Thinking.* Oxford: Clarendon Press, 1947. (See Chapter 5.)
Carson, Thomas. "Happiness and the Good Life." *Southwestern Journal of Philosophy* 9 (1978):73-88.
_____. "Happiness and Contentment: A Reply to Benditt." *The Personalist* 59 (1978):101-107.
_____. "Happiness and the Good Life: A Rejoinder to Mele." *Southwestern Journal of Philosophy* 10 (1979):189-192.
_____. "Happiness, Contentment, and the Good Life." *Pacific Philosophical Quarterly* October, 1981.
Carver, Thomas Nixon. *Essays in Social Justice.* Cambridge: Harvard University Press, 1915.
Casellato, S. *Giovanni S. Mill e l'Utilitarismo Inglese.* Padova: Cedam, 1951.
Cash, Arthur Hill. *Sterne's Comedy of Moral Sentiments: The Ethical Dimension of the Journey.* Pittsburgh: Duquesne University Press, 1966.
Castaneda, Hector-Neri. "A Problem for Utilitarianism." *Analysis* 28 (1968):141-142.
_____. "Ought, Value and Utilitarianism." *American Philosophical Quarterly* 6 (1969): 257-275.
Cerf, Walter, "Value Decisions." *Philosophy of Science* 18 (1951):26-34.
Champlin, T. S. and Walker, A. D. M. "Tendencies, Frequencies and Classical Utilitarianism." *Analysis* 35 (1974):8-12.
Chandler, Hugh S. "Hedonism." *American Philosophical Quarterly* 12 (1975):223-233.
Chapman, John. "Justice and Fairness." In *Nomos VI: Justice,* edited by C. Friedrich. New York: Atherton Press, 1963.
Charvet, J. "Criticism and Punishment." *Mind* 75 (1966):573-579.
Chipman, J. S. "Foundations of Utility." *Econometrica* 28 (1960):193-224.

Choppra, Y. N. "The Consequences of Human Actions." *Proceedings of the Aristotelian Society* 67 (1966-67):147-166.
Churchman, C. West. *Prediction and Optimal Decision.* Englewood Cliffs, N. J.: Prentice-Hall, 1961.
Clark, George A. "Mill's 'Notorious Analogy'." *Journal of Philosophy* 56 (1959): 652-655.
Clark, J. B. *The Distribution of Wealth.* New York: Macmillan, 1899.
Clark, John P. *The Philosophical Anarchism of William Godwin.* Princeton: Princeton University Press, 1977.
Clark, Michael. "The Moral Graduation of Punishment." *Philosophical Quarterly* 21 (1971): 132-140.
Clark, Pamela M. "Some Difficulties in Utilitarianism." *Philosophy* 29 (1954): 244-252.
Coates, Willson H. "Benthamism, Laissez Faire, And Collectivism." *Journal of the History of Ideas* 11 (1950): 357-363.
Coburn, J. B. "Rules and Consequences." *Mind* 78 (1969):136.
Coddington, Alan. "Utilitarianism Today." *Political Theory* 4 (1976):213-226.
Cody, A. B. "Can A Single Action Have Many Different Descriptions?" *Inquiry* 10 (1967): 164-180.
Cohen, Brenda. "Some Ambiguities in the Term 'Hedonism'." *Philosophical Quarterly* 12 (1962):239-247.
Cohen, Carl. "Defending Civil Disobedience." *Monist* 54 (1970):469-487.
Coleman, Jules L., and Derloff, Michael. "On the Purported Inconsistency of Act-Utilitarianism." *Philosophical Studies* 28 (1975):297-298.
Cooper, Neil. "Mill's 'Proof' of the Principle of Utility." *Mind* 78 (1969):278-279.
_____. "The Only Possible Morality." *Aristotelian Society Supplementary Volume* 50 (1976):43-68.
Cooper, Wesley E.; Nielsen, Kai; and Patten, Steven, eds. *New Essays on John Stuart Mill and Utilitarianism. Canadian Journal of Philosophy, Supplementary Volume* 5 (1979).
Copleston, Frederick C. *A History of Philosophy: Volume 8 — Bentham to Russell.* Glen Rock: Newman Press, 1966.
Copp, David. "The Iterated-Utilitarianism of J. S. Mill." In *New Essays on John Stuart Mill and Utilitarianism,* edited by Wesley E. Cooper, Kai Nielsen, and Steven C. Patten, pp. 75-98. *Canadian Journal of Philosophy, Supplementary Volume* 5 (1979).
Corkey, R. "Benevolence and Justice." *Philosophical Quarterly* 9 (1959):152-163.
Cornman, James W. and Dirnbach, Boris J. "Utilitarianism and the Obligation to do Exactly One Act." *Analysis* 34 (1973):20-23.
Cosby, Grant. "Abortion: An Unresolved Moral Problem." *Dialogue* (Canada) 17 (1978): 106-121.
Cowan, Joseph Lloyd. *Pleasure and Pain: A Study in Philosophical Psychology.* London: Macmillan, 1968.
Cox, Kendall B. "The Relevance of Promises to Obligations on Act Utilitarianism." *Michigan Academician* 6 (1974):333-349.
Cranston, Maurice. *John Stuart Mill.* Writers and Their Works Series 99. New York: British Book Center, 1960.
Creel, Richard E. "An Apology for John Stuart Mill." *Kinesis* 1 (1968):22-28.
Crocker, Lawrence. "Egoistic Hedonism." *Analysis* 36 (1976):168-176.
Crocker, Lester G. *Nature and Culture: Ethical Thought in the French Enlightenment.* Baltimore: Johns Hopkins Press, 1963.
Crosland, C. A. R. *The Future for Socialism.* London: Macmillan, 1955, 1957.
Crossley, David J. "Bradley's Utilitarian Theory of Punishment." *Ethics* 86 (1976):200-213.
Cumming, Robert Denoon. *Human Nature and History: A Study in the Development of Liberal Political Thought.* Chicago: University of Chicago Press, 1969.
Cummins, Robert. "Better Total Consequences: Utilitarianism and Extrinsic Value." *Metaphilosophy* 7 (1976):286-306.

Cunningham, Robert L. "Is It Necessary or Useful to Randomize?" *Analysis* 26 (1966):103.
──── , editor. *Situationism and the New Morality*. New York: Appleton-Century-Crofts, 1970.
────. "Justice: Efficiency or Fairness?" *Personalist* 52 (1971):253-281.
Cupples, Brian. "A Defense of the Received Interpretation of J. S. Mill." *Australasian Journal of Philosophy* 50 (1972):131-137.
Curzie, Kathleen L. "Analysis of the Utilitarian Maxim: 'The Greatest Good for the Greatest Number'." *Dialogue* (Phi Sigma Tau) 12 (1970):30-33.
Dahl, Norman O. "Is Mill's Hedonism Inconsistent?" *American Philosophical Quarterly*, Monograph 7 (1973):37-54.
Dahl, R., and Lindblom, C. *Politics, Economics and Welfare*. New York: Harper & Brothers, 1953.
Danhof, Clarence H. "Economic Values in Cultural Perspective." In *Goals of Economic Life*, edited by Dudley Ward, pp. 84-117. New York: Harper & Brothers, 1953.
Daniels, Norman, ed. *Reading Rawls: Critical Studies of A Theory of Justice*. Oxford: Blackwell, 1975.
Danielson, Peter. "Theories, Intuitions and the Problem of World-Wide Distributive Justice." *Philosophy of the Social Sciences* 3 (1973):331-338.
D'Arcy, J. E. *Human Acts: An Essay in Their Moral Evaluation*. Oxford: The Clarendon Press, 1963.
Darwall, Stephen L. "Pleasure as Ultimate Good in Sidgwick's Ethics." *Monist* 58 (1978): 475-489.
Dasgupta, Partha. "On Some Problems Arising from Professor Rawls' Conception of Distributive Justice." *Theory and Decision* 4 (1974):325-344.
David, Lawrence. "The Intelligibility of Rule Utilitarianism." *Philosophical Studies* 24 (1973):343-349.
Davidson, Donald; McKinsey, J. C. C.; and Suppes, Patrick. "Outlines of a Formal Theory of Value." *Philosophy of Science* 22 (1955):140-160.
──── ; Suppes, Patrick; and Siegel, Sidney. *Decision-Making: An Experimental Approach*. Stanford: Stanford University Press, 1957.
Davidson, William Leslie. *Political Thought in England: The Utilitarians from Bentham to J. S. Mill*. Oxford: Oxford University Press, 1915.
Davis, Walter T. "Economic Individualism and Social Disorder: The Power of Submerged Ideology." *Second Order: An African Journal of Philosophy* 6 (1977):21-43.
Day, J. P. "Retributive Punishment." *Mind* 87 (1978):498-516.
Dayton, Eric. "Towards a Credible Act-Utilitarianism." *American Philosophical Quarterly* 16 (1979):61-66.
────. "Utility Maximizers and Cooperative Undertakings." *Ethics* 90 (1979):130-141.
────. "Course of Action Utilitarianism." *Canadian Journal of Philosophy* 9 (1979):671-684.
DeGeorge, Richard T., ed. *Ethics and Society: Original Essays on Contemporary Moral Problems*. Garden City: Anchor, 1966.
DeMarco, Joseph P., and Richmond, Samuel A. "A Fault in the Utilitarian Theory of Conduct." *Southern Journal of Philosophy* 13 (1975):275-279.
DeNicola, Daniel R. "A Typology of Conceptions of the Good." *Personalist* 59 (1978): 38-46.
DeSousa, Ronald B. "The Good and the True." *Mind* 81 (1974):534-551.
Devine, Philip E. "The Moral Basis of Vegetarianism." *Philosophy* 53 (1978):481-505.
────. "The Conscious Acceptance of Guilt in the Necessary Murder." *Ethics* 89 (1979): 221-239.
Devlin, Lord Patrick. *The Enforcement of Morals*. Oxford: Oxford University Press, 1965.
Diamond, P. A. "Cardinal Welfare, Individualistic Ethics, and Interpersonal Comparisons of Utility: A Comment." *Journal of Political Economy* 75 (1967):765-766.

Diesing, Paul. "The Nature and Limitations of Economic Rationality." *Ethics* 61 (1950): 12-26.
Dietze, Gottfried. *In Defense of Property*. Chicago: Henry Regnery, 1963.
Diggs, B. J. "A Technical Ought." *Mind* 69 (1960):301-317.
———. "Rules and Utilitarianism." *American Philosophical Quarterly* 1 (1964):32-44.
———. "A Comment on 'Some Merits of One Form of Rule Utilitarianism'." In *Readings in Contemporary Ethical Theory*, edited by K. Pahel and M. Schiller, pp. 307-317. Englewood Cliffs, N. J.: Prentice-Hall, 1970.
DiIanni, Albert R. "The Direct/Indirect Distinction in Morals." *Thomist* 41 (1977): 350-380.
Donagan, Alan. "Is There a Credible Form of Utilitarianism?" In *Contemporary Utilitarianism*, edited by Michael Bayles, pp. 187-202. Garden City: Doubleday and Company, Inc., 1968.
———. "Sidgwick and Whewellian Intuitionism: Some Enigmas." *Canadian Journal of Philosophy* 7 (1977):447-465.
———. "A New Sidgwick?" *Ethics* 90 (1980):282-295.
Dorman, Neil. "The Refutation of the Generalization Argument." *Ethics* 74 (1963-64): 150-154.
Downie, R. S. "Social Roles and Moral Responsibility." *Philosophy* 39 (1964):29-36.
———. "Mill on Pleasure and Self-Development." *Philosophical Quarterly* 16 (1966):69-71.
———. "Moral Problems in a Market Economy: A Reappraisal of Adam Smith." *Dalhousie Review* 57 (1977):424-436.
Downs, A. *An Economic Theory of Democracy*. New York: Harper & Brothers, 1957.
Doyle, J. F. "Justice and Legal Punishment." *Philosophy* 42 (1967):53-67.
Draughon, W. E. "Liberty: A Proposed Analysis." *Social Theory and Practice* 5 (1978): 29-44.
Dryer, D. P. "Utilitarianism For and Against." *Canadian Journal of Philosophy* 4 (1975): 549-559.
Ducasse, C. J. "The Nature and Function of Theory in Ethics." *Ethics* 51 (1940):22-37.
Duncan, Graeme C. *Marx and Mill*. London: Cambridge University Press, 1973.
Duncan-Jones, A. "Utilitarianism and Rules." *Philosophical Quarterly* 7 (1957):364-367.
Duncker, Karl. "On Pleasure, Emotion and Striving." *Philosophy and Phenomenological Research* 1 (1941):391-430.
Dworkin, Gerald. "Marx and Mill: A Dialogue." *Philosophy and Phenomenological Research* 26 (1966):403-414.
———. "Paternalism." *Monist* 56 (1972):64-84.
———. and Blumefeld, D. "Punishment for Intentions." *Mind* 75 (1966):396-404.
Dworkin, Ronald. "Lord Devlin and the Enforcement of Morals." *Yale Law Journal* 75 (1965-1966):986-1005.
———. "The Original Position." *University of Chicago Law Review* 40 (1973):500-533.
———. *Taking Rights Seriously*. London: Duckworth, 1977.
Dwyer, William. "Egoism and Renewed Hostilities." *Personalist* 57 (1976):279-289.
Dybikowski, J. C. "False Pleasure and the *Philebus*." *Phronesis* 15 (1970):147-165.
———. "Lord Devlin's Morality and Its Enforcement." *Proceedings of the Aristotelian Society* 75 (1974-75):89-109.
Ebisch, Glenn. "Nationality and Moral Obligations." *Journal of Social Philosophy* 9 (1978): 5-10.
Eckhoff, Torstein. "Justice and Social Utility." In *Legal Essays: Festskrift for Frede Castberg*, pp. 74-93. Oslo, 1963.
Edgeworth, F. Y. *Mathematical Psychics*. London: Kegan Paul, 1881. Reprinted New York: A. M. Kelly, 1961.
Edwards, Rem B. "Do Pleasures and Pains Differ Qualitatively?" *Journal of Value Inquiry* 9 (1975):270-281.

———. *Pleasures and Pains: A Theory of Qualitative Hedonism.* Ithaca: Cornell University Press, 1979.
Eggerman, Richard W. "Moral Theory and Practicality." *Ethics* 84 (1974):174-179.
Ehman, Robert. "Rawls and Nozick: Justice Without Well-Being." *Journal of Value Inquiry* 14 (1980):7-21.
Ehring, Douglas E. "A Defense of Lyon's Reduction Thesis." *Kinesis* 8 (1977):26-43.
Ellery, John Blaise. *John Stuart Mill.* New York: Twayne Publishers, 1964.
Ellsberg, D. "Classic and Current Notions of 'Measurable Utility'." *Economic Journal* 64 (1954):528-556.
Ely, Richard T. *Property and Contract in Their Relations to the Distribution of Wealth.* New York: Macmillan, 1908.
Emmet, D. "Justice-II." *Aristotelian Society Supplementary Volume* 43 (1969):121-140.
Emmons, Donald C. "Justice Reassessed." *American Philosophical Quarterly* 4 (1967):144-151.
———. "Act vs Rule-Utilitarianism." *Mind* 82 (1973):226-233.
Ericsson, Lars O. *Justice In the Distribution of Economic Resources.* Stockholm: University of Stockholm, 1976.
———. "Some Reflections on Extended Utilitarianism." *Theoria* 43 (1977):145-156.
Everett, Charles Warren. *Jeremy Bentham.* London: Weidenfeld Nicholson, 1969.
Ewing, Alfred Cyril. "Punishment as a Moral Agency, An Attempt to Reconcile the Retributive and the Utilitarian View." *Mind* 36 (1927):292-305.
———. *The Definition of Good.* New York: Macmillan, 1947.
———. "Utilitarianism." *Ethics* 58 (1948):100-111.
———. *Ethics.* London: English Universities Press, 1953. (See Chapters 2, 3, and 5.)
———. "What Would Happen If Everybody Acted Like Me?" *Philosophy* 28 (1953):16-29.
———. "Armstrong and the Retributive Theory." *Mind* 72 (1963:121-124.
———. "Political Differences." *The Philosophical Quarterly* 13 (1963):333-343.
Ezorsky, Gertrude. "Review of *Generalization in Ethics* by Marcus Singer." *The Journal of Philosophy* 60 (1963):323-333.
———. "Utilitarianism and Rules." *Australasian Journal of Philosophy* 43 (1965):225-229.
———. "Review of *The Forms and Limits of Utilitarianism* by David Lyons." *The Journal of Philosophy* 65 (1968):533-544.
———, ed. *Philosophical Perspectives on Punishment.* Albany: State University of New York Press, 1972.
———. "Punishment and Excuses." In *Punishment and Human Rights,* edited by M. Goldinger, pp. 99-115. New York: Schenkman Publishing Company, 1974.
———. "Unconscious Utilitarianism." *Monist* 58 (1974):468-474.
Faidherbe, A. J. *La justice distributive.* Paris: Librairie du Recueil Sirey, 1934.
Falk, W. David. "Morality, Self and Others." In *Morality and the Language of Conduct,* edited by H. Castaneda and G. Nakhnikian, pp. 25-67. Detroit: Wayne State University Press, 1963.
Feeley, Malcolm. "A Solution to the 'Voting Dilemma' in Modern Democratic Theory." *Ethics* 84 (1974):235-242.
Feinberg, Joel. "The Forms and Limits of Utilitarianism." *Philosophical Review* 76 (1967):368-381.
———. *Doing and Deserving.* Princeton: Princeton University Press, 1971.
———. "Duty and Obligation in the Non-Ideal World." *Journal of Philosophy* 70 (1973):263-275.
———. *Social Philosophy.* Englewood Cliffs, N. J.: Prentice-Hall, Inc., 1973.
Feldman, Fred. "On the Extensional Equivalence of Simple and General Utilitarianism." *Nous* 8 (1974):185-194.

———. "World Utilitarianism." In *Analysis and Metaphysics*. edited by Keith Lehrer, pp. 255-271. Dordrecht: Reidel, 1975.
———. *Introductory Ethics*, Englewood Cliffs, N. J.: Prentice-Hall, 1978.
Findlay, J. N. *Values and Intentions*. London: George Allen & Unwin, 1961. (See Chapters 6 and 7.)
Firth, Roderick. "Ethical Absolutism and the Ideal Observer." *Philosophy and Phenomenological Research* 12 (1952):317-345.
Fishburn, Peter C. "Utility Theory." *Management Science* 14 (1968):335-378.
———. *Utility Theory for Decision Making*. New York: John Wiley, 1970.
———. "Utility Theory with Inexact Preferences and Degrees of Preference." *Synthese* 21 (1970):204-221.
———, and Roberts, Fred S. "Mixture Axioms in Linear and Multilinear Utility Theories." *Theory and Decision* 9 (1978):161-171.
Fisher, Franklin M., and Rothenberg, Jerome. "How Income Ought to be Distributed: A Paradox Lost." *Journal of Political Economy* 69 (1961):162-180.
———, and Rothenberg, Jerome. "How Income Ought to be Distributed: Paradox Enow." *Journal of Political Economy* 70 (1962):88-93.
Flathman, Richard E. *The Public Interest: An Essay Concerning the Normative Discourse of Politics*. New York: Wiley, 1966.
———. "Forms and Limits of Utilitarianism." *Ethics* 76 (1966):309-317.
———. *Political Obligation*. New York: Atheneum, 1972.
Fleisher, Martin, ed. *Machiavelli and the Nature of Political Thought*. New York: Atheneum, 1972.
Flew, Anthony. "The Justification of Punishment." *Philosophy* 29 (1954):291-307.
Flubacher, Joseph Francis. *The Concept of Ethics in the History of Economics*. New York: Vantage Press, 1950.
Foot, Philippa. "Abortion and the Doctrine of Double Effect." *Oxford Review* 5 (1967). Reprinted in Rachels, James, ed., *Moral Problems* (New York: Harper & Row, 1971) pp. 29-41.
Fowler, T. "Professor Sidgwick on 'Progressive Morality'." *Mind* 10 (old series) (1885):481-486.
Franke, Gunter. "Expected Utility with Ambiguous Probabilities and 'Irrational' Parameters." *Theory and Decision* 9 (1978):267-283.
Frankel, Charles. "Empiricism and Moral Imperatives." *Journal of Philosophy* 50 (1953): 257-268.
———. "Justice and Rationality." In *Philosophy, Science and Method*, edited by S. Morgenbesser, P. Suppes, and M. White, pp. 400-414. New York: St. Martin's Press, 1969.
———. "Justice, Utilitarianism and Rights." *Social Theory and Practice* 3 (1974):27-46.
Frankena, William K. "Henry Sidgwick." In *Encyclopedia of Morals*, edited by Vergilius T. A. Ferm. New York: Philosophical Library, 1956.
———. *Ethics*. Englewood Cliffs, N. J.: Prentice-Hall, 1963.
———. "Comments on Charles Baylis' 'C. I. Lewis' Theory of Value and Ethics'." *Journal of Philosophy* 61 (1964):567-570.
——— "The Concept of Morality." *Journal of Philosophy* 63 (1966):688-696.
——— "Sidgwick and the Dualism of Practical Reason." *Monist* 58 (1974):449-467.
———. "Methods of Ethics, 1977." *Ratio* 21 (1979):125-134.
Freed, Lan. "A New Review of *Principia Ethica*." *Philosophical Quarterly* 6 (1956): 315-326.
Freeman, H. "Egoism, Community and Rational Moral Education." *Educational Philosophy and Theory* 9 (1977):1-8.
Freeman, James B. "Fairness and the Value of Disjunctive Actions." *Philosophical Studies* 24 (1973):105-111.
Freund, Hans. *The Balanced Life: An Essay in Ethics*. New York: Philosophical Library, 1959.

Frey, R. G. "On Casual Consequences." *Canadian Journal of Philosophy* 4 (1974):365-379.
_____. "Circumstances and Consequences." *Personalist* 57 (1976):34-42.
_____. "Can Act-Utilitarianism Be Put Into Practice?" *Journal of Value Inquiry* 11 (1977): 49-58.
_____. "Act-Utilitarianism: Sidgwick or Bentham and Smart?" *Mind* 86 (1977):95-100.
Fried, Charles. *An Anatomy of Values*. Cambridge: Harvard University Press, 1970.
_____. *Right and Wrong*. Cambridge: Harvard University Press, 1978.
Fried, Marlene Gerger. "Marxism and Justice." *Journal of Philosophy* 71 (1974):612-613.
Friedman, Milton J. "Choice, Chance, and the Personal Distribution of Income." *Journal of Political Economy* 61 (1953):277-292.
_____, and Savage, L. J. "The Utility Analysis of Choices Involving Risk." *Journal of Political Economy* 56 (1948):279-304.
Friedrich, Carl J., ed. *Nomos IV: Liberty*. New York: Atherton Press, 1962.
_____, ed. *Nomos V: The Public Interest*. New York: Atherton Press, 1962.
_____. *Man and His Government*. New York: McGraw-Hill, 1963. (See Chapter 6.)
Fuchs, Alan. "The Role of the Formal Constraints of the Concept of Right in Rawls' Theory." Paper read at the Eastern Division of the American Philosophical Association, 1975.
Fuller, Lon L. *The Morality of Law*. New Haven: Yale University Press, 1964.
Fullinwider, Robert K. "On Mill's Analogy Between Visible and Desirable." *Southern Journal of Philosophy* 10 (1972):17-22.
Fulmer, Gilbert. "Skinner's Values." *Journal of Value Inquiry* 10 (1976):106-118.
Fuss, Peter. "Sense and Reason in Butler's Ethics." *Dialogue* (Canada) 7 *(1968):180-193*.
Gallagher, Neil. "Utilitarian Blame: Retrospect and Prospects." *Journal of Value Inquiry* 12 (1978):13-23.
Gardenfors, Peter. *Group Decision Theory*. Lund: Studentlitteratur, 1974.
Gardner, Michael. "Rawls on the Maximin Rule and Distributive Justice." *Philosophical Studies* 27 (1975): 255-270.
Garin, E. *L'illuminismo inglese: i moralisti*. Milano: Fratelli Bocca, 1941.
Garner, Richard T. "Some Remarks on Act Utilitarianism." *Mind* 78 (1969):124-128.
Garnett, Arthur Campbell. *The Moral Nature of Man: A Critical Evaluation of Ethical Principles*. New York: Ronald Press, 1952.
_____. "Virtues, Rules and Good Reasons." *Monist* 47 (1963):545-562.
Garvin, Lucius. "Pleasure Theory in Ethics and Esthetics." *Journal of Philosophy* 39 (1942): 57-63.
_____. "Retributive and Distributive Justice." *Journal of Philosophy* 42 (1945):270-277.
_____. "Normative Utilitarianism and Naturalism." *Ethics* 60 (1949):49-54.
_____. *A Modern Introduction to Ethics*. New York: Houghton Mifflin, 1953 (See Chapters 10 and 11.)
Gauthier, David P. *Practical Reasoning*. Oxford: Clarendon Press, 1963.
_____. "Rule Utilitarianism and Randomization." *Analysis* 25 (1965):68-69.
_____. "Progress and Happiness: A Utilitarian Reconsideration." *Ethics* 78 (1967):77-82.
_____. "Brandt on Egoism." *Journal of Philosophy* 69 (1972):697-698.
_____. "Justice and Natural Endowment: Toward a Critique of Rawls' Ideological Framework." *Social Theory and Practice* 3 (1974):3-26.
_____. "Reason and Maximization." *Canadian Journal of Philosophy* 4 (1975):411-433.
_____. "Coordination." *Dialogue* (Canada) 14 (1975):195-221.
_____. "The Social Contract as Ideology." *Philosophy & Public Affairs* 6 (1977):130-164.
_____. "Critical Notice of Harsanyi's *Essays on Ethics, Social Behavior and Scientific Explanation.*" *Dialogue* (Canada) 17 (1978):696-706.
_____. "Social Choice and Distributive Justice." *Philosophia* 7 (1978):239-253.
_____. "Economic Rationality and Moral Constraints." *Midwest Studies in Philosophy* 3 (1978):75-96.

———. "The Social Contract: Individual Decision or Collective Bargain." In *Foundations and Applications of Decision Theory*, Vol. II, edited by C. A. Hooker, J. J. Leach, and E. F. McClennen. Dordrecht: Reidel, 1978.
———. "David Hume, Contractarian." *Philosophical Review* 88 (1979):3-38.
Gavison, Ruth. "The Enforcement of Morals and the Status of the Principle of Liberty." (In Hebrew.) *IYYUN* 27 (1976-77):274-294.
Geddes, Leonard. "On the Intrinsic Wrongness of Killing Innocent People." *Analysis* 33 (1973):93-97.
Gendin, Sidney. "Comments on Smart's *An Outline of A System of Utilitarian Ethics*." *Australasian Journal of Philosophy* 45 (1967):207-213.
———. "A Plausible Theory of Retribution." *Journal of Value Inquiry* 5 (1970):1-16.
Georgescu-Roegen, Nicolas. "Choice, Expectations and Measurability." *Quarterly Journal of Economics* 68 (1954):503-534.
Gerber, William. "Johnson's Analysis of the Good." *Journal of Philosophy* 51 (1954):325-327.
Gewirth, Alan. "The Generalization Principle." *The Philosophical Review* 73 (1964):229-242.
Gibbard, Allan F. "Rule Utilitarianism: Merely An Illusory Alternative?" *Australasian Journal of Philosophy* 43 (1965):211-220.
———. "Doing No More Harm Than Good." *Philosophical Studies* 24 (1973):158-173.
Gibson, A. Boyce. "The Goodness of Producing and the Good Produced." *Australasian Journal of Philosophy* 18 (1940):232-245.
Gide, C., and Rist, C. *A History of Economic Doctrines from the Times of the Physiocrats to the Present Day*. Translated by R. Richards. Boston: Heath and Company, 1938. (2nd edition, 1948.)
Gill, Emily R. "Responsibility and Choice in Robert Nozick: Sins of Commission and of Omission." *Personalist* 59 (1978):344-357.
Ginsberg, Morris. "The Concept of Justice." *Philosophy* 38 (1963):91-116.
Girshick, Meyer A. "An Elementary Survey of Statistical Decision Theory." *Review of Educational Research* 24 (1954):448-466.
Glossup, Ronald J. "Review of *Distributive Justice* by Nicholas Rescher." *The Journal of Philosophy* 66 (1969):213-221.
———. "Is Hume a 'Classical Utilitarian'?" *Hume Studies* 2 (1976):1-12.
Godlovitch, Roslind. "Animals and Morals." *Philosophy* 46 (1971):23-33.
Godwin, William. *Political Justice*. 1793.
Golding, Martin Philip. *Philosophy of Law*. Englewood Cliffs, N. J.: Prentice-Hall, 1975.
Goldinger, Milton. "Punishment, Justice, and the Separation of Issues." *Monist* 49 (1965):458-474.
———. "Rule-Utilitarianism and Criminal Reform." *Southern Journal of Philosophy* 5 (1967):103-109.
———. "Is Population Control a Difficulty for the Utilitarian?" *Personalist* 54 (1973):355-360.
———. "Mill's Attack on Moral Conservatism." *Midwest Studies in Philosophy* 1 (1976):61-67.
Goldman, Alan H. "Can a Utilitarian's Support of NonUtilitarian Rules Vindicate Utilitarianism?" *Social Theory and Practice* 4 (1977):333-345.
Goldman, Alvin I. *A Theory of Human Action*. Englewood Cliffs, N. J.: Prentice-Hall, 1970.
Goldman, Holly S. "The Generalization Principle In Ethics." Ph.D. dissertation, University of Michigan, 1972.
———. "David Lyons on Utilitarian generalization." *Philosophical Studies* 26 (1974):77-95.
———. "The 'Collective' Interpretation of Utilitarian Generalization." *Philosophical Studies* 34 (1978):207-209.
———. "Utilitarianism and Future Acts." In *Values and Morals: Essays In Honor of Charles*

L. Stevenson, William K. Frankena, and Richard B. Brandt, edited by J. Kim and A. Goldman. Dordrecht: Reidel, 1978.

Goldschmidt, Walter. "Values and the Field of Comparative Sociology." *American Sociological Review* 18 (1953):287-293.

Goldstein, Irwin. "Happiness: The Role of Non-Hedonistic Criteria in its Evaluation." *International Philosophical Quarterly* 13 (1973):523-534.

Goldstick, D. "Assessing Utilities." *Mind* 80 (1971):531-541.

Goldworth, Amnon. "The Meaning of Bentham's Greatest Happiness Principle." *Journal of History of Philosophy* 7 (1969):315-321.

_____. "Bentham's Concept of Pleasure: Its Relation to Fictitious Terms." *Ethics* 82 (1972): 334-343.

Goodrich, T. "The Morality of Killing." *Philosophy* 44 (1969):127-139.

Gordon, Scott. "John Rawls' Difference Principle, Utilitarianism, and the Optimum Degree of Inequality." *Journal of Philosophy* 70 (1973):275-280.

_____. "The Quality Problem in Utilitarianism." *Mill News Letter* 10 (1975):9-13.

Gorovitz, S., ed. *Mill: Utilitarianism, With Critical Essays*. Indianapolis: The Bobbs-Merrill Company, Inc., 1971.

Gosling, Justin Cyril Bertrand. *Pleasure and Desire: The Case for Hedonism Reviewed*. Oxford: Clarendon Press, 1969.

Gottlieb, Gidon. *The Logic of Choice*. New York: Macmillan Company, 1968.

Gourevich, Victor. "Rawls on Justice." *Review of Metaphysics* 28 (1975):485-519.

Govier, Trudy. "What Should We Do About Future People?" *American Philosophical Quarterly* 16 (1979):105-113.

Graaff, Johannes de Villiers. *Theoretical Welfare Economics*. Cambridge: Cambridge University Press, 1967.

Graham, William. *English Politics from Hobbes to Maine*. London: E. Arnold, 1899.

Gray, John N. "On the Contestability of Social and Political Concepts." *Political Theory* 5 (1977):331-348.

Grean, Stanley. "Self-Interest and Public Interest in Shaftesbury's Philosophy." *Journal of the History of Philosophy* 2 (1964):37-46.

Green, T. H. "Hedonism and Ultimate Good." *Mind* 2 (old series) (1887):266-269.

Greenberg, Allan. "On a Concept of Happiness." *Philosophy and Phenomenological Research* 16 (1955-56):286-287.

Grice, Godfrey Russell. *The Grounds of Moral Judgment*. New York: Cambridge University Press, 1967.

Griffin, James P. "Consequences." *Proceedings of the Aristotelian Society* 65 (1965):167-182.

_____. "Are there Incommensurable Values?" *Philosophy & Public Affairs* 7 (1977): 39-59.

_____. "Is Happiness Morally More Important than Unhappiness?" *Philosophical Quarterly* 29 (1979): 47-55.

Griffin, Nicholas. "Cooper's Reconstruction of Mill's 'Proof'." *Mind* 81 (1972): 142-143.

Griffin-Collart, E. "Le Principe D'Utilité et L'Egalité: Bentham et J. S. Mill." *Revue Internationale de Philosophie* 25 (1971):312-330.

Griffiths, A. Phillips. "Justifying Moral Principles." *Proceedings of The Aristotelian Society* 58 (1958):103-124.

_____. "Review of *Generalization In Ethics* by Marcus Singer." *Philosophical Books* 3 (1962):18-21.

Griffiths, Leslie. "Social Morality and the Law." *Journal of Social Philosophy* 2 (1971): 8-10.

Grimm, Robert H., and MacKay, Alfred F., eds. *Society: Revolution and Reform*. Cleveland: Case Western Reserve University Press, 1971.

Grisez, Germain, "Methods of Ethical Inquiry." *Proceedings of the American Catholic Philosophical Association* 41 (1967):160-168.
———. "The Moral Basis of Law." *Thomist* 32 (1968):283-306.
Grover, Robinson A. "The Ranking Assumption." *Theory and Decision* 4 (1974): 277-299.
Guyau, M. *La morale anglaise contemporaine: morale de l'utilité et de l'évolution.* Paris: F. Alcan, 1879.
Halévy, Elie. *The Growth of Philosophic Radicalism.* Translated by Mary Morris. London: Faber & Gwyer, 1928.
Hall, Everett W. "The 'Proof' of Utility in Bentham and Mill." *Ethics* 60 (1949):1-18.
———. "Justice as Fairness: A Modernized Version of the Social Contract." *Journal of Philosophy* 64 (1957):662-670.
Hall, J. C. "Quantity of Pleasure." *Proceedings of the Aristotelian Society* 67 (1966-67):35-52.
Hallett, Garth. "Happiness." *Heythrop Journal* 12 (1971):301-303.
Halliday, Richard John. *John Stuart Mill.* New York: Barnes & Noble, 1976.
Hallowell, John Hamilton. *Main Currents In Modern Political Thought.* New York: Holt, 1950.
Hamburger, Joseph. *Intellectuals in Politics: John Stuart Mill and the Philosophic Radicals.* Yale Studies in Political Science, No. 14. New Haven: Yale University Press, 1965.
———. *James Mill and the Art of Revolution.* New Haven: Yale University Press, 1965.
Hamlyn, D. W. "The Obligation to Keep a Promise." *Proceedings of the Aristotelian Society* 62 (1961-62):179-194.
Hammond, Albert L. "Euthyphro, Mill, and Mr. Lewis." *Journal of Philosophy* 49 (1952): 377-391.
Hammond, Peter J. "Why Ethical Measures of Inequality Need Interpersonal Comparisons." *Theory and Decision* 7 (1976): 263-274.
Hampshire, Stuart. *Morality and Pessimism.* London: Cambridge University Press, 1972.
Hancock, Roger N. *Twentieth Century Ethics.* New York: Columbia University Press, 1972.
———. "Mill, Saints and Heroes." *Mill News Letter* 10 (1975):13-15.
Handy, Rollo. "A Need Definition of Value." *The Philosophical Quarterly* 10 (1960):156-163.
Haney, Lewis H. *Value and Distribution.* New York: Appleton-Century-Crofts, 1939.
Hanink, J. G. "On the Survival Lottery." *Philosophy* 51 (1976):223-225.
Hardin, Garrett. "The Tragedy of the Commons." *Science* 162 (1968):1243-1248.
———. "Lifeboat Ethics: The Case Against Helping the Poor." In *Morality and World Hunger,* edited by William Aiken and Hugh La Follette. Englewood Cliffs, N. J.: Prentice-Hall, 1977.
Hardin, Russell. "Collective Action as an Agreeable n-Person Prisoners' Dilemma." *Behavioral Science* 16 (1971):472-481.
Harding, D. W. *Social Psychology and Individual Values.* London: Hutchinson's, 1953.
Hare, Richard Mervin. *Freedom and Reason.* New York: Oxford University Press, 1963 (see Chapter 7).
———. *Essays on Philosophical Method.* Berkeley: University of California Press, 1971.
———. "Rules of War and Moral Reasoning." *Philosophy & Public Affairs* 1 (1972):166-181.
———. "Principles." *Proceedings of the Aristotelian Society* 73 (1972-73):1-18.
———. "Rawls': A Theory of Justice—I." *Philosophical Quarterly* 23 (1973):144-155.
———. "Rawls': A Theory of Justice—II." *Philosophical Quarterly* 23 (1973):241-252.
———. "Ethical Theory and Utilitarianism." In *Contemporary British Philosophy*, Fourth Series, edited by H. D. Lewis. London: Allen & Unwin, 1976.
———. "Justice and Equality." (In Polish) *Etyka* 15 (1977):143-161.
———. "What Is Wrong With Slavery." *Philosophy & Public Affairs* 8 (1979):103-121.
———. "On Terrorism." *The Journal of Value Inquiry* 13 (1980):241-249.

Harman, Gilbert. "Moral Relativism Defended." *Philosophical Review* 84 (1975):3-22.
_____. "Relativistic Ethics: Morality as Politics." *Midwest Studies in Philosphy* 3 (1978): 109-121.
Harris, John "Williams on Negative Responsibility and Integrity." *Philosophical Quarterly* 24 (1974):265-273.
_____. "The Survival Lottery." *Philosophy* 50 (1975):81-87.
Harris, N. G. E. "Nondeliberative Utilitarianism." *Ethics* 82 (1972):344-348.
Harrison, Jonathan. "Utilitarianism, Universalization and Our Duty To Be Just." *Proceedings of the Aristotelian Society* 53 (1953):105-134.
_____. "The Place of Moral Goodness In A Teleological Ethical Theory." *Australasian Journal of Philosophy* 48 (1970):190-196.
_____. "The Right and the Just in Mill's 'Utilitarianism'." *Canadian Journal of Philosophy Supplementary Volume* 1 (1974):93-107.
Harrison, Ross. "The Only Possible Morality." *Proceedings of the Aristotelian Society Supplementary Volume* 50 (1976):21-42.
Harrod, R. F. "Utilitarianism Revised." *Mind* 45 (1936):137-156.
Harsanyi, John C. "Cardinal Utility in Welfare Economics and in the Theory of Risk-Taking." *Journal of Political Economy* 61 (1953):434-435.
_____. "Cardinal Welfare, Individualistic Ethics, and Interpersonal Comparisons of Utility." *Journal of Political Economy* 63 (1955):309-321. Reprinted in his *Essays on Ethics, Social Behavior, and Scientific Explanation.* Dordrecht: Reidel, 1976.
_____. Ethics in Terms of Hypothetical Imperatives." *Mind* 67 (1958):305-316.
_____. "Nonlinear Social Welfare Functions." *Theory and Decision* 6 (1975):311-332.
_____. "Advances in Understanding Rational Behavior." In his *Essays on Ethics, Social Behavior, and Scientific Explanation.* Dordrecht: Reidel, 1976.
_____. "The Problem Solving Ability of the Rule Utilitarian Approach Should Not Be Underestimated: Comments on Scanlon's Paper." *Erkenntnis* 11 (1977):435-438.
_____. "Rule Utilitarianism and Decision Theory." *Erkenntnis* 11 (1977):25-53.
_____. "Morality and the Theory of Rational Behavior." *Social Research* 44 (1977):625-656.
_____. "Preferences and Utilitarian Theory: Some Comments." *Erkenntnis* 13 (1978):397-399.
_____. "Bayesian Decision Theory, Rule Utilitarianism, and Arrow's Impossibility Theorem." *Theory and Decision* 11 (1979):298-317.
_____. "Rule Utilitarianism, Rights, Obligations and the Theory of Rational Behavior." *Theory and Decision* 12 (1980):115-133.
Hart, H. L. A. "Are There Any Natural Rights?" *Philosophical Review* 64 (1955):175-191.
_____. "Immorality and Treason." *The Listener* 62 (1959).
_____. *The Concept of Law.* Oxford: Clarendon Press, 1961.
_____. *Law, Liberty, and Morality.* Stanford, Calif.: Stanford University Press, 1963.
_____. *Punishment and Responsibility: Essays in the Philosophy of Law.* Oxford: Oxford University Press, 1968.
Hart, W. A. "Freedom Versus Reason." *Philosophical Quarterly* 24 (1974):245-260.
Haslett, D. W. *Moral Rightness.* The Hague: Nijhoff, 1974.
Havard, William C. *Henry Sidgwick and Later Utilitarian Political Philosophy.* Gainesville: University of Florida Press, 1959.
Haworth, Lawrence. "Utility and Rights." In *American Philosophical Quarterly Monograph 1: Studies in Moral Philosophy*, edited by Nicholas Rescher. Oxford: Basil Blackwell, 1968.
Hazlitt, Henry. *The Foundations of Morality.* Princeton, N. J.: Van Nostrand, 1964.
Hearn, Thomas K., Jr., ed. *Studies in Utilitarianism.* New York: Appleton-Century-Crofts, 1971.
Held, Virginia. "Rationality and Social Value in Game Theoretical Analysis." *Ethics* 76 (1966):215-220.

——. "On the Meaning of Trust." *Ethics* 78 (1968):156-159.
Henderson, H. D. *Supply and Demand.* New York: Harcourt Brace and Co., 1922.
Henry, N. O. "Political Obligation and Collective Goods." In *Nomos XII: Political and Legal Obligation,* edited by J. R. Pennock and J. W. Chapman, pp. 263-287. New York: Atherton Press, 1970.
Henson, Richard G. "Utilitarianism and the Wrongness of Killing." *Philosophical Review* 80 (1971):320-337.
Hicks, G. Dawes. "Die englische Philosophie." In *Friederich Ueberwegs Grundriss der Geschichte der Philosophie.* Part 5, *Die Philosophie des Auslandes vom Beginn des 19. Jahrhunderts.* 12th edn. edited by T. K. Oesterreiche. Berlin: E. S. Mittler u. Sohn, 1928.
Hicks, J. R. "The Foundations of Welfare Economics." *Economic Journal* 49 (1939):696-712.
——. "The Valuation of Social Income." *Economica* 7 (1940):105-124.
——. *The Social Framework: An Introduction to Economics.* London: Oxford University Press, 1942.
——. *Value and Capital,* 2nd ed. Oxford: The Clarendon Press, 1946.
——. *The Theory of Wages.* London: Macmillan, 1951.
Hill, John. *The Ethics of G. E. Moore: A New Interpretation.* Assen: Van Gorcum, 1976.
Hilliard, Albert L. *The Forms of Value: The Extension of a Hedonistic Axiology.* New York: Columbia University Press, 1950.
Hillinger, C. "Measurement of Utility." *Review of Economic Studies* 35 (1969):111-116.
Hilton, John. *Rich Man, Poor Man.* London: Allen & Unwin, 1944.
Hirshleifer, Jack. *Price Theory and Applications.* Englewood Cliffs, N. J.: Prentice-Hall, 1976.
Hiskes, Richard P. "Has Hume a Theory of Social Justice?" *Hume Studies* 3 (1977):72-93.
Hobhouse, L. T. *Elements of Social Justice.* New York: Henry Holt, 1922.
Hodges, H. A. "Things and Persons." Part II *Aristotelian Society Supplementary Volume* 22 (1948):190-201.
Hodgson, D. H. *Consequences of Utilitarianism: A Study in Normative Ethics and Legal Theory.* Oxford: Clarendon Press, 1967.
Hoerster, N. "Is Act-Utilitarian Truth-Telling Self-Defeating?" *Mind* 82 (1973):413-416.
Höffe, Otfried. "Zur Rolle Der Entscheidungstheorie Bei Der Rechfertigung Von Gerechtigkeitsprinzipien: Kritische Übelegungen Im Anschluss An Rawls." *Erkenntnis* 11 (1977):411-425.
——. "Einige Schwierigkeiten in Harsanyi's Praferenz-Utilitarismus." *Erkenntnis* 11 (1977):431-432.
Hogan, Richard. "Was Socrates a 'Utilitarian'?" *Auslegung* 5 (1978):118-131.
Holmes, R. L. "On Generalization." *The Journal of Philosophy* 60 (1963):317-323.
Holtzman, Irving. "Patenting Certain Forms of Life: A Moral Justification." *Hastings Center Report* 9 (1979):9-11.
Honderich, Ted. *Punishment: The Supposed Justifications.* London: Hutchinson, 1969.
Hook, Sidney, ed. *Law and Philosophy.* New York: New York University Press, 1964.
——. *Human Values and Economic Policy.* New York: New York University Press, 1967.
Horowitz, Irving Louis. *Claude Helvetius: Philosopher of Democracy and Enlightenment.* New York: Paine-Whitman, 1954.
Horwich, Paul. "On Calculating the Utility of Acts." *Philosophical Studies* 25 (1974):21-31.
Hospers, John. *Human Conduct: An Introduction to the Problems of Ethics.* New York: Harcourt, Brace and World, Inc., 1961.
——. "Rule Egoism." *Personalist* 54 (1973):391-395.
Hotelling, H. "The General Welfare in Relation to Problems of Taxation and of Railway and Utility Rates." *Econometrica* 6 (1938):242-269.
Hourani, George F. *Ethical Value.* Ann Arbor, Mich.: University of Michigan Press, 1956.

Hubin, D. Clayton. "The Scope of Justice." *Philosophy & Public Affairs* 9 (1979):3-24.
Huff, Thomas. "Self-Interest and Benevolence in Hume's Account of Moral Obligation." *Ethics* 83 (1972):58-70.
Hughes, George E. "The Ethical Relevance of Consequences." *Proceedings of the Aristotelian Society* 48 (1948):59-74.
Hume, David. *A Treatise of Human Nature.* 1739-1740.
_____. *An Enquiry Concerning the Principles of Morals.* 1751.
Hunt, W. Murray. "The Inadequacy of Kalin's Views on 'The Inadequacy of Contemporary Moral Philosophy'." *The Journal of Value Inquiry* 13 (1979):145-148.
Hutchinson, T. W. *A Review of Economic Doctrines.* Oxford: The Clarendon Press, 1953.
Irvine, William. "Shaw, the Fabians, and the Utilitarians." *Journal of the History of Ideas* 8 (1947):218-231.
Isenberg, A. I. "Comments on Pleasure and Falsity." *American Philosophical Quarterly* 1 (1964):96-100.
_____. "Deontology and the Ethics of Lying." *Philosophy and Phenomenological Research* 24 (1964):463-480.
Itzkin, Elissa S. "Bentham's 'Chrestomathia': Utilitarian Legacy to English Education." *Journal of the History of Ideas* 39 (1978):303-316.
Jack, Henry H. "Utilitarianism and Ross's Theory of 'Prima Facie' Duties." *Dialogue* (Canada) 10 (1971):437-457.
Jackson, Reginald. "Bishop Butler's Refutation of Psychological Hedonism." *Philosophy* 18 (1943):114-139.
Jeffrey, R. C. *The Logic of Decision.* New York: Wiley, 1965.
_____. "Ethics and the Logic of Decision." *Journal of Philosophy* 62 (1965):528-538.
_____. "On Interpersonal Utility Theory." *Journal of Philosophy* 68 (1971):647-656.
Jenkins, Iredell. "The Analysis of Justice." *Ethics* 57 (1946):1-13.
_____. "Some Large Scale Moral Theorizing." *Review of Metaphysics* 5 (1951):309-326.
Jennings, R. E. "A Utilitarian Semantics for Deontic Logic." *Journal of Philosophical Logic* 3 (1974):445-456.
Jevons, W. Stanley. *The Theory of Political Economy.* London: Macmillan, 1885. 4th edition, 1911.
Johnson, Oliver A. "Rightness, Moral Obligation, and Goodness." *Journal of Philosophy* 50 (1953):597-607.
_____. *Rightness and Goodness.* The Hague: Martinus Nijhoff, 1959.
Jones, Hardy. "Fairness, Meritocracy, and Reverse Discrimination." *Social Theory and Practice* 4 (1977):211-226.
_____. "Mill's Argument for the Principle of Utility." *Philosophy and Phenomenological Research* 38 (1978):338-354.
Jouvenel, Bertrand, Jr. *The Ethics of Redistribution.* Cambridge: Cambridge University Press, 1951.
Kading, Daniel. "On Promising Without Moral Risk." *Philosophical Studies* 11 (1960):58-62.
Kaiser, Nolan. "Distributive Justice and Rule Utilitarianism." *Philosophical Studies* (Ireland) 20 (1972):144-151.
Kaldor, Nicholas. "Welfare Propositions in Economics." *Economic Journal* 46 (1939):549-552.
_____. "Alternative Theories of Distribution." *Review of Economic Studies* 23 (1955-56):83-100.
_____. *Essays on Value and Distribution.* London: Duckworth & Co., 1960.
Kaler, Emil. *Der Ethik des Utilitarianisms.* Hamburg and Leipzig: L. Voss, 1855.
Kalin, Jesse. "On Ethical Egoism." *American Philosophical Quarterly Monograph* 1: *Studies in Moral Philosophy* (1968):26-41.
_____. "Two Kinds of Moral Reasoning: Ethical Egoism as a Moral Theory." *Canadian Journal of Philosophy* 5 (1975):323-356.

——. "Grice's Contract Ground and Moral Obligation: The Inadequacy of Contractualism." *Philosophical Studies* 29 (1976):115-128.
——. "Lies, Secrets, and Love: The Inadequacy of Contemporary Moral Philosophy." *Journal of Value Inquiry* 10 (1976):253-265.
Kant, I. *Groundwork of the Metaphysics of Morals*. Translated by H. J. Paton. New York: Harper and Row, 1964.
Kantor, Paul, and Nelson, Raymond J. "Social Decision Making in the Presence of Complex Goals, Ethics and the Environment." *Theory and Decision* 10 (1979):181-200.
Kaplan, Morton A. "Some Problems of the Extreme Utilitarian Position." *Ethics* 70 (1960): 228-232.
——. "Restricted Utilitarianism." *Ethics* 71 (1961):301-302.
Katz, Eric. "Utilitarianism and Preservation." *Environmental Ethics* 1 (1979):357-364.
Kaufman, Arnold S. "Anthony Quinton on Punishment." *Analysis* 20 (1959):10-13.
Kaufmann, Walter. "The Origin of Justice." *Review of Metaphysics* 23 (1969):209-239.
Kavka, Gregory S. "Rawls on Average and Total Utility." *Philosophical Studies* 27 (1975): 237-253.
——. "Extensional Equivalence and Utilitarian Generalization." *Theoria* 41 (1975):125-147.
——. "Deterrence, Utility, and Rational Choice." *Theory and Decision* 12 (1980):41-60.
Keat, David, and Miller, David. "Understanding Justice." *Political Theory* 2 (1974):3-31.
Keeney, Ralph, and Raiffa, Howard. *Decisions with Multiple Objectives: Preferences and Value Tradeoffs*. New York: Wiley, 1976.
Keeton, G. W., and Schwartzenberger, Georg, eds. *Jeremy Bentham and the Law*. London: Stevens & Sons, 1948.
Kelly, Jack. "Virtue and Pleasure." *Mind* 82 (1973):401-408.
Kemp, John. "Pain and Evil." *Philosophy* 29 (1954):13-26.
Kennick, W. E. "Comments on 'Pleasure and Falsity'." *American Philosophical Quarterly* 1 (1964):92-95.
Kenny, Anthony J. P. *Action, Emotion and Will*. London: Routledge and Kegan Paul, 1963.
——. "Happiness." *Proceedings of the Aristotelian Society* 66 (1966):93-102.
Kerner, George C. "The Immorality of Utilitarianism and the Escapism of Rule-Utilitarianism." *Philosophical Quarterly* 21 (1971):36-50.
Keynes, J. M. *The General Theory of Employment, Interest, and Money*. London: Macmillan, 1936.
Keynes, J. N. *The Scope and Method of Political Economy*. London and New York: Macmillan, 1891.
Keyt, David. "Singer's Generalization Argument." *The Philosophical Review* 72 (1963): 466-476.
Kim, Jaegwon, and Goldman, Alvin, eds. *Values and Morals: Essays in Honor of Charles L. Stevenson, William K. Frankena, and Richard B. Brandt*. Dordrecht: Reidel Publishing Co., Inc., 1978.
King, J. Charles. "The Inadequacy of Situation Ethics." *Thomist* 34 (1970):423-437.
King-Farlow, John "Justice in Abundance and Despair." *Philosophical Papers* 6 (South Africa) (1977):1-10.
Kleinig, John. "The Fourth Chapter of Mill's *Utilitarianism*." *Australasian Journal of Philosophy* 48 (1970):197-205.
——. "The Concept of Desert." *American Philosophical Quarterly* 8 (1971):71-78.
Knight, Frank H. *The Ethics of Competition*. New York and London: Harper and Brothers Publishers, 1935.
——. "Short Cuts to Justice and Happiness." *Ethics* 57 (1947):199-205.
Koch, Adrienne. *Philosophy of Thomas Jefferson*. New York: Columbia University Press, 1943.

Konstan, David. *Some Aspects of Epicurean Psychology.* Leiden: Brill, 1973.
Kordig, Carl R. "Structural Similarities Between Utilitarianism and Deontology." *Journal of Value Inquiry* 8 (1974):52-56.
Kretzmann, Norman. "Desire As the Proof of Desirability." *Philosophical Quarterly* 8 (1958):246-258.
Kuklick, Bruce. "The Mill Analogy and Its Critics." *Philosophical Journal* 6 (1970):74-80.
Kupfer, Joseph. "Universalization in Berkeley's Rule-Utilitarianism." *Revue Internationale de Philosophie* 28 (1974):511-531.
Kupperman, Joel J. "Do We Desire Only Pleasure?" *Philosphical Studies* 34 (1978):451-454.
Kutschera, Franz V. "Comments on John C. Harsanyi's Paper." *Erkenntnis* 11 (1977):433-434.
Lacey, A. R. "Sidgwick's Ethical Maxims." *Philosophy* 34 (1959):217-228.
Ladd, Everett C., Jr. "Helvetius and d'Holbach: 'La Moralisation de la Politique'." *Journal of the History of Ideas* 23 (1962):221-238.
Ladd, John. "Comments" on Symposium on Utilitarianism and Moral Obligation. *Philosophical Review* 61 (1962):320-326.
_____. "The Ethical dimensions of the Concept of Action." *The Journal of Philosophy* 62 (1965):633-645.
_____, ed. *Ethical Issues Relating to Life and Death.* New York: Oxford University Press, 1979.
Ladenson, Robert F. "Does the Deterrence Theory of Punishment Exist? A Response to Nozick." *Philosophy Research Archives* 2 (1976): No. 1090.
_____. "Mill's Conception of Individuality." *Social Theory and Practice* 4 (1977):167-182.
Lafleur, Lawrence. "A Dialectical Dissolution of Psychological Hedonism." *Review of Metaphysics* 7 (1954):368-378.
_____. "In Defense of Ethical Hedonism." *Philosophy and Phenomenological Research* 16 (1956):547-550.
Laird, John. *An Enquiry into Moral Notions.* London: George Allen & Unwin, 1935 (especially Chapter 17).
_____. "Other People's Pleasures and One's Own." *Philosophy* 16 (1941):39-55.
Lamont, W. D. "Justice: Distributive and Collective." *Philosophy* 16 (1941):3-18.
Lancaster, Lane W. *Masters of Political Thought.* Boston: Houghton Mifflin, 1960.
Landesman, Charles. "A Note on Act Utilitarianism." *Philosophical Review* 73 (1964): 243-247.
_____. "Promises and Practices." *Mind* 75 (1966):239-243.
Lang, Beryl, and Stahl, Gary. "Mill's Howlers and the Logic of Naturalism." *Philosophy and Phenomenological Research* 29 (1968-1969):562-574.
Lange, Oskar. "The Determinateness of the Utility Function." *Review of Economic Studies* 1 (1934):218-225.
_____. "The Foundations of Welfare Economics." *Econometrica* 10 (1942):215-228.
La Rosa, Guiseppina Sindoni. "Note Storiche Sulla Filosofia nel Periodo Preshaftesburiano." *Teoresi* 27 (1972):123-125.
Laux, Helmut, and Schneeweiss, Hans. "On the Onassis Problem." *Theory and Decision* 2 (1972):353-370.
Lawrence, Nathaniel. "Benevolence and Self-Interest." *Journal of Philosophy* 45 (1948): 457-462.
Leach, James; Butts, Robert; and Pearce, Glenn, eds. *Science, Decision and Value: Proceedings of the Fifth Anniversary of Western Ontario Philosophy Colloquium.* Boston: D. Reidel, 1973.
Leacock, S. B. *The Unsolved Riddle of Social Justice.* New York: John Lane Co., 1920.
Legros, Robert. "L'Egalité dans La Pensée Politique de L'Utilitarisme." *Revue Internationale de Philosophie* 28 (1974):391-405.

Lemos, Ramon M. "Psychological Egoism." *Philosophy and Phenomenological Research* 20 (1960):540-546.
Lensky, Gerhard E. *Power and Privilege: A Theory of Social Stratification*. New York: McGraw-Hill, 1966.
Lerner, A. P. "The Concept of Monopoly and the Menace of Monopoly Power." *Review of Economic Studies* 1 (1934):157-175.
———. *The Economics of Control*. New York: Macmillan, 1944.
Lerner, Daniel, and Lasswell, Harold D. *The Policy Sciences*. Palo Alto: Stanford University Press, 1951.
Lessnoff, Michael G. "John Rawls' Theory of Justice." *Political Studies* 19 (1971):65-80.
———. "Two Justifications of Punishment." *Philosophical Quarterly* 21 (1971):141-148.
———. "Justice, Social Contract and Universal Prescription." *Philosophical Quarterly* 28 (1978):65-73.
Letwin, Shirley Robin. *The Pursuit of Certainty: David Hume, Jeremy Bentham, John Stuart Mill, Beatrice Webb*. New York: Cambridge University Press, 1965.
Levi, Albert William. "The Value of Freedom: Mill's Liberty (1859-1959)." *Ethics* 70 (1959):37-46.
Levin, D. M. "Some Remarks on Mill's Naturalism." *Journal of Value Inquiry* 3 (1969):291-297.
Levin, Michael E. "Animal Rights Evaluated." *Humanist* 37 (1977):12, 14-15.
Levy, David. "Libertarian Communists, Malthusians, and J. S. Mill Who Is Both." *Mill News Letter* 15 (1980):2-16.
Lewis, Clarence Irving. *An Analysis of Knowledge and Valuation*. La Salle, Ill. Open Court, 1950 (see especially Chapters 16 and 17).
Lewis, David *Convention*. Cambridge, Massachusetts: Harvard University Press, 1969.
———. "Utilitarianism and Truthfulness." *Australasian Journal of Philosophy* 50 (1972):17-19.
———. "Reply to McMichael's 'Too Much of a Good Thing: A Problem in Deontic Logic'." *Analysis* 38 (1978):85-86.
———. "Prisoners' Dilemma Is a Newcomb Problem." *Philosophy & Public Affairs* 8 (1979):235-240.
Lewis, Thomas T. "Humanistic Eudaemonism: An Interpretation of Utilitarianism." *Religious Humanism* 13 (1979):64-71.
Leys, Wayne Albert Risser. *Ethics for Policy Decisions: The Art of Asking Deliberative Questions*. New York; Prentice-Hall, 1952.
———. "Justice and Equality." *Ethics* 67 (1956):17-24.
Lindsay, Alexander Dunlop. *The Modern Democratic State*. New York: Oxford University Press, 1947.
———. Introduction to *Mill's Utilitarianism, Liberty and Representative Government*. New York: Dutton, 1950.
Lipsey, R. G., and Lancaster, Kalvin. "The General Theory of the Second Best." *Review of Economic Studies* 24 (1956-57):11-32.
Little, Ian M. D. "Economic Behavior and Welfare." *Mind* 58 (1949):195-209.
———. *A Critique of Welfare Economics*. Oxford: The Clarendon Press, 1950, 2nd edition, 1957.
Locke, Don. "The Many Faces of Punishment." *Mind* 72 (1963):568-572.
———. "Why the Utilitarians Shot President Kennedy." *Analysis* 36 (1976):153-155.
Lockwood, Michael. "Singer on Killing and the Preference for Life." *Inquiry* 22 (1979):157-170.
Loftsgordon, Donald. "On 'Inadequate' Definitions." *Analysis* 21 (1961):109-114.
———. "Present-Day British Philosophers of Punishment." *The Journal of Philosophy* 63 (1966):341-353.
Long, Douglas G. *Bentham on Liberty: Jeremy Bentham's Idea of Liberty in Relation to His Utilitarianism*. Toronto: University of Toronto Press, 1977.

Long, W. H. "The Legend of Mill's Proofs." *Southern Journal of Philosophy* 5 (1967):36-47.
Loring, L. M. "Moore's Criticism of Mill." *Ratio* 9 (1967):84-90.
Luce, R. Duncan. "Conditional Expected, Extensive Utility." *Theory and Decision* 3 (1972):101-106.
_____, and Raiffa, Howard. *Games and Decisions*. New York: John Wiley and Sons, 1957.
Lyons, Daniel. "Is Hart's Rationale for Legal Excuses Workable?" *Dialogue* (Canada) 8 (1969):496-502.
Lyons, David Barry. *Forms and Limits of Utilitarianism*. Oxford: Clarendon Press, 1965.
_____. "On Sanctioning Excuses." *Journal of Philosophy* 66 (1969):646-660.
_____. "Rights, Claimants, and Beneficiaries." *American Philosophical Quarterly* 6 (1969): 173-185.
_____. "Rawls Versus Utilitarianism." *Journal of Philosophy* 69 (1972):535-545.
_____. *In the Interest of the Governed: A Study in Bentham's Philosophy of Utility and Law*. Oxford: Clarendon Press, 1973.
_____. "On Justifying Enforced Requirements: A Reply to Baier." *Journal of Value Inquiry* 9 (1975):42-58.
_____. "Review of Robert Nozick, *Anarchy, State, and Utopia*." *Philosophical Review* 85 (1976):208-215.
_____. "Mill's Theory of Morality." *Nous* 10 (1976):101-120.
_____. "Human Rights and the General Welfare." *Philosophy & Public Affairs* 6 (1977): 113-129.
_____. "Mill's Theory of Justice." In *Values and Morals: Essays in Honor of Charles L. Stevenson, William K. Frankena, and Richard B. Brandt*, edited by J. Kim and A. I. Goldman. Dordrecht: Reidel, 1978, pp. 1-20.
_____. "Liberty and Harm to Others." *Canadian Journal of Philosophy Supplementary Volume* 5 (1979):99-114.
_____. "Utility as a Possible Ground of Rights." *Nous* 14 (1980):17-28.
Mabbott, J. D. "Punishment." *Mind* 48 (1939):152-167.
_____. "Is Anthropology Relevant to Ethics?" Part II. *Aristotelian Society Supplementary Volume* 20 (1946):85-93.
_____. "Moral Rules." *Proceedings of the British Academy* 39 (1953):97-118.
_____. "Professor Flew on Punishment." *Philosophy* 30 (1955):256-265.
_____. "Free Will and Punishment." In *Contemporary British Philosophy*, Third Series, edited by H. D. Lewis. London: Allen & Unwin, 1956, pp. 287-309.
_____. "Interpretations of Mill's 'Utilitarianism'." *Philosophical Quarterly* 6 (1956):115-120.
_____. *An Introduction to Ethics*. London: Hutchinson University Library, 1966.
MacBeath, A. *Experiments in Living*. London: Macmillan, 1952 (see Chapter 2).
MacDonald, R. D. "Pursuing Happiness." *Personalist* 58 (1977):179-181.
MacIntyre, Alasdair C. "Pleasure as a Reason for Action." *Monist* 48 (1965):215-233.
_____. *A Short History of Ethics*. New York: Macmillan, 1966.
Mack, Mary Peter. "The Fabians and Utilitarianism." *Journal of the History of Ideas* 16 (1955):76-88.
_____. *Jeremy Bentham: An Odyssey of Ideas*. London: Heinemann, 1962, and New York: Columbia University Press, 1963.
MacKay, Alfred F. "Interpersonal Comparisons." *Journal of Philosophy* 72 (1975):535-549.
MacKenzie, Nollaig. "A Note on Rawls' Decision Theoretic Argument for the Difference Principle." *Theory and Decision* 8 (1977):381-385.
Mackie, J. L. "The Disutility of Act-Utilitarianism." *Philosophical Quarterly* 23 (1973): 289-300.

──── . "Sidgwick's Pessimism." *Philosophical Quarterly* 26 (1976):317-327.
Mackinnon, Donald M. "Things and Persons." Part I. *Aristotelian Society Supplementary Volume* 22 (1948):179-189.
──── . *A Study in Ethical Theory*. London: Adam and Charles Black, 1957 (see Chapter 2).
Macklin, Ruth. "Actions, Consequences and Ethical Theory." *Journal of Value Inquiry* 1 (1967):72-80.
──── . "A Rejoinder." *Journal of Value Inquiry* 1 (1967):135-138.
MacLagen, W. G. "Punishment and Retribution." *Philosophy* 14 (1939): 282-298.
──── . "Self and Others: A Defense of Altruism." *Philosophical Quarterly* 4 (1954):109-127.
MacLeod, A. M. "Critical Notice of Rawls' *A Theory of Justice*." *Dialogue* (Canada) 13 (1974):139-159.
MacPherson, C. B. *The Real World of Democracy*. Oxford: Clarendon Press, 1966.
──── . "Democratic Theory: Ontology and Technology." In *Political Theory and Social Change*, edited by David Spitz, pp. 203-220. New York: Atherton Press, 1967.
──── . "The Maximization of Democracy." In *Philosophy, Politics and Society*, 3rd Series, edited by P. Laslett and W. G. Runciman, pp. 83-103. New York: Barnes and Noble, 1967.
MacPherson, Thomas. "Punishment: Definition and Justification." *Analysis* 28 (1967-1968):21-27.
MacRae, Duncan, Jr. "Utilitarian Ethics and Social Change." *Ethics* 78 (1968):188-198.
Madden, Edward H. *Chauncey Wright and the Foundations of Pragmatism*. Seattle: University of Washington Press, 1963.
──── . *Civil Disobedience and Moral Law in Nineteenth-Century American Philosophy*. Seattle: University of Washington Press, 1968.
──── . "Oberlin's First Philosopher." *Journal of the History of Philosophy* 6 (1968): 57-66.
──── ; Handy, Rollo; and Farber, Marvin, eds. *Philosophical Perspectives on Punishment*. Springfield, Ill.: Charles C. Thomas, 1968.
──── , and Hare, Peter. "C. J. Ducasse's Progressive, Universal Hedonism." *Philosophy and Phenomenological Research* 34 (1973-74):36-50.
Madell, Geoffrey. "Hare's Prescriptivism." *Analysis* 26 (1965):37-41.
Majumdar, Tapas. *The Measurement of Utility*. London: Macmillan, 1958.
Malinovich, Stanley. "The Happiness Criterion." *Philosophia* (Israel) 2 (1972):195-203.
Mandelbaum, Maurice. "On Interpreting Mill's *Utilitarianism*." *Journal of the History of Philosophy* 6 (1968):35-46.
──── . "Two Moot Issues in Mill's Utilitarianism." In *Modern Studies in Philosophy: John Stuart Mill*, edited by J. B. Schneewind. Garden City: Doubleday Anchor, 1968, pp. 206-233.
Manser, A. R. "It Serves You Right." *Philosophy* 37 (1962):293-306.
Margolis, Joseph. "On the Principle of Benevolence." *Personalist* 46 (1965):39-44.
──── . "Rule Utilitarianism." *Australasian Journal of Philosophy* 43 (1965):220-225.
──── . "Mill's Utilitarianism Again." *Australasian Journal of Philosophy* 45 (1967):179-184.
──── . Human Acts and Moral Judgments." *Ethics* 80 (1969):56-61.
──── . Egoism and the Confirmation of Metamoral Theories." *American Philosophical Quarterly* 7 (1970):260-266.
──── . *Values and Conduct*. Oxford: Oxford University Press, 1971.
──── . "Animals Have No Rights and Are Not the Equal of Humans." *Philosophical Exchange* 1 (1974):119-123.
──── . "Two Concepts of Happiness." *Humanist* 35 (1975):22-24.
Marshak, Jacob. "Rational Behavior, Uncertain Prospects, and Measurable Utility." *Econometrica* 18 (1950):307-327, 373-396.

Marshall, Alfred. *Principles of Economics.* London: Macmillan, 1890, 8th edn. 1920
Marshall, John. "Punishment for Intentions." *Mind* 80 (1971):597-598.
———. "The Proof of Utility and Equity in Mill's Utilitarianism." *Canadian Journal of Philosophy* 3 (1973-1974):13-26.
Martin, Michael, and Ruf, Henry. "A Utilitarian Kantian Principle." *Philosophical Studies* 21 (1970):90-91.
———, and ———. "Silverstein's defense of Cornman." *Philosophical Studies* 23 (1972): 319-323.
Martin, John N. "The Concept of the Irreplaceable." *Environmental Ethics* 1 (1979):31-48.
Martin, Rex. "On the Logic of Justifying Legal Punishment." *American Philosophical Quarterly* 7 (1970):253-259.
———. "A Defense of Mill's Qualitative Hedonism." *Philosophy* 47 (1972):140-151.
Martin, Richard M. *Intension and Decision.* Englewood Cliffs, N.J.: Prentice-Hall, 1963.
Maxwell, J. C. "Disinterested Desires." *Mind* 52 (1943):39-46.
———. "Ethics and Politics in Mandeville," *Philosophy* 26 (1951):242-252.
Mazlish, Bruce. *James and John Stuart Mill: Father and Son in the Nineteenth Century.* London: Hutchinson, 1975.
McAllister, W. K. "Toward a Re-examination of Psychological Hedonism." *Philosophy and Phenomenological Research* 13 (1953):499-505.
McCall, Storrs. "Quality of Life." *Social Indicators Research* 2 (1975):229-248.
McCloskey, H. J. "An Examination of Restricted Utilitarianism." *Philosophical Review* 66 (1957):466-485.
———. "The Complexity of the Concepts of Punishment." *Philosophy* 37 (1962):307-325.
———. "Mill's Liberalism." *Philosophical Quarterly* 13 (1963):143-156.
———. "A Note on Utilitarian Punishment." *Mind* 72 (1963):599.
———. "A Non-Utilitarian Approach to Punishment." *Inquiry* 8 (1965):249-263.
———. "'Suppose Everybody Did the Same'." *Mind* 75 (1966):432-433.
———. "Egalitarianism, Equality and Justice." *Australasian Journal of Philosophy* 44 (1966):50-69.
———. "Utilitarian and Retributive Punishment." *Journal of Philosophy* 64 (1967):91-110.
———. "Some Arguments for a Liberal Society." *Philosophy* 43 (1968):324-344.
———. *Meta-Ethics and Normative Ethics.* The Hague: Martinus Nijhoff, 1969.
———. "'Two Concepts of Rules' – A Note." *Philosophical Quarterly* 22 (1972):344-348.
———. "Utilitarianism: Two Difficulties." *Philosophical Studies* 24 (1973):62-63.
———. "The Right To Life." *Mind* 84 (1975):403-425.
———. "A Right to Equality." *Canadian Journal of Philosophy* 6 (1976):625-642.
———. "Rights – Some Conceptual Issues." *Australasian Journal of Philosophy* 54 (1976): 99-115.
———. "Universalized Prescriptivism and Utilitarianism: Hare's Attempted Forced Marriage." *Journal of Value Inquiry* 13 (1979):63-76.
McDonald, Michael F. "Autarchy and Interest." *Australasian Journal of Philosophy* 56 (1978):109-125.
———. "Can Serious Rights Be Taken Seriously?" *Canadian Journal of Philosophy* 9 (1979):23-41.
McGill, V. J. *The Idea of Happiness.* New York: Praeger, 1967.
McGreal, Ian. "A Naturalist Analysis of Duty." *Philosophical Review* 58 (1949):221-233.
———. "A Naturalistic Utilitarianism." *Journal of Philosophy* 49 (1950):520-525.
———. *The Art of Making Choices.* Dallas: Southern Methodist University Press, 1953.
McNaughton, Robert. "A Metrical Concept of Happiness." *Philosophy and Phenomenological Research* 14 (1953-54):172-183.
McNeilly, F. S. "Pre-Moral Appraisals." *Philosophical Quarterly* 8 (1958):97-111.
McNiece, Gerald. "Shelley, John Stuart Mill, and the Secret Ballot." *Mill News Letter* 8 (1973):2-7.

Mead, Dale C. "Profit Maximization Strategies in Russian Roulette: Rawls and Utilitarianism." *Dialogue* (Phi Sigma Tau) 19 (1977):52-57.
Meehl, Paul. "The Selfish Voter Paradox and the Thrown-Away Vote Argument." *American Political Science Review* 71 (1977):11-30.
Melden, A. I. "Two Comments on Utilitarianism." *Philosophical Review* 60 (1951):508-524.
_____. "Utility and Moral Reasoning." In *Ethics and Society*, edited by Richard T. DeGeorge, pp. 173-196. New York: Anchor, 1966.
Mele, Alfred R. "On 'Happiness and the Good Life'." *Southwestern Journal of Philosophy* 10 (1979):181-187.
Merino, David B. *Natural Justice and Private Property*. St. Louis: B. Herder, 1923.
Mew, Peter. "Doubts About Moral Principles." *Inquiry* 18 (1975):289-308.
Michalos, Alex C. "Postulates of Rational Preference." *Philosophy of Science* 34 (1967):18-22.
_____. "Cost-Benefit Versus Expected Utility Acceptance Rules." *Theory and Decision* 1 (1970):61-88.
Mill, James. *Analysis of the Phenomena of the Human Mind*, 2nd edition, edited by John Stuart Mill, 1869. 1st edition, 1829.
Mill, John Stuart. *On Liberty*. 1859.
_____. *Utilitarianism*. 1861.
_____. *The Letters of John Stuart Mill*, edited by H. S. R. Elliot. London: Longmans, Green, and Co., 1910.
_____. *The Later Letters of John Stuart Mill 1849-1873*, edited by Francis E. Mineka and Dwight N. Lindley, *Collected Works of John Stuart Mill*, Volume XVI. Toronto: University of Toronto Press, 1972.
Miller, Frank, and Sartorius, Rolf. "Population Policy and Public Goods." *Philosophy & Public Affairs* 8 (1979):148-174.
Miller, Fred D. "Can Pleasures Be False? (*Philebus* 36C-41B)" *Southwestern Journal of Philosophy* 2 (1971):51-71.
Miller, Leonard G. "Rules and Exceptions." *Ethics* 66 (1956):262-270.
Miller, Richard W. "Rawls and Marxism." *Philosophy & Public Affairs* 3 (1974):167-191.
_____. "Rawls, Risk, and Utilitarianism." *Philosophical Studies* 28 (1975):55-61.
Miller, W. A. "A Theory of Punishment." *Philosophy* 45 (1970):307-316.
Milo, Ronald D. "Bentham's Principle." *Ethics* 84 (1974):128-139.
Mitchell, Dorothy. "Mill's Theory of Value." *Theoria* 36 (1970):100-115.
Mitchell, W. C. "Bentham's Felicific Calculus." *Political Science Quarterly* 33 (1918):161-183.
Moberly, Walter. *The Ethics of Punishment*. London: Faber and Faber, 1968.
Monro, David Hector. "In Defense of Hedonism." *Ethics* 60 (1950):285-291.
_____. *Godwin's Moral Philosophy: An Interpretation of William Godwin*. London: Oxford University Press, 1953.
_____. "Mill's Third Howler." In *Contemporary Philosophy in Australia* edited by R. Brown and C. D. Rollins, pp. 190-203. London: Allen & Unwin, 1969.
Montague, Roger. "Happiness." *Proceedings of the Aristotelian Society* 67 (1966-1967):87-102.
Moore, G. E. *Principia Ethica*. Cambridge: Cambridge University Press, 1903.
_____. *Ethics*. Oxford: Oxford University Press, 1966.
Moore, Ronald. "What Hath Rawls Got?" *Journal of Chinese Philosophy* 4 (1977):143-160.
Morawetz, Thomas. "Goodness and Benefit." *Journal of Value Inquiry* 9 (1975):1-11.
Morris, Bertram, and others. *University of Colorado Studies, Series in Philosophy, No. 1: Studies in Ethical Theory*. Boulder, Col.: University of Colorado Press, 1958.
Morris, Charles W. "Axiology as the Science of Preferential Behavior." In *Value: A*

Cooperative Inquiry edited by Ray Lepley, pp. 211-222. New York: Columbia University Press, 1949.
Morrison, Alasdair. "Justice." *Aristotelian Society Supplementary Volume* 43 (1969):109-122.
Moser, Shia. "Utilitarian Theories of Punishment and Moral Judgments." *Philosophical Studies* 8 (1957):15-18.
———. "A Comment on Mill's Argument for Utilitarianism." *Inquiry* 6 (1963):308-318.
Mothershead, John L., Jr. *Ethics: Modern Conceptions of the Principles of Right.* New York: Holt, 1955.
Mott, Omer. "Utility as the Norm of Law." *The New Scholasticism* 15 (1941):377-390.
Mueller, Dennis C. "Intergenerational Justice and the Social Discount Rate." *Theory and Decision* 5 (1974):263-273.
———; Tollison, Robert D.; and Willett, T. D. "The Utilitarian Contract: A Generalization of Rawls' Theory of Justice." *Theory and Decision* 4 (1974):345-365.
Mueller, Iris Wessel. *John Stuart Mill and French Thought.* Urbana: University of Illinois Press, 1956.
Muller, Anselm W. "Radical Subjectivity: Morality Versus Utilitarianism." *Ratio* 19 (1977):115-132.
Mundle, C. W. K. "Punishment and Desert." *Philosophical Quarterly* 4 (1954):216-228.
Murakami, Yasusuke. *Logic and Social Choice.* London: Routledge and Kegan Paul, 1968. New York: Dover Publications.
Murphy, Frances H. "What Sort of Freedom Does Moral Responsibility Presuppose?" *Philosophical Review* 53 (1944):575-580.
Murphy, Jeffrie G. "Three Mistakes About Retributivism." *Analysis* 31 (1971):166-169.
———. "Marxism and Retribution." *Philosophy & Public Affairs* 2 (1973):217-243.
Murray, A. R. M. *An Introduction to Political Philosophy.* New York: Philosophical Library, 1953.
Myers, Gerald E. "Ryle on Pleasure." *Journal of Philosophy* 54 (1957):181-187.
Myint, Hla. *Theories of Welfare Economics.* London: Longmans Green, 1948.
Nagel, Thomas. *The Possibility of Altruism.* Oxford: Oxford University Press, 1970.
———. "War and Massacre." *Philosophy & Public Affairs* 1 (1972):123-144.
———. "Rawls on Justice." *Philosophical Review* 82 (1973):220-234.
Nakhnikian, George. "Value and Obligation in Mill." *Ethics* 62 (1951):33-40
———. "Generalization in Ethics." *The Review of Metaphysics* 17 (1963-1964):436-461.
Nandi, S. K. "Moore's Refutation of Sidgwick's Pleasure Theory: A Critical Examination." *Philosophical Quarterly* (India) 30 (1955):41-47.
Narveson, Jan F. "The Desert Island Problem." *Analysis* 23 (1963):63-67.
———. "Utilitarianism and Formalism." *Australasian Journal of Philosophy* 43 (1965):58-72.
———. "Utilitarianism and New Generations." *Mind* 76 (1967):62-72.
———. *Morality and Utility.* Baltimore: Johns Hopkins Press, 1967.
———. "Utilitarianism and Moral Norms." *Journal of Value Inquiry* 4 (1970):273-282.
———. "Promising, Expecting and Utility." *Canadian Journal of Philosophy* 1 (1971):207-234.
———. "Aesthetics, Charity, Utility, and Distributive Justice." *Monist* 56 (1972):527-551.
———. "Moral Problems of Population." *Monist* 57 (1973):62-86.
———. "An Overlooked Aspect of the Fairness-Utility Controversy." *Journal of Value Inquiry* 8 (1974):124-130.
———. "Utilitarianism, Group Action, and Coordination." *Nous* 10 (1976):173-194.
———. "Animal Rights." *Canadian Journal of Philosophy* 7 (1977):161-178.
———. "Liberalism, Utilitarianism, and Fanaticism: R. M. Hare Defended." *Ethics* 88 (1978):250-259.

———. "Review of *Pleasures and Pains: A Theory of Qualitative Hedonism* by Rem B. Edwards." *Mill News Letter* 15 (1980):28-31.
Nathan, N. M. L. "A Difficulty about Justice." *Mind* 80 (1971):227-237.
———. *The Concept of Justice*. London: Macmillan, 1971.
———. "On the Justification of Democracy." *Monist* 55 (1971):89-120.
Neave, Edwin H. "On Arbitration Schemes for a Wealth Distribution Problem." *Theory and Decision* 9 (1978):295-312.
Neblett, William R. "A Note on Love and Obligation (and Utility)." *International Journal of the Philosophy of Religion* 1 (1970):124-125.
Nelson, R. J. "Ethics and Environmental Decision Making." *Environmental Ethics* I (1979): 263-278.
Neumann, Michael. "Killing and Average Utility." *Analysis* 40 (1980):35-36.
New, Christopher. "Saints, Heroes and Utilitarians." *Philosophy* 49 (1974):179-189.
Nickel, James W. "On Banishing Ethics from Our Minds." *Journal of Value Inquiry* 8 (1974):204-214.
Nielsen, Kai. "Ethical Egoism and Rational Action." *Journal of Philosophy* 69 (1972): 698-700.
———. "Monro on Mill's 'Third Howler'." *Australasian Journal of Philosophy* 51 (1973):63-69.
———. Hedonism and the Ends of Life." *Philosophical Journal* 10 (1973):14-26.
———. "Some Puzzles About Formulating Utilitarianism." *Ratio* 15 (1973):256-262.
———. "Hedonism, Utilitarianism and the Naturalistic Fallacy." *Midwest Journal of Philosophy* 2 (1974):1-8.
———. "Distrusting Reason." *Ethics* 87 (1976):49-60.
———. "Rationality and Preference." *Second Order* 6 (1977):21-30.
———. On Formulating the Utility Principle." *Indian Philosophical Quarterly* 6 (1979):427-435.
Norman, Richard. *Reasons for Actions: A Critique of Utilitarian Rationality*. New York: Barnes and Noble, 1971.
Noxon, James. "Hazlitt as Moral Philosopher." *Ethics* 73 (1963):279-283.
Nowell-Smith, P. H. *Ethics*. London: Penguin Books, 1954.
———. "Utilitarianism and Treating Others as Ends." *Nous* 1 (1967):81-90.
———. "On Sanctioning Excuses." *Journal of Philosophy* 67 (1970):609-619.
———. "Some Reflections on Utilitarianism." *Canadian Journal of Philosophy* 2 (1973): 417-431.
Nozick, Robert. "Distributive Justice." *Philosophy & Public Affairs* 3 (1973):45-126.
———. *Anarchy, State and Utopia*. New York: Basic Books, 1974.
Nute, Donald E. "Extensional Equivalence of Simple and General Utilitarian Principles." *Notre Dame Journal of Formal Logic* 20 (1979):32-36.
Oake, Roger B. "Montesquieu's Religious Ideas." *Journal of the History of Ideas* 14 (1953): 548-560.
Ogden, C. K. Introduction to his edition of Bentham's *The Theory of Legislation*. London: Routledge and Kegan Paul, 1931. French edition, Trubner and Co., 1931.
Oldenquist, Andrew. "Rules and Consequences." *Mind* 75 (1966):180-192.
Oliver, Henry M., Jr. "Economic Value Theory as a Policy Guide." *Ethics* 68 (1958):186-193.
Olscamp, Paul J. "Some Suggestions About the Moral Philosophy of George Berkeley." *Journal of the History of Philosophy* 6 (1968):147-156.
———. *The Moral Philosophy of George Berkeley*. The Hague: Nijhoff, 1970.
Olson, Mancur. *The Logic of Collective Action*. Cambridge, Mass.: Harvard University Press, 1971.
Olson, Robert G. "Ethical Egoism and Social Welfare." *Philosophy and Phenomenological Research* 21 (1961):528-536.

_____. *The Morality of Self-Interest.* New York: Harcourt Brace World, 1965.
Opp, Karl-Dieter. "Social Evolution: Learning Theory Applied to Group Action." *Theory and Decision* 10 (1979):299-243.
Oppenheim, Felix E. "Rational Choice." *Journal of Philosophy* 50 (1953):341-350.
Ossowska, Maria. "Remarks on the Ancient Distinction Between Bodily and Mental Pleasures." *Inquiry* 4 (1961):123-127.
Overvold, Mark C. *Self Interest, Self Sacrifice, and the Satisfaction of Desires.* Unpublished Ph.D. Dissertation, University of Michigan.
_____. "Self-Interest and the Concept of Self-Sacrifice." *Canadian Journal of Philosophy* 10 (1980):105-118.
Pahel, Kenneth R. "Is Sartorius Getting Away With Doing the Moral Thing?" *Southern Journal of Philosophy* 16 (1978):95-103.
Paley, William. *The Principles of Moral and Political Philosophy.* 1786.
Palmer, P. A. "Benthamism in England and America." *American Political Science Review* 35 (1941):855-871.
Pareto, Vilfredo. *Manuel d'économie politique.* Translated from Italian by Alfred Bonnet. Paris: V. Girad and E. Brière, 1909.
Parfit, Derek. "Personal Identity." *Philosophical Review* 80 (1971):3-27.
_____. "Later Selves and Moral Principles." In *Philosophy and Personal Relations*, edited by Alan Montefiore, pp. 137-169. Montreal: McGill-Queens University Press, 1973.
_____. "Innumerate Ethics." *Philosophy & Public Affairs* 7 (1978):285-301.
Park, Roy. "Hazlitt and Bentham." *Journal of the History of Ideas* 30 (1969):369-384.
Parsons, Talcott. *Structure of Social Action.* Glencoe, Ill.: The Free Press, 1961.
Paskins, Barrie. "Some Victims of Morality." *Proceedings of the Aristotelian Society* 76 (1975-1976):89-108.
Paul, Ellen Fankel. "W. Stanley Jevons: Economic Revolutionary, Political Utilitarian." *Journal of the History of Ideas* 40 (1979):267-283.
Penelhum, Terence. "The Logic of Pleasure." *Philosophy and Phenomenological Research* 17 (1956-1957):488-503.
_____; Kennick, W. E.; and Isenberg, A. I. "Symposium: Pleasure and Falsity." *American Philosophical Quarterly* 1 (1964):81-100.
Pennock, J. Roland. "Democratic Political Theory: A Typological Discussion." *Monist* 55 (1971):61-88.
Pepper, Stephen C. *Ethics.* New York: Appleton-Century-Crofts, 1960.
Perelli-Minetti, C. R. "Nozick on Sen: A Misunderstanding." *Theory and Decision* 8 (1977): 387-393.
Perelman, Chaim. *The Idea of Justice and the Problem of Argument.* London Routledge and Kegan Paul, 1963.
_____. *Justice.* New York: Random House, 1967.
Perkins, Lisa H. "Suggestion for a Justification of Punishment." *Ethics* 81 (1970):55-61.
Perry, Charner M. "Bases, Arbitrary and Otherwise, For Morality: A Critique Criticized; the Arbitrary as a Basis For Rational Morality." *International Journal of Ethics* 43 (1933):127-166.
_____. "Principles of Value and the Problem of Ethics." *Revue internationale de philosophie* 1 (1939):666-683.
Perry, David L. *The Concept of Pleasure.* New York: Humanities Press, 1967.
_____. "Pleasure and Justification." *Personalist* 51 (1970):174-189.
Perry, John. "The Importance of Being Identical." In *The Identities of Persons*, edited by Amelie O. Rorty, pp. 67-90. Berkeley: University of California Press, 1976.
Peterfreund, Sheldon P. "A Note On Supererogation and Utilitarianism." *Personalist* 57 (1976):290-291.
_____. "On Mill's Higher and Lower Pleasures." *Personalist* 57 (1976):411-412.
Pettit, Philip. "A Theory of Justice?" *Theory and Decision* 4 (1974):311-324.

Phelps, E. S., ed. *Economic Justice.* Baltimore: Penguin Books, 1973.
Phillips, Herbert J. "Sanctions and Obligations in Naturalistic Ethics." *Philosophy and Phenomenological Research* 7 (1947):612-620.
Pigou, A. C. *Wealth and Welfare.* London: Macmillan, 1912.
_____. *Economics of Welfare.* London: Macmillan, 1932.
_____, and Georgescu-Roegen, N. "Marginal Utility of Money and Elasticities of Demand." *Quarterly Journal of Economics* 50 (1936):532-539.
Pincoffs, Edmund L. *The Rationale of Legal Punishment.* New York: Humanities Press, 1966.
Pingel, Martha M. *An American Utilitarian: Richard Hildreth as a Philosopher.* New York: Columbia University Press, 1948.
Piper, Adrian M. S. "Utility, Publicity, and Manipulation." *Ethics* 88 (1978): 189-206.
Plamenatz, John. *Mill's Utilitarianism.* New York: Macmillan, 1949.
_____. *The English Utilitarians.* London: Oxford University Press, 1958.
Plant, Raymond. "The Greatest Happiness." *Journal of Medical Ethics* 1 (1975):104-106.
Pole, David. "On Practical Reason and Benevolence." *Proceedings of the Aristotelian Society* 68 (1968):129-144.
Popkin, Richard H. "A Note on the 'Proof' of Utility in J. S. Mill." *Ethics* 61 (1950):66-68.
Postow, B. C. "Generalized Act Utilitarianism." *Analysis* 37 (1977):49-52.
_____. "Rule Utilitarianism in Partial Compliance Theory." *Analysis* 38 (1978):187-193.
Poupko, Chana. "Political Ideas Underlying the Utilitarian Approach to Punishment." *Philosophy Today* 18 (1974):285-292.
Powers, Lawrence H. "A More Effective Average: A Note on Distributive Justice." *Philosophical Studies* 24 (1970):74-78.
Prawitz, Dag. "A Discussion Note on Utilitarianism." *Theoria* 34 (1968):76-84.
_____. "The Alternatives to an Action." *Theoria* 36 (1970):116-126.
Prichard, H. A. *Moral Obligation.* Oxford: The Clarendon Press, 1957.
Primorac, Igor. "Utilitarianism and Self-Sacrifice of the Innocent." *Analysis* 38 (1978): 194-199.
Pritchard, Michael S. "Rawls' Moral Psychology." *Southwestern Journal of Philosophy* 8 (1977):59-72.
Quinn, Warren S. "Pleasure—Disposition or Episode." *Philosophy and Phenomenological Research* 28 (1967-1968):578-586.
_____. "Theories of Intrinsic Value." *American Philosophical Quarterly* 11 (1974):123-132.
Quinton, Anthony Meredith. "On Punishment." *Analysis* 14 (1954):133-142.
_____. *Utilitarian Ethics.* London: Macmillan, 1973.
Quirk, J. P., and Saposnik, R. "Admissibility and Measurable Utility Functions." *Review of Economic Studies* 29 (1962):140-146.
Rabassi, Eduardo A. "Acerca de Una Prueba Posible de los Primeros Principios Eticos." *Revista Latinamericana de Filosofia* 4 (1978):21-38.
Radcliff, P., ed. *Limits of Liberty.* Belmont, Calif.: Wadsworth Publishing Company, 1966.
Rader, Melvin Miller. *Ethics and Society: An Appraisal of Social Ideals.* New York: Holt, 1950.
Rader, Trout. "Existence of a Utility Function to Represent Preferences." *Review of Economic Studies* 30 (1963):229-232.
Ralls, Anthony. "Rational Morality for Empirical Man." *Philosophy* 44 (1969):205-216.
Randall, John Herman, Jr. "The Wrong and the Bad." *Journal of Philosophy* 51 (1954): 764-775.
_____. "T. H. Green: The Development of English Thought from J. S. Mill to F. H. Bradley." *Journal of the History of Ideas* 27 (1966):217-244.
Raphael, David Daiches. "Equality and Equity." *Philosophy* 21 (1946):118-132.
_____. *The Moral Sense.* London: Oxford University Press, 1947.
_____. "Justice and Liberty." *Proceedings of the Aristotelian Society* 51 (1951):167-196.

———. *Moral Judgment.* London: George Allen & Unwin, 1955 (see Chapter 5).
———. "Fallacies In and About Mill's Utilitarianism." *Philosophy* 30 (1955):344-357.
———, ed. *British Moralists 1650-1800,* 2 volumes. London: Oxford University Press, 1969.
———. "Adam Smith and 'The Infection of David Hume's Society'." *Journal of the History of Ideas* 30 (1969):225-248.
———. "Hume and Adam Smith on Justice and Utility." *Proceedings of the Aristotelian Society* 73 (1972-1973):87-103.
———. "Sidgwick on Intuitionism." *Monist* 58 (1974):405-419.
———. "The Standard of Morals." Presidential Address, *Proceedings of the Aristotelian Society* 75 (1974-1975):1-12.
———. "Utilitarismo E Giustizia." *Rivista Intenazionale Di Filosofia Del Diritto* 54 (1977): 875–886.
Rapoport, Anatol. *Fights, Games, and Debates.* Ann Arbor: University of Michigan Press, 1960.
———. *Strategy and Conscience.* New York: Harper and Row, 1964.
———, and Chammah, Albert M. *Prisoner's Dilemma.* Ann Arbor: University of Michigan Press, 1965.
Rashdall, Hastings. "Can There Be a Sum of Pleasures?" *Mind* 8 (1899):357-382.
———. "Professor Sidgwick's Utilitarianism." *Mind* o.s. 10 (1885):200-206.
———. *The Theory of Good and Evil.* Oxford: Oxford University Press, 1924.
Rauch, Leo. "Mill's Secular Religion." *Journal of Critical Analysis* 3 (1972):178-187.
Rawls, John. "Outline of a Decision Procedure for Ethics." *Philosophical Review* 60 (1951): 177-197.
———. "Two Concepts of Rules." *Philosophical Review* 64 (1955):3-32.
———. "Justice as Fairness." *Philosophical Review* 67 (1958):164-194.
———. "Constitutional Liberty and the Concept of Justice." In *Nomos VI: Justice,* edited by C. Friedrich and John W. Chapman, pp. 98-125. New York: Atherton, 1963.
———. "The Sense of Justice." *The Philosophical Review* 72 (1963):281-305.
———. "Legal Obligation and the Duty of Fair Play." In *Law and Philosophy,* edited by S. Hook, pp. 3-18. New York: New York University Press, 1964.
———. "Distributive Justice." In *Philosophy, Politics and Society,* Third Series, edited by P. Laslett and W. G. Runciman, pp. 58-82. Oxford: Basil Blackwell, 1967.
———. "Distributive Justice: Some Addenda." *Natural Law Forum* 13 (1968):51-71.
———. "The Justification of Civil Disobedience." In *Civil Disobedience,* edited by H. Bedau, pp. 240-255. New York: Pegasus, 1969.
———. *A Theory of Justice.* Cambridge, Mass.: Belknap Press, 1971.
———. "Reply to Lyons and Teitelman." *Journal of Philosophy* 69 (1972):556-557.
———. "The Kantian Conception of Equality." *Cambridge Review* (1975):94-99.
———. "Fairness to Goodness." *Philosophical Review* 84 (1975):536-554.
———. "The Basic Structure as Subject." *American Philosophical Quarterly* 14 (1977): 159-165.
Reder, M. W. *Studies in the Theory of Welfare Economics.* New York: Columbia University Press, 1942.
Reed, T. M. "The Paneuthanasia Argument." *Personalist* 58 (1977):84-87.
———. "On Sterba's 'Retributive Justice'." *Political Theory* 6 (1978):373-376.
———. "The Poverty of Prescriptivism." *Personalist* 60 (1979):243-252.
Rees, John Collwyn. *Mill and His Early Critics.* Leicester: University College Press, 1956.
Reeve, E. G. "'Suppose Everyone Did The Same'–A Note." *Mind* 78 (1969):280.
Regan, Donald. *Utilitarianism and Cooperation.* Oxford: Clarendon Press, 1980.
Rein'l, Robert. "The Limits of Utility." *Journal of Philosophy* 53 (1956):549-555.
Rescher, Nicholas. *Distributive Justice.* Indianapolis: Bobbs-Merrill Co., Inc., 1965.

———. "Notes on Preference, Utility, and Cost." *Synthese* 16 (1966):332-343.
———. *Introduction to Value Theory.* Englewood Cliffs, N.J.: Prentice-Hall, Inc., 1969.
———. *Welfare, the Social Issues in Philosophical Perspective.* Pittsburgh: Pittsburgh University Press, 1972.
———. *Unselfishness: The Role of the Vicarious Affects in Moral Philosophy and Social Theory.* Pittsburgh: Pittsburgh University Press, 1975.
———. "Economics vs. Moral Philosophy: the Pareto Principle as a Case Study of Their Divergent Orientation." *Theory and Decision* 10 (1979):169-179.
Restaino, Franco. "Polemiche Antilluministiche in Inghilterra Intorno al 1830." *Giornale Critico Della Filosofia Italiana* 48 (1969):332-385.
Rice, Philip Blair. "'Public' and 'Private' Factors In Valuation." *Ethics* 54 (1943):41-52.
Richards, David A. J. *A Theory of Reasons for Action.* Oxford: Clarendon Press, 1971.
Rickertsen, Bryan C. "The Myth of the Super Pleasure Helmet." *Journal of Thought* 11 (1976):240-244.
Riddle, G. K. "The Place of Benevolence in Butler's Ethics." *Philosophical Quarterly* 9 (1959):356-362.
Roberts, Fred S. "What if Utility Functions Do Not Exist?" *Theory and Decision* 3 (1972):126-136.
Roberts, Tom Aerwyn. *The Concept of Benevolence: Aspects of Eighteenth-Century Moral Philosophy.* London: Macmillan, 1973.
Robertson, D. H. *Utility and All That.* London: Allen & Unwin, 1952.
Robbins, Lionel. *An Essay on the Nature and Significance of Economic Science.* London: Macmillan, 1932. 2nd edition, 1935.
———. "Interpersonal Comparisons of Utility: A Comment." *Economic Journal* 48 (1938):635-641.
Robins, Michael H. "Hare's Golden-Rule Argument: A Reply to Silverstein." *Mind* 81 (1974):578-581.
Robson, John Mercel. *The Improvement of Mankind: The Social and Political Thought of John Stuart Mill.* Toronto: University of Toronto Press, 1968.
———, ed. *Collected Works of John Stuart Mill,* Volume X: *Essays on Ethics, Religion and Society.* Toronto: University of Toronto Press, 1969.
———, and Laine, Michael, eds. *James and John Stuart Mill: Papers of the Centenary Conference.* Toronto: University of Toronto Press, 1976.
Rockmore, Tom. "The Moral Philosophy of J. S. Mill Revisited." *Personalist* 55 (1974):380-387.
Rohatyn, Dennis Anthony. "Hall and Mill's Proof." *Southwestern Journal of Philosophy* 2 (1971):113-118.
———. "A Note on Kaufmann and Justice." *Mill News Letter* 6 (1971):23-25.
———. "Mill, Kant, and Negative Utility." *Philosophia* 5 (1975):515-522.
Rosen, Bernard. "Rules and Justified Moral Judgments." *Philosophy and Phenomenological Research* 30 (1969-1970):436-443.
Rosenbaum, Alan S. "The Idea of Liberalism and J. S. Mill." *Philosophy in Context* 5 (1976):50-65.
Ross, Geoffrey. "Utilities for Distributive Justice: The Meshing Problem and a Solution To It." *Theory and Decision* 4 (1974):239-258.
Ross, W. D. "The Ethics of Punishment." *Philosophy* 4 (1929):205-211.
———. *The Right and the Good.* Oxford: Oxford University Press, 1930.
Rossi, M. M. "Utilitarismo." *Enciclopedia Filosofica* 4. Venezia: Instituto per la collaborazione culturale, 1957-58.
Rothenberg, Jerome. *The Measurement of Social Welfare.* Englewood Cliffs, N. J.: Prentice-Hall, 1961.
Ruf, Henry L. "On Being Morally Justified." *Journal of Value Inquiry* 3 (1969):1-18.
Runciman, W. G. *Relative Deprivation and Social Justice.* Harmondsworth: Penguin, 1972.

———, and Sen, A. K. "Games, Justice and General Will." *Mind* 74 (1965):554-562.
Russell, Bertrand. "John Stuart Mill." *Proceedings of the British Academy* 4 (1955):43-59.
Russell, L. J. "Is Anthropology Relevant to Ethics?" Part I. *Aristotelian Society Supplementary Volume* 20 (1946):61-84.
Ryan, Alan. "Mr. McCloskey on Mill's Liberalism." *The Philosophical Quarterly* 14 (1964): 253-260.
———. "John Stuart Mill's Art of Living." *The Listener* 71 (1965):620-622.
———. "Mill and the Naturalistic Fallacy." *Mind* 75 (1966):422-425.
———. *The Philosophy of John Stuart Mill*. London: Macmillan, 1970.
———. "Two Kinds of Morality." *Hastings Center Report* 5 (1975):5-7.
Ryan, John A. *A Living Wage: Its Ethical and Economic Aspects*. New York: Macmillan, 1906. 2nd edition, 1920.
———. *Distributive Justice*. New York: Macmillan, 1916. 3rd edition, 1942.
Ryan, Louis A. "Charity and the Social Order (Part II)." *Thomist* 4 (1942):70-120.
Sams, Henry W. "'Reflection'." *Philosophical Review* 52 (1943):400-408.
Samuelson, Paul Anthony. "Welfare Economics and International Trade." *American Economic Review* 28 (1938):261-266.
———. *Foundations of Economic Analysis*. Cambridge, Mass.: Harvard University Press, 1947.
———. *Foundations of Welfare Economics*. Cambridge, Mass.: Harvard University Press, 1948.
Santoni, Ronald E. "Ducasse's 'Criterion' of Morality—An Exploration and Critique." *Personalist* 53 (1972):425-437.
Sartorius, Rolf. "Book Review: *The Logic of Choice* by Gidon Gottlieb." *Harvard Law Review* 82 (1969):1783-1793.
———. "Utilitarianism and Obligation." *Journal of Philosophy* 66 (1969):67-81.
———. "Individual Conduct and Social Norms: A Utilitarian Account." *Ethics* 82 (1972): 200-218.
———. "Book Review: *In the Interest of the Governed* by David Lyons." *Journal of Philosophy* 71 (1974):779-787.
———. *Individual Conduct and Social Norms: A Utilitarian Account of Social Union and the Rule of Law*. Encino, Calif.: Dickenson, 1975.
———. "Moral Theories and Moral Judgments." *Midwest Studies in Philosophy* 1 (1976):68-71.
———. "The Limits of Libertarianism." In *Law and Liberty: Essays in Honor of F. A. Hayek*, edited by Robert Cunningham. Indianapolis: Liberty Press, 1978.
Sasieni, Maurice; Jospur, Arthur; and Friedman, Lawrence. *Operations Research: Methods and Problems*. New York: Wiley, 1959.
Saydah, J. Roger. *The Ethical Theory of Clarence Irving Lewis*. Athens, Ohio: Ohio University Press, 1969.
Scanlan, James P. "Nikolaj Cernysevskij and Soviet Philosophy." *Studies in Soviet Thought* 7 (1967):1-27.
Scanlon, T. M. "Rights, Goals and Fairness." *Erkenntnis* 11 (1977):81-95.
Scarpelli, Uberto. "Moore in Italia." *Revista Di Filosofia* 61 (1970):289-301.
Schaefer, David Lewis. "A Critique of Rawls' Contract Doctrine." *Review of Metaphysics* 28 (1974):89-115.
Schapiro, J. Salwyn. "John Stuart Mill, Pioneer of Democratic Liberalism in England." *Journal of the History of Ideas* 4 (1943):127-160.
———. *Liberalism and the Challenge of Fascism: Social Forces in England and France 1815-1870*. New York: McGraw-Hill, 1949.
Schelling, Thomas C. *The Strategy of Conflict*. Cambridge, Mass.: Harvard University Press, 1960.
———. "Game Theory and the Study of Ethical Systems." *Journal of Conflict Resolution* 12 (1968):34-44.
Scheltons, D. "De Contracttheorien en de Rechtvaardigheidsbeginselen." *Tijdschrift Voor Filosofie* 38 (1976):203-235.

Schick, Frederic. "Arrow's Proof and the Logic of Preference." *Philosophy of Science* 36 (1969):127-144.
_____. "Beyond Utilitarianism." *Journal of Philosophy* 68 (1971):657-666.
_____. "A Justification of Reason." *Journal of Philosophy* 69 (1972):835-840.
_____. "Toward a Logic of Liberalism." *Journal of Philosophy* 77 (1980):80-98.
Schlick, Moritz. *Problems of Ethics.* New York: Dover Publications, 1962 (especially Chapter 4).
Schneewind, J. B. "First Principles and Common Sense Morality in Sidgwick's Ethics." *Archiv für Geschichte der Philosophie* Bd. 45 (1963):137-156.
_____, ed. *Mill's Ethical Writings.* London: Collier-Macmillan Ltd; New York: Collier Books, 1965.
_____. "Henry Sidgwick." *Encyclopedia of Philosophy* 7, edited by P. Edwards, pp. 434-436. New York: Macmillan and The Free Press. London: Collier Macmillan, 1967.
_____. *Backgrounds of English Victorian Literature.* New York: Random House, 1970.
_____. "Sidgwick and the Cambridge Moralists." *Monists* 58 (1974):371-404.
_____. "Two Unpublished Letters of John Stuart Mill to Henry Sidgwick." *Mill News Letter* 9 (1974):9-11.
_____. *Sidgwick's Ethics and Victorian Moral Philosophy.* Oxford: Clarendon Press, 1977.
Schneider, Herbert W. "Obligations and the Pursuit of Happiness." *Philosophical Review* 61 (1952):312-319.
Schrattenholzer, A. *Soziale Gerechtigkeit.* Graz: U. Moser, 1934.
Schuh, Edward. "Comparative, Relative, and Normal Value." *Philosophy and Phenomenological Research* 16 (1955):229-236.
Schuller, Bruno. "Anmerkungen Zu Dem Begriffspaar 'Teleologisch-Deontologisch'." *Gregorianum* 57 (1976):740-755.
Schumpeter, Joseph. *Capitalism, Socialism and Democracy.* London: Allen & Unwin, 1943.
Schwartz, Adina. "Moral Neutrality and Primary Goods." *Ethics* 83 (1973):294-307.
Schwartz, Thomas. "On the Possibility of Rational Policy Evaluation." *Theory and Decision* 1 (1970):89-106.
_____. "Von Wright's Theory of Human Welfare: A Critique," written in 1973-1974 for P. A. Schilpp, ed. *The Philosophy of Georg Henrik von Wright,* forthcoming.
_____. "On the Utility of MacKay's Comparisons." *Journal of Philosophy* 72 (1975):549-551.
_____. "Welfare Judgments and Future Generations." *Theory and Decision* 11 (1979): 181-194.
Schwayder, D. S. "Moral Rules and Moral Maxims." *Ethics* 67 (1957):269-285.
Schwyzer, Herbert. "Rules and Practices." *The Philosophical Review* 78 (1969):451-467.
Scitovsky, T. "A Note on Welfare Propositions in Economics." *Review of Economic Studies* 9 (1941):77-88.
_____. *Welfare and Competition.* London: Allen & Unwin, 1952.
_____. *Papers on Welfare and Growth.* London: Allen & Unwin, 1964.
Scott-Taggart, M. J. "Mandeville: Cynic or Fool?" *Philosophical Quarterly* 16 (1966):221-232.
_____. "It Makes No Difference Whether or Not I Do It." Part II. *Aristotelian Society Supplementary Volume* 49 (1975):191-209.
Self, Donnie J. "Philosophical Foundations of Various Approaches to Medical Ethical Decision Making." *Journal of Medicine and Philosophy* 4 (1979):20-31.
Seligman, E. *The Income Tax.* 2nd rev. ed. New York: Macmillan, 1921.
_____. *The Shifting and Incidence of Taxation.* 4th rev. ed. New York: Columbia University Press, 1921.
Sen, A. K. *Collective Choice and Social Welfare.* San Francisco: Holden-Day, 1970.
_____. *On Economic Inequality.* New York: W. W. Norton, 1973.

_____. "Rawls Versus Bentham: An Axiomatic Examination of the Pure Distribution Problem." *Theory and Decision* 4 (1974):301-309.
_____. "Rational Fools: A Critique of the Behavioral Foundations of Economic Theory." *Philosophy & Public Affairs* 6 (1977):317-344.
_____. "Utilitarianism and Welfarism." *Journal of Philosophy* 76 (1979):463-489.
Sesonske, Alexander. "Moral Rules and the Generalization Argument." *American Philosophical Quarterly* 3 (1966):282-290.
Seth, James. "Is Pleasure the Summum Bonum?" *International Journal of Ethics* 6 (1895-1896):409-424.
_____. "The Ethical System of Henry Sidgwick." *Mind* 10 (1901):172-187.
_____. "The Alleged Fallacies in Mill's *Utilitarianism*." *Philosophical Review* 17 (1908):469-488.
Shaida, S. A. "Moore's Evaluation of Sidgwick's Hedonism." *Indian Philosophical Quarterly* 1 (1974):112-123.
_____. "Moore's Criticism of Sidgwick's Utilitarianism." *Visva-Bharati Journal of Philosophy* 8 (1971):51-57.
Sharp, Frank Chapman. *Good Will and Ill Will: A Study of Moral Judgments*. Chicago: University of Chicago Press, 1950.
Shaw, P. D. "Self Interest and the Theory of Demand." *Philosophy of the Social Sciences* 7 (1977):77-89.
Sheldon, Mark. "Community, History and Proof." *Mill News Letter* 14 (1979):9-14.
Sheldon, W. H. "The Absolute Truth of Hedonism." *Journal of Philosophy* 47 (1950):285-303.
Sher, George. "An Unsolved Problem About Punishment." *Social Theory and Practice* 4 (1977):149-165.
Shue, Henry. "The Current Fashions: Trickle-Downs By Arrow and Close-Knits By Rawls." *Journal of Philosophy* 71 (1974):319-327.
Sidgwick, Henry. *Elements of Politics*. London: Macmillan, 1890. 2nd ed., 1897.
_____. *Outlines of the History of Ethics for English Readers*. Boston: Beacon Press, 1960.
_____. *The Methods of Ethics* (7th edition) Reprinted by Dover and the University of Chicago Press, 1907, 1966.
Siegler, Frederick Adrian. "Lyons on Sanctioning Excuses." *Journal of Philosophy* 67 (1970):620-628.
Sikora, R. I. "Unforeseeable Consequences." *Analysis* 29 (1969):89-91.
_____. "Utilitarianism: The Classical Principle and the Average Principle." *Canadian Journal of Philosophy* 5 (1975):409-419.
_____. "Negative Utilitarianism: Not Dead Yet." *Mind* 85 (1976):587-588.
_____. "Towards a Satisfactory Formulation of Utilitarianism." *Ratio* 19 (1977):68-69.
_____. "Utilitarianism, Supererogation and Future Generations." *Canadian Journal of Philosophy* 9 (1979):461-466.
Silverstein, Harry S. "Reply to Martin and Ruf." *Philosophical Studies* 23 (1972):324-326.
_____. "Simple and General Utilitarianism." *Philosophical Review* 83 (1974):339-363.
_____. "Horwich's Reformulation of Lyons." *Philosophical Studies* 28 (1975):63-66.
_____. "Goldman's 'Level-2' Act Descriptions and Utilitarian Generalization." *Philosophical Studies* 30 (1976):45-55.
_____. "Utilitarianism and Group Coordination." *Nous* 13 (1979):335-360.
Simon, Herbert A. *Models of Man, Social and Rational*. New York: Wiley, 1957.
Simon, Yves R. *Philosophy of Democratic Government*. Chicago: University of Chigago Press, 1951.
Simons, Henry C. *Personal Income Taxation*. Chicago: University of Chicago Press, 1938.
_____. *Federal Tax Reform*. Chicago: University of Chicago Press, 1950.

Simpson, Robert W. "Happiness." *American Philosophical Quarterly* 12 (1975):169-176.
Sinclair, A. G. *Der Utilitarismus bei Sidgwick und bei Spencer.* Heidelberg: C. Winter, 1907.
Singer, Marcus George. *Generalization in Ethics: An Essay in the Logic of Ethics, With the Rudiments of a System of Moral Philosophy.* New York: A. A. Knopf, 1961 (see Chapter 7).
―――. "The Golden Rule." *Philosophy* 38 (1963):293-314.
―――. "The Many Methods of Sidgwick's Ethics." *Monist* 58 (1974):420-448.
―――. "On Rawls On Mill On Liberty and So On." *Journal of Value Inquiry* 11 (1977):141-148.
―――. "The Principle of Consequences Reconsidered." *Philosophical Studies* 31 (1977): 391-410.
―――. "Actual Consequence Utilitarianism." *Mind* 86 (1977):67-77.
Singer, Peter. "Is Act-Utilitarianism Self-Defeating?" *Philosophical Review* 81 (1972):94-104.
―――. "Famine, Affluence and Morality." *Philosophy & Public Affairs* 1 (1972):229-243.
―――. "Sidgwick and Reflective Equilibrium." *Monist* 58 (1974):490-517.
―――. "All Animals Are Equal." *Philosophical Exchange* 1 (1974):103-116.
―――. "Utility and the Survival Lottery." *Philosophy* 52 (1977):218-222.
―――. "A Reply to Professor Levin's 'Animal Rights Evaluated'." *Humanist* 37 (1977): 13, 16.
―――. "Anglin On the Obligation to Create Extra People." *Canadian Journal of Philosophy* 8 (1978):583-585.
―――. "Killing Humans and Killing Animals." *Inquiry* 22 (1979):145-156.
Sinha, A. P. "On Sidgwick's Reconciliation of Ethical Theories." *Indian Philosophical Quarterly* 6 (1979):149-158.
Skinner, B. F. "The Ethics of Helping People." *Humanist* 36 (1976):7-11.
Skorupski, John. "Sidgwick's Ethics." *The Philosophical Quarterly* 29 (1979):158-169.
Slote, Michael. "The Morality of Wealth." In *World Hunger and Moral Obligation*, edited by William Aiken and Hugh LaFollette. Englewood Cliffs, N. J.: Prentice-Hall, 1977.
Smart, Alwynne. "Mercy." *Philosophy* 43 (1968):345-359.
Smart, John Jamieson Carswell. "Extreme and Restricted Utilitarianism." *Philosophical Quarterly* 6 (1956):344-354.
―――. *An Outline of A System of Utilitarian Ethics.* Melbourne: Melbourne University Press, 1961.
―――. "Extreme Utilitarianism: A Reply to M. A. Kaplan." *Ethics* 71 (1961):133-134.
―――. "Free Will, Praise, and Blame." *Mind* 70 (1961):291-306.
―――. "The Methods of Ethics and the Ethics of Science." *Journal of Philosophy* 62 (1965):344-348.
―――. "Utilitarianism." *The Encyclopedia of Philosophy* 8, edited by Paul Edwards, pp. 206-212. New York: Macmillan and the Free Press, 1967.
―――. "Benevolence as an Over-Riding Attitude." *Australasian Journal of Philosophy* 55 (1977):127-135.;
―――. "Utilitarianism and Justice." *Journal of Chinese Philosophy* 5 (1978):287-299.
―――. "Hedonistic and Ideal Utilitarianism." *Midwest Studies in Philosophy* 3 (1978): 240-251.
―――, and Williams, Bernard. *Utilitarianism: For and Against.* London: Cambridge University Press, 1973.
Smart, R. N. "Negative Utilitarianism." *Mind* 67 (1958):542-543.
Smart, W. *The Distribution of Income.* London: Macmillan, 1899.
Smith, Constance I. "Bentham's Second Rule." *Journal of the History of Ideas* 31 (1970): 462-463.
Smith, J. M. "Punishment: A Conceptual Map and A Normative Claim." *Ethics* 75 (1964-1965):285-290.

Smith, James Ward. "Intrinsic and Extrinsic Good." *Ethics* 58 (1948): 195-208.
____. "The British Moralists and the Fallacy of Psychologism." *Journal of the History of Ideas* 11 (1950):159-178.
Smith, Nicholas M., Jr. "A Calculus for Ethics; A Theory of the Structure of Value." *Behavioral Science* 1 (1956): Parts 1 and 2, 111-142, 186-211.
____ ; Walters, Stanley S.; et al. "The Theory of Value and the Science of Decision; A Summary." *Journal of the Operations Research Society of America* 1 (1953):103-113.
Smith, Wilson. *Professors and Public Ethics: Studies of Northern Moral Philosophers Before the Civil War*. Ithaca, N. Y.: Cornell University Press, 1956.
Snare, Frank. "John Rawls and the Methods of Ethics." *Philosophy and Phenomenological Research* 36 (1975):100-112.
Snyder, Richard C.; Bruck, H. W.; and Sapin, Burton. *Decision-Making as an Approach to the Study of International Politics*. Princeton: Princeton University Press, 1954.
____ ; ____ ; ____. "A Decision-Making Approach to the Study of Political Phenomena." In *Approaches to the Study of Politics*, edited by Roland Young, pp. 3-38. Evanston: Northwestern University Press, 1958.
Sobel, Jordan Howard. "'Everyone', Consequences and Generalization Arguments." *Inquiry* 10 (1967):373-404.
____. "Rule-Utilitarianism." *Australasian Journal of Philosophy* 46 (1968):146-165.
____. "Utilitarianisms: Simple and General." *Inquiry* 13 (1970):394-449.
____. "Value, Alternatives, and Utilitarianism." *Nous* 5 (1971):373-384.
____. "Interaction Problems for Utility Maximizers." *Canadian Journal of Philosophy* 4 (1975):677-688.
____. "Utility Maximizers in Iterated Prisoner's Dilemmas." *Dialogue* 15 (1976):38-53.
____. "Utilitarianism and Past and Future Mistakes." *Nous* 10 (1976):195-219.
Soble, Alan. "Deception in Social Science Research: Is Informed Consent Possible?" *Hastings Center Report* 8 (1978):40-46.
Sorley, W. R. "Henry Sidgwick." *International Journal of Ethics* 11 (1900-1901):168-174.
Sosa, Ernest. "Mill's *Utilitarianism*." In *Mill's Utilitarianism*, edited by J. M. Smith and E. Sosa, pp. 154-172. Belmont, Calif.: Wadsworth, 1969.
Spence, G. W. "The Psychology Behind J. S. Mill's 'Proof'." *Philosophy* 63 (1968):18-28.
Spengler, J. J. "Sociological Presuppositions in Economic Theory." *Southern Economic Journal* 7 (1940-41):131-157.
Sprigge, Timothy L. S. "A Utilitarian Reply to Dr. McCloskey's 'A Non-Utilitarian Approach to Punishment'." *Inquiry* 8 (1965):264-291.
____. "Professor Narveson's Utilitarianism." *Inquiry* 11 (1968):332-345.
Stace, Walter Terence. *The Concept of Morals*. New York: Macmillan, 1937 (see Chapters 7 and 10).
Stearns, J. Brenton. "Ideal Rule Utilitarianism and the Content of Duty." *Kantstudien* 56 (1965):53-70.
____. "Ecology and the Indefinite Unborn." *Monist* 56 (1972):612-615.
____. "Bentham on Public and Private Ethics." *Canadian Journal of Philosophy* 5 (1975): 583-594.
Steinberg, Ira S. "Economics: Value Theory in the Spirit of Bentham." *Proceedings: Philosophy of Education Society* 25 (1969):38-44.
Steintrager, James. "Morality and Belief: The Origin and Purpose of Bentham's Writings on Religion." *Mill News Letter* 6 (1971):3-15.
____. *Bentham*. Ithaca: Cornell University Press, 1977.
Stegenga, James A. "J. S. Mill's Concept of Liberty and the Principle of Utility." *Journal of Value Inquiry* 7 (1973):281-289.
Stephen, James Fitzjames. *Liberty, Equality, Fraternity*, edited by R. J. White. London: Cambridge University Press, 1967.
Stephen, Sir Leslie. *The English Utilitarians*. 3 vols. London: Duckworth & Co., 1900; reprinted in one volume. New York: Peter Smith, 1950.

———. "Henry Sidgwick." *Mind* 10 (1901):1-7.
———. "Sidgwick's *Methods of Ethics.*" *Frazer's Magazine* 41 (1875):306-325.
Sterba, James P. "Prescriptivism and Fairness." *Philosophical Studies* 29 (1976):141-148.
———. "Retributive Justice." *Political Theory* 5 (1977):349-362.
———. "In Defense of Rawls Against Arrow and Nozick." *Philosophia* 7 (1978):293-303.
———. "Can a Person Deserve Mercy?" *Journal of Social Philosophy* 10 (1979):11-14.
Stern, Kenneth. "Testing Ethical Theories." *Journal of Philosophy* 63 (1966):234-238.
Stern, Laurence. "Deserved Punishment, Deserved Harm, Deserved Blame." *Philosophy* 45 (1970):317-329.
Stigler, G. J. "The New Welfare Economics." *American Economic Review* 33 (1943):355-359.
———. "The Goals of Economic Policy." *The Journal of Business* 31 (1958):169-176.
Stocker, Michael. "Consequentialism and Its Complexities." *American Philosophical Quarterly* 6 (1969):276-289.
———. "Mill on Desire and Desirability." *Journal of the History of Philosophy* 7 (1969):198-199.
———. "Moral Duties, Institutions, and Natural Facts." *Monist* 54 (1970):602-624.
———. Rightness and Goodness: Is There a Difference?" *American Philosophical Quarterly* 10 (1973):87-98.
———. "The Schizophrenia of Modern Ethical Theories." *Journal of Philosophy* 73 (1976):453-466.
Stokes, Eric. *English Utilitarians and India.* Oxford: Clarendon Press, 1959.
Stone, Julius. *The Province and Function of Law: Law As Logic, Justice and Social Control, A Study in Jurisprudence.* Cambridge: Harvard University Press, 1950.
Stout, A. K. "But Suppose Everyone Did the Same." *Australasian Journal of Philosophy* 32 (1954):1-29.
Strang, Colin. "What If Everyone Did That?" *Durham University Journal* 53 (1960):5-10.
Strawson, P. F. "Social Morality and Individual Ideal." *Philosophy* 36 (1961):1-17.
———. *Freedom and Resentment.* London: Methuen, 1974.
Stroll, Avrum. "Mill's Fallacy." *Dialogue* 3 (1964-1965):385-404.
Strotz, Robert. "How Income Ought To Be Distributed: Paradox Regained." *Journal of Political Economy* 69 (1961):271-278.
Sturgeon, Nicholas L. "Altruism, Solipsism, and the Objectivity of Reasons." *Philosophical Review* 74 (1973):374-402.
Sumner, L. W. "Consequences of Utilitarianism." *Dialogue* (Canada) 7 (1969):639-642.
———. "Cooperation, Fairness and Utility." *Journal of Value Inquiry* 5 (1971):105-119.
———. "More Light on the Later Mill." *Philosophical Review* 83 (1974):504-527.
———. "A Matter of Life and Death." *Nous* 10 (1976):145-171.
———. "Mill and the Death Penalty." *Mill News Letter* 11 (1976):2-6.
——— "Rawls and the Contract Theory of Civil Disobedience." In *New Essays in Contract Theory,* edited by K. Nielsen and R. A. Shiner, pp. 1-48. Guelph: Canadian Association for Publishing in Philosophy, 1977.
———. "The Good and the Right." *Canadian Journal of Philosophy Supplementary Volume* 5 (1979):99-114.
———. "Review of *Sidgwick's Ethics and Victorian Moral Philosophy* by J. B. Schneewind." *Mill News Letter* 14 (1979):22-25.
Suppes, Patrick. "Behavioristic Foundations of Utility." *Econometrica* 29 (1961):186-202.
———. "The Philosophical Relevance of Decision Theory." *Journal of Philosophy* 58 (1961):605-614.
Surber, Jere Paul. "Obligations to Future Generations: Explorations and Problemata." *Journal of Value Inquiry* 11 (1977):104-116.

Suter, Ronald, "Moore's Defense of the Rule 'Do No Murder'." *Personalist* 54 (1973):361-374.
Swabey, William Curtis. "Non-Normative Utilitarianism." *Journal of Philosophy* 40 (1943):365-373.
———. "Benevolence and Virtue." *Philosophical Review* 52 (1943):452-467.
Sweezy, Alan R. "The Interpretation of Subjective Value Theory in the Writings of the Austrian Economists." *Review of Economic Studies* 1 (1934):176-185.
Sylvester, Robert P. "Pleasures: Higher and Lower." *Personalist* 56 (1975):129-137.
Talmage, R. Stephen. "Utilitarianism and the Morality of Killing." *Philosophy* 47 (1972):55-63.
Tännsjö, Torbjörn. "The Morality of Abstract Entities." *Theoria* 44 (1978):1-18.
Tatarkiewicz, Wladyslaw. "Psychological Hedonism." *Synthese* 8 (1949-1951):409-434.
———. "Happiness and Time." *Philosophy and Phenomenological Research* 27 (1966):1-10.
Tawney, R. H. *Equality*. London: Allen & Unwin, 1931. 4th edition, 1952.
Taylor, C. C. W. "Pleasure." *Analysis* 23 Supplement (1963):2-19.
Taylor, Gwennyth. "On Doing What One Wants To Do." *Canadian Journal of Philosophy* 5 (1975):435-447.
Taylor, Paul W. "Justice and Utility." *Canadian Journal of Philosophy* 1 (1972):327-350.
Taylor, Richard. *Good and Evil: A New Direction*. New York: Macmillan, 1970.
Teitelman, Michael. "The Limits of Individualism." *Journal of Philosophy* 69 (1972):545-556.
Temkin, J. "Actual Consequence Utilitarianism: A Reply to Professor Singer." *Mind* 87 (1978):412-414.
Ten, C. L. "Mr. Thompson On the Distribution of Punishment." *The Philosophical Quarterly* 17 (1967):253-254.
———. "Mill on Self-Regarding Actions." *Philosophy* 43 (1968):29-37.
———. "Self-Regarding Conduct and Utilitarianism." *Australasian Journal of Philosophy* 55 (1977):105-113.
———. "Jim's Utilitarian Mission." *Philosophy* 54 (1979):221-222.
Tennessen, Herman. "Happiness is for the Pigs: Philosophy Versus Psychotherapy." *Journal of Existentialism* 7 (1966-67):181-214.
Thalberg, Irving. "False Pleasures." *The Journal of Philosophy* 59 (1962):65-74.
Thomas, D. A. Lloyd. "Consequences." *Analysis* 28 (1968):133-141.
———. "Happiness." *Philosophical Quarterly* 18 (1968):97-113.
Thomas, Sid B., Jr. "Morality As Institutionalized Benevolence." *Ethics* 74 (1964):269-280.
———. "The Status of the Generalization Principle." *American Philosophical Quarterly* 5 (1968):174-182.
Thompson, D. F. "Retribution and the Distribution of Punishment." *Philosophical Quarterly* 16 (1966):59-63.
Thompson, George. "Game Theory and 'Social Value' States." *Ethics* 65 (1964):36-39.
Thompson, William. *Inquiry into the Principles of the Distribution of Wealth*. London: Longman, 1824. 2nd edition by W. Pare, London: Orr and Co., 1850.
Thomson, Judith Jarvis. "Killing, Letting Die, and the Trolley Problem." *Monist* 59 (1976):204-217.
Thornton, J. C. "Can the Moral Point of View Be Justified?" *Australasian Journal of Philosophy* 42 (1964):22-34.
Thrall, Robert M. "Multidimensional Utility Theory." In *Decision Processes*, edited by R. M. Thrall, et al. New York: Wiley, 1954.
———; Coombs, Clyde H.; and Davis, Robert L., eds. *Decision Processes*. New York: Wiley, 1954.
Thurow, L. C. "The Income Distribution as a Pure Public Good." *Quarterly Journal of Economics* 85 (1971):327-336.

Thurstone, L. L., and Jones, Lyle V. "The Rational Origin for Measuring Subjective Values." *Journal of the American Statistical Association* 52 (1957):458-471.
Toulmin, S. E. *An Examination of the Place of Reason in Ethics*. Cambridge: The University Press, 1950.
———. "Is There a Fundamental Problem In Ethics?" *Australasian Journal of Philosophy* 33 (1955):1-19.
Trammell, Richard L. "Saving Life and Taking Life." *Journal of Philosophy* 72 (1975):131-137.
———, and Wren, Thomas E. "Fairness, Utility and Survival." *Philosophy* 52 (1977):331-337.
Trianosky, Gregory W. "Rule-Utilitarianism and the Slippery Slope. *Journal of Philosophy* 75 (1978):414-424.
Tullock, Gordon. "The Prisoners' Dilemma and Mutual Trust." *Ethics* 77 (1967):229-230.
Urmson, J. O. "The Interpretation of the Moral Philosophy of J. S. Mill." *Philosophical Quarterly* 3 (1953):33-39.
Van Holthoon, F. L. *The Road to Utopia: A Study of John Stuart Mill's Social Thought*. Assen: Van Gorcum, 1971.
Varian, Hal R. "Distributive Justice, Welfare, Economics, and the Theory of Fairness." *Philosophy & Public Affairs* 4 (1975):223-247.
Vendler, Zeno. "Effects, Results and Consequences." In *Analytical Philosophy*, First Series, edited by R. J. Butler, pp. 1-15. Oxford: Basil Blackwell, 1962.
Vetter, Hermann. "The Production of Children as a Problem of Utilitarian Ethics." *Inquiry* 12 (1969):445-447.
———. "Utilitarianism and New Generations." *Mind* 80 (1971):301-302.
Vickers, John M. "Utility and Its Ambiguities." *Erkenntnis* 9 (1975):287-311.
Vickrey, W. S. "The Goals of Economic Life." In *Goals of Economic Life*, edited by A. D. Ward, pp. 148-177. New York: Harper and Row, 1953. Reprinted in *Economic Justice*, edited by E. S. Phelps, pp. 35-61. Baltimore: Penguin Books, 1973.
———. "Utility, Strategy, and Social Decision Rules." *Quarterly Journal of Economics* 74 (1960):507-535.
———. "Risk, Utility, and Social Policy." *Social Research* 28 (1961):205-217. Reprinted in *Economic Justice*, edited by E. S. Phelps, pp. 286-297. Baltimore: Penguin Books, 1973.
Viner, Jacob. "Bentham and J. S. Mill." *American Economic Review* 39 (1949):360-392, reprinted in *The Long View and the Short*, edited by Jacob Viner, pp. 306-331. Glencoe, Ill.: The Free Press, 1953.
Vlastos, Gregory. "Justice." *Revue Internationale de Philosophie* 11 (1957):324-343.
———. "Justice and Equality." In *Social Justice*, edited by R. Brandt, pp. 31-72. Englewood Cliffs, N. J.: Prentice-Hall, 1962.
von Neumann, John; and Morgenstern, Oskar. *Theory of Games and Economic Behavior*. Princeton, N. J.: Princeton University Press, 1946. 2nd edition, 1953.
Von Wright, G. H. *The Varieties of Goodness*. London: Routledge and Kegan Paul, 1963.
Waldner, Ilmar. "The Empirical Meaningfulness of Interpersonal Utility Comparisons." *Journal of Philosophy* 70 (1972):87-103.
———. "The Possibility of Rational Policy Evaluation." *Theory and Decision* 4 (1973):85-90.
———. "Bare Preference and Interpersonal Utility Comparisons." *Theory and Decision* 5 (1974):313-328.
———. "Value Neutrality." *Theory and Decision* 5 (1974):333-334.
Walker, A. D. M. "Negative Utilitarianism." *Mind* 83 (1974):424-428.
Wall, George B. "Primitive Cultures and Ethical Universals." *International Philosophical Quarterly* 7 (1967):470-482.
———. "Cultural Perspectives on the Punishment of the Innocent." *Philosophical Forum* (Boston) 2 (1971):489-499.

_____. "More on the Equivalence of Act and Rule Utilitarianism." *Philosophical Studies* 22 (1971):91-95.
Wallace, James. "Pleasure as an End of Action." *American Philosophical Quarterly* 3 (1966): 312-316.
Wallis, Wilson D. "Utilitarianism and Self Realization." *Journal of Philosophy* 39 (1942): 717-719.
Walras, Léons. *Eléments d'économie politique pure.* Lausanne: L. Corgez & Cie, 1874-1877.
Wand, Bernard. "Hume's Non-Utilitarianism." *Ethics* 72 (1962):193-196.
Ward, A. D., ed. *Goals of Economic Life.* New York: Harper & Brothers, 1953.
Warnock, Geoffrey James. *The Object of Morality.* London: Methuen, 1971.
Warnock, Mary. Introduction to her edition of Mill, J. S., *Utilitarianism, On Liberty, Essay on Bentham. Together with Selected Writings of Jeremy Bentham and John Austin.* Cleveland: World Publishing Co., 1962.
Washburne, N. F., ed. *Decisions, Values and Groups,* Volume II. New York: Pergamon Press, 1962.
Wasserstrom, Richard A. "Strict Liability in the Criminal Law." *Stanford Law Review* 12 (1960):731-745.
_____. *The Judicial Decision: Toward a Theory of Legal Justification.* Palo Alto, Calif.: Stanford University Press, 1961.
_____. "Disobeying the Law." *Journal of Philosophy* 58 (1961):641-652.
Watkins, J. W. N. "Negative Utilitarianism." Part II *Aristotelian Society Supplementary Volume* 37 (1963):95-114.
Watson, Donald S., and Holman, Mary A. *Price Theory and Its Uses,* 4th edition. Boston: Houghton Mifflin, 1977.
Wedar, Sven. *Duty and Utility: A Study in English Moral Philosophy.* Lund: C. W. K. Gleerup, 1952.
Wedgewood, J. *The Economics of Inheritance.* London: G. Routledge & Sons, 1929.
Weinberger, Ota. "'Begrundung Oder Illusion: Erkenntnis Kritische Gedanken zu John Rawls Theorie Der Gerechtigkeit." *Zeitschrift fur Philosophische Forschung* 31 (1979):234-251.
Weinryb, Elazar. "Omissions." (In Hebrew) *IYYUN* 27 (1976-77):249-273.
Weinstock, Henry R. "Utilitarianism: A Common Issue For the Sciences and Humanities." *Journal of Thought* 1 (1966):15-18.
Weiss, Donald D. "Wollheim's Paradox: Survey and Solution." *Political Theory* 1 (1973): 154-170.
_____. "An Incredible Utilitarianism." *Journal of Value Inquiry* 8 (1975):308-312.
Wellmann, Carl. "A Reinterpretation of Mill's Proof." *Ethics* 69 (1959):268-276.
_____. "On Terrorism Itself." *The Journal of Value Inquiry* 13 (1980):250-258.
Wennberg, Robert N. "Act Utilitarianism, Deterrence and the Punishment of the Innocent." *Personalist* 56 (1975):178-194.
Wenz, Peter S. "Act-Utilitarianism and Animal Liberation." *Personalist* 60 (1979):423-428.
Werner, Louis. "A Note About Bentham on Equality and About the Greatest Happiness Principle." *Journal of the History of Philosophy* 11 (1973):237-251.
Wertheimer, Alan. "Should Punishment Fit the Crime?" *Social Theory and Practice* 3 (1975):403-423.
_____. "Deterrence and Retribution." *Ethics* 86 (1976):181-199.
_____. "Punishing the Innocent: Unintentionally." *Inquiry* 20 (1977):45-65.
Wertz, S. K. "Composition and Mill's Utilitarian Principle." *Personalist* 52 (1971):417-431.
West, Henry R. "Reconstructing Mill's 'Proof' of the Principle of Utility." *Mind* 81 (1972): 256-257.
_____. "Comparing Utilitarianisms." *Philosophy Research Archives* 1 (1975):No. 1047.
_____. "Mill's Naturalism." *Journal of Value Inquiry* 9 (1975):67-69.

———. "Mill's Moral Conservatism." *Midwest Studies in Philosophy* 1 (1976):71-79.
———. "Mill's Qualitative Hedonism." *Philosophy* 51 (1976):97-101.
———. "Justice and Utility." In *Moral Philosophy: Classic Texts and Contemporary Problems*, edited by Joel Feinberg and Henry West, pp. 338-343. Belmont, Calif.: Dickenson Publishing Company, Inc., 1977.
Westphal, Fred. "Utilitarianism and 'Conjunctive Acts': A Reply to Professor Castaneda." *Analysis* 32 (1972):82-85.
Whiteley, C. H. "Morality and Egoism." *Mind* 85 (1976):90-96.
Whittemore, Robert C. "Positivistic Paths to Value." *Tulane Studies in Philosophy* 21 (1972):159-190.
Wicksteed, Philip Henry. *An Essay on the Co-ordination of the Laws of Distribution*. London: Macmillan, 1894. Photoprinted, series of reprints of Scarce Tracts in Economic and Political Science, No. 12. London School of Economics and Political Science, 1932.
———. *Common Sense of Political Economy*. 1st edition. London: Macmillan, 1910. Revised edition, London: Routledge and Kegan Paul, 1933.
Wilker, David, and Nelson, Jack. "Pleasure and the Intrinsically Desired." *Analysis* 35 (1975):152-159.
Willey, Basil. *Nineteenth Century Studies: Coleridge to Matthew Arnold*. New York: Columbia University Press, 1949.
———. *The English Moralists*. London: Chatto and Windus. New York: Norton, 1964.
Williams, Bernard A. O. *Morality: An Introduction to Ethics*. New York: Harper and Row, 1972.
Williams, Gardner. "The Moral Insignificance of the Total of All Value." *Ethics* 55 (1945):216-221.
———. "Individual, Social, and Universal Ethics." *Journal of Philosophy* 45 (1948):645-655.
———. "Normative and Naturalistic Ethics." *Journal of Philosophy* 47 (1950):324-330.
———. "Hedonism, Conflict, and Cruelty." *Journal of Philosophy* 47 (1950):649-656.
———. "Universalistic Hedonism vs. Hedonic Individual Relativism." *Journal of Philosophy* 52 (1955):72-76.
———. "Subjective Ethics and the Subconscious Value Judgments of the Average Citizen." *Philosophy and Phenomenological Research* 25 (1964):201-207.
Willner, Dorothy, ed. *Decisions, Values and Groups* Volume I. New York: Pergamon Press, 1960.
Wilson, J. "Why Should Other People Be Treated As Equal?" *Revue Internationale de Philosophie* 25 (1971):272-286.
Wilson, John. "Happiness." *Analysis* 29 (1968):13-21.
Winter, Ernst S. F. *Henry Sidgwick's Moralphilosophie*. Flensburg: L. P. H. Maass, 1904.
Wittman, Donald. "A Diagrammatic Exposition of Justice." *Theory and Decision* 11 (1979):207-237.
Wolff, Robert Paul. "Reflections on Game Theory and the Nature of Value." *Ethics* 72 (1962):171-179.
———. "A Refutation of Rawls' Theorem on Justice." *Journal of Philosophy* 63 (1966):179-190.
———. *The Poverty of Liberalism*. Boston: Beacon Press, 1968.
———. "Maximization of Expected Utility as a Criterion of Rationality in Military Strategy and Foreign Policy." *Social Theory and Practice* 1 (1970):99-111.
Wollheim, Richard, and Berlin, Isaiah. Symposium: "Equality." *Proceedings of the Aristotelian Society* 56 (1955-1956):281-326.
Wood, David. "Rawls's Maximin Argument." *Personalist* 60 (1979):221-227.
Wootton, Barbara. *Social Foundations of Wage Policy*. London: Allen & Unwin, 1955.

Yilmaz, Mustafa R. "Multiattribute Utility Theory: A Survey." *Theory and Decision* 9 (1978):317-347.
Zellner, Harold. "Required by a Rule." *Ethics* 85 (1975):164-169.
Zemach, Eddy M. "Love Thy Neighbor As Thyself or Egoism and Altruism." *Midwest Studies in Philosophy* 3 (1978):148-158.
Zink, Sidney. "The Principles of Inclusiveness and Harmony in Perry's Theory of Value." *Philosophical Review* 53 (1944):185-194.
____. *The Concepts of Ethics.* New York: St. Martins Press, 1962.
Zinkernagel, Peter. "Revaluation of J. S. Mill's Ethical Proof." *Theoria* 18 (1952):70-77.

Index

Index

Act utilitarianism: defined, 5, 44-45, 225, 242; Mill as proponent of, 5, 44; requirements of cooperation, 16, 208, 212-218, 224$n8$; and aid to others, 17, 208, 225-240, 245, 246, 250, 251; refutation of by counterexample, 76, 86-87; moral rules lack independent authority, 107; as social morality, 107, 111, and moral freedom, 108; and respect for persons, 108; as moral action guide, 108-110; and social engineering, 112; and justice, 113; excluded by rationality and impartial concern, 208; sacrifice required by, 217, 250, 251; and self-interest, 242; and case for equality, 242; similarity on aid to Carson's (A) and (G), 245-246. *See* Aid; Mill, John Stuart; Utilitarianism; Utility

Actions: function of desires and beliefs, 185 $n15$; relevance to self-interest, 188-189

Acts: vs. omissions, 236. *See* Doing vs. letting happen

Aid: act-utilitarian requirements, 17, 208, 225-240, 245, 246, 250, 251; who owes, 226; is requirement conditional, 226; issues for theory of, 226-227; kinds and amounts owed, 226, 228; to whom owed, 226, 227, 228; involuntary system of, 226, 229; organ transfer, 226, 229, 239; three test cases, 228; limits to obligation, 228-231 *passim*, 234, 237-239, 240$n3$, 251; obligation to prevent harm, 231; to relieve suffering, 231; forfeitability of entitlement to 232-233; ideal of decency, 234; Brazen Rule, 231, 234-235; doing vs. letting happen, 236; to impoverished societies, 243; Carson's (A) and (G), 245-246; compelling justified, 251

Aquinas, St. Thomas: background conditions of justice, 120

Arbitrator: model for moral agent, 152; fair compromise among individual preferences, 159; ignorance of own identity, 159; decision paralleled by impartial choice, 160

Aristotelian principle: irrelevance in Rawls, 140

Aristotle: welfare and functional value, 204

Arrow, Kenneth: Harsanyi compared with, 151; theorem, 151, 163$n12$

Art of life, 20, 24, 33$n12$. *See* Mill, John Stuart

Assistance. *See* Aid

Atkinson, R. F.: "happiness" and "desirable" in Mill, 33$n11$

Autonomy: in Mill's conception of happiness, 44, 46, 61; not unbridled liberty, 102-103; and social morality, 102, 104-106 *passim*, 114; no special importance in act utilitarianism, 107; important human good, 108; utilitarian base insecure, 113; secured by contractualism, 114; in Kant, 124; and independence of

303

utility maximization, 231; and responsibility for choices, 232; and moral rights, 232
Aversion. *See* Desire

Bargain. *See* Choice; Impartiality; Rational bargain
Barry, Brian: anticipates Narveson, 142$n1$; Rawls guarantees no satisfactory minimum, 143$n6$; Rawls on maximin, 143$n8$; Rawls's utility assumptions, 143$n10$; disagreement with Olson, 213; on imperceptible effects, 214
Bayesian decision theory: when no interpersonal interaction, 146; in prisoners' dilemmas, 148; excludes consideration of utility dispersion, 153; compared with rational bargaining, 153, 155
Becker, Lawrence: views summarized, 17; defeat of dilemma, 208; disagreement with Sartorius, 208
Belief: in desire-satisfaction, 172
Beneficence: not obligation, 6; not justice, 20, 42; as imperfect obligation, 46-47; positive, 48-51 *passim*, 60, 61; on Mill's treatment of paternalism, 62; and rights, 62-67
Benevolence: aims at happiness, 14, 166; source of act utilitarianism, 107; and moral freedom, 107; enlightened, 108; and total happiness, 112; and subordination of ideals, 114; and voluntary cooperation, 211, 213. *See* Equibenevolence
Benevolent utilitarianism. *See* Act utilitarianism
Bentham, Jeremy: as hedonist, 23; on utilitarianism, value and reason, 144; pleasure and pain on throne, 183; analysis of welfare, 204
Berger, Fred: harm-prevention in Mill, 70$n11$, 70$n15$
Bodily parts. *See* Aid
Brandt, Richard: qualified attitude method, 9, 84$n10$; three theories of good, 13-14; summarized, 13-15; rule-utilitarian theory, 84$n7$; function of ethical system, 127$n7$; happiness defined, 166; want-analysis of utility, 186
Braybrooke, David: Rawls as utilitarian, 143$n13$
Brazen rule. *See* Aid
Broad, C. D.: self-referential altruism, 251-252$n7$

Brock, Dan: act utilitarianism and aid, 17, 226
Brown, D. G.: conflict with Lyons, 43-44, 55; Mill's principle of liberty (L), 53; principle of enforcing morality (M), 54; examination of (M), 54-59; principle of wrong (P), 55; refinement of (L), 55; on sanctions and wrong, 56
Buchanan, Allen: free rider dilemma, 223$n5$
Buchanan, James M., cooperation as example, 216$n11$; mentioned, 163$n31$
Butler, Joseph: enjoyment and altruistic desires, 173; wanting enjoyment, 176

Calculation. *See* Prisoners' dilemma
Carson, Thomas: summarized, 17, 208; duty to befriend friendless, 240-241$n7$
Categorical imperative: and Carson's (G), 246; (CI), 247-248; Carson's (C), 248; Kant's formulations, 252$n11$
Choice: maximin strategy, 11, 12, 137, 138, 250; impartiality in moral, 12, 155; in ignorance of one's own identity, 12, 13, 132, 158, 159; under uncertainty, 138, 159; measured by utilities, 145; true preferences, 145; rational constraint and ethics, 148; personal preference, 150; moral, 150; from individual to social, 150, 152, 155; social includes moral and constitutional, 151; logical problem for moral, 152; arbitrator in moral, 152; fair compromise in moral, 152, 159; egalitarian preferences and distribution, 155; Harsanyi's operationalization of impartiality in moral, 155-158; rationality of in Harsanyi, 160; and bargain, 160-161. *See* Harsanyi; Original position; Rational bargain; Utility
Civil society: problem of, 211
Coercion: justification, 61; and cooperation, 212, 216, 221, 224$n7$. *See* Liberty; Paternalism; Prisoners' dilemma
Common-sense morality: relation of to utilitarianism, 6-9: not consciously utilitarian, 7-8, 72, 73, 86; some felicific tendency, 8, 72, 95, 97; relation to utilitarianism in Sidgwick, 71-74, 91-98; coincidence with utilitarianism, 73, 82, 89, 111; distortions in, 73, 83; authority of, 82, 87, 90, 92, 98; defended by utilitarian reasoning, 89; at heart utilitarian, 89; systematized by utilitarianism, 92-93; inconsistent with act utilitarianism, 111.

INDEX 305

See Mill, John Stuart; Rule utilitarianism; Sidgwick; Sidgwickian equilibrium; Sidgwick's thesis; Social morality; Utilitarianism
Compensation: interpersonal, 240; intrapersonal and concept of persisting self, 240
Congruence argument: limited use in contractarian theory, 127$n11$
Considered judgments: and utilitarian requirements of aid, 226-227. *See* Rawls
Contract. *See* Contractarianism
Contractarianism: in Mill, 5; and utilitarianism, 5, 10, 100, 101, 107, 109, 111, 113, 131, 132, 162; concept of morality in, 10, 100, 111, 116, 117, 235; conditions of correct moral rules, 100, 111; as moral philosophy, 101; and reasonableness, 107-108; and fairness, 107-108; and social morality, 107-111; right to moral respect, 113; guards moral freedom, 114; moral equality for natural inequality, 114; pure procedural justice in, 125; as basis for cooperation, 208; Carson's definition of, 244
Contractualism. *See* Contractarianism
Conviviality. *See* Solidarity
Cooperation. *See* Voluntary cooperation
Copp, David: on Mill, 70$n3$
Counterexample. *See* Act utilitarianism; Sidgwick's thesis; Utilitarianism
Cultural lag. *See* Common-sense morality; Sidgwick's thesis
Cumberland, Richard: first utilitarian, 169

Decision. *See* Choice
Declining marginal utility: of primary goods, 11, 134-135, 139, 141; as basis for fundamental guarantees, 113; not of utility, 154; supports equality, 242
Democratic decision-making: and preference satisfaction, 206
Deontological. *See* Teleological
Desirable. *See* Desire
Desire: actual vs. corrected (qualified or ideal), 13, 16, 166, 171, 173, 174, 178, 197-198; pertinent to own welfare, 15, 173, 187, 188, 189-191, 199-200; as evidence of desirable, 26, 27, 28, 32, 37; and intrinsic good, 28; does not confer desirability, 28; pleasure an end of, 28; and idea of pleasure, 29; 34$n19$; pleasure makes desirable, 29; connection with happiness (Whewell), 33$n9$; defective, 166, 192, 195-199; alters, 166, 174, 178, 179; to have at a time, 170; dispositional property, 170-171; intrinsically desired, 171; simultaneous, 171; aversions, 171, 178; and frustration, 171; families of , 172, 184$n8$; strength of, 172, 175; altruistic, 173; time of, 174-175; stable, 175, 183; second order, 178; retrospective, 181; of dead, 184-85$n14$; restriction to rational in Overvold, 191; causal consequences of, 192$n7$
——satisfaction: utility or welfare as, 13-16 *passim*, 166, 172-187, 195; as goal of morality, 114; coherence of maximizing, 166; utility as power of, 170; need to know meaning of, 171, 184$n7$, 193$n3$; does not imply knowledge of, 171, 193$n3$; does not imply pleasure in, 171, 193$n3$; with pleasure, 172; with belief, 172; higher level of, 172; restrictions on definition, 172-173; of living, 172; further variations in utility as, 173-174; difficulty for utility as, 174; and happiness, 176-177; how to maximize difficult to determine, 177; utility$_{DS}$ maximization and change of desire, 178; utility$_{DS}$ and second-order desires, 178; example of difficulty of, 178-179; no plausible program of, 178; in terms of actual desires, 178; conception of maximization elusive, 179; possible maximizing procedures, 179-182; procedure (a) 179-182; procedures (b) and (c) simpler than (a), 180; (c) better than (b), 180; and asymmetry for utility of past and future desires, 180; plausibility of ignoring past desires, 180; ignoring future desires, 181; programs dt_1 and dt_2, 181; dt_2 preferred to (b), 182; dt_1 most appealing, 182; procedure dt_1 and stable desires, 183; dt_1 as rule of thumb for promoting utility$_H$, 184; of intrinsic desires and utility, 184$n6$; (a) sets no date on, 184$n14$; utility as, self-interest and self-sacrifice, 186-187; Brandt's former theory of utility as, 186; as subjectivist conception of welfare, 195; welfare as certain enduring means of, 201
Desire theory of utility. *See* Desire; Utility
Difference Principle: relation to general happiness in Mill, 39; acceptance of losses, 132; admissible nonutilitarian theory

of moral preference, 152; generalized form rejected, 152, 163n16. *See* Rawls
Diggs, B. J.: conditions of social morality summarized, 13
Dilemma of collective action. *See* Free rider problem; Prisoners' dilemma
Distribution. *See* Bayesian decision theory; Choice; Primary goods; Rational bargain; Rationality; Redistribution
Distributive justice. *See* Choice; Difference principle; Justice; Mill, John Stuart; Rawls; Redistribution
Doing vs. letting happen: and requirements of aid, 236; greater responsibility for doing, 237
Dominance, in decision theory, 147, 211
Donagan, Alan: counterexample to act utilitarianism, 76
Duties. *See* Obligation
Dworkin, Ronald: on congruence, 127n3

Egoism: rival to utilitarianism, 84n4, 92; way to maximize welfare, 217; dissatisfaction with, 217, 222n1
Emotivism, 170
Enjoyment. *See* Happiness
Epicurus, 169
Epistemic position: ideal circumstances, 8-9; idea introduced, 79; and Sidgwickian equilibrium, 79. *See* Sidgwick; Sidgwickian equilibrium
Equal opportunity. *See* Equality
Equality: in Mill, 5, 20, 30, 31, 35, 37, 39, 40; moral equality in place of natural inequality, 114; of opportunity in Rawls, 134, 136; of nations in Rawls, 249-250. *See* Equibenevolence
Equibenevolence: parental in Mill, 37; required by Mill's principle, 37; and impartial spectator, 38. *See* Equality
Equiprobability: distinguished from indifference, 138; in original position, 138-139; model of moral choice, 156; model and average utilitarianism, 158. *See* Choice; Original position; Rawls
Essential needs. *See* Needs
Ethical Choice. *See* Choice
Ethical theory: positive impartial consideration required, 144, 208; and theory of rational behavior, 144, 148; and interpersonal situations, 146; properly contractarian, 13, 161. *See* Ethics

Ethical worth: and utility, 153-154; and welfare, 153-154
Ethics: Harsanyi's account, 150; and rationality, 150; and positive, impartial concern, 144, 208; place revealed by prisoners' dilemma, 208. *See* Harsanyi; Morality; Rawls
Expediency. *See* Utility
Ezorsky, Gertrude, 98n6

Fair compromise. *See* Choice, Rational bargain
Fairness: and cooperation in Mill, 50; and choice of rules, 100; as condition of morality, 107-108; and equiprobability model, 156; and ignorance of identity, 160. *See* Choice; Impartiality; Justice as fairness; Morality; Rawls
Falk, W. D.: choice of morality, 127n4
Fallacy of composition: in Mill, 36
Fidelity: and reciprocity in Mill, 66
Firth, Roderick: ideal observer theory, 84n10
Formal constraints. *See* Right
Frankena, William: informed choice, 127n4
Fraternity. *See* Solidarity
Free rider: and self-interest, 210, 221. *See* Free rider problem; Prisoners' dilemma; Public goods
Free rider problem: conditions of, 209; and invisible hand, 217; and public goods, 217; second level in Becker's solution, 221
Fried, Charles: friendship and morality, 240n6
Fuchs, Alan: summarized, 10-11; mentioned, 100
Functional value. *See* Aristotle; Welfare

Game theory: and utility maximization, 146
Gauthier, David: discussion summarized, 12-13; on Rawls's contractees, 142n5, 143n11; prisoners' dilemma and ethics, 208; insurance system, 237
General agreement, 211
General happiness: as sum, 4, 5, 20, 30, 32, 36, 41n3; desirability, 4, 30; good to aggregate, 5, 25-26, 30-31, 37, 45n3; and equibenevolence, 37-38. *See* Mill, John Stuart
Generosity. *See* Beneficence; Mill, John Stuart

Gibbard, Allan: discussion summarized, 8-9; mentioned, 21
Golden rule: and utilitarianism, 244; and Carson's (G), 246; ambiguous, 246; Carson's (GR), 247
Good: what is, 3; and right, 3; to a person, 5, 30-31; indefinable quality, 13-14, 170; of each and every, 114; as satisfaction of rational desire, 139; intrinsically, 242. See Desire; General happiness; Happiness; Utility; Value; Welfare
Good for: varieties of, 201-203
Good samaritan: obligation in Mill, 6, 50, 52, 63, 64. See Aid; Mill, John Stuart
Governmental control. See Coercion
Griffin, James: defends desire theory, 170

Hall, E. W.: refutes Moore, 33$n11$
Happiness: pleasure or absence of pain, 4, 23; a good, 4, 25, 30; only thing desirable as end, 4, 23, 31; as a sum, 4, 5, 20, 30, 32, 36, 41$n3$; bearing on morality in Mill, 4, 5, 24, 31, 39, 40, 45, 88, 89; equal claim to in Mill, 5, 20, 30, 31, 35, 37, 39, 40; as utility or welfare, 13-15, 166, 174-176; advantages of happiness account, 14-15, 183; as aim of benevolence, 14, 166; connection with desire, 28, 29, 33$n9$, 34$n19$; autonomy part of, 44, 46, 61; conceived as enjoyment, 174; qualities of pleasure, 174; levels of, 174; intensity, 174; utility$_H$ maximization, 175-176; correlation of utility$_H$ and utility$_{DS}$, 176-177; influence on desires, 177; not form of utility$_{DS}$, 182; asymmetry of past and future desires, 180; dt_1 and, 184; common end of human activities, 185$n17$. See Desire; General happiness; Utility; Welfare
Hardin, Garrett: on cooperation, 211-212
Hare, R. M.: on Rawls, 127$n3$, 127$n9$; desire theory, 170
Harm: prevention of, 6, 43, 49-53, 65-67, 231, 244; avoidance of, 43, 49-53, 65-67, 231, 244; knowledge of, 61; and universal interests, 61; not all injustice, 67
Harman, Gilbert, 244-245
Harris, John: organ redistribution, 241$n12$
Harsanyi, John: moral judgments, 12; Gauthier's discussion of summarized, 12-13; defense against contractualism, 100; conceptions of value and reason, 144-146; problem of impartiality, 148; ethics, 150; rationality in ethics, 150; arguments for utilitarianism, 150-160; first argument for weak utilitarianism, 150-155; premises, 150; personal and moral preferences, 150-155 *passim*, 160; first argument deemed valid, 151; ethical worth, 153-154; rejects egalitarian preferences, 155; first argument rejected, 155; second argument for strong utilitarianism held unsound, 156; operationalization of impartiality, 155, 158; apparent vindication of second argument, 158; social utility and preference, 170; utility as qualified desire satisfaction, 173; true preferences, 173
Hart, H. L. A.: on "obligation," 64; not all rights violations unjust, 70$n16$; background conditions of justice, 120
Health: and welfare, 203
Hedonism: Mill's theory of life, 23. See Desire; General happiness; Happiness; Mill, John Stuart; Utility
Hirshliefer, Jack: policy and want satisfaction, 170; utility rank ordering of preference, 170
Hobbes, Thomas: compared with Rawls, 122; state of nature, 211
Human-welfare value. See Value; Welfare
Hume, David: utilitarianism and common sense, 6-7, 20, 87; sentiment of justice, 83; background conditions of justice, 120, 127$n5$; compared with Rawls, 122; on reason, 146

Impartial spectator: misunderstood by Rawls, 38
Impartiality: positive impartial concern for individual preferences, 12, 144, 152, 208; ignorance as a condition of, 12-13, 155-158, 238, 245; and individuality, 13, 38, 159; derived from utility, 39-40; and compatibility of ethics with rationality, 148; operationalization of, 155-158; and equiprobability model, 156; distinguished in bargaining and choice, 160-161; and denial of right not to be killed, 238. See Choice; Desire, Harsanyi; Justice; Justice as fairness; Rational bargain; Rawls
Incentives: as limit on aid, 230; constraint on equality, 243

308 INDEX

Individuality: sacrificed in ignorance of who one is, 13, 159
Initial factor endowments: and market optimum, 161; imposed distribution of redistributive, 161; require protective state, 162
Interests: universal, vital human, 61; knowledge of, 61; distinguished from desire, 166
Intrinsically desired. See Desire
Intuition: rejected by Mill, 27; Ross, 78; Sidgwick's rejection of dogmatic, 91
Invisible hand: reconciling egoism and utilitarianism, 217

Justice: as constraint on production of good, 3; presupposes community, 3; presupposes persons, 3; and utility, 3, 39-40, 88, 112-113, 128, 133-136; correlated with rights by Mill, 6, 44, 46, 64, 69, 88; Rawls's concept of, 10, 121-126; Rawls's special conception of, 10, 134, 136, 140, 141, 143n7; and public policy, 16; as standard of distribution, 16, 83, 129; not whole of morality, 42; and avoidance of harm, 43, 49-53, 65-67, 231, 244; category overpopulated by Mill, 64-65, 68; evolutionary advantage to consensus on, 83; and perfect obligation in Mill, 88; and political rights, 113; adjudication of differing conceptions, 117; background conditions of, 122-123; as virtue of institutions, 129; Rawls's general conception, 133
Justice as fairness: described, 10, 121-126; compared with Mill's concept of general happiness, 5, 38-39; vs. utilitarianism, 117; not relativistic, 125; concept acceptable to utilitarians, 129-130

Kant, Immanuel: source of contractarianism, 10; and Rawls, 124. See Categorical imperative
Kantian procedure. See Rawls
Killing vs. letting die: moral relevance of, 236, 244. See Doing vs. letting happen

Law of nations: in Rawls, 249-250; Carson's (WDP), 250
Lensky, Gerhard E.: evolution of moral beliefs, 85n11

Liberty:
—— in Mill, 43-44, 49-59 *passim*; 70n5; and harm-prevention, 49-56; Brown's reading of Mill (L), 53-54; Lyon's reading of Mill (L*), 55-56; and paternalism in Mill, 59-62
—— in Rawls: principle of greatest equal liberty, 10; priority of, 10, 136, 140; and equality of nations, 250. See Autonomy; Mill, John Stuart; Rawls
Life value, 205. See Value; Welfare
Lyons, David: Reading of Mill summarized, 5-6, 20; cited on Mill's theory of morality, 41

McClelland, David: past enjoyments, 177
MacLeod, A. M.: on Rawls, 142n1, 142n5
McNaughton, Robert: intensity of enjoyment, 174; problem with, 175
Market: theory of and utilitarianism, 161-162
Marshall, John: discussed, 5, 20; criticized, 34n24
Marx, Karl: concern with malconditioned preferences, 196
Maximin. See Choice
"Metaphysical": means psychological, 29
Mill, James: "metaphysical," 29; on desire, 34n16, 34n19
Mill, John Stuart: classical source, 4; West's reading summarized, 4-5, 20; happiness pleasure or absence of pain, 4, 23; happiness to a good, 4, 25, 30; only thing desirable as end, 4, 23, 31; principle of evidence, 4, 24, 26, 27, 35, 36; proof of principle of utility, 4, 20, 23-27, 35, 91; psychological hedonism, 4, 25; inference from good of happiness of each to good of general happiness, 4, 25-26, 30-31; general happiness as sum, 4, 20, 30, 32, 36, 41n3; utility and morality, 4, 5, 24, 31, 39, 40, 45, 88, 89; as act utilitarian, 4, 5, 36, 44, 45; Marshall's reading summarized, 5, 20; Lyons summarized, 5-6, 20; equal claim to happiness, 5, 20, 30, 31, 35, 37, 39, 40; good to person or aggregate, 5, 25-26, 31, 37, 41n3; and Rawls, 5, 38, 39; as rule utilitarian, 5, 45, 70n4; beneficence not obliga-

tion, 6; harm prevention, 6, 43, 49-53, 65-67; good samaritan obligations, 50, 52, 63, 64; justice and rights, 6, 44, 46, 64-69, 88; and Sidgwick, 6-8, 20, 90, 91; nonjustice obligations, 6, 42, 46, 48, 50-52, 65-69; supererogation, 6, 20, 45; varieties of obligation, 6, 50-52, 65; and Hume, 6, 20; utility and commonsense morality, 7-8, 87-90; Socrates and fool, 12, 157; art of life, 20, 24, 33$n12$; beneficence not justice, 20, 42; desire as evidence of desirable, 26, 27, 28, 32; no direct proof of utility, 23-24, 91; sensibility, 27; will is child of desire, 27; desire and pleasure, 28-29; on James Mill, 29; measuring pleasure, 32; desire does not confer desirability, 32; "happiness" and "desirable," 33$n11$; psychological egoism, 36; justice not whole of morality, 42; justice and harm avoidance, 43, 49-53, 65-67; division of morality, 43, 45-48, 69; negative utilitarian obligation, 43, 48-49; liberty, 43-44, 49-59 passim, 70$n5$; paternalism, 44; internal and external sanctions, 44, 54, 56, 57; perfect and imperfect obligations, 46-48, 63-65, 88; beneficence as imperfect obligation, 46-47; positive beneficence, 48-51 passim, 60, 61; enforcement of morality, 49, 50, 54, 57, 58, 59; Brown's interpretation examined, 53-59; Brown's formulation of liberty (L), 53; formulation of enforcing morality (M), 54; formulation of wrong conduct (P), 55; Brown's formulations refined (L*) (P*), 55-56; liberty and paternalism, 59-62; beneficence and paternalism, 62; beneficence and rights, 62-67 passim
Mitchell, Dorothy: "desirable" and "good," 33$n7$
Moore, G. E.: naturalistic fallacy, 26, 33$n11$; on good, 13-14, 170
Moral act. See Rational behavior
Moral attitudes: justification, 80-81, 84$n10$
Moral beliefs. See Common-sense morality
Moral choice. See Choice; Ethics; Impartiality; Rationality

Moral community, 3, 106, 111
Moral decision. See Choice; Ethics; Impartiality; Rationality
Moral epistemologies: pertinence to Sidgwick's thesis, 8-9, 79-81
Moral equality. See Equality
Moral freedom. See Autonomy
Moral reasoning. See Bayesian decision theory; Choice; Desire; Rational bargain
Moral rights. See Justice; Mill, John Stuart; Rawls; Rights
Moral rules: felicitous, 74; as Humean conventions, 110; as landmarks, 110; as action-guides, 110; See Commonsense morality; Contractarianism; Mill, John Stuart; Rawls; Rule utilitarianism; Utilitarianism; Utility
Moral sense. See Intuition
Morality: Rawls's concept, 10, 116-117, 235; and art of life, 24; and expediency in Mill, 39-40; division of in Mill, 43, 45-48, 69; why be moral, 193; and prudence, 193; and voluntary cooperation, 212. See Commonsense morality; Contractarianism; Social morality
Mutual advantage. See Optimality
Mutual coercion. See Coercion

Nagel, Thomas: on veil of ignorance, 127$n9$
Narveson, Jan: discussion summarized, 11, 12
Naturalistic fallacy, 26, 33$n11$, 33$n12$
Needs: and welfare, 16, 201; true needs, 196
von Neumann-Morgenstern (vNM) utility function, 146, 150, 153, 178
Nozick, Robert: sacrifice in Rawls, 142$n4$

Obligation. See Aid; Fairness; Harm; Hart; Mill, John Stuart; Rights; Sanctions; Supererogation; Utilitarianism; Utility
Olson, Mancur: on collective action, 213-214, 223-224$n6$
Omissions, 236. See Doing vs. letting happen
Optimality (Pareto): and utility maximization, 148, 161; and prisoners' dilemma, 148, 211; in bargaining the-

ory, 153; sacrificed by egalitarian preferences, 155; bearing on ethics and rationality, 161, 162
Organ transfer. *See* Aid
Original position: described, 10-11; role in justification, 10, 115, 116; as theoretical construct, 119, 120-121; controversial features of, 123-125; choice strategy in, 137-138; and equiprobability, 139; law of nations, 249-250. *See* Choice; Equiprobability; Fairness; Justice; Justice as fairness; Rawls
Overvold, Mark C.: summarized, 15-16; desires pertinent to self-interest, 15, 18n29, 173; self-sacrifice, 166; psychological egoism, 166

Pareto-optimality. *See* Optimality
Parfit, Derek: personality identity, 241n17
Paternalism: sanctioned by utilitarianism, 231. *See* Mill, John Stuart
Perry, R. B.: desire theory, 169
Personal identity. *See* Parfit; Self
Persons: and concern to produce good, 3; and justice, 3; and rights, 3, 239; "good to," 5, 30-31; respect for and social morality, 104, 105, 106; respect for and utilitarianism, 111, 154, 239; differences among, 17, 154, 239; inviolability, 239
Plan of life: distinguished from style, 231
Plato: concern with malconditioned preferences, 196
Pleasure. *See* Desire; Happiness; Hedonism; Mill, John Stuart; Utility
Preference. *See* Choice; Desire; Harsanyi; Utility
Primary goods: characterized, 10; and utility, 12, 39, 131, 134-135, 139-141, 186; neutral between utilitarianism and contractarianism, 39; and social intervention in Mill, 61-62; eliminate need for interpersonal utility comparisons, 131; maximization not required by utilitarianism, 134; desire-satisfaction utility extrapolated from, 186. *See* Desire; Rawls; Utility
Principle of indifference: assumed by maximizing strategy in original position, 138, 143n8
Principle of utility. *See* Choice; Mill, John Stuart; Rawls; Sidgwick; Sidgwick's thesis; Utilitarianism; Utility
Prisoners' dilemma: matrix, 147, 210-211, 223; and utilitarianism, 147-150, 161, 208, 210-214; and rationality, 148, 208, 217-218, 223n5; defeat of, 208, 219, 220, 222; and free rider, 209, 210, 217, 221; assumption excluding example setting, 215; and invisible hand, 217; and rational self-maximizing, 217-218, 223n5; calculation as source, 218; means of escape, 219; solution, 219-220; cooperation to defeat, 221; mutual coercion defeat by, 224n7; explicated, 222-223n3. *See* Free rider; Free rider problem
Prudence: conflict with morality resolved, 193
Psychological egoism: substantive thesis, 15, 166, 192-193; in Mill, 36; not espoused by Rawls, 123; and subjectivist welfare, 199; objections to, 200
Psychological hedonism. *See* Mill, John Stuart
Public goods: require productive state, 162; and act-utilitarian requirements, 208, 210-214; examples, 209, 217; defined, 209-210, 217; voluntary cooperation in production of, 212; free rider problem, 217; motives for supplying, 214; by one person, 214, 215, 216n2, 223n5; where voluntary provision not desired, 223n4
Public goods dilemma. *See* Free rider problem; Prisoners' dilemma
Public policy: and welfare, 16, 205; limited to primary goods, 62
Publicity. *See* Rawls

Qualified attitude method, 9, 85n14

Rachels, James: on killing and letting die, 244
Raphael, D. D.: on unconscious utilitarianism, 98n6
Rashdall, Hastings: good as indefinable quality, 170
Rational act: distinguished from self-interested and moral, 193
Rational agent: defined, 146
Rational bargain: as model of moral choice, 12, 153, 161, 163n19; theory of and Bayesian decision, 153, 155; as alternative to Harsanyi, 153; distinguished from choice, 160; maximizes where production and distribution independent, 162; optimum may not be welfare maximum,

162. *See* Choice; Desire; Harsanyi; Optimality
Rational behavior: general theory of and ethics, 144, 145, 161
Rational self-maximization: and cooperation, 217, 219; absence the problem, 221; and individualist political theory, 222. *See* Choice; Egoism; Rationality
Rationality: in decision theory, 12, 160-161; in interpersonal situations, 146; in private behavior, 152, 160; in moral decision, 152, 160; Bayesian theory inferior in ethics, 153, 155; full information required for, 191; in desires, 191; perspective for resolving morality and prudence, 193; in preferences, 196; abandonment of, 222
Rawls, John: and utilitarianism, 10-11, 115, 116, 128, 129, 131-133, 141, 142, 143$n5$, 244; considered judgments, 10, 78, 84$n10$, 226-227; primary goods, 10-12, 131, 134-135, 139-141; special conception of justice, 10, 134, 136, 140, 141, 143$n7$; principles of justice, 10-11, 134, 136-141, 249; justice as fairness described, 10, 121-126; morality modeled by original position, 10, 115-116, 118, 120, 121, 123, 124, 125; veil of ignorance as element of original position, 11; formal constraints of right, 11, 126, 127$n12$, 130, 142$n3$; conception of justice a distributive standard, 16, 83, 129; justice as fairness and Mill, 38; fair play, 70$n14$; justification of moral attitudes, 80; summary rules, 89; Kantian interpretation of justice as fairness, 101; considered judgments a Socratic procedure, 115-117; defends contractarian normative theory, 115, 235; Kantian procedure, 115, 116, 117; adjudication of different conceptions, 117; contract theory excludes reflective equilibrium, 117-118; Kantian procedure as moral geometry, 117, 124; apparent fallacy in geometric method, 118; original position as theoretical construct, 118, 120-121; support for grounds of theory, 118; two arguments for construct, 120-121; concept/conception distinction, 121-125; function of justice, 122; background of justice, 122, 123; controversial features of original position, 123-125; thin vs. thick veil, 123; veil and fairness, 124-125; use of pure procedural justice and reflective equilibrium, 125; weakness of assumptions, 126; justice virtue of institutions, 129; interpersonal utility assumptions, 131, 135-137 *passim*, 141, 142; utilitarianism and persons, 132, 143$n5$; self-interest problematic behind veil, 132, 143$n5$; Two Principles and losses, 132-133, 138; general conception of justice, 133; Two Principles and satisfactory minimum, 133, 138, 143$n6$; principles and utility on different levels, 134; arguments for Two Principles examined, 136-141; choice strategy in original position, 137-138; generalized difference principle, 152, 153, 162; desire theory of utility, 169, 186; contract and deciding valid claims, 233; utilitarian adaptation of argument, 239; on law of nations, 249-250
Reason: acceptable conception and utilitarianism, 144; received account, 145; in Harsanyi, 146. *See* Choice; Desire; Harsanyi; Rational agent; Rational behavior; Rationality
Reasonable agreement: and social morality, 106, 107, 108. *See* Social morality
Reciprocity. *See* Fairness; Mill, John Stuart; Rawls
Redistribution: not justified by mutual advantage, 161. *See* Harsanyi; Optimality; Utilitarianism
Responsibility. *See* Autonomy
Reflective equilibrium. *See* Considered judgments; Rawls; Sidgwickian equilibrium
Respect for persons: and social morality, 12, 104, 105, 109; and utilitarian requirements of aid, 17, 231, 239; promotes general good, 108; act-utilitarian accommodation of, 108; basic to contractualism, 113; first moral duty, 114. *See* Persons
Right: relation of good to, 3; formal constraints of, 11, 126, 127$n12$, 130, 142; RU-right, 75; Carson's general account (G), 245-246
Rights: and persons, 3, 113, 231-232, 236, 239; and moral community, 3, 113; as constraints on production of good, 3; can utilitarianism accommodate them, 3; and autonomy, 231-232; not to be killed, 236; to our bodies, 236. *See* Equality; Fairness; Justice; Mill, John Stuart

312 INDEX

Ross, Sir David: moral beliefs as apprehensions, 8, 78; counterexample to act utilitarianism, 76; intuitionism, 78; and Sidgwick's thesis, 78-79

Rousseau, J. J.: source of contractarianism, 10; *Social Contract* as moral philosophy, 101; moral and legal equality for natural inequality, 114

Rule utilitarianism: Mill as proponent, 5, 45, 70$n4$; and best explanation argument, 6-7; domestic, 9, 75; Gibbard's (RU), 75; supported by Sidgwick's thesis, 79, 80, 81, 82; with class bias, 82; Gibbard's satisficing (RU), 84$n8$; Rawls not variant of, 141; basis for cooperation, 208, 212; held unacceptable by Sartorius, 212; not advocated by Becker, 222; extensionally equivalent to Carson's (C), 248

Sanctions: reconciling moral consciousness and utilitarianism, 110. See Mill, John Stuart

Sartorius, Rolf: summarized, 16-17, 208; desire theory, 170; mentioned in Becker, 218, 224$n8$

Satisfaction. See Desire

Scanlon, Thomas: on Rawls, 241$n10$

Schelling, Thomas: on agreement in bargaining, 83

Schneewind, Jerome: on Mill's proof, 23; on Sidgwick, 83$n1$, 98$n4$; mentioned, 17$n6$

Schwartz, Thomas: summarized, 16, 167

Self: concept of explains intrapersonal trade-offs, 240

Self-interest: Overvold's account summarized, 15-16, 166; notion problematic behind veil of ignorance, 132, 143$n5$; and self-sacrifice, 173; comprises motley collection, 186; aspect of wants, 186; promotion need not be selfish, 187, 191; desires pertinent to, 188; distinguished from rationality in general, 193; and free rider, 210; served by not calculating, 218-219; no special weight for act utilitarian, 242. See Choice; Desire

Selfishness: distinct from promotion of self-interest, 187; alleged condition of prisoners' dilemma, 211

Self-referential altruism, 251-252$n5$

Self-sacrifice: Overvold's treatment, 15-16, 173, 191, 192; rationality of, 132; problem for desire-satisfaction utility, 166, 186-187; and self-interest, 173; coherent notion, 191, 192; excluded by subjectivist account of welfare, 200; required by utilitarianism, 217, 226, 250-251; and aid, 229

Sen, Amartya K., 163$n14$

Sensibility, 27

Sidgwick, Henry: common-sense morality and utilitarianism, 7-8, 20, 71-73, 91-98; cites Adam Smith, 18$n12$; on Mill's proof, 37; arguments for utilitarianism examined, 74-83, 91-98; egoism only systematic rival of utilitarianism, 84$n4$; anticipated by Mill, 90; rejection of dogmatic intuitionism, 91; his object in *Methods*, 91, 98$n4$; utilitarianism cannot be strictly proved, 91-92; proof *ad hominem*, 92; proof negative, 92; cannot convince egoist, 92; unconscious utilitarianism held necessary to his argument, 95; universal happiness end of human activities, 185$n17$. See Common-sense morality; Sidgwickian equilibrium; Sidgwick's thesis; Utilitarianism; Utility

Sidgwickian equilibrium: and epistemic position, 8, 79; and ideal justification, 8-9, 81; introduced, 9, 74-75; not reflective equilibrium, 78; Gibbard's assumptions concerning, 84$n6$; Gibbard's satisficing equilibrium, 84$n8$. See Sidgwick's thesis

Sidgwick's thesis: introduced, 7-9, 21, 71; evidence of unconscious ends, 7, 96; normative relevance, 8, 74; bearing on Ross's intuitionism, 78-79; bearing on epistemic position, 8, 79; bearing on justification of moral attitudes, 8-9, 81; bearing on utilitarianism, 8, 76-77, 79-81, 86; implications for normative relevance of nonutilitarian tendency, 8, 83; truth of, 9, 82, 97-98; sociological and psychological, 72; examined, 74-83, 95-98; and counterexamples, 76; bearing on rule utilitarianism, 79, 80, 81, 82; use depends on refined rationalism, 84$n5$; without assuming unique equilibrium point, 84$n8$; difficult to argue for, 95; manifest felicific tendency of moral rules, 95; myriad alternatives to thesis, 96; bearing on synthesis argument, 98

Simmons, A. John, 7, 17$n6$, 21, 84$n3$

Singer, Peter: Sidgwick's object, 98$n4$; Sidgwick's appeal to common sense,

98n5; utilitarian treatment of duty and charity, 222n2
Skinner, B. F.: concerned with malconditioned preferences, 196
Slote, Michael: Brazen rule, 232
Smart, J. J. C.: on satisfaction, 184n7
Smith, Adam: Sidgwick cites, 18n12
Smith, John Maynard: stability of conventions, 85n13
Social choice. *See* Choice
Social engineering: and act utilitarianism, 112
Social goals, 209. *See* Public goods
Social goods, 209. *See* Public goods
Social ideals: in utilitarianism, 113
Social morality: descriptive sense, 12, 101; shared views and dispositions, 102; normative acceptability, 102; and moral freedom, 102, 104-106 *passim*, 114; entails cooperation, 103; involves compromise, 103, 106; free and reasonable subscription, 103, 104, 106, 114; as practical ideal, 104-105, ideal of and respect for persons, 104-105, 106; possibility of achieving, 105; reality of, 107; captured by Rawls's method, 126; *See* Common-sense morality; Morality
Socialization: moral rules and act utilitarianism, 110
Sociobiology, 85n12
Socrates: dissatisfied, 12, 157
Socratic procedure, 115-117. *See* Rawls
Solidarity: feeling offsets costs of cooperation, 17, 206, 219; provided by cooperation, 218; depends on others' cooperation, 221-222
Spencer, Herbert: Mill's answer to, 40
Spontaneity: utility of, 218
State of nature: Hobbes's, 211
Subjective value, 204. *See* Value
Subjectivism: theories described, 16, 195; avoidance of defective preference in, 197; welfare as preference satisfaction, 198; best ploy of, 198-199; form of psychological egoism, 199. *See* Welfare
Suffering: obligation to relieve, 231. *See* Aid; Mill, John Stuart
Sumner, L. W.: on Mill, 70n3; on act-utilitarian cooperation, 216n13, 224n6
Supererogation: vs. obligation, 226; required by utilitarianism, 243. *See* Aid; Mill, John Stuart; Utilitarianism
Sympathy: requirement of moral decision, 152. *See* Harsanyi; Mill, John Stuart

Tarski, Alfred, 184n7
Teleological: utilitarianism as, 130-131; contrast with deontological a red herring, 131. *See* Rawls
Theory of aid. *See* Aid
Theory of rational bargaining. *See* Rational bargain
Threshold effects: defined, 213; and voluntary cooperation, 213-214
Trammell, Richard: criticized Harris, 241n12
Troland, L. T.: past enjoyments and present wants, 177

Uncertainty. *See* Choice; Rawls
Unconscious utilitarianism. *See* Common-sense morality; Mill, John Stuart; Sidgwick; Sidgwick's thesis; Utilitarianism
Utilitarian ethical theory. *See* Harsanyi; Utilitarianism
Utilitarianism: traditional questions, 3; a consequentialist theory of right, 3, 20, 23, 107, 139, 146, 169; direct and indirect, 3, 35, 100, 110, 149; and respect for persons, 3, 17, 108, 111, 154, 239; and justice, 3, 39-40, 88, 112-113, 128, 133-136; and rights, 3, 238; and contractarianism, 5, 10, 100, 101, 107, 109, 111, 113, 131-132, 162; and common-sense morality, 6-9, 20, 71-73, 82, 86-87, 89, 91-98, 110-111; unconscious, 7, 8, 72-73, 86, 87, 89, 91-98; and Rawls's theory, 10-11, 115-116, 128, 129, 131-133, 141-142, 143n5, 244; and primary goods, 12, 39, 134, 135, 139-141, 186; average, 12, 35, 142n2, 150, 156, 158-159, 163, 163n26; and aid to others, 17, 208, 225-240, 245, 246, 250, 251; and welfare maximization, 35, 148, 149, 166, 169, 205, 242; and counterexample, 76, 86-87; and egoism, 84n4, 92; and benvolence, 107, 108, 112, 114; and moral freedom, 107, 113, 231-234; and liberty, 107, 113, 231-234; assumes interpersonal utility function, 135; and rationality, 145, 147-148, 150, 152-153, 160-161; weak theory, 146-147, 150; strong theory, 147, 156; and institutional design, 149, 161; Harsanyi's arguments for, 150-160; vs. rational theory of bargaining, 152-153, 162; and modern economic theory, 152-153, 160-161; stringency of, 217, 226, 250-251; and

supererogation, 226, 243; tested against considered judgments, 226-227; and paternalism, 231; and self preference, 240n5, 242; view of personal identity supporting, 241n17; and antiegalitarian considerations, 243. *See* Act utilitarianism; Harsanyi; Mill, John Stuart; Rawls; Rule utilitarianism; Sidgwick; Sidgwick's thesis; Utility

Utility: of commitment to moral rules, 5; and primary goods, 11, 12, 39, 131, 134-135; 139-141, 186; interpersonal comparison of, 12, 131, 134-137 *passim*, 146-147, 166; expected, 12, 146, 169; total or average as standard, 12, 163n26; of situation for person vs. for chooser of being person in situation, 12, 157, 246; distribution of, 12, 153-155, 162; question of nature, 13, 166, 169; diminishing marginal and justice, 113; interpersonal comparison and justice, 113; interpersonal in Rawls, 131, 135-137 *passim*, 141, 142; prospects primary objects of, 145; as measure of personal preference, 145, 150; welfare as function of, 146; maximization inconsistent with that of welfare, 147; no diminishing marginal utility of, 154; and urgency of needs, 154; interpersonal measure not requiring single preference ordering, 159; need for ethical constraint on maximization, 160; mutual disadvantage of direct maximization, 161; possibility frontier, 161; social and preference, 170; as rank ordering of preference, 170; interpersonal comparison in Brandt, 166; not appropriate for public policy, 205-206; diminishing marginal of income, 243. *See* Desire; Happiness; Value; Welfare

Value: acceptable conception of and utilitarianism, 144; utility maximizing implications of received account, 145; as identical with utility, 145; of prospect for a valuer, 145; human welfare as value for, 203; value-for goal relative, 203-204; subjective value, 204; functional value, 204; welfare value, 204; self-interest value, 204-205; life value, 205. *See* Choice; Desire; Ethical worth; Utility; Welfare

Veil of ignorance: as feature of original position, 11; thin vs. thick veil, 123; formulation in categorical imperative, 148; insures impartiality, 245. *See* Original position, Rawls

Voluntary cooperation: in provision of public goods, 16, 208; moral conditions of, 16-17, 214; costs of, 208, 209-222 *passim*; as condition of social goals, 209; moral basis of, 212-218; required only where perceptible difference made, 214; act-utilitarian requirements, 214, 216n13, 223n6; values in, 218; self-maximizers would promote, 219; promotion of would include, 219; costs offset by attitudes toward, 219; to defeat dilemma, 221-223. *See* Prisoners' dilemma; Public goods

Wants: satisfaction of should govern property, 170

Wealth: nontransferability, 243

Welfare: linear function of individual utilities, 146; definition induces interpersonal comparisons of utility, 146; as weighted sum of utilities, 146; maximization inconsistent with utility maximization, 147; measure of social preference, 150; maximization constraint on utility maximization, 160; maximum not necessarily coincident with optimum, 161; as desire satisfaction, 166-167, 170-174; as happiness, 172-176; motley collection of elements, 186; Brandt's want analysis of, 186; utilitarian conception of as subjectivist, 195, 199, 200; not nondefective self-regarding preference, 200; not nonethical preference, 200; enduring means of satisfaction, 201; minimum requisites of good living, 201; special case of good for, 202; functions constituting, 203; and health, 203; relatives of, 203-205; as value for, 203; special case of functional value, 204; not utility, 205; importance of, 205-206; more plausible for maximization than utility, 206. *See* Desire; Happiness; Utility; Value

Welfare economists: want satisfaction as utility, 186

Welfare state, 162

West, Henry: standard account of Mill defended, 4-5, 20

Whewell, William: quoted by Mill, 33*n9*
Will: is child of desire, 27
Wolff, Robert Paul, 143*n9*
Wren, Thomas: critique of Harris, 241*n12*

von Wright, Henrik: good of man, 186

Young, P. T.: past enjoyments and present wants, 177

Harlan B. Miller and **William H. Williams** are associate professors of philosophy at Virginia Polytechnic Institute and State University.